MUSEUM PIECES

McGill-Queen's/Beaverbrook Canadian Foundation
Studies in Art History

Series editors: Sandra Paikowsky and
Martha Langford

Recognizing the need for a better understanding of
Canada's artistic culture both at home and abroad,
the Beaverbrook Canadian Foundation, through its
generous support, makes possible the publication
of innovative books that advance our understanding
of Canadian art and Canada's visual and material
culture. This series supports and stimulates such
scholarship through the publication of original and
rigorous peer-reviewed books that make significant
contributions to the subject. We welcome submis-
sions from Canadian and international scholars for
book-length projects on historical and contemporary Canadian art and visual and material culture,
including Native and Inuit art, architecture, photography, crafts, design, and museum studies. Studies
by Canadian scholars on non-Canadian themes will
also be considered.

The Practice of Her Profession
Florence Carlyle, Canadian Painter
in the Age of Impressionism
Susan Butlin

Bringing Art to Life
A Biography of Alan Jarvis
Andrew Horrall

Picturing the Land
Narrating Territories in Canadian
Landscape Art, 1500 to 1950
Marylin J. McKay

The Cultural Work of Photography in Canada
Edited by Carol Payne and Andrea Kunard

Newfoundland Modern
Architecture in the Smallwood Years, 1949–1972
Robert Mellin

The Codex Canadensis *and*
the Writings of Louis Nicolas
The Natural History of the New World,
Histoire Naturelles des Indes Occidentals
Edited and with an Introduction by François-Marc
Gagnon, Translation by Nancy Senior,
Modernization by Réal Ouellett

Museum Pieces
Toward the Indigenization of Canadian Museums
Ruth B. Phillips

MUSEUM PIECES

Toward the Indigenization of
Canadian Museums

RUTH B. PHILLIPS

McGill-Queen's University Press
Montreal & Kingston | London | Ithaca

© McGill-Queen's University Press 2011
ISBN 978-0-7735-3905-1 (cloth)
ISBN 978-0-7735-3906-8 (paper)

Legal deposit fourth quarter 2011
Bibliothèque nationale du Québec

Printed in Canada on acid-free paper that is 100%
ancient forest free, processed chlorine free

McGill-Queen's University Press acknowledges
the support of the Canada Council for the Arts for
our publishing program. We also acknowledge the
financial support of the Government of Canada
through the Canada Book Fund for our publishing
activities.

LIBRARY AND ARCHIVES CANADA
CATALOGUING IN PUBLICATION

Phillips, Ruth B. (Ruth Bliss), 1945–
Museum pieces : toward the indigenization of
Canadian museums / Ruth B. Phillips.

(McGill-Queen's/Beaverbrook Canadian
Foundation studies in art history ; 7)
Includes index.
ISBN 978-0-7735-3905-1 (bound).
ISBN 978-0-7735-3906-8 (pbk.)

1. Native peoples – Museums – Canada.
2. Museums and Indians – Canada.   3. Museums
– Social aspects – Canada.   4. Museums – Political
aspects – Canada.   I. Title.   II. Series: McGill-
Queen's/Beaverbrook Canadian Foundation studies
in art history ; 7.

E76.85.P55 2012   305.897'071074   C2011-904117-0

Set in 10.5/13 Minion with Trade Gothic & Meta+
Book design & typesetting by Garet Markvoort

To the members of the   and in memory of Michael Ames
Task Force on Museums and First Peoples

CONTENTS

ILLUSTRATIONS

ACKNOWLEDGMENTS

A great many people have generously given their time and help during this book's long gestation. They include friends and colleagues in Canadian museums and as well as a larger international community. The several decades over which the essays were written and the different venues and forms in which they have been presented make the otherwise welcome opportunity to express my gratitude a formidable task, and I apologize for the inevitable failures of memory that will prevent me from thanking everyone individually.

In writing the individual chapters I have benefited from opportunities to talk to scholars, curators, and participants in the research and projects I discuss. I am very grateful for the guidance of Norman Hillmer and H. Blair Neatby in framing parts of the Introduction. Sherry Brydon's collaboration was critical to chapter 1, and Judy Thompson and Bernadette Driscoll Engelstad reviewed chapter 2, while Lindy Allen, Stephen Augustine, Philip Batty, Michael Green, Penny Ikinger, Diana Loren, and Ron Vanderwal provided valuable perspectives and information for chapter 7. Judy Thompson, Judy Hall, and Leslie Tepper took time to discuss their work for chapter 10; as did Gerald Conaty and Anita Herle for chapter 11, Andrea Laforet and Jolene Rickard for chapter 12, Lilly Koltun and Johanna Mizgala for chapter 13, Linda Grussani, Denise Leclerc, and Matthew Teitelbaum for chapter 14, Sue Rowley and my GRASAC collaborators, Heidi Bohaker, Alan Corbiere, John Borrows, Darlene Johnston, and Cory Willmott, for chapter 15, and Anna Edmundson for chapter 16. Research for the book has also been supported by fellowships at the National Gallery of Canada and the Humanities Research Centre of the Australian National University and by visiting professorships at the Cambridge University Museum of Anthropology and Archaeology and Harvard University, where I was hosted by the Department of History and the Weatherhead Centre for International Affairs. Grants from the Social Sciences and Humanities Research Council of Canada, the Leverhulme Foundation, and the British Academy also supported particular aspects of the research.

Artists, designers, and photographers generously gave permission for the publication of their work, and I thank Bill McLennan, Gerald McMaster, Kent Monkman, Tanya Harnett, Rebecca Belmore, Terrance Houle, the heirs of Joane Cardinal-Schubert, Reich and Petch, and Dixon Jones Ltd. It is particularly hard to acknowledge adequately the members of the staff of the University of British Columbia's Museum of Anthropology. My years there were tremendously enriched by the opportunity to work with each of them and to come, through them, to a deeper understanding of how museums work and what they, at their best, can accomplish.

I am especially indebted to Janet Berlo, Miriam Clavir, Andrea Laforet, Diana Nemiroff, Trudy Nicks, Aldona Jonaitis, Moira McCaffrey, and Judy Thompson for their friendship and collegiality over many years and, most recently, for reading and commenting on drafts of the chapters as they came together in their present form. The suggestions of the anonymous readers for McGill-Queen's University Press and the editorial counsel of Jonathan Crago have made important contributions to its shaping. I thank Mary Newberry for her fine work in creating the index. The work of bringing these museum pieces together was immeasurably facilitated by Kate Higginson's editorial help and Stacey Loyer's research assistance. As with every project that works its way through my life and my head and then on to paper, the willingness of my husband, Mark, to listen, read, and critique enabled in myriad ways the process of writing this book.

A NOTE ON NAMES AND TERMS

In the course of the history that is described here a number of verbal usages have changed, some in response to demands for greater accuracy and some as part of the search for an acceptable way of representing the fictitious collectivities imposed on Indigenous peoples. The term "Indian," which originates in a geographical misunderstanding of European explorers who did not know where they were, is still used in common parlance by many Indigenous North Americans, particularly in the United States. In Canada, although it was adopted by the Indigenous advisers of the Indians of Canada Pavilion at Expo 67, it has been replaced successively by "Native," "Aboriginal," "First Peoples," "First Nations," and "Indigenous." In the early twenty-first century, Aboriginal is more commonly used in central and eastern Canada, while First Nations is more widespread in western Canada. "Indigenous" is preferred by some people today above either of these two. As there is no clear consensus, I use all three in this book.

Since much of my research has been conducted with the Indigenous peoples of the Great Lakes, the peoples of this region are referred to particularly frequently in the chapters of this book, and it will be helpful to explain the different names that refer to them. The peoples who have been known as Ojibwe (or Chippewa in the United States), Odawa (Ottawa), Potawatomi, Algonquin, and some groups of Cree now normally prefer Anishinaabe (meaning "people"), the term used in their own languages. It can be spelled in various ways, depending on regional differences of pronunciation. The six nations who have collectively been known as Iroquois – Mohawk, Onondaga, Seneca, Oneida, Cayuga, and Tuscarora – generally prefer Onkwehonwe ("the real people"). Hodenosaunee ("People of the Longhouse") is also frequently used, but as it refers to those Onkwehonwe who follow the traditional Longhouse religion, it is not as inclusive a term. In editing already published essays for this book, I have changed names and terms in several to reflect current usages.

Categorical English terms can also be problematic. In the course of developing the collaborative work of the Great Lakes Research Alliance for the Study of Aboriginal Arts and Cultures (GRASAC), discussed in chapter 14, for example, Indigenous colleagues called into question the use of "object" for entities they may regard as possessing qualities of personhood. In Indigenous languages the terms used for the same entities are often animate, referring to other-than-human persons, to use anthropologist Irving Hallowell's term. I discuss the conundrum this presents in chapter 15, but as it remains a challenge for the future, I have not attempted to change these usages in chapters written during past years in order to underline their status as artifacts of a history that continues to unfold.

MUSEUM PIECES

A Preface – by Way of an Introduction

The term Canadian means so many different things to the people of Canada, be they white or red.
– *Harold Cardinal (1977)*[1]

Borders and Crossings

Canada's collaborative models of museum practice have arisen as organically from its history as the canoe or the snowmobile. In recent decades these innovative practices have become a major export, carried abroad by Canadian consultants, lecturers, and expatriate Canadian-trained curators and studied on site by visitors from other countries. Yet the impact of Canadian museology is more widely recognized abroad than at home. Most Canadians have become more accustomed to hearing about the activities of their museums when the latest protest or demonstration hits the national media. The furor of the moment might surround a demand to remove a familiar piece of art whose colonial content has come to seem offensive, an exhibition accused of misrepresenting a particular constituency, or the spending of public funds on a new museum or work of art that, some feel, does not adequately serve the nation as a whole.

Not surprisingly, given Canada's long struggle to define its own image, what such controversies have in common is that they revolve around issues of identity, diversity, and public representation. Should we boycott an exhibition sponsored by a company that is drilling for oil on land claimed by a First Nation (1988)? Is an exhibition that explores Canadian involvement in the colonization of Africa demeaning to African Canadians (1989)? Why did the National Gallery spend a large sum of Canadian taxpayers' money on a painting by an American artist (1990)? Would the inclusion of a Holocaust gallery in the new Canadian War Museum overshadow the history of Canada's military and the genocidal experiences of other diasporic communities (1997–98)? Should the Indian scout kneeling at the feet of Samuel de Champlain on an early twentieth-century Ottawa monument be removed because it suggests Aboriginal complicity in colonial conquest (1997)? Was the Canadian Museum of Civilization wrong to have tried to postpone an exhibition of art by Arab Canadians scheduled to open right after the bombing of the World Trade Center (2001)? Does the National Gallery of Canada's definition of artistic excellence unfairly exclude artists from diasporic communities (2010)? Whose injustices should be represented in the new Canadian Museum of Human Rights (2011)? Where, if at all, should the government build a new national portrait gallery (ongoing)?

Although I cannot support the statement with statistics, I would be willing to wager that Canada has seen a disproportionately large number of such museum-based contestations and that they receive an exceptional amount of coverage in the national media. Museums and public monuments, it seems, have come to serve as primary barometers of the manner in which public institutions – and, by association, their governmental sponsors – interpret laws and policies related to cultural diversity. Since the 1980s the development of new ways to work with both the Indigenous and diasporic "originating communities" from whom museums have acquired their collections has been a positive result of the volatile atmosphere in which Canadian museums have been operating. The chapters in this book explore this history of contestation, innovation, and change, as well as the structural relationships that link processes of decolonization, inclusivity, and reform at the micro-level of the museum with those that have been unfolding at the macro-level of Canadian society and politics.

In light of these goals it will be important, especially for the non-Canadian reader, to provide a summary, however brief, of key late twentieth-century trends and events that define these larger patterns of change. Because I have been a participant in a number of the episodes of museum change I discuss, it will also be helpful for me to position myself in the story. In this prefatory chapter I thus find myself deviating from the advice I give to students writing theses. "Tell your readers how you came to the project in the preface," I suggest, "and put the intellectual framing into the introduction." Instead, I offer here a preface by way of an introduction – or perhaps an introduction by way of a preface. My excuse for the inconsistency is that the trajectory of my professional career has been so closely interwoven with the story of change in Canadian museums that an account which combines analysis with a personal documentation of events as I experienced them seems both more honest and more useful.

Contingencies of biography enter, of course, into every scholarly and critical project, and personal experience always determines the angles of reflection that both open up and limit the resulting narratives. Yet the four decades of change in Canadian museums since the mid-1960s that are discussed in these chapters seem to me to have a particularly tight connection to the events that shaped the political and social consciousness of my generation. I came of age in the United States during the 1960s, and my academic formation was inevitably influenced by the upheavals and activist movements that marked that decade – the civil-rights movement, the anti–Vietnam War protests, and the women's movement. The Vietnam War was the cause of my husband's and my immigration to Canada in 1968. Once arrived in Toronto to resume graduate studies, we encountered a new and unfamiliar set of social and political dynamics. The atmosphere of nationalist pride and the exhilaration generated by the previous year's centennial celebrations still lingered, but the residual euphoria mingled uneasily with the growing momentum of Quebec nationalism. Indigenous resistance to colonial policies and territorial infringements had been renewed following World War II and intensified during the 1960s. A further factor that complicated national and local politics was the increased pace of demographic diversification brought about by postwar immigration. I vividly remember my first months in Canada, when the Ontario Ministry of Culture and Communication gave me a temporary job dispensing information about programs for new Canadians at its booth at the Canadian National Exhibition. Each day for nearly three weeks, in the space adjacent to our booth, a different group of young people came to demonstrate the music and dance of the ethnic group to which they belonged. Accustomed to thinking of "immigrants" as largely elderly people who had arrived in North America in the early twentieth century and whose children had long fled the inner-city neighbourhoods where their parents still resided for the assimilated life of the suburbs, I found the energy of these demonstrations amazing. Both their vitality and the official government sponsorship impressed me as evidence of a much more celebratory attitude toward cultural diversity. As I argue in these pages, the challenge posed to the traditional construct of Canada as a settler nation rooted in French and British colonial histories by increasingly effective Aboriginal activism and the growth of diasporic communities provided not just the backdrop to a history of museum change but, rather, its enabling conditions.

The year 1969 saw a defining shift in the relationship of Aboriginal people to the Canadian state when a highly effective group of political activists forced the federal government to withdraw its White Paper, or "Statement of the Government of Canada on Indian Policy." The proposed new policy centred on the repeal of the Indian Act, a piece of nineteenth-century legislation that, although many times amended, continued to define Indigenous people as wards of the Crown and to control their lives in myriad ways. As a classic liberal gesture, the White Paper was intended to make In-digenous people equal to all other Canadians under the law. Yet from an Indigenous perspective, as argued by Aboriginal political activists in their Red Paper (formally entitled "Citizens Plus"), such an action would constitute the capstone of the government's century-old policy of assimilation.[2] By eliminating the economic benefits and special status historically granted to Aboriginal people in exchange for all that had been taken away, it would prevent their recovery from a century of oppressive assimilationist policies and the scourge of residential schooling and would impede the restoration and preservation of indigenous cultural traditions.

Two Founding Races and Multiculturalism

The epochal nature of the shift in national historical consciousness that these events foreshadowed has become clear with the passage of time, but in 1969 the distinctive nature of Aboriginal claims was a case that still had to be made. The special status of Native peoples among the demographic minorities within Canada has become accepted only as a result of sustained political activism and negotiation during the next three decades. Aboriginal political leaders gained affirmation from the global struggles for decolonization, national liberation, civil rights, and restorative justice of the late twentieth century. They also forced federal and provincial governments to recognize that their claims to vast tracts of land within Canada for which treaties had never been signed would have to be resolved before major power projects and resource development critical to the Canadian economy could go ahead.

Official settler histories have traditionally inscribed an origin story of Canada as the product of two founding "races" or "nations," the French and the British. Aboriginal activism helped to rupture this narrative. Their adoption of the collective terms First Peoples and First Nations is a pointed corrective to this historical construct, and they were joined in their revisionist project by members of other minority groups. The crucible in which a new and more pluralist amalgam of Canadian identity was formed was, unexpectedly, the Royal Commission on Bilingualism and Biculturalism. The B and B Commission, as it is commonly known, had been established in 1963 by Prime Minister Lester Pearson to counter the threat to Canadian federalism posed by Quebec's Quiet Revolution and growing nationalist movement. It was mandated to "inquire into and report upon the existing state of bilingualism and biculturalism in Canada and to recommend what steps should be taken to develop the Canadian Confederation on the basis of an equal partnership between the two founding races, taking into account the contribution made by the other ethnic groups to the cultural enrichment of Canada and the measures that should be taken to safeguard that contribution."[3] The commission was chaired by a French Canadian, André Laurendeau, and an English Canadian, Davidson Dunton, and its members included representatives of Canada's ten provinces. Early in the commission's deliberations, Aboriginal people raised vigorous objections to the notion of "two founding races" because of the erasure it implied of their own status as the primordial founding peoples of the country. Representatives of other minorities also objected to the dualism of the commission's guiding mandate, and it was a Ukrainian-Canadian senator who first proposed the term "multicultural" as a better way to characterize Canadian society.[4] The shift in historical consciousness that resulted was evidenced by the decision of the members of the royal commission to add a fourth volume to their final report entitled *The Cultural Contribution of the Other Ethnic Groups.*[5]

When Prime Minister Pierre Elliott Trudeau addressed Parliament in 1971 to announce his government's acceptance of the B and B Commission's recommendations in volume 4, he officially endorsed this new model of multiculturalism:

> It was the view of the Royal Commission, shared by the government and, I am sure, by all Canadians, that there cannot be one cultural policy for Canadians of British and French origin, another for the original peoples and yet a third for all others. For although there are two official languages, there is no official culture, nor does any ethnic group take precedence over any other. No citizen or group of citizens is other than Canadian, and all should be treated fairly … A policy of multiculturalism within a bilingual framework commends itself to the government as the most suitable means of assuring the cultural freedom of Canadians. Such a policy should help to break down discriminatory attitudes and cultural jealousies. National unity if it is to mean anything in the deeply personal sense, must be founded on confidence in one's own individual identity; out of this can grow respect for that of others and a willingness to share ideas, attitudes and assumptions. A vigorous policy of multiculturalism will help create this initial confidence. It can form the base of a society which is based on fair play for all.[6]

Trudeau's notion of multiculturalism, like that of the commission, remained framed within and subsidiary to the language-based dualism of the report's major recommendations. It was also strongly federalist, asserting an overarching national identity that would subsume all other individual and group differences. Although official multiculturalism has been the subject of lively critique in subsequent years, the introduction of a more pluralist concept of the country opened a space for a more fundamental redefinition of Canadian identity, one that has widened in subsequent decades.[7] As a new century dawned, this broadening was manifested when, for example, successive Liberal governments broke the long-standing tradition of alternating French- and English-Canadian appointments to the office of governor general by naming a Chinese Canadian and a Haitian Canadian (both of whom had come to Canada as immigrants), although the tradition of alternating francophones and anglophones was maintained.[8]

During the 1970s and 1980s the demands of Quebec nationalists and Aboriginal peoples for the recognition of their sovereignty continued to complicate federal politics. Both issues came to a head as the Trudeau government proceeded with its efforts to eliminate the last legislative remnant of Canada's own colonial status by patriating the country's constitution, which had remained an act of the British Parliament since Confederation. Aboriginal people succeeded in entrenching recognition of their sovereignty in the new constitution that became law in 1982, but the matter of Quebec's status within Canada proved impossible to resolve. And as these political negotiations were taking place, immigration from all over the globe continued to increase the country's cultural diversity. Prior to World War II, immigrants who came to Canada from outside the traditional northern European mother countries had remained largely ghettoized within the dominant anglophone and francophone communities. The image of Canada as a mosaic, which had first been proposed in the 1930s, achieved broad currency in 1965 with the publication of John Porter's sociological study *The Vertical Mosaic*. The idea of the mosaic assumed a positive valence in the popular imagination as a mark of Canada's difference from the "melting pot" ideal promoted in the United States, despite Porter's argument that the Canadian model perpetuated the economic and social dominance of the older immigrant groups.[9]

In 1988 the official policy of multiculturalism that had first been announced by Trudeau in 1971 was enshrined in law with the passage of the Act for the Preservation and Enhancement of Multiculturalism in Canada. Compliance with the act is monitored by the Department of Canadian Heritage, and its own programs and policies, which include funding for museums, galleries, and other cultural institutions, have been reconfigured to support its guarantees. Federal patronage has thus encouraged the implementation of the ideal of "recognition" affirmed by Trudeau in 1971 and subsequently given a genealogy in the liberal philosophical tradition by Charles Taylor in his widely read essay "The Politics of Recognition."[10] Although multicultural policies have also come to define Australia, New Zealand, and other settler nations, as well as former imperial mother countries such as Great Britain and France, polls consistently show that Canadians have come to embrace multiculturalism as a core aspect of their identity to an exceptional degree.

Essaying Indigenization

This summary of a complex matrix of political and social forces, however simplified, suggests the ways in which the four decades of change in Canadian museums traced here have been informed by broader political and social movements. As publicly funded institutions, museums have, at different times and in various parts of the country, been picketed, boycotted, and criticized for perpetuating colonial ideologies and oppressive policies; they have been called upon by governments to implement official multicultural policies; and some have also chosen to play proactive roles by advocating more radical forms of social intervention and reform. The activation of museums, traditionally bastions of high culture and research that valued their academic freedom and detachment from real-world politics, as sites for wider social and political transformation has proved alternately perplexing, frustrating, painful, and exhilarating for those involved.

I began my own professional career in the 1980s in the art history department at Carleton University. Aboriginal artistic traditions were then a kind of academic no man's land. They had been largely abandoned by the anthropologists who had formerly studied them within the sub-field of material culture, and very few art history departments had yet come to include non-Western and especially Indigenous arts in their curricula. In keeping with the practice of many academic art historians, I also took on occasional assignments as a guest curator, and I soon found that Aboriginal arts also fell between two stools in the museum world. Neither historic nor contemporary "Indian" arts had found their way into the collections and permanent exhibitions of art galleries, while contemporary Indigenous art realized in Western genres was uneasily and erratically collected by a few ethnographic museums. In both the academy and the museum I soon found myself caught up in episodes of contestation and revisionism. In the midst of often confusing and challenging events and debates I have found the opportunities for reflection and analysis provided by the conference paper, the review, and the essay to have been not only constructive and cathartic but also necessary complements to active practice. These are the "museum pieces" I gather together in this book.

The chapters were written over a period of twenty years, some for publication and some as conference papers or lectures that have not previously been published. Because most were written *in medias res*, the book has elements of both the chronicle and the analytical study. One purpose in gathering these museum pieces together is to make them newly or more easily accessible. I have left them in their original form as much as possible to preserve their value as artifacts that testify to the way I and many others responded to issues as they unfolded. The revisions I have made in both the published and unpublished texts are intended to clarify arguments, eliminate repetition, or correct information. I have not tried to update references comprehensively, as the enormous expansion of the literature on museums would make doing so too formidable a task.

I have grouped the chapters into four sections that are intended to trace the evolving politics of contestation, theorization and disciplinary revision, and practice over four decades, beginning in 1967. Part One addresses three successive and revealing moments of Indigenous contestation at the site of the museum. The second part examines the complementary process of disciplinary revisionism that such protests helped to stimulate and that has in turn facilitated change. Part Three brings together short reviews and longer discussions of exhibitions that are representative of the processes of critique and experimentation that followed. Each intervened in key modernist museological practices and representational conventions established in earlier years. The final part explores new challenges, opportunities, and directions that define the context in which museums are working in the early twenty-first century.

I also have a larger purpose in bringing these pieces together in the sequence found here. By selecting and ordering them as I have, I hope to make the argument that is suggested by the second part of my title. In my view, the process of change we have witnessed in Canada since Expo 67 can be understood as one of indigenization, in two senses of the word. In a literal sense, indigenization refers to the incorporation into the mainstream museum world of concepts, protocols, and processes that originate in Aboriginal societies. These include ways of thinking about key issues that are central to museum work, such as the nature of materiality, spirituality, community, and history. They also include traditional Aboriginal modes of decision making whose goal is to arrive at consensus through discussions that involve careful and respectful listening and in which all interested parties have equal opportunities to speak. The result of indigenization in this sense has been a kind of hybridization, leading us toward more dialogical ways of determining how the public representation of distinctive cultural traditions should be enacted.

In a second sense, however, I also use the term to refer to a characteristically Canadian model of pluralist negotiation that arises from a unique history of interaction among Indigenous peoples, French and English colonizers and settlers, and diasporic immigrant communities. Such negotiations often privilege a pragmatic capacity for compromise, on the one hand, and, on the other, a case-by-case approach that acknowledges the uniqueness of individual communities and their needs. Repeatedly, the case studies I discuss evidence the ways in which contestation, mediation, and resolution in the museum have followed models of process similar to those that unfold in Canadian society more generally, and they display similar patterns of adaptation and individuation. The culture of negotiation and the ability to tolerate anomalies and ambiguities that characterize Canadian politics on both the macro- and the micro-levels may well be key components of the national identity that we continue to try to define.

Indigenization in both senses flows from the status of Indigenous people as Canada's "significant Other," a structural position occupied elsewhere by other groups whose claims arise from different national and colonial histories – African Americans in the United States, for example, or North Africans in France. The model of partnership between museums and originating communities that has been central to the new Canadian museology is, arguably, derived from the historical relationships between Indigenous peoples and early European colonists that were critical to the fur trade, the central economic activity of the early contact period. As Sherry Brydon and I write in chapter 1, for example, this egalitarian model was invoked in the revisionist historical narrative presented by the Aboriginal curators of the Indians of Canada Pavilion at Expo 67. More recently, it has been urged by John Ralston Saul in his book *A Fair Country: Telling Truths about Canada.*[11] Although such collaborative practices were first developed in response to the demands and needs of Aboriginal peoples, museums soon began to apply the partnership model with equal success to their work with diasporic communities. In this sense, the unique ways in which multiculturalism has been embraced and developed in Canada are owed as much to Aboriginal claims for land and sovereignty and the unfinished business of Quebec nationalism as they are to the sheer size and diversity of "new Canadian" communities.[12]

Opportunities Missed and Taken

To my lasting regret, I just missed seeing the first major public staging of a contestatory history of Aboriginal-settler relationships. In June 1967 my husband and I celebrated the *rite de passage* of university graduation by driving from Boston to Montreal to visit Expo 67. In the fall I would begin graduate work in art history with the goal of specializing in African art. Focused as I was on that part of the world, I failed to visit the Indians of Canada Pavilion, one of the surprise hits of the fair. The anti-colonial critique of standard museum narratives presented by the members of the pavilion's Aboriginal advisory committee was an early warning signal of the struggles over power and representation that were to come, and it can be seen in retrospect as having prepared the ground for the 1969 Red Paper. Despite the buzz of excitement that surrounded the pavilion, however, few visitors are likely to have realized just how precocious and revolutionary its installations were in relation to standard twentieth-century museum exhibits. Canadian museums, furthermore, failed to build on the new approaches to representation it introduced. As I argue in chapter 2, their lack of response testifies to a constitutional resistance to change in institutions such as museums and universities that would have to be confronted in subsequent years.

The renegotiation of power in Canadian museums did not begin in earnest until two decades later, when hands were forced in Canada and abroad by an international boycott of one of the major cultural events of the 1988 Winter Olympics in Calgary. *The Spirit Sings: Artistic Traditions of Canada's First Peoples* was a super-show that brought back to the country hundreds of the oldest extant examples of Aboriginal art, most of which had left Canada in earlier centuries. I had shifted the focus of my research and teaching from African to Native North American art history in the early 1980s, after completing fieldwork in Sierra Leone and a dissertation on Mende women's masquerade traditions. I had also curated *Patterns of Power: The Jasper Grant Collection and Great Lakes Indian Art of the Early Nineteenth Century* for the McMichael Canadian Collection to mark the 1984 bicentennial of the settlement of Ontario by Loyalists from the American colonies.[13] That exhibition, like *From the Four Quarters*, the larger show of Indigenous and settler art organized for the bicentennial at the Art Gallery of Ontario, would likely be criticized today as an appropriation of Indigenous heritage to a settler historical commemoration, especially as no Indigenous consultation or curatorial collaboration was involved. In 1984, however, both exhibitions were shown without incident.[14] When I was invited to serve as one of the six curators of *The Spirit Sings*, I had no reason to anticipate that things would be different.

It is clearer today that events occurring elsewhere were portents of the new role which museum representation would soon assume as a site of postcolonial critique. In 1984, even as the two Ontario bicentennial exhibits of Canadian Aboriginal art were in progress, an explosive controversy erupted around the Museum of Modern Art's exhibition *"Primitivism" in 20th Century Art: Affinity of the Tribal and the Modern*. Its celebration of modern artists' appropriations of Primitive Art galvanized the academic and museum worlds and generated furious debates in the press and academic journals. As I discuss in chapter 2, although these debates influenced the different approach to contextualization developed for *The Spirit Sings*, they did not prepare those involved for the far more activist forms that protest would take when an international boycott of the exhibition was called in support of an unresolved land claim that had brought great suffering to a band of Alberta Cree.

The *Spirit Sings* boycott proved pivotal for Canadian museum history because of the constructive process of deliberation and new policy formulation to which it led. This process resulted from the formation of a national Task Force on Museums and First Peoples, which was mandated to examine the wide range of problems that the boycott had brought to light. Sponsored by the Canadian Museums Association and the Assembly of First Nations (the major national Aboriginal political organization), it was funded through the federal Department of Communications.[15] The task force was chaired by two widely respected museum professionals, one Aboriginal and the other non-Aboriginal – Tom Hill, the director of the museum at the Woodlands Cultural Centre, and Trudy Nicks, curator of anthropology at the Royal Ontario Museum. Its members were drawn in equal numbers from the ranks of Aboriginal and non-Aboriginal professionals working in museums, cultural centres, and heritage organizations. (I, as the only academic member, was something of an anomaly.)

In its composition, mandate, and process the task force was thus a typically Canadian response to a looming crisis or thorny issue of major national importance, and its bicultural structure displays striking parallels to that of the B and B Commission. Meetings were hosted by both Aboriginal and non-Aboriginal institutions and held in different regions of the country. At each venue Indigenous elders conducted opening rituals that engendered an atmosphere of respect and carefulness. Coming in the wake of a divisive national confrontation over power in museums, the task force provided members of the Canadian museum and Aboriginal communities with a cooling-off period, away from the full glare of public scrutiny, during which they could collect facts, sample opinions, identify common interests, investigate alternative models, and propose possible solutions. During the three years of task force meetings, the wounds that the *Spirit Sings* boycott had left in its wake began to heal, making new beginnings possible.

The task force report, issued in 1992, reconceptualized the ways in which Canadian museums and Indigenous peoples should work together in the future.[16] A comparison with the approach taken in the United States around the same time is revealing, although that process addressed only the issue of repatriation, rather that the more comprehensive set of problems covered by the task force. A number of Canadian analysts have argued that the federal law passed by the United States Congress, the Native American Graves Protection and Repatriation Act (NAGPRA), was a better solution than the repatriation guidelines included in the task force report because it has more "teeth." I argue in chapter 7 that both strategies have advantages and disadvantages and both have fostered dialogue and stimulated new practices. Yet I would also argue that the task force process is indigenous to Canada in the sense that it offers the wider latitude for negotiation, interpretation, and case-by-case consideration that has historically suited Canadian needs and temperaments.

The experience of serving on the task force was, for me, profoundly formative, teaching me a great deal about the nature and pace of institutional change. I also came to appreciate the importance of showing up, being there, and listening at moments of discord and crisis. I began to understand the value of dialogue and the simple truth that change is a process that cannot be hurried past investments of time, patience, and respect. This is, I think, what the late Métis-Cree artist and educator Bob Boyer meant when we encountered each other briefly during a coffee break at the meeting that led to the establishment of the task force, the "Preserving Our Heritage" conference, held at Carleton University in Ottawa in November 1988. The meeting took place during the last days of *The Spirit Sings* at its second and final venue, hosted in Ottawa by the Canadian Museum of Civilization, and the conference sessions were suffused with the raw emotions and residual tensions that had been generated by the boycott. Friends and colleagues who had found themselves on different sides of the issues were still barely on speaking terms. But when Bob saw me he said, simply, "You're here. That's good, you're okay."

In the late 1980s museum colleagues in other countries tended to greet the news of the boycotts and debates organized around both *The Spirit Sings* and, the following year, *Into the Heart of Africa* at Toronto's Royal Ontario Museum with a reaction of "There but for the grace of God go I," but its lessons were also quickly learned. One American curator who was organizing a major exhibition of Native American art and culture to mark her state's centennial celebration was spurred to expand its consultative process in order to avoid similar problems.[17] A curator in Britain, who was creating a permanent exhibit about diasporic immigrant communities for a large urban museum, followed the ROM controversy carefully to identify possible pitfalls in her project.[18] The task force process and its report thus excited widespread interest and proved to have enduring value. It has provided a model both as a process of response and as a set of recommended practices that have influenced the work of museums in Australia, Europe, and elsewhere in important ways.

The Spirit Sings and the task force turned me from an art historian who occasionally dabbled in curatorial work into a hybrid art historian–critical museologist. Together they persuaded me, in other words, that academic research, writing, and teaching cannot be kept in a separate compartment either from the politics of identity or from the problems of public representation. This new orientation led, in turn, to a term as a full-time museum professional when I became director of the UBC Museum of Anthropology (MoA) in 1997. Four months after my arrival, Canada took its turn as host of the meeting of Asia-Pacific Economic Cooperation (APEC). The federal government had chosen MoA, with its magnificent architecture and natural setting, as the site of the APEC leaders' meeting. That event, as many will remember, sparked the first of the large anti-globalization protests that have since become regular features of economic summits. The UBC protests were staged right outside the museum's doors, and widely publicized police infringements of the protestors' civil rights resulted in an equally well-publicized public inquiry. In chapter 3 I discuss a less well-known backstory involving a serious breach of the protocol agreements that the museum and the university had worked hard to develop with local First Nations in the years after the release of the task force report. I explore this incident as an object lesson that illustrates the delicate balance between the museum's vulnerability to appropriation and its ability to advocate for social justice.

During the decade that followed the task force report, Canadian museums began to experiment with ways of implementing its guidelines. Its central recommendation was that museums and originating communities should henceforth work together as partners, but the all-important details of what partnership meant in practice remained to be worked out. Similarly, there were few models for implementing its recommendations for handling sacred items, adjudicating repatriation claims, creating Aboriginal training programs, or improving access to collections. Equally, the principle of respect for Aboriginal knowledges required a rethinking of definitions of authority, "expertise," and, consequently, the contributions that could be made by academically trained specialists. The chapters in Part Two explore the critical re-evaluation of modern Western disciplinary traditions that had to be undertaken in order to respond to such questions.

In the heat of contestation there was a tendency for critics, both Aboriginal and non-Aboriginal, to issue totalizing condemnations of Western scholarly traditions – views that continue to be voiced today. The implicit and explicit burden of argument in many of the chapters in this book is that such a position is not only wasteful but also impossible. Even apart from the value of Western disciplinary formations and methods of archival research and material culture study, Western ways of knowing have become inextricably interwoven with Indigenous ways in the course of several centuries of contact and colonialism: they have been "indigenized" in the opposite sense from the way I have used the term thus far. Trained in the same schools and universities as non-Aboriginal people and armed with the same tools of post-structuralist and postcolonial analysis, contemporary Indigenous scholars have deployed these methods in the service of their own goals. At the same time, however, non-Aboriginal scholars and museum professionals have also been learning the value of balancing Western disciplinary knowledges with traditional Indigenous perspectives. Although there are certainly Indigenous academics and activists who would disagree, in my view indigenization is a process of hybridization that works and has always worked, in two directions. Western scholars have, however, been far more reluctant to recognize and profit from the methods and insights embedded in Indigenous knowledge traditions. In this context, the most exciting products of new partnership arrangements in museums have been the creative, innovative, hybrid, and effective solutions contributed by Indigenous collaborators out of their historical experience and knowledge of traditional principles, protocols, and practices. The chapters in Part Three examine several experimental collaborations between museums and Aboriginal artists and communities that featured such Indigenous critiques and innovations.

The last section of the book includes chapters on several early twenty-first-century museum projects that illustrate possible future directions for history, art, and anthropology museums. It begins with a discussion of the plans for the Aboriginal component of the projected Portrait Gallery of Canada, for which I served as a guest curator. Although this new and innovative national museum became a casualty of wasteful political jealousies on Parliament Hill and arrived in the world stillborn, even as a paper creation it usefully illustrates the challenges posed by inclusivity. Thus far, Western genres and media have largely been assumed as the standards to which the newly included will adhere. How might a Western genre such as the portrait be translated into non-Western traditions of thought and representation? In chapter 14 I continue to explore twenty-first-century approaches to inclusivity and genre in relation to two groundbreaking early twenty-first-century installations of Canadian art, one at the National Gallery of Canada and the other at Art Gallery of Ontario.

Chapter 15 returns me to my years at the UBC Museum of Anthropology and to a major redesign of its facilities conceived specifically to support the collaborative models of work that have become normative in Canadian anthropology museums. Our project was stimulated by the creation of a new federal fund to support the creation of innovative research infrastructure in Canadian non-profit institutions. The availability of this resource spurred us to think not only about the built environment of the museum but also about how electronic networks could be mobilized to transform access to museum collections. In order to apply for the new money, we also had to make a compelling argument for the value of the museum as a research institution, something that would not have had to be justified in earlier years but today must be reasserted after years of academic neglect and Indigenous critique. Our success in the grant competition made it possible for MoA and its three First Nations partners to realize and build further on these plans. When I returned to Carleton University and the academic world of teaching and research in 2003, I was able to initiate a parallel electronic network that supports collaborative research in my own area of specialization, Great Lakes Aboriginal arts and cultures. As chapter 15 also recounts, the preliminary results of this project suggest how Western and Indigenous knowledge traditions can complement each other to produce new understandings of Indigenous heritage.

The last chapter in the book considers the positive value of controversy itself. Using the work of Bruno Latour and other actor-network theorists, I argue that museums should work *with*, rather than try to avoid, the heterogeneous entanglements that have produced episodes of museum contestation and disruption. The tremendous revelatory power such events have had, as these chapters demonstrate, has been due in part to the ways in which they have illuminated the nature of the museum's agency and its connectedness to larger social processes. Heterogeneity and hybridity have also come to characterize the approaches to installation and representation of many museums in a more literal way. Here too I find the concepts advanced through actor-network theory useful in understanding these practices as products of controversy. Museums, I urge, should be willing to risk even greater messiness in the future by seeking direct social engagements and opportunities for experimentation. In a period when they have to work with less and less government support, such a willingness can mean foregoing the slickness and professional gloss in presentation that have come to seem indispensable.

As I write this preface, the daily listserv of the Canadian Museums Association offers up an example. An article describes an exhibit entitled *From Manila to Manitoba*, which is about to open at the Manitoba Museum in Winnipeg. It seems to exemplify the auto-ethnographic work of "recognition" that Trudeau advocated four decades ago, however much he may also have sought at the time to contain its power. The Winnipeg exhibition is community-curated, the writer explains, put together largely by volunteers from the local Filipino community in order to foster understanding of their community's immigrant experience. Darlene Bautistia, one of the volunteer curators, tells the journalist that, although born in Winnipeg, she has been asked all her life where she is from. "'It's tiring being the perpetual stranger,' says the young woman, who feels that many Manitobans lump Filipinos in with other Asians and lack understanding of the "culture of migration" that has propelled thousands of Filipinos to seek better lives in Canada.[19]

The exhibit, it is clear, was developed with very few resources. It consists of "27 large display panels, some tracing events in the Philippines and some documenting the evolution of the community in Winnipeg. The panels combine text, personal and historical photographs, quotations from interview subjects and enlarged newspaper clippings. 'It's our story,' says Maria Monica de Castro, 21, a member of the research team who immigrated here when she was eight years old. 'It's a way for future generations to know what their parents have been through.'"[20] Despite its modest scale, low budget, and global diasporic focus, *From Manila to Manitoba* is, I would argue, a direct descendant of the Indians of Canada Pavilion at Expo 67. It shares the politics of voice and the activist spirit that were first manifested in that much larger, more expensive, and more elaborately produced project, where the indigenization of Canadian museums began.

History + Theory + Practice = Critical Museology

There is a conversation I have found myself having at regular intervals during the past ten years. Typically, it takes place between me in my persona as a hybrid academic–museum professional and a museum curator working with university students who are writing papers or theses about exhibits in her museum. The conversation goes like this:

> CURATOR. "You know, Student X gave me a draft of her thesis chapter on our museum the other day," or "I talked to a museum studies class Professor Y brought over here last week and then they wrote papers on our new exhibition." (*Pregnant pause.*)
>
> ME. You mean she/they started from the assumptions that any representation in a museum obviously had to be an example of neo-colonial and hegemonic oppression of the Other and that you had never talked to an Aboriginal person in the course of creating it … Oh, and also they took it as a given that any right-thinking person would agree that the museum should just give everything back to Aboriginal people?
>
> CURATOR, *eagerly*. Yes! They don't seem to understand that (a) we had no final control over those captions because the interpretive planners rewrote them, or (b) our Aboriginal consultants made the very decisions they criticized, or (c) we've received very few requests for repatriation and a lot of the things in the collection were made to sell for the tourist trade anyway.
>
> ME, *sympathetically but also guiltily*. Yes, well, you know today's students have been brought up on the literature of critical museology assigned by people like me, and a lot of it is written by academic theorists with little or no experience working in museums, so the students naturally apply what they've read and offer simple solutions to complicated situations.

The conversation usually concludes with a mutual agreement that such black-and-white forms of analysis and understanding are inadequate and that we need to find ways to encourage more complex and nuanced kinds of analysis.

On one level, such exchanges are evidence of a positive development: the rapid maturing of an interdiscipline of critical museology that did not exist in the early 1980s, when I first began to do curatorial work. Since then, museums have become popular subjects of academic study and critique, not only within museum studies programs (of which there were relatively few in the 1980s) but also in art history, anthropology, sociology, history, communications, cultural studies, and numerous other fields. The museum has become both a site of practice for which multiple forms of specialized professional training are required and a kind of whetstone for sharpening tools of representational analysis and postcolonial critique. My own movements back and forth between the museum and the academy have persuaded me that our most effective studies of museums are those that are informed by history *and* theory *and* practice. In addition to documenting a history of museum change, then, I offer the chapters in this book to demonstrate the usefulness of this mix. As suggested by the imagined scenario with which I began this section, I also hope to complicate the seductive but ever-present temptation – to which I have myself succumbed more than once – to force the irregular profiles of real-world museum dilemmas into one-size-fits-all theoretical boxes. I will suggest ways to bridge the gap that currently exists between theoretical and practical approaches in two ways. First, I will offer a brief discussion of key texts that have shaped my understanding of museum representation. Secondly, I will propose a case-study approach to museum pedagogy that combines theoretical and historical perspectives with experiences of practice.

Museums became the subject of academic scrutiny rather suddenly during the 1990s, as evidenced by the tremendous growth of the small existing literature on museums. The rapidity with which the critique of the museum progressed was due in part to the heated debates around exhibitions that erupted during the late 1980s, but it was also a product of the reflexivity fostered by the development of critical theory and cultural studies during the previous two decades (see chapter 5). It is impossible to do justice to the now extensive literature on critical museology in a few paragraphs, and I will, rather, point to a set of pioneering works published during the 1990s that provided me with a tool kit with which I continue to think and teach. Even within these limits, the body of work I outline here is not intended to be either comprehensive or representative, but is instead a personal compilation of texts that I encountered early on and found particularly illuminating.

Late twentieth-century writing on museums, I would argue, displays three distinct approaches: deconstruction, effective history, and reconstruction. They developed, generally speaking, as a progressive unfolding of theory into practice. The deconstructive impulse is well represented by a number of widely cited essays in the influential 1991 anthology edited by Ivan Karp and Steven D. Lavine, *Exhibiting Cultures: The Poetics and Politics of Museum Display*.[21] Papers such as James Clifford's "Four Northwest Coast Museums," Stephen Greenblatt's "Resonance and Wonder," Barbara Kirshenblatt-Gimblett's "Objects of Ethnography," and Svetlana Alpers's "The Museum as a Way of Seeing" denaturalize the modernist paradigms and technologies of display and the ways in which they have privileged particular kinds of knowledge and empowered particular social groups. Together with Susan Vogel's innovative exhibition publication *Art/artifact: African Art in Anthropology Collections* and Sally Price's *Primitive Art in Civilized Places*,[22] they have stood as key points of reference for the analysis of Western ideals of aesthetic experience and scientific objectification. They also illuminate how resulting hierarchies are being renegotiated through postcolonial, feminist, and other critiques of established regimes of power.

Arjun Appadurai's groundbreaking *The Social Life of Things* stimulated a revival of anthropological interest in the study of material culture. His introduction and Igor Kopytoff's essay "The Cultural Biography of Things: Commoditization as Process" made strong arguments for the role of material objects in social formations and for the insights gained into larger social processes by tracing transformations in the meanings associated with objects as they move through time and across cultures.[23] James Clifford's work in *Writing Culture: The Poetics and Politics of Ethnography* (co-edited with George E. Marcus) and his essay collections *The Predicament of Culture* and *Routes: Travel and Translation in the Late Twentieth Century* extended the reflexive consideration of anthropological discourse. His much cited essays identify the interlocking nature of the institutions of art and culture, the role served by museums as "contact zones," the legacies of modernist primitivism, and the impact of global and colonial patterns of travel and circulation on the cultural politics of the late twentieth century.[24] The work of Nicholas Thomas and Annie Coombes has been important in deepening understanding of the role played by art and material culture in the making and unmaking of colonial regimes of power. Coombes's *Reinventing Africa* is a highly original and penetrating investigation of the historical reception of Benin brasses not only in Britain but also in Africa and its diaspora, while Thomas's explorations of processes of exchange and circulation in the Pacific in *Entangled Objects* and *Colonialism's Cultures* develop paradigmatic studies of the cultural biography of things and the kinds of agency objects acquire in museums.[25]

As an art historian, I am drawn to such historical and diachronic accounts as a primary mode of explanation. Uncovering the many micro-histories that lie behind museums and their collections seems a necessary first step in understanding how we have come to have certain kinds of material evidence of the past rather than others – not only objects but also buildings and spaces of display – and historical analyses also make us aware of the limitations and opportunities that arise from our inherited forms of documentation and representation. In this context, the literature on collecting history has been indispensable, notably the key early compilation *The Origins of Museums*, edited by Oliver Impey and Arthur MacGregor, and studies of curiosity collecting and display by Krzysztof Pomian and Horst Bredekamp.[26] Equally important has been work on nineteenth- and early twentieth-century anthropological collecting, such as George W. Stocking Jr's edited volume *Objects and Others* and the detailed account of the development of scholarship and collecting within the Smithsonian Institution's Bureau of American Ethnology provided by Curtis Hinsley in *Savages and Scientists*.[27]

These and other related works provided the basis for several compelling theorizations of the social functions that Western museums have performed since the Renaissance. Eilean Hooper-Greenhill's *Museums and the Shaping of Knowledge* rewrites the history of museums in terms of Foucault's notion of "effective history" and his theorization of the epistemic shifts of Western knowledge formation. Tony Bennett also draws on Foucault in *The Birth of the Museum*, using his theorizations of institutional surveillance and discipline to analyse the kinds of spectatorial spaces created by public exhibitions. Both he and Carol Duncan, in *Civilizing Rituals: Inside Public Art Museums*, argue that during the nineteenth century the public museum became a key institution for the production of the kinds of citizens required by emerging democratic nation states. Duncan also draws on anthropological theories of ritual process to explicate the ways in which the organization of a museum's displays and visitor path cause members of the public to interiorize narratives productive of a sense of national identity. Their insights continue to explain how museums do the work of social reproduction, whether they are in Calgary, Canberra, London, or Alert Bay.[28]

The third strand in the literature of critical museology, which I term "reconstructive," models and makes available for future use the innovative practices and processes through which museums have been responding to such deconstructive analyses, as well as to Indigenous contestations and interventions. During the 1990s, participants in such projects began to share their experiences through exhibition publications, articles, and conference papers. It is even harder here to single out individual examples, but Aldona Jonaitis's *Chiefly Feasts* and particularly her introductory essay and that of her chief collaborator, Kwakwaka'wakw curator Gloria Cranmer Webster, are good examples.[29] The exhibition project engaged contemporary Kwakwaka'wakw community members in the interpretation of the important collections made by Franz Boas and George Hunt for the American Museum of Natural History during the early twentieth century. The curators' reflections demonstrated the power of community collaboration in recovering orally transmitted knowledge and community memory and in making available new kinds of historical perspectives.

If there is one book, however, that precociously envisioned the possibility of a major paradigm shift in the work of museums it must be Michael Ames's *Cannibal Tours and Glass Boxes: The Anthropology of Museums* (1992), an expanded and revised version of his 1985 book *Museums, the Public and Anthropology*.[30] In the preface to the second edition Ames writes that the essays "document my own struggles to achieve a practical understanding of a cultural complex in which I was also actively involved, to relate experience to critique and then to action."[31] The emphasis on the practical and on action reflect the innovative environment in which Ames and his staff had been working at the UBC Museum of Anthropology throughout the 1980s. He had early insisted on the need for museums to practise reflexivity and self-critique, urging museum workers to examine their institutions as cultural artifacts of the societies that produced them and to study themselves as an "exotic tribe" of museum professionals. Ames argued that such analyses reveal the inherent contradictions of the museum as a product of late modern political and economic systems – displaying both impulses toward further popularization and democratization and the increasing dominance of consumer-oriented economics. Influenced not only by theorists such as Gramsci, Althusser, and Foucault but also by the populist activism of Paolo Freire and writing on the sociology of organizations, Ames used his analyses of the deep structures of power and organizations to invent innovative approaches to museum administration. The commitment to action was, for him, an ethical imperative, a part of an individual's and a museum's responsibility to society. Criticism, he believed, had, in the end, to be "useful." I inherited Ames's strong legacy when I followed him as director of the UBC Museum of Anthropology, and many others have also benefited from it.

Ames's work brings me, finally, to the challenge that is posed by critical museum studies as a basis for training museum professionals. I privilege case studies in this book because of their potential for providing historical perspective *and* a site for theoretical analysis *and* models of innovative practices. Not all case studies, of course, attend to all of these aspects, and those that I have sketched here certainly fall short of the fully developed forms which, I believe, are needed in order to develop a new pedagogy in critical museology. Museum training can, I would argue, profitably borrow from the kind of case-study method used to teach in schools of business, medicine, social work, and other fields. Such an approach would provide students with full details regarding the development and reception of exhibitions and other projects, ideally allowing them to trace a project from the initial proposal through its formulation and budgeting in grant applications to its development by the full range of museum professionals whose contributions lead to the final realization. The dossier for an exhibition would document the selection of works and the success or failure of loan requests; the development of the storyline from its original scripting to the modifications introduced through focus groups, interpretive planners, and others; the process and products of consultations with collaborators; the design process and its adaptation in different venues; the text panels and captions; a full visual documentation of the installations; details of the marketing and public relations campaigns, the educational programs; the design of websites and blogs; the souvenirs sold in the museum shop; and copies of the reviews and visitor comments. Such dossiers would make evident the mediated nature of the final forms in which museum representations reach the public and prepare students to recognize not only potential pitfalls but also sources of creativity and resiliency.[32]

Case studies are, in this sense, micro-histories that have the potential both to model best practices and to raise awareness of the consequences of such problems as poor communication among staff, failure to adapt to sudden changes in the external environment, pressures to "dumb down" content to meet arbitrary profiles of the "average" visitor, and shortfalls in funding. Such training would inoculate students against the expectation of total control acquired in the individualistic culture of the academy. At the heart of this methodology, too, is a recognition of the distinctive quality of the network of people, politics, and resources in which each museum is situated. The pluralist world in which we live, it seems to me, requires that we approach each new museum project by tailoring it to the unique combination of history and needs in which it is embedded through the respectful process of negotiation and compromise that I have framed as indigenization.

As I noted at the beginning of this introduction, for the past twenty-five years Canadians have lived with ambiguities and anomalies that result from the desires for special status and the protection of their distinctive cultures of francophone Quebecers and First Nations. They also, increasingly, live with the logical contradictions that arise from Canada's self-identification as both a single nation and a multicultural entity. The dynamic mixture that results is volatile and threatening as well as fertile and productive, not only on the political but also on the cultural-institutional level. It has pushed the Canadian museum community to develop new practices adequate to the ways in which the peoples who live in Canada want and need to represent themselves to each other. In museums, as in broader political processes, the negotiation of new relationships with francophones and Indigenous peoples provides models for the accommodation of pluralism more broadly. Together with many colleagues in the Canadian museum and academic communities, I have been challenged and privileged to observe and participate in a historic process of museological contestation, negotiation, and reinvention. Although much has changed, much still remains to be changed. It ceased, years ago, to be the work of any one generation.

PART ONE   CONFRONTATION AND CONTESTATION

Undoing the Settler Museum:
Showing Off and Showing Up

It has become a normative aspect of public culture to plan major exhibitions in conjunction with an important historical anniversary or the hosting of a major international event. These "show times" begin as occasions for the nation to "show off" its colourful history, its modern and enlightened present, and its confident expectation of an even better future.[1] Museums welcome such events as opportunities to mount projects that would normally be beyond their scope. A simple formula usually applies: the bigger the event, the bigger the budget and the more ambitious the exhibition. In Canada during the past four decades, such moments have also become strategically useful to the decolonizing campaigns of Indigenous people. The three chapters in this section narrate the postcolonial reform of the Canadian museum in terms of the Indigenous contestations of settler histories of the nation staged at three moments when Canada put itself on display before the international community.

Whether the focus of an exhibition is art, history, sport, or something else, the exhibitions organized at show times invite a greater than usual temporal, cultural, and geographic breadth. Because the stories told on such occasions tend to be larger and more comprehensive, successful contestations have a greater potential to embarrass the institutions and their government backers. Predicated on the availability of corporate sponsorship and/or special allocations of public money, such exhibitions are conceived from the start on a scale well beyond normal levels of institutional and

governmental funding. At show times, then, the museum's ties to the business and political establishments are unusually tight and transparent. Like a raking light, the glare of publicity picks out the sponsors' logos on posters, advertising, and exhibition signage, laying open to public scrutiny relationships of dependency that are normally at least partly masked.

The high public profile of these special exhibitions has provided members of disempowered and marginalized groups with a valuable opportunity for "showing up" in two senses of the phrase. On one level, Aboriginal people have shown up bodily, organizing demonstrations, counter-exhibitions, and public debates. On another, they have used these occasions to initiate projects of analysis and critique that show up the inaccuracies, silences, or misrepresentations embedded in the exhibitions or public representations. The three moments of protest I examine in this section were provoked by museological displays that focused on Indigenous arts, cultures, and histories. Spanning a thirty-year period, they both illustrate a range of different settings and strategies and demonstrate the ways in which each contestation changed the terms of engagement for the next.

In chapter 1 Sherry Brydon and I discuss the Indians of Canada Pavilion organized for Montreal's Expo 67. In this case the contestation occurred within the government agencies charged with developing the official displays about Canada for the world's fair. As we demonstrate, a successful palace coup staged by Indigenous people brought in to work on the pavilion led to their successful takeover of power. The pavilion that resulted constituted the first large-scale public representation of Indigenous Canadian history and contemporary societies authored by Indigenous people. Chapter 2 discusses what is perhaps the most famous museum controversy in Canadian history, the boycott and protest that arose around the exhibition organized by the Glenbow Museum for the Calgary Winter Olympics of 1988, *The Spirit Sings: Artistic Traditions of Canada's First Peoples*. Here, as I will argue, the organizers and curators (myself included) failed to assimilate the lessons that could have been learned from the Indians of Canada Pavilion. Equally, as I will also argue, the sizable body of critical writing stimulated by the exhibition fails to recognize the ways in which the exhibition intervened innovatively in the standard modernist paradigms for the display of Indigenous arts and histories that had located them in a frozen "ethnographic present," and that, to a degree, had still been in evidence in the Expo 67 pavilion.

In a number of its aspects, *The Spirit Sings* set a standard that subsequent exhibitions would build on. Chapter 3 focuses, not on an exhibition per se, but on the implications of the government of Canada's use of the University of British Columbia's Museum of Anthropology as the site for the 1997 APEC (Asia-Pacific Economic Cooperation) leaders' meeting. In this case the museum's newly minted protocols for working respectfully with Indigenous First Nations, developed during the preceding decade as a direct result of the *Spirit Sings* debates and

within the framework of the *Report of the Task Force on Museums and First Peoples* of 1992, were disabled and suspended by the government's actions, revealing the slippage that increasingly occurs between official and museological modes of interaction.

These events and exhibitions are not, of course, the only ones that have stimulated revisionism, protest, or controversy. The chapters in this section can be read in conjunction with chapter 8, in which I discuss *Indigena* and *Land, Spirit, Power*, two landmark exhibitions of contemporary Indigenous art organized in 1992 by the Canadian Museum of Civilization and the National Gallery of Canada in conjunction with the Columbus quincentennial. Other important protests have targeted longstanding installations of particular works of art. In 1996, for example, the Assembly of First Nations successfully orchestrated a campaign to have the kneeling figure of the generic Indian scout removed from the base of the early twentieth-century monument erected to Samuel de Champlain on Ottawa's Nepean Point. Similarly, after years of protest, in 2007 First Nations succeeded in forcing the removal of historical murals painted for the British Columbia legislature by George Southwell in 1932, which, in their view, contain demeaning images of Indigenous people. Such contestations of public monuments and major exhibitions have attracted national attention, raising consciousness not only of the perspectives of Indigenous critics but also of their activism and determination to effect change, not just in relation to public art and exhibitions but also in negotiations of land claims, sovereignty, and social programs.

Taken together, these moments of protest comprise a mini-history of change that is historically significant and irreversible, though also uneven and incomplete. It illustrates not an uninterrupted vector of progress toward decolonization but, rather, an uneven line whose dips and rises mirror swings from liberalism to reaction in Canadian politics. In the mid-1960s, where I begin this history of focused protest, there was, as Karen Coody Cooper has written, "a closed loop of information serving to exclude American Indian knowledge and sensitivities."[2] Thirty years later, when the APEC meeting took place, Indigenous peoples' rights to control or at least to collaborate meaningfully in public representations of their cultures had been widely recognized by Canadian and American museums. The analysis of this period, then, provides an opportunity to explore more general patterns of relationship between the staging of exhibitions, the broader formulation of national policies, and the politics of pluralism.

In recent years, museums have become increasingly cautious about exhibitions that could spark controversies.[3] This is, in my view, the wrong lesson to be learned from the three case studies in this section. If we need convincing, we need only to ask what capacity museums and their sponsoring institutions would today have to respond to and represent the demands of an increasingly diverse society if it had not been for the public debates stimulated by Expo 67,

The Spirit Sings, and the APEC protests. Perhaps the most dramatic proof of the cumulative changes these events helped to bring about was at the opening ceremonies of the 2010 Vancouver Winter Olympics, when millions around the world watched as First Nations dancers offered the first welcome to the foreign visitors to Canada and the chiefs of the four host nations, dressed in their traditional regalia, sat together with the prime minister and the governor general. I will return to the topic of controversy and its value to the socially activist museum in the last part of this book.

1

"Arrow of Truth"

The Indians of Canada Pavilion at Expo 67

WITH SHERRY BRYDON

Those Indians of Canada have bowed ... an arrow of truth at the Canadian government and white man – telling "le monde entier" just what they think of us.
– *Michael McGarry in the* Winnipeg Tribune *(1967)*

The government really wanted a positive image in that pavilion and what they got was the truth. That's what really shocked them the most.
– *Tom Hill, Seneca artist and curator (1976)*

The year 1967 was a time of nationalist euphoria in Canada. The country was celebrating the one-hundredth anniversary of Confederation, its union as a new nation formed out of a group of British colonies. Within fifteen years Canada would complete the process begun in 1867 by patriating the British North America Act, a piece of British parliamentary legislation that had served as the country's effective constitution since then. During the centennial year a wave of constructive energy swept the country, leaving behind new hockey rinks, museums, civic buildings, roads, acres of fresh paint, and the memories of a thousand parties. The most dazzling of all the construction projects, and the biggest birthday party of all, was, of course, Expo 67, the Montreal world's fair.

One of the highlights of the fair was the Indians of Canada Pavilion, and it was perhaps typical of the decade of the sixties that its popularity was produced by dissonance rather than harmony (fig. 1.1). Inside the pavilion, visitors were confronted with the abstention of Canadian peoples from the general celebration and with the message that for these peoples the century since Confederation had been one of repression, loss, and deterioration in lifestyle.[1] In contrast to earlier exhibitions, the installations affirmed the contemporary value of cultural difference and the survival of traditional values and beliefs in the face of great odds.[2] The evidence of this survival – and of successful adaptations to the modern world – was expressed most vibrantly and concretely by the remarkable assemblage of contemporary Indian art commissioned for the pavilion's exterior and also displayed inside.

1.1   The Indians of Canada Pavilion at Expo 67, with mural by George Clutesi. © Government of Canada; reproduced with the permission of the Minister of Public Works and Government Services Canada (2011). Library and Archives Canada, Canadian Corporation for the 1967 World Exhibition fonds/ e001096685

Anniversary celebrations such as the Canadian centennial are, as Tony Bennett has observed, "events intended to mark the historical time of the nation," and he notes that "the initiatives such celebrations call forth are predominantly historical in orientation."[3] The Indians of Canada Pavilion framed its messages in the form of a revisionist historical narrative that refuted the venerable doctrine of progress through assimilation inscribed by official government policy, academic texts, and museum displays. In the early twenty-first century the radical nature both of the interior installations and of the politics of self-empowerment that made them possible seem to prefigure many of the issues of pluralism and representation that have engaged the Canadian museum community most urgently during the intervening decades.

Scholars interested in the history of contemporary Native art have studied the pavilion project because of its pivotal importance to the history of contemporary Canadian Indigenous art. Yet, despite the pavilion's historical significance, no comprehensive published record exists of its installations and their development apart from Sherry Brydon's article on its program of contemporary art.[4] Although this lack is characteristic of world's fairs, which are by definition ephemeral events, the gap is, nonetheless, a serious one, especially because the afterlife of the pavilion project has extended well beyond its brief existence as the physical embodiment of a contestatory self-representation.[5] In the years since Expo 67 many Indigenous people who worked on the pavilion have identified the experience as a formative moment in the development of an activist Indian cultural politics. The project forged a sense of common purpose among the participating artists, organizers, and activists from across Canada, and the experience of effective collaboration left a legacy of self-confidence and a sense of possibility. This chapter documents the process by which the Indians of Canada Pavilion at Expo 67 was developed and reconstructs its architecture, art, and interior installations from the extant archival records. It relies heavily on exhaustive archival research conducted by Brydon in the early 1990s, which makes possible the analysis of the pavilion's significance in light of the more recent politics of Aboriginal representation.[6]

Bureaucrats and Activists: The Genesis of a Separate Pavilion

Planning for the Canadian contributions to Expo 67 began in the early 1960s under the auspices of three separate governmental agencies: the Centennial Corporation for World Exhibitions (CCWE), a Crown corporation established to oversee the development of a broad range of centennial projects, including Expo; the Centennial Commission; and the Department of Citizenship and Immigration, whose Indian Affairs Branch took on specific responsibility for projects concerning Canadian Indians.[7] Initial plans were grounded in the assumption that, as at previous fairs, the stories of Aboriginal peoples and other "ethnic groups" within Canada would be folded into the master narrative of a single Canada Pavilion. One bureaucrat urged, in this context, a "balanced portrayal," which would "prevent the over-stressing of the accomplishments of a particular group." He envisioned, for example, that "Indian paintings should be a part of the general Art Exhibit and that Indian handicraft should be shown along with the handicraft of the other elements of our population. Again, the contribution of the Indian, of maize, potatoes, and tobacco might be part of a general display of agricultural achievements, as his use and design of sleds, birch-bark canoes, toboggans and snowshoes might be part of a general story of the development of transportation."[8] The initial concept was thus a conventional, totalizing vision of Canadian history in which distinct groups within the population were subsumed as "contributors" within a single linear narrative of development.[9] Early plans from 1963 also indicate that within the Canada Pavilion the contributions of Indigenous peoples would be temporally distanced by locating them in the pre-Confederation period. Indians were thus to be effectively excluded from the main story – the century since Confederation – that was the focus of the celebration. Inside the building, as one bureaucrat envisioned it, "some Indian artifacts [would] be dimly spotlighted amidst 'a dreamworld forest.'"[10]

Early in the planning process, the initial concept of a single pavilion was reconceptualized as a complex of buildings, including the Canada Pavilion, individual pavilions for the provinces and regions, and the Indians of Canada Pavilion.[11] The representation of Indians through an autonomous structure – the separating out of the First Peoples from the rest of the Canadian mosaic – was itself an important break with the patterns laid down in previous international expositions. Although representations of Indigenous peoples had been a standard feature of the Canadian sections of fairs from the time of London's Great Exhibition of 1851, these displays had always been marginalized and presented as minor footnotes to the main focus on Euro-Canadian agriculture, industry, and cultural life.[12] Federal officials also recognized fairly early a need to involve Indians in the development of the built environment and the storyline. Expo was, furthermore, seen as an opportunity to correct previous misrepresentations. As pre-publicity for the fair noted, many foreign visitors "have been vaguely aware of the North American Indian, and … will wish to learn something of their history and culture," although "what is known is often erroneous and misleading." The Expo installations were "to present an encompassing, respectful, and dignified picture of the true Indian."[13]

During the initial phase of planning, the National Indian Council, the main Aboriginal political organization of the day, was also engaged in attempting to coordinate the representation of Indigenous people at Expo. It was hampered, however, by its relative weakness as a national organization during the mid-1960s because its political base was largely urban. It included both status and non-status Indians in an uneasy coalition, and the different political agendas of these groups, exacerbated by the lack of a strong representation from reserve communities, would lead to its dissolution in 1968.[14] This situation undoubtedly contributed to the comparatively fluid and informal collaborations between government agencies and Aboriginal individuals and groups that developed over the next few years.

Because of their distrust of the National Indian Council's ability adequately to represent Indian interests, government agencies proposed the involvement of other Aboriginal individuals and groups in the development of the pavilion. Throughout the project the government's interventions were, however, in tension with its desire to keep an arm's-length relationship from the representational process. As one bureaucrat wrote, "at no time should the impression be given that a government agency … has a directing or even subjective role to play in your relations with the Indian group." He defined the role of the Indian Affairs Branch as a resource available to help "the Corporation and the Indians in a discrete manner" whenever required.[15] The ambivalence felt by Indian Affairs officials over the degree of control they should assume – or should appear to assume – is evident in other documents. An Indian Affairs report of 1964 titled "Participation in Canada's Centennial by People of Indian Ancestry" acknowledged the colonial attitudes of racial superiority that had obtained in the past. It cautioned that "the traditional image of the federal Indian Affairs Branch is not a good one among Indians," adding that "until very recently the Branch was a true reflection of the blind attitude of cultural superiority from which Indians were viewed by other Canadian groups." Despite this acknowledgment, the report continued, it was important to work with the "right sort" of Aboriginal people. It was judged that the NIC was "committed to the 'Canadian ideal' and will cooperate," while "there is no guarantee that the Indian organization which would replace NIC, in the event of the latter's demise, would be friendly or constructive."[16]

These concerns gained resonance, finally, in the context of the tumultuous multicultural politics of the 1960s, described in the report as "a time when the country is in a state of crisis over its inability to reconcile the divergent cultural and regional demands which arise out of the pluralistic character of our nation."[17] The government's fear of being accused of favouring one Aboriginal group over another translated into efforts to neutralize political tensions among them. Andrew Delisle, a prominent Mohawk chief who later became commissioner general of the Indians of Canada Pavilion, also linked this concern to a long-standing desire on the part of government (and non-natives in general) to see all Indians as the same and to its refusal to recognize the cultural diversity of the First Peoples.[18]

As the NIC was foundering, a new Centennial Indian Advisory Committee (CIAC) was formed, made up of officials from different branches of government. The need to negotiate a delicate balance between intervention and a hands-off arrangement now became an even more complex task. CIAC was under direct pressure from the overarching coordinating body, the Centennial Commission, which wanted to be kept informed "as to the degree of acceptance and dissension among the various sectors of the Indian population."[19] It also now had to motivate and coordinate the efforts of many different interest groups and Native associations without the mediation of a national Aboriginal organization. CIAC constructed a series of working committees, including one for "celebrations," that were largely staffed by Aboriginal people.

During the deliberations of these groups, the desire for a separate representation at the fair had been steadily growing, and at the end of 1965 the first official announcement was made that the Indians of Canada would have their own pavilion at Expo 67. The Department of Indian Affairs and Northern Development (DIAND), which had played a behind-the-scenes role throughout the first phase of planning, now began to intervene more directly. It appointed a Task Force on Expo 67 to develop plans for the building and organize their implementation and, following this, an Indian Advisory Council (IAC, also known as the National Indian Advisory Board), which DIAND recognized as its main consultative body in the development of the storyline.[20] The surviving archival records evidence struggles for control over both design and storyline during the crucial next phase. These records can be, and have been, read in different ways. Two prominent Aboriginal leaders of the period have, for example, published divergent accounts. Harold Cardinal denied the importance of the Indian Advisory Council because its members operated as individuals and not as community representatives and because its recommendations were not binding on DIAND.[21] George Manuel and Michael Posluns, however, considered the process of consultation and committee work to have been effective, even if in an unforeseen manner, and argued that "the greatest single value that the meetings of the National Indian Advisory Council offered was that the Indian leadership from all across Canada got to know one another, and to discover where our common interests lay."[22] It is also important to note that, despite a tendency to regard DIAND and other governmental bodies as monolithic entities, the documents also reveal a considerable diversity of opinion among the civil servants involved.

Manuel, a chief of the Shuswap nation and president of the North American Indian Brotherhood of British Columbia from 1959 to 1963, was a member of the IAC from 1959 to 1967. He later described an incident that illustrates the internal process of empowerment which was, in retrospect, a critical precondition to the radical nature of the pavilion installations. Initially, he wrote, CIAC appointed the members and the chair of the IAC and set the agendas for meetings without any consultation with Aboriginal people. After IAC members protested and threatened to walk out and take their complaints to the press, they won the right to chose their vice-chair and set their own agendas. The CIAC-appointed chair then resigned in favour of the vice-chair, effectively affirming to government officials the determination of the Aboriginal participants to assume control over the process of pavilion development.[23] The IAC played the critical role in developing the storyline that was ultimately adopted, but DIAND officials continued to monitor the whole process closely.

Architecture and Art: Sixties Formalism and Sixties Semiotics

The site assigned to the Indians of Canada Pavilion was located at one side of the Canadian section of the fair, between the Atlantic Pavilion and the colourful display of massed flags that marked the United Nations Pavilion. Although coincidental, the proximity to the UN pavilion was to prove opportune, for it gave the Aboriginal people who worked at the Indians of Canada Pavilion valuable opportunities to make contacts with the many international officials who came to visit the neighbouring building. The fortuitous juxtaposition also reinforced the "independent status" desired by its Native organizers, a status that had been affirmed by their successful lobbying to have Chief Andrew Delisle appointed commissioner general of the Indians of Canada Pavilion on a par with the heads of other national pavilions, rather than commissioner like the heads of provincial pavilions.[24]

By the time the Indian Advisory Council began to meet, the architectural plans for the building commissioned by DIAND from its in-house architect, J.W. Francis, were already well under way. DIAND countered the IAC's complaints that Indian artists had not been adequately consulted in its design with the argument that pressure of time had made it necessary to begin the process earlier. After protesting the lack of consultation and insisting that future modifications "must rely more fully on participation by Indian artists," the IAC approved the plans, recognizing that because of "the major effort and expensive costs involved to date in producing this design and model [and] in the face of a pressing deadline as well, it would be irresponsible to reject the work done so far." At this meeting the architect also reported that "a seminar consisting of a number of Indian artists was held in December, 1965, in order to obtain some ideas for a pavilion," and that their sketches (which he displayed to the IAC) had been reviewed by the architects before they produced the preliminary drawings.[25]

Francis's design sought to make maximum use of the relatively modest space available and also to create a building that would attract attention amid the sensory overload of a world's fair. As he noted, visitors entered from "the general turmoil of the Exhibition grounds" and were faced with the "vast complex" of the Canadian buildings.[26] "The first impression they get of the Pavilion," he wrote, "must be sufficiently inviting and obviously 'Indian' for them to wish to take a closer look." His solution was "a tower-like figure, fashioned in a manner that would be vaguely reminiscent of the teepee form – an Indian dwelling that would be uppermost in the public's mind."[27] It was a neat solution to the problem as Francis conceived it. The verticality of the teepee would make the building stand out, while its form would send out clear semiotic signals of Indianness. In his choice of tempered steel panels to reinterpret a prototype traditionally made of hide or birchbark, the architect was guided by one of the main themes of the storyline, the coexistence of traditional values with technological modernity. The symbolic references of the pavilion's architecture were further reinforced by its subsidiary forms and interior and exterior detailing. Through the design of the interior spaces, the architect aimed to suggest other traditional Indian dwellings, such as longhouses. As Francis explained, "none are truly realistic, but like the teepee figure, all retain something of the spirit of their historical character."[28]

The vision of harmonious unity among Indian peoples dear to the hearts of DIAND officials is also evident in his statement that "these dwellings merge into a series of six identical hexagonal shapes, linked in hexagonal progression around the teepee figure, suggesting the unifying influence of the various Indian cultures in today's world … all are blended together visually to produce a coherent and unifying whole, and, we hope, a strong Indian identity."[29] To those aware of other centennial projects, the ring of hexagons encircling the base of the teepee would have carried a further, though more subtle, political reference. They echoed the architecture of the newly completed National Arts Centre in Ottawa, whose plan was also based on an additive sequence of low-rise hexagonal forms. The NAC was the federal government's major centennial construction project for the national capital, and Francis, as an Ottawa-based architect, would have been well aware of its design. His use of similar forms at Expo thus allied the Indian Pavilion, for all its separateness, with the architectural project that most represents 1960s federalism.

The teepee form of the Indians of Canada Pavilion seems to have been well accepted by Aboriginal people. It was also entirely in keeping with the conventional appeal that much world's fair architecture makes to national stereotypes. In semiotic terms, however, the pavilion sits squarely within the long-standing, totalizing Western construction of Indianness. By privileging the teepee over other potential architectural prototypes, it assimilated all the Aboriginal peoples of Canada to the romanticized nineteenth-century "noble savage" image of the Plains Indian, the image that also lies at the heart of the dominant twentieth-century stereotype – the Hollywood Indian. Neil Harris has written of large international fairs that, like the city, they "were designed for a new sensibility, a product of this new era of transportation, communication, and mass production. And that sensibility was the tourist's."[30] A further conjuring of stereotypes that were specifically touristic occurred as the result of the positioning near the entrance of a magnificent totem pole, carved for the pavilion by master Kwakwaka'wakw carvers Henry and Tony Hunt. The juxtaposition of totem pole and conical Indian dwelling thus collapses architectural forms from the Woodlands, Plains, and Northwest Coast. It would have been familiar to visitors from the repetition of these iconic images in popular culture, and specifically from the countless wigwams and totem poles erected by owners of souvenir shops across North America and the miniature replicas sold to tourists.

Susan Stewart has theorized the rhetorical significance of the variable scales through which images are materialized. "We find the miniature at the origin of private, individual history," she writes, "but we find the gigantic at the origin of public and natural history."[31] The strategy of gigantism adopted by the pavilion thus removed Indians from the realm of the private and situated them in the arena of public events. Stewart has further suggested that invocations of the gigantic are related to particular forms of historical consciousness. "In contrast to the still and perfect universe of the miniature, the gigantic represents the order and disorder of historical forces. The consumerism of the miniature is the consumerism of the classic; it is only fitting that consumer culture appropriates the gigantic whenever change is desired."[32] At Expo 67 the fantasy landscape of a world's fair thus provided a space in which to enlarge the scale of a sign that in previous decades had existed only as miniature or as commodity. The gigantic scale of the teepee presented the Indian presence as public and active and announced the pavilion's more serious intentions, setting a stage for the rhetoric of social reform urged by the curators in its interior installations.

The architecture of the pavilion also participated in the sensibility of late sixties pop art. It fitted the two models of popular vernacular architecture identified by postmodern architectural theorist Robert Venturi and his colleagues, the "duck" and the "billboard."[33] Like the Big Duck building built by a Long Island duck farmer, it communicated its symbolic meaning through its architectural form. Like a billboard, its blank walls were used as surfaces on which to hang another set of signifying images.[34]

The Art: Tradition and Modernity

The "signs" added to the exterior of the Indians of Canada Pavilion consisted of an ambitious program of commissioned murals, paintings, and sculptures made by artists from across the country. These works of art articulated the cultural diversity of Indigenous artistic traditions and thus to some extent deconstructed the stereotype of homogeneous Indianness invoked by the architecture. In addition to the monumental totem pole, three large wall murals were painted on the trapezoidal vertical walls of the large building adjacent to the central teepee. George Clutesi, a Tseshaht artist from British Columbia, painted *West Coast*, a composition featuring thunderbird and whale crests based on a traditional Nuchahnulth house front painting.[35] Anishinaabe painters Norval Morrisseau and his assistant Carl Ray, both from northern Ontario, contributed *Earth Mother with Her Children*, depicting human and animal figures executed in a graphic style derived from Great Lakes rock painting and birchbark scrolls. Francis Kagige, another Anishinaabe painter from Manitoulin Island, painted *The Land*, a composition of birds and pictographic motifs communicating a vision of the primordial harmony of the natural world. In their scale and locations these large murals were the most prominent of the art works ornamenting the pavilion. The kinds of images they privileged was almost certainly deliberate, for all three murals drew on ancient oral traditions and spiritual concepts. Because they were figurative rather than abstract, they were accessible to a broad public; because they appeared "traditional," they were among the most recognizably "Indian" of the commissioned works, inscribing in the pavilion a primary message of the survival of traditional spirituality.

The exterior of the pavilion also displayed a series of round panel paintings, nine and a half feet in diameter, fixed to the sides of the five hexagonal bays surrounding the base of the teepee. Alex Janvier, a Chipewyan artist from Alberta, created an abstract composition of rhythmic, flowing linear passages to which he gave a typically ironic title, *The Unpredictable East*.[36] Noel Wuttunee, a Plains Cree artist from Saskatchewan, contributed a decorative composition derived from floral beadwork that bordered on abstraction. It was entitled (probably not ironically) *The Garden of Indians*. Both Gerald Tailfeathers, a Kainai (Blood) from Alberta who was well-known for his meticulous figurative paintings illustrating earlier Indian life on the Plains, and Ross Woods, a Lakota from Manitoba who was also known as a figurative artist, created geometric compositions for the pavilion that were atypical of their work. Tailfeathers's painting, *Blackfoot Design*, was based on the motifs of traditional bead- and quillwork. Woods's painting, *Fading*

Colours, also drew on historic embroidery motifs and was intended to convey the idea that "the Indian is here to stay with his colours even though the buffalos are gone."[37] Tom Hill, a Seneca from Ontario, created a geometric composition entitled *Tree of Peace*. It was executed in ceramic by the Huron artist Jean-Marie Gros-Louis and interpreted a centrally important Onkwehonwe symbol that occurs in historic wampum belts.

In 1967 the average Expo visitor's expectation of "Indian art" was still conditioned largely by tourist arts. The vitality of the contemporary art displayed at the pavilion must have come as a revelation to some viewers, while provoking in others questions about its authenticity. In either case, the use of modernist abstract styles by many of the artists sent messages about the readiness of Aboriginal artists to participate in the world of contemporary fine art. In a complementary fashion, the works newly created in traditional idioms countered the still-widespread impression that traditional Indian art – and culture – had disappeared. From a distance, the works of Janvier, Hill, Tailfeathers, and Wuttunee could be read as abstract compositions, inviting comparison with the late modernist minimalist, hard-edge, and colour-field styles that dominated the mainstream art centres of New York and Toronto during the late 1960s.

Yet, in contrast with the practices of mainstream artists, the Aboriginal painters who made work for Expo 67 referred unambiguously to historic forms of Indigenous art through titles and accompanying texts that invited viewers to read their images as continuous with historic traditions. In this sense they diverged from the avant-gardist postures of rupture with tradition that had been fundamental to Western modernist art since the beginning of the twentieth century. As would become still clearer in later years, a political agenda that asserted the survival and vitality of Aboriginal traditions has been central to Indigenous modernism, even as it sought to negotiate the stylistic conventions and aesthetic modes of contemporary Western art. As a number of art historians have argued more recently, the spiritual and political references in the Western modernist art that inspired this first generation of Aboriginal modernists were largely suppressed by the formalist criticism of the 1960s.[38] In this sense the works presented at the Indians of Canada Pavilion at Expo 67 stand at the beginning of a shift that would lead both Indigenous and non-Indigenous contemporary artists to produce explicitly referential works of political, social, and spiritual critique in the years that followed.

"A Sense of the Power of Artists"

The art project of the Indians of Canada Pavilion brought together Aboriginal artists of different generations and from different parts of Canada for the first time. George Clutesi, Henry Hunt, Francis Kagige, and Gerald Tailfeathers belonged to an older generation. They represented the small group of artists who had managed to continue to make "Indian art" through the darker period of the 1940s and 1950s, when the doctrines of assimilationism were dif-

ficult to contest in public venues. Morrisseau and Janvier were in their thir-
ties and represented the first generation to achieve success in the mainstream
art galleries of Toronto and Edmonton, providing a powerful inspiration to
younger artists.[39] Morrisseau, a charismatic mystic with no formal training,
had achieved sudden fame five years earlier with a show of work widely received and appreciated as a survival of the "primitive."[40] Janvier, one of the
first Indian artists to attend art school, was known for his cooler and more
controlled abstract canvases.[41] The less established group of artists, many of
whom were in their twenties, included Wuttunee, Hill, Woods, Gros-Louis,
and Tony Hunt as well as the Ontario Anishinaabe painter Carl Ray, who assisted Morrisseau.[42] For many of these artists the Expo project provided their
first major official commissions.[43]

No collaboration of Indian artists on this scale had occurred prior to Expo.
The impact on the artists was expressed some years later by Alex Janvier,
who recalled that "when we started out there was someone called Bill Reid
on the west coast, Gerald Tailfeathers in the South, who I never really met.
There were only a few names around – they were struggling entirely on their
own."[44] Tom Hill considers that the pavilion project "brought a sense of the
power of the artists, people all of a sudden realized what they could do, as
artists, to communicate ideas."[45] In retrospect, the gathering at Expo also
established a powerful precedent for future national Native artists' organizations such as SCANA (the Society of Canadian Artists of Native Ancestry)
and its successor, the Aboriginal Curatorial Collective, both of which have,
among other things, lobbied effectively to loosen the exclusive hold of ethnographic museums on contemporary Aboriginal art and to insert it into Canada's major art galleries.

In the climate of militant confrontation that characterized the national
liberation politics of the late 1960s, the mentoring of the older artists provided valuable models of another sort. The desire of government officials to
monitor the content of the pavilion extended to the art program and generated considerable tension. The artists' contracts provided for an unusual
level of surveillance as work progressed, and officials felt free to suggest "appropriate" subjects to artists, often in paternalistic tones. Tom Hill recalled
one exchange between Morrisseau and Expo officials: "When questioned
about the content for the mural by one of the theme coordinators, he stated
that it would depend upon the forces within him … He then accused the
coordinator of trying to tell him what to paint. 'When I paint,' he said to his
hushed audience, 'it is as if a force inside of me starts pouring out. I don't
know what my mural will look like. It could be a thunderbird, wolves or a
moose.'"[46] Alex Janvier related a similar experience to a journalist: "When
the government asked the artists to paint a positive, cheery picture, he and
the other native artists bristled. 'How come our people are dying in the jails
and rotting in the mental hospitals and here we're going to tell the world
we're doing great?' they asked. 'Let's tell it as it is.'"[47] Hill has recalled how
Clutesi intervened in a meeting when the whole project seemed to be about
to come apart: "[When] native artists were on the verge of beating up another

participant (not an artist) it was George Clutesi with his fatherly image that held it all together. One afternoon everyone had enough and we were quitting, but George said, 'Look, this is our chance!'"[48] The artists involved in the Expo 67 pavilion thus assumed a position of overt political activism that has continued to the present day. They belonged to the generation that Chief Dan George termed our "new warriors," strategically invoking a Western ideal of artistic freedom in the service of forms of empowerment that extended well beyond traditional enclaves of fine art production.[49]

The Installations: History Lessons

The tensions surrounding the creation of the art program mirrored the process that was going on in the creation of the installations for the interior. Here too there was an alternation between confrontation and moderation, and here too the displays ultimately strove to achieve a balanced representation of the survival of traditions and participation in modernity and between generalized stereotypes and local particularities that paralleled that expressed in the art and architecture. If the effect of the exterior visual ensemble was to attract visitors and draw them inside the structure through references to the familiar, the interior presented them with something they had not seen before. It expressed, with very little compromise, the answers to the question that had been put to Indians across Canada by the writers of the storyline: "What do you want to tell the people of Canada and the world when they come to Expo in 1967?"[50]

The storyline was created by an apparently harmonious collaboration between the non-Native writer contracted by CIAC, Robert Marjoribanks, and the members of the Indian Advisory Council. In March and April of 1966 Marjoribanks and other members of the team had taken their initial draft across the country, holding meetings in Vancouver, Edmonton, Montreal, and Amherst, Nova Scotia, with what would today be called focus groups composed of "Indian leaders, craftsmen, artists and others." Their initial idea for the storyline seems to have been well-received at these meetings, although some modifications were made in response to the consultants' comments. Andrew Delisle, a member of the touring CIAC group, also recalled that in comparison with today's frankness, there was at the time a general reluctance to criticize government openly for fear of later repercussions.[51] Nevertheless, this hurried and informal tour constituted one of the first attempts at a broadly conceived national sampling of Aboriginal opinion, and the organizers were careful to make clear in their exhibition texts that the authority with which they spoke was derived from this broad, consultative process. Marjoribanks, for example, described this process in the first paragraph of the brochure distributed to visitors.[52] As with so many of the features of the pavilion project, this community consultation prefigured practices that would become general only after reforms were set in motion twenty years later following the boycott of the *Spirit Sings* exhibition.

The critique of historical and contemporary relations between Natives and non-Natives in Canada contained in the pavilion was by far the most comprehensive that had ever been presented in such a public and officially authorized forum. Because of their breadth and scope, the pavilion's installations should be assessed, therefore, in relation not only to earlier fairs but also to standard textbook accounts and museum displays of the period.[53] Mid-twentieth-century museum representations of Aboriginal culture had changed little from those of the late Victorian period, continuing to locate a "pure" and "authentic" era of Aboriginal culture in the remote past and to assume both the inevitability and the benefits of assimilation. In contrast, the Indians of Canada Pavilion stressed the negative aspects of contact and the currency and value of traditional practices and values. The guiding principle, was that "the Past should not dominate the Present and the Future; the Present is the crucial part which should be projected."[54] The shift in emphasis was evidenced, first of all, by the allocation of space within the pavilion. After entering a reception area where they were introduced to the six large cultural groupings of Canadian Indians, visitors proceeded up a ramp into the two introductory rooms, which presented Indian life in the pre-contact era, the period usually given centre stage in prior representations. From these areas the visitor entered a large central space where the focus was squarely on the present and the recent past.

Although no complete visual or textual record of the pavilion's installations was made, they can be largely reconstructed from extant archival photographs and documents and from the recollections of the project organizers. The first of the introductory areas was entitled "The Land." Tom Hill recalls that this area consisted of a bridge placed amidst forest-like scenery.[55] It was conceived as "a beautiful, serene, peaceful environment in which the visitor will be able to share some of the Indians' love of the land, his kinship with the wild creatures, the harmony of the natural world which is an important part of his values and beliefs."[56] The themes of pervasive spiritual presence and of a primordial harmony among "men" and between people and nature are noted in the description of this section in the pavilion brochure, which concludes with the assertion that "in many villages today The People have not forgotten the ways of their fathers."[57] The second of the two pre-contact sections, "The Awakening of the People," was "a five-sided brilliantly coloured room in which varying tones of gold and yellow predominate."[58] It contained displays about the adaptations of Indians to their different environments and featured photographs and functional objects such as snowshoes, baskets, and paddles. The room articulated the theme of cultural diversity, emphasizing that "the Indians in all parts of Canada had their own local cultures, their own way of doing things, but at the same time were united by an underlying feeling of kinship."[59]

From these sections the visitor entered the main area of the pavilion inside the teepee proper, a lofty space extending upward to the roof. The room's title, "The Drum," referred to a ritual object sacred to all the Aboriginal peoples of Canada. The idea of the drum also contained a further reference to the powwow, the major communal ceremonial of modern times that was actively being revived across Canada and the United States during the 1960s. In the six bays that opened out of the central space a series of thematic displays addressed the impacts of European contact. These installations both rewrote standard historical narratives and provided an exposé of contemporary living conditions. The installations were lit with spotlights, creating a dramatic chiaroscuro environment broken up by the outlines of the objects on display and the shadows they projected onto the walls. The first bay introduced the arrival of the Europeans, illustrated by early trade objects and the gifts of Indian food, tools, and canoes that were essential to European exploration. As the brochure commented, "The Europeans never could have travelled more than a few days from the sea and the great rivers without the help of The People, whom they mistook for 'Indians.'" The critique of the term "Indian" contained in this sentence is one of a series of deconstructive interventions into standard Euro-Canadian discourse put forward by the exhibition's brochure and text panels.[60]

The second bay addressed the changing political, economic, and military roles assumed by Indigenous peoples during the early nineteenth century, as well as the rapid disintegration of their traditional ways of life once Euro–North Americans no longer required their support as military allies. In the third bay of "The Drum" the impact of missionaries was presented. The carved items displayed included historic Iroquoian False Face masks and a contemporary sculpture of a celestial bear carved by Nathan Montour (fig. 1.2). Although based on a traditional Lenape (Delaware) image, it had a broader general reference, since in the spiritual beliefs of many Indigenous North Americans the bear is a being of great physical and spiritual power. The installation constructed around this image was the most politically charged in the pavilion. A shaft of light in the form of a Christian cross was projected onto Montour's sculpture to represent the imposition of foreign beliefs on Indigenous spiritual systems. The text panel behind the bear read: "The early missionaries thought us pagans. They imposed upon us their own stories of god, of heaven and hell, of sin and salvation." The installation could thus be read as subverting the supremacy of Christianity by linking Christ's sacrifice with a sacred Aboriginal image. Across from this panel another text panel affirmed the validity of Aboriginal spirituality. It displayed historic pictographs and read, "… but we spoke with God the Great Spirit in our own way. We lived with each other in love, and honoured the holy spirit in all living things." The official brochure reiterated the same messages, but softened them somewhat by acknowledging that despite the "paternalism and lack of understanding" of missionaries, many were also dedicated and giving individuals. DIAND officials were initially concerned that this section of the pavilion would offend Catholic French Canadians. That, rather surprisingly, no concerted protest materialized may reflect, in part, the anti-clericalism that informed Quebec's own Quiet Revolution of the 1960s.

1.2   Display about the impact of missionaries, at the Indians of Canada Pavilion, Expo 67. © Government of Canada; reproduced with the permission of the Minister of Public Works and Government Services Canada (2011). Library and Archives Canada, Canadian Corporation for the 1967 World Exhibition fonds/e001096685

Following this display, the visitor came to a bay entitled "The Government and the Indians," illustrated by a large geopolitical map of Canada showing the locations of reserves. Photo-murals depicting Aboriginal people from different parts of the nation illustrated how various communities had fared within Canada. A journalist noted the diversity that was represented, "ranging from the very small to the very large, the most remote to the almost-urban, the virtual slums, to the well-ordered communities."[61] The intention of this section was to make clear the importance of the reserve to Aboriginal peoples, one of the most important messages that had emerged from the national consultations in 1966.[62] As a text panel read, "the reserve is our last grip on the land, many of our people fear that, if the reserve should disappear, the Indian would disappear with it."[63] The brochure further emphasized the historic responsibility of government to Indians. "They feel they have a special claim to consideration because of the loss of vast tracts of land which were their inheritance," the pamphlet explained. "It appears, however, that they

1.3   Display on work life, at the Indians of Canada Pavilion, Expo 67. © Government of Canada; reproduced with the permission of the Minister of Public Works and Government Services Canada (2011). Library and Archives Canada, Canadian Corporation for the 1967 World Exhibition fonds/e001096685

have other concerns which affect them more profoundly – the retention of an Indian identity, a sense of independence, the right to manage their own affairs, and to determine their own destiny."[64] In what was probably a comment added at the behest of DIAND officials, the passage concluded that government had "begun to recognize" these concerns through the "philosophy of community development."[65]

The next bay, representing "Work Life," was constructed in the form of a barrel vault on which photo panels were mounted portraying Indians engaged in a wide range of occupations ranging from trapping to nursing and teaching. The brochure pointed out that even though Aboriginal people engaged in the same range of activities as non-Natives, there were an "abnormally high number living on government relief," and it also raised the particular problems affecting non-status Indians. The last image the visitor saw on leaving this bay was a large photograph of an unsmiling and poorly dressed woman standing with her four small children at the door of their log cabin (fig. 1.3). The final bay addressed the problem of education, focusing on the challenge facing the Native child in "the white man's school, an alien land for an Indian child." This alienness was spelled out in one of the text panels: "Dick and Jane in the storybook are strangers to an Indian boy. An Indian child begins school by learning a foreign tongue. The sun and the moon mark passing time in the Indian home. At school, minutes are important and we jump to the bell. Many precious hours are spent in a bus going to a distant school and coming home again."[66] Adjacent to these texts the public was confronted with "large blown-up photographs of tattered, unhappy-looking Indian children placed beside pictures of white Canadian children playing in the comfort of suburbia."[67] The impact of the harsh realities described in this section was only somewhat softened by the inclusion, requested by DIAND officials, of three displays presenting statistics showing progressive increases of student enrolments in the years 1946, 1956, and 1966.[68]

From "The Drum," stairways and ramps led visitors up into the final exhibition space, "The Future." As the *Indian News* reported, "Looking down, our attention is focused on a symbolic fire that lies directly under the peak of the teepee. Permeating the air with the rising smoke from the council fire is taped background music and voices of the Indian people. Feelings of despair, hope, and confidence intermingle but the emphasis will be on the upbeat, the feeling that the Indian will succeed in grasping the future with one hand while preserving certain values with the other."[69] Telephone headsets were arranged around this fire. When visitors picked them up, they heard a message, spoken in an archaic poetic diction, that summarized the themes that had been presented and articulated a vision of the future: "Some of my people see in the dark coals a world where the Indian is a half-remembered thing and the ways of the old men are forgotten. But I see another vision, I see an Indian, tall and strong in the pride of his heritage. He stands with your sons, a man among men. He is different, as you and I are different, and perhaps it will always be so. But, in the Indian way, we have many gifts to share." The message went on to urge the importance of mutual respect and sharing, but it also stressed the necessity of separation and distinctiveness. Its final line underlined the rejection of the paternalistic policies of the past that had been expressed throughout the exhibition: "The trail we walk is our own, and we bear our own burdens. That is our right."[70]

Unfinished Business: Gender, Voice, and Culture

As we have noted throughout this chapter, the Indians of Canada Pavilion at Expo 67 constituted a moment of dramatic rupture with many key conventions of colonialist representation. This break was not, and could not have been, total, and in several important ways the pavilion's installations continued to employ the patriarchal discourse characteristic not only of the dominant society but also of Expo 67, whose theme was "Man and His World." As in the passage just cited from the "Future" installation, the masculine voice was used exclusively. Throughout the pavilion, text panels spoke of fathers, brothers, and sons, not mothers, sisters, and daughters. The Indian was always "he," despite the presence of women and girls in many of the photographs used as visuals. Although the privileging of the masculine was typical of non-Native discourse during the 1960s, its use in the pavilion seems particularly relentless. All the commissioned artists were men, and there were no women on the IAC, despite the fact that talented women with similar levels of achievement, such as Odawa painter Daphne Odjig or Gitk'san painter Judith Morgan, were available to fill these positions. In retrospect, this exclusion seems an omen of the degree to which gender would become a site of difficulty in Aboriginal politics in the years to come.

An oscillation between the directness of first-person voice and the objectifying third person was also characteristic of the texts that accompanied the installations. While the text panels addressed the visitors in the first person, speaking directly as "we" to "you," the brochure spoke in the third person of how "the Indian" had fared in the past and of "his" goals for the future. Because the pamphlet, which was issued by the government printing office, was the take-home souvenir of the pavilion experience, its use of the third person was a particularly striking example of continuing paternalism. Although, as we have seen, its content seems to have been a remarkably faithful summary of the community consultations and advisory committee discussions, it also filtered these statements through the standard tropes of the ethnographic tradition and the reportorial voice of the public relations consultant. During the transitional period of the late 1960s, compromises such as this are not surprising, and they indicate that although a new process had begun, it was not yet possible to discard the dominant society's categories. During the first meeting of the IAC the members had visited the National Museum of Canada, where ethnologists had "delivered a series of briefings on the sources and migrations to this continent of the first inhabitants, the linguistic affiliations of Canadian Indians and their cultural groupings."[71] Although the use of quotation marks in the text panels and brochure ironized and distanced words such as Indian, many such standard terms continued to be employed. Similarly, the use of the conventional anthropological cultural-area concept as an organizing principle limited the degree to which totalizing representations could be deconstructed (fig. 1.4). The conventional Western construction of the pre-contact past as a romanticized, Edenic paradise free of conflict or want was, furthermore, appropriated and invoked rather than contested in the pavilion. The opening lines for "The Beginning" in the pavilion brochure – "All the creatures of the world lived, one with another, in harmony and order. All owed each other respect and reverence" – read very much like an animist version of Genesis. At other moments the use of a Longfellowian English to evoke an ideal future – "Sit now by the fire and rest, my brother, We will talk of the time to come" – was equally striking, though not surprising. As Homi Bhabha has observed, "Colonized countries have had to construct their cultural forms by hybridizing the Indigenous culture with the

1.4   Introductory installation at the Indians of Canada Pavilion, Expo 67.
© Government of Canada; reproduced with the permission of the Minister of Public
Works and Government Services Canada (2011). Library and Archives Canada,
Canadian Corporation for the 1967 World Exhibition fonds/e001096685

colonizer's culture … Strategies of resistance, of identification and of mimicry all came into play. But mimicry can be subversive; you use the language
of the master in an alloyed form, in order to deflect the dominating ideologies being imposed on you."[72] The Indians of Canada Pavilion at Expo 67
was a mixture of colonial mimicry, in Bhabha's sense, and more overt contestation. The issues of voice, anthropological objectification, and historical
agency that it raised would become the subject of increasingly comprehensive
critique in future years.

Staging Decolonization

There is evidence that before the Indians of Canada Pavilion opened, some
government officials, as could have been predicted, wanted to modify its
"negative" tone. A senior DIAND official reported to the director of Indian
Affairs on the pavilion just prior to its opening. Although favourably im-

pressed by its art and architecture, he considered that its displays were "not as objective as they should be and appear to be purposely showing the past history giving very little attention to the progress which has taken place and the increasing assistance being provided by the Government."[73] Commissioner General Andrew Delisle believed that the texts would not have received final approval without the direct intervention of Montreal's mayor, Jean Drapeau, and Prime Minister Lester Pearson.[74] By the end of the fair, however, the pavilion's popularity and the enthusiasm of the 15,000 visitors who viewed it daily caused DIAND to revise its opinion. In his report to the Privy Council, Assistant Deputy Minister of Indian Affairs R.F. Battle wrote that the pavilion had sparked many requests for further information about Indians and that visitors had appreciated "the Government's action in providing the Indian people with the opportunity of telling their story in their own way," and had generally "responded positively to the theme of diversity and to the contemporary art."[75] The pavilion's success was probably an important stimulus both for DIAND's strong support of contemporary Indian art in subsequent years and for its retention of the model of community consultation that the pavilion's organizers had pioneered. Museums and other institutions were, however, slower to pick up the challenges raised by the pavilion. It would require the passage of two more decades and the crisis provoked by a national boycott of Canada's next comprehensive presentation of Indigenous cultures to a large international audience before the issue of museum representation would be addressed seriously on a national scale.

What accounts for the opening up in 1967 of a space in which Aboriginal people could successfully contest colonial representations of their history? The answer to this question must lie in large part in the extraordinary nature of that year. It was a time of confidence and expansiveness in Canada, as most coming-of-age celebrations are. The maturing of the non-Anglo-Saxon immigrant communities that had entered the country in large numbers after World War II had stimulated the formalization of a new ethos of multiculturalism and a new national self-image of Canada as a cultural mosaic. The economy was strong, and the country was in a generous mood. Canada could afford to be self-critical. The international politics of the late 1960s, too, created a mood in which the liberal governments of the Western democracies were adopting strategies of accommodation toward their historically marginalized visible minorities in an attempt to contain the threats of civil disorder and violence that were perceived to exist in a range of different social and political locations. The American counter-culture, the Vietnam resistance, the Black Power movement, and the activities of the American Indian Movement spilled over into Canada, as indicated in one journalist's reaction to the pavilion: the Indians' "message is quite simple and packs the punch of a thousand Cassius Clays."[76]

As noted earlier, these external influences combined with the renewed activism initiated by Canadian Aboriginal people who had fought and sacrificed alongside other Canadians during World War II and were no longer willing to return to the status quo ante. The pavilion's bold break with many colonial representations of Indianness, its rejection of assimilationist policies, and its stress on the value of difference and the need to preserve distinct cultural heritages were all validated by their representation before the broad national and international publics that came together at Expo 67. The Indians of Canada Pavilion constitutes the first act in a drama which, twenty years later, would reach a kind of denouement when Canada entrenched Aboriginal sovereignty in its constitution and, a decade after that, began to introduce new forms of Aboriginal self-government in the Arctic and northern British Columbia.

According to Neil Harris's typology, Expo 67 was a "Post-Modern Fair ... [that,] lacking any totally confident vision of the future, could not project a sympathetic view of the past."[77] Yet on the evidence of the Indians of Canada Pavilion, as well as other innovative displays and features, it also varied from this pattern. The political world of the 1990s has seen the progressive dismantling of old empires and the proliferation of new nationalisms. In this context, too, Expo 67 and the Indians of Canada Pavilion were prefigurations. The surreal atmosphere of the fair provided the backdrop against which dramas of decolonization could be acted out. As a global spectacle, Expo 67 permitted gestures of postcolonial detachment that were, in a partial sense, premature and illusory – Canada at last independent of Britain and the United States, and the First Peoples and Quebec distinct from Canada. These acts of representation were fantasies, but they were also portents.

2

Moment of Truth

The Spirit Sings as Critical Event and the
Exhibition Inside It

The Spirit Sings as Critical Event

Virtually all Canadian writers on museums and Indigenous peoples have positioned *The Spirit Sings: Artistic Traditions of Canada's First Peoples* as the point of departure for the postcolonial project of museum reform that has been underway during the past two decades.[4] Staged by the Glenbow Museum as the centrepiece of the Calgary Winter Olympics in 1988, the exhibition assembled over 650 examples of Aboriginal art from museums around the world. Most had been collected during the early years of European contact, and many had rarely been exhibited or published and were unknown to Indigenous people, curators, and scholars. In 1986, three years after work on the exhibition had begun and two years before its opening, the project was engulfed by a boycott and a controversy that sent shock waves around the world. In the international museological literature the show continues to be referenced alongside three other controversial exhibitions of the 1980s – *"Primitivism" in 20th Century Art: Affinity of the Tribal and the Modern* (Museum of Modern Art, New York, 1984), *Magiciens de la Terre* (Centre Pompidou, Paris, 1989), and *Into the Heart of Africa* (Royal Ontario Museum, Toronto, 1989) – as a key stimulus for the reflexive critique of the exhibitionary practices of Western museums.

One of the most recent assessments of the impact of *The Spirit Sings* was made by Cherokee museologist Karen Coody Cooper in her 2008 book, *Spirited Encounters: American Indians Protest Museum Policies and Practices*: "The exhibition was a watershed for North American Indian/museum relationships. Had it not been for the Lubicon boycott which

The irony of using a display of North American Indian artifacts to attract people to the Winter Olympics being organized by interests who are still actively seeking to destroy the Indian people seems painfully obvious.
– *Bernard Ominayak, chief of the Lubicon Lake First Nation (1986)*[1]

I believe that it is this Olympic connection which will draw attention to the real concerns of Canadian Native peoples, as it is in the context of the exhibition that the richness and depth of Canada's Native culture will be emphasized.
– *Duncan Cameron, director of the Glenbow Museum (1986)*[2]

The exhibiting of "other cultures" – often performed with the best of liberal intentions – has proved controversial. The questions – "Who should control the power to represent?" – "Who has the authority to re-present the culture of others?" – have resounded through the museum corridors of the world, provoking a crisis of authority.
– *Stuart Hall (2005)*[3]

drew worldwide attention and created a call for action to which Canada responded in an enlightening fashion while the world watched, positive changes in policy and practice regarding First Nations (and, quite likely, indigenous people throughout the world) would have been, I believe, slower to come, and not as extensive as the progress that has been made since the exhibition's protest."[5]

The immediate cause of the *Spirit Sings* boycott was the Glenbow Museum's announcement of Shell Oil as the exhibition's major corporate sponsor. During the early 1980s, the Lubicon Lake Cree First Nation in Alberta, which had been overlooked when reserves were being assigned during the early twentieth century, had been seeking a way to put pressure on the governments of Alberta and Canada to resolve their stalled land claim. Forced to leave their traditional lands and way of life when oil companies began to drill during the 1970s, band members had suffered a rapid and drastic deterioration in their health and well-being. After the Winter Olympics were awarded to Calgary, Lubicon leaders tried without success to marshal international support for a general boycott of the games. The announcement that one of the companies exploiting the oil on their traditional lands was to fund an exhibition celebrating the glories of early contact-period Aboriginal cultures struck Lubicon strategists as the ultimate hypocrisy. The exhibition also presented a tailor-made opportunity to draw international attention to their land claim.

Like a magnet set down among iron filings, the contention over corporate sponsorship quickly attracted to itself a host of other issues that have stuck to the exhibition ever since. Although some of these problems, such as the inappropriate display of ceremonial items, the retention of human remains, and claims for the return of cultural property, were of long standing, only a few museums had yet begun to address them.[6] Other, more general issues of Indigenous voice and power in the representation of their own cultures had come into focus more recently as a result of the comprehensive postcolonial critique of the Western disciplines that had been sweeping through the humanities and social sciences since the 1970s. As far as I know, neither the justice of the Lubicons' cause nor the urgent need to alleviate their sufferings was disputed by anyone connected with the exhibition. Their grievous problems seemed to mirror in microcosm the post-contact history of Aboriginal peoples in many parts of Canada. Rather, the debates weighed the nature of the museum as a space of public representation that could provide access to the material artifacts of Aboriginal history against the leverage a boycott could provide for the rectification of specific injustices, and they questioned whether political advocacy was the proper role for the museum. One prominent defender of the exhibition, Michael Ames, then director of the UBC Museum of Anthropology, opposed the boycott as an infringement on academic freedom which, he argued, should apply not only to universities and professors but also to museums and curators.[7]

The Spirit Sings went ahead largely as planned, despite strong support for the boycott among activist groups, academics, and Aboriginal organizations

2.1   A cartoon published
on 15 January 1988, the day
after the opening of *The
Spirit Sings*, on the editorial
page of the *Calgary Sun*.
© Sun Media Corporation

(fig. 2.1). It was shown as planned at the Glenbow Museum
from 15 January to 1 May and at the Canadian Museum of
Civilization in Ottawa from 1 July to 6 November 1988. Although some museums refused to lend, most of the loan requests were granted – in several cases, because of the efforts
of Canadian government representatives who negotiated
with the museums' governing agencies. The loan requests
also created divisions within the international community;
although phrased in general terms, the resolution passed by
ICME, the UNESCO-sponsored International Committee for
Museums of Ethnography, at its 1986 meeting in Argentina
was undoubtedly a response to the controversy. It stated that
"museums, which are engaged in activities relating to living
ethnic groups, should whenever possible, consult with the
appropriate members of those groups, and such museums

should avoid using ethnic materials in any way which might be detrimental and/or offensive to such groups."[8]

The most far-reaching response of the museum community, however, was initiated at a conference convened during the last days of the exhibition's Ottawa showing by the Canadian Museums Association, the Canadian Museum of Civilization, and the Assembly of First Nations with funding from the federal Department of Communications (now the Department of Canadian Heritage). The purpose of "Preserving Our Heritage: A Working Conference for Museums and First Peoples" was to provide a forum in which the full range of issues brought to the fore by the boycott could be aired and debated. It opened up a new and crucial process of dialogue and revealed a collective will to find positive solutions, as articulated by George Erasmus, one of Canada's most prominent Aboriginal leaders, in his opening address to the conference: "*The Spirit Sings* exhibition sparked a fair amount of controversy in Canada. It raised questions that museums had to deal with and a lot of questions that Native people had to address ... What kind of role should Native people play in the presentation of their own past, their own history? ... When the exhibition came to Ottawa we had to ask the indigenous community what we were going to do. We could have continued with the boycott. But we needed to get beyond that. What we are embarking on now is the beginning of a different kind of relationship between two potentially strong allies."[9] The conference participants agreed to create a national Task Force on Museums and First Peoples charged with formulating guidelines for the future.[10] Its report, issued in 1992, recommended changes to existing protocols, practices, and power structures informed by a new model of partnership between First Nations and Canadian museums.[11] The process of change mandated by the task force report continues to unfold, not only in Canada but also internationally.[12]

Defined in terms of the controversy it provoked, *The Spirit Sings* was thus undoubtedly, in anthropologist Veena Das's terms, a "critical event" that "establishes new modalities of social action."[13] Yet the polemical nature of the published literature has had the effect of defining the exhibition *only* as a critical event, understood in terms of its after-effects and their contribution to museological reform. At their most strident, the critiques have identified the exhibition with all the sins of modernist museology – the dehumanizing objectification of the artifact paradigm, the inscription of evolutionary and racialized cultural hierarchies, the freezing of Indigenous peoples in a remote "ethnographic present," the denial of their contemporary authenticity, and complicity with the agendas of state and corporate sponsors. In this vein, for example, Robyn Gillam has written reductively of the exhibition as an "astonishing collection of goods displayed in exchange for international cooperation, cultural empathy or 'understanding,' and economic gain through tourism for the city of Calgary and perhaps for the local Native community."[14]

It is a paradox of the boycott that it prevented many of those best qualified to conduct informed evaluations from seeing the exhibition. It is equally paradoxical that the long afterlife of the controversy has made it necessary for many of the critics to base their post-mortems on second- or third-hand reports. As a result, we have lost sight of *The Spirit Sings* as an *exhibit*, rather than a critical event. Exhibitions are complex theatrical assemblages that exist for defined periods in real time and space, and they are experienced by visitors on many different levels. The individual shape and style of each exhibition is created through a unique alchemy of storyline, object selection, written texts, design elements, colour, light, sound, educational programming, publications, graphic branding, a marketing campaign, and a souvenir shop. In a large institution, each of these components is the product of a particular professional expertise and communicates its message in its own way. To allow a demonized and flattened cardboard representation of *The Spirit Sings* to stand unchallenged is to lose a valuable opportunity to learn about the dynamics of interaction through which major public representations are produced. Just as a tear in a garment reveals to the naked eye the threads, interfacings, and modes of construction that are normally hidden by the lining with which it is finished, so do breakdowns in normal exhibition processes offer us valuable opportunities to see how these complex compositions are put together. Analysis of the processes of translation and transformation that occur through the overlays and interactions of different exhibitionary components add to our understanding of the historical evolution of museology and provide insight into how institutions interpellate different kinds of patrons. Like the "notes" given to actors by stage directors, such analyses also equip us to manage future projects more effectively.

I will argue in the remainder of this chapter that an examination of the exhibitionary strategies of *The Spirit Sings* reveals it to have been a transitional, intentionally hybrid, and in many ways innovative project, rather than a conventional ethnographic installation. As such, it responded to challenges to modernist paradigms of display and historical representation that were beginning to emerge during the 1980s, opening them up to, rather than closing them off from, scrutiny. I will also maintain that the exhibition's negotiation of the conventional art and artifact paradigms was not, ultimately, successful and that its embedded contradictions may have helped to fan the flames of the controversy. Finally, I will suggest that, in addition to the constructive changes stimulated by that controversy, *The Spirit Sings* left other valuable legacies that we need to acknowledge. It helped to stimulate the revival of museum-based research that is now in full swing but that, in the 1980s, had been largely dormant for many decades. It also left a legacy of knowledge about the historical travels and contemporary locations of Indigenous heritage that continues to be mined by Indigenous and non-Indigenous researchers.

I will organize my discussion in terms of four propositions: first, if *The Spirit Sings* controversy had not taken place, it would have had to be invented; second, although *The Spirit Sings* has been condemned as a traditional ethnographic exhibition, it was, in fact, a new kind of hybrid that intentionally blurred art and artifact display paradigms; third, the lack of alignment of curatorial messages with those transmitted by graphic branding and marketing strategies exacerbated the controversy surrounding the exhibition; and, finally, the legacy of research and publication left by *The Spirit Sings* laid an important basis for subsequent collaborative projects for the recovery of historical heritage.

These lines of argument reflect my own positioning vis-à-vis *The Spirit Sings*, just as the views of the exhibition's critics reflect theirs. I served as guest curator of the Northern Woodlands section, and my participation in the project was a major watershed in my life. For me, as for my fellow curators, the controversy was very painful. It has made the retrospective analysis of the exhibition a necessary and integral process in my subsequent work, leading me to re-examine fundamental assumptions of my training as an art historian, to make the study of museum representation a focus of my academic research, to participate in the task force and other processes of change that *The Spirit Sings* set in motion, and to work for a time in a museum. The nature of my involvement gives me not only a personal investment in the process of analysis but also a particular angle of vision. I had the opportunity to witness the development of the curatorial component over a five-year period and to interact with designers and other professionals. I saw the show not only in Calgary but also in Ottawa, where I visited it weekly during the autumn of 1988 with students in a seminar focusing on the exhibition. I was not, however, privy to the Glenbow's internal process, and I have supplemented my own notes and memories by selectively consulting the many shelves of meeting minutes, photographs, and other documentation deposited in the Glenbow Archives. The discussion that follows will inevitably reflect this personal investment and the privileges and limitations attached to my role.

First Proposition: Power and Politics

By proposing that, if the *Spirit Sings* had not taken place, it would have had to be invented, I seek to situate the exhibition within a larger history of post–World War II Aboriginal activism around land claims, restitution, and social justice. As part of this process, Aboriginal people had for some years sought to intervene in aspects of museum practice that would be problematized by the Lubicon boycott, insisting on the need for Aboriginal voice in the representation of their own histories, asking for the removal of sacred objects from public display, and requesting the repatriation of heritage that had left Aboriginal communities in illegal or improper ways. Although these interventions tended to be local, intermittent, and little publicized, we can see now that they combined to build up the head of steam that would power the 1988 protest.

The most notable exception to the localized nature of previous Aboriginal activism was, as we have seen, the Indians of Canada Pavilion at Expo 67. Although this project is discussed in detail in chapter 1, it is worth pointing to specific links between its revisionist nature and the *Spirit Sings* controversy. As we saw, the creation of a separate pavilion under the control of an Aboriginal committee was the result of a palace coup staged by Indigenous activists working within the Department of Indian and Northern Affairs. As also noted, in formulating the pavilion's storyline and themes, the Indian Advisory Committee conducted a groundbreaking, if brief, cross-country tour in 1966 to consult members of Indigenous communities about the key messages that needed to be transmitted. This process anticipated by three decades the consultative models that would become fundamental to the collaborative exhibition practice now normative for Canadian anthropology museums. Through its exhibits and displays of contemporary art, the pavilion also placed new emphasis on the survival of Indigenous people and their modern-day lives. As we have seen, one of the critiques of *The Spirit Sings* was its choice of a historical focus, in contrast to the model presented by the Expo 67 pavilion.

There were, however, other ways in which *The Spirit Sings* and the Indians of Canada Pavilion made use of a shared repertoire of the modernist conventions used in ethnographic representation. Both presented culture through didactic installations of artifacts displayed in glass cases, and both adopted the culture-area system of anthropological classification.[15] Most strikingly, both exhibitions featured ceremonial items that hold spiritual meaning for Indigenous people, another flashpoint of the 1988 controversy. On the day *The Spirit Sings* opened in Calgary, representatives of the Kahnawake Mohawk won a temporary injunction forcing the Glenbow to remove from display an Onkwehonwe (Iroquois) *ga:goh:sah*, or "False Face" mask, on the grounds that, as a sacred object, its public exhibition "violates the intended purpose of the mask and its sacred functions, constitutes a desecration, and ridicules and misrepresents the spiritual beliefs and practices of the Iroquois."[16] Although the mask was removed while the court case was being heard, the judge did not uphold the Mohawk request and the mask was replaced in its case. (The Canadian Museum of Civilization did, however, substitute a replica carved by Chief Jacob Thomas during the Ottawa showing.) The judge noted, among other things, that the mask had been publicly displayed several times without incident.[17] Twenty years earlier, at Expo 67, a similar *ga:goh:sah* had been exhibited in the Indians of Canada Pavilion without incident, despite the many people who visited the pavilion from Kahnawake, located only a few miles away, and despite the fact that the pavilion's commissioner general, Andrew Delisle, was himself a Kahnawake Mohawk. As we will see in chapter 6, Onkwehonwe had approached the National Museum of Man in Ottawa during the 1970s to request the removal of their *ga:goh:sah* masks from display, establishing a precedent for their actions in 1988. This example, I would suggest, illustrates the cumulative histories behind many late twentieth-century examples of political activism and contestation. Just as the organizers of the Lubicon boycott of 1986–88 opened up a host of issues that had not been identified in their initial call for action, so the success of the Expo 67 pavilion and the defeat of the federal government's assimilationist White Paper on Indian Affairs a year later had enabled Aboriginal representatives to broaden the scope of their critique in the succeeding years.

The 1960s and 1970s also saw renewed activism in relation to the repatriation of cultural property from museums. The most famous case involves the campaign waged by descendants of Kwakwaka'wakw chief Dan Cranmer for the return of their family's potlatch regalia, illegally confiscated in 1922. This restitution, as Gloria Cranmer Webster has stated, was motivated, not by a need to recover regalia for use, but by a desire to "rectify a terrible injustice that is part of our history."[18] The campaign proceeded on a number of fronts, including the production of a film about the confiscation and its aftermath that was widely shown in anthropology classes during the 1970s.[19] According to Donna McAlear's research, the return by the National Museum of Canada of its share of the confiscated treasures was agreed to in 1975 as a result of pressure put on the museum by the federal Department of Indian Affairs and Northern Development, rather than because of a determination of rightful ownership by the museum.[20] It seems highly likely that DIAND's role reflected, at least in part, both the internal political activism of the Indigenous people within DIAND and the popular success of the Expo 67 pavilion.

These examples of the persistence of modernist art and artifact paradigms, the display of sacred objects, and repatriation activism, although by no means exhaustive, help to explain why, as the Lubicon boycott proceeded, it quickly became identified with a wider set of grievances and demands that transformed a protest which targeted corporate sponsorship and a land claim into one that was much more comprehensive.[21] *The Spirit Sings* protest was, then, a controversy waiting to happen. If the opportunity had not offered itself in 1988, a similar spectrum of issues would very likely have erupted the next time a project representing Aboriginal culture converged with a public relations opportunity and the taint of corporate sponsorship. It would surely not have been long before such an occasion arose, for, as Mohawk cultural impresario John Kim Bell memorably said at the "Preserving Our Heritage" conference, "All money is dirty, and the dirtiest money of all is that which comes from the federal government." Indeed, as we will see, four years later, during the Columbus quincentennial year of 1992, Aboriginal contemporary artists, writers, and curators would build on the politics of contestation generated around *The Spirit Sings* to carry their issues forward in major exhibitions of Indigenous art at the National Gallery of Canada and the Canadian Museum of Civilization. That the moment of truth came in 1988 was also due, I would argue, to the expected federal election which was called in November, just after the exhibition closed in Ottawa. Native political leaders were quick to exploit the connections between the issues the exhibition had raised and the underlying questions of sovereignty on their larger political agenda.

Second Proposition: Neither Art nor Artifact, or We Are All Hybrid Now

Although *The Spirit Sings* has been condemned as a traditional ethnographic exhibition, it was, in fact, a new kind of hybrid that intentionally blurred art and artifact modes of display. My second proposition seeks to position the exhibition within the lively debates of the period over the merits of the two modernist installation paradigms that had evolved during the twentieth century for the presentation of Indigenous and other world arts.[22] The art display focuses the viewer's attention on the object's singularity and formal properties through the use of dramatic lighting, neutral colours, minimalist exhibition furniture, and the avoidance of distracting texts and images. The artifact display, in contrast, presents objects as representative types, specimens of culture from which information can be derived through scientific study. It communicates these meanings to the public with lengthy text panels, photographs, maps, dioramas, and films and videos. Until the 1980s, art and artifact modes of display had generally been viewed as pure and mutually exclusive options that were suited, respectively, to the production of aesthetic or cognitive experience. When work began on *The Spirit Sings*, virtually all Western museums displayed Indigenous art and material culture in one or the other of these modes. Yet by the 1980s the two paradigms had also begun to influence each other. As Aldona Jonaitis has shown, for example, New York's influential American Museum of Natural History had been incorporating aestheticizing display strategies for some time.[23] During the 1980s, *The Spirit Sings* was bracketed by two widely discussed New York exhibitions which, in different ways, focused on the decade's preoccupation with installation. The first of these was *"Primitivism" in 20th Century Art: Affinity of the Tribal and the Modern* at the Museum of Modern Art in 1984, which sparked a heated controversy that was in full swing as work on *The Spirit Sings* began.[24] The exhibition was angrily attacked for appropriating to the Western construct of "primitive art" works possessing different and complex meanings within their own societies. In 1988, a week after *The Spirit Sings* opened in Calgary, New York's Center for African Art opened *Art/artifact: African Art in Anthropology Collections*. This highly influential touring exhibition featured simulated installations of Indigenous works presented as curiosity, artifact, and art, and it subjected these paradigms to searching reflexive analysis.[25]

In 1980s Canada, however, virtually all permanent exhibitions of Indigenous arts were produced by museums or departments of anthropology, which displayed them according to the artifact mode. One notable exception to this pattern was the University of British Columbia Museum of Anthropology, which broke ranks with conventional ethnographic displays in 1976 when it opened its new building, designed to present Northwest Coast carvings as works of art.[26] Its highly aestheticized installations had, in turn, been inspired both by the Vancouver Art Gallery's *Arts of the Raven*, a celebrated temporary exhibition mounted for the centennial in 1967, and by the exhibition of Northwest Coast art organized by the MoA's founding curator, Audrey Hawthorn, for the *Man and His World* exhibition that succeeded Expo 67 in Montreal the following year.[27]

At the Glenbow itself another precedent for display had been established a few years earlier when the museum hosted *Treasures of Ancient Nigeria*, a landmark international touring exhibition of historic Ife and Benin brasses and terracottas dating back to the twelfth century. As one British reviewer wrote when the exhibition opened at London's Royal Academy, it was groundbreaking "not only because it contained superb sculpture but because it demonstrated a willingness to accept the creations of Black Africa as art, to be judged on the same basis as those of the classical or renaissance worlds or of China or Japan."[28] In retrospect, it is clear that from the start the Glenbow's director and staff saw their Olympics project as an opportunity to build on these examples. They conceptualized *The Spirit Sings* as a blockbuster "treasures" show along the lines of the Nigerian exhibition and saw it as an opportunity to redefine Canadian Indigenous material culture as art. These intentions were, for their time, the progressive and liberal options available to a Western museum. As James Clifford has observed, within the established dichotomies of great civilizations versus small-scale societies and art versus craft, the redefinition of a society's material culture as art is a compliment of the highest order.[29] This compliment, as we have seen, had not yet been paid to the vast majority of Canadian Indigenous works, for apart from the innovative displays of Northwest Coast carvings and paintings noted earlier, the quillwork, beadwork, baskets, painted hide clothing, and carved pipe bowls and clubs from other parts of Canada were still defined as material culture, craft, and decorative or applied art.[30]

At the same time, however, the Glenbow's curators were aware of the dangers of appropriation and radical decontextualization that had been revealed by the Museum of Modern Art's *"Primitivism"* show, and as anthropologists they were professionally predisposed to privilege cultural contextualization. The Glenbow staff and the members of the scientific committee (as the guest curators were termed) were in agreement that *The Spirit Sings* would aim to combine elements of both approaches. A memo of July 1986 summarizes this solution: "The overriding design principle would be to keep the installation as simple as possible. The objects would essentially be exhibited as 'art' objects with contextual references to geography and enivronment."[31] In a more detailed memo written a month later, the Glenbow's chief designer, Rick Budd, elaborated further: "Photo-murals and/or illustrations may be used to accentuate the reality of the landscape and to add humans to an otherwise object-oriented installation. Sound effects will be used as environmental ambience appropriate to each geographic and cultural region. Human and/or natural sounds will be used to add dimension to the exhibits" (fig. 2.2). Distractions, he emphasized, would be avoided, allowing the "objects to demand all the attention of the visitor."[32]

Arguably, Budd's final design achieved a successful convergence in some aspects while introducing new problems in others. He avoided the radical decontextualization, homogenizing effect, and ahistoricity of the modernist "white cube" art display by changing wall and case colours from section to section. Colours deemed appropriate to each region were chosen in consultation with the curators and were more intense than the neutral tones as-

2.2   Introductory section of *The Spirit Sings*. Photo © Glenbow Museum, Calgary

sociated with 1980s art gallery spaces – a reddish tone reminiscent of ochre in the Woodlands, a sand colour for the prairies, blue for the Arctic, and so on. Budd also deviated from the art-exhibition model in his use of gobos to create patterns of light and shade suggestive of leaves, waves, and other natural features. The component of sound was added by a carefully researched soundscape composed of Indigenous music and soft natural and animal noises. Internal memos explicitly instructed staff to make sure none of the chosen music was sacred.[33]

The case designs used in most of the exhibition, however, inadvertently reinforced older objectifying display paradigms. Influenced by the postmodern historicism in vogue during the 1980s, Budd "quoted" the wood-framed artifact cases used in nineteenth- and early twentieth-century anthropology and natural history museums in order to reference the ways in which many of the items in the exhibition had originally been displayed[34] (fig. 2.3). In order to distance the older museological paradigm, he rendered the cases in metal and painted them in the signifying colours of each section. The historicist reference and ironic inflection of his design seems, however, to have been lost on the exhibition's critics – and probably on most visitors – who read the installation either as reinscribing the objectifying and deadening habits of past museums or as conveying the ineffable sadness of lost worlds (fig. 2.4). To add to the ambiguity, a more modern art-museum case design featuring simple pedestal bases

2.3 (*above and colour plate 1*)   Northern Woodlands section of *The Spirit Sings*.
Photo © Glenbow Museum, Calgary

2.4 (*below*)   Beothuk installation at *The Spirit Sings*. Photo © Glenbow Museum, Calgary

2.5 (*see also colour plate 2*)   Northwest Coast installation of *The Spirit Sings*. Photo © Glenbow Museum, Calgary

and clear glass tops was used in the Northwest Coast and Arctic sections (fig. 2.5). Since these were the two regions most clearly associated with the production of fine art, both historic and contemporary, it is hard not to read into this choice a judgment that some Indigenous traditions were more "art-like" than others.

In retrospect, and despite the progressive intentions behind the design choices for the exhibition, its hybrid approach to the art and artifact display paradigms and its mixture of different case designs undercut the curatorial messages and probably exacerbated the critique that the exhibition constituted a conservative reaffirmation of the artifact paradigm through which Indigenous material heritage had long been represented. The dangers of relying on a strategy of postmodern historicism and quotation to critique museum and collecting histories would be fully revealed a year later, in the aftermath of another boycott and controversy that developed around the Royal Ontario Museum's *Into the Heart of Africa*.[35] Linda Hutcheon's conclusion regarding that exhibition also applies to installation features of *The Spirit Sings*: "There are times when a reflexive, ironic challenge is either not appropriate or simply not strong enough, no matter how demystificatory it might be of modernity's assumptions."[36]

Such insights, however, are the products of hard retrospective thinking and analysis and do not reflect the climate of reception in 1988. The responses of ordinary visitors and reviewers for the popular press were overwhelmingly positive, while also expressing a sense of loss and sadness that was engendered by the exhibition. The great majority of the many comment cards written by both non-Indigenous and Indigenous visitors, now preserved in the archives of the Glenbow Museum and the Canadian Museum of Civilization, are appreciative and respectful, and they deserve a far more systematic analysis than is possible in this chapter.

Even a sampling, however, suggests the emotional intensity of many visitors' reactions and the mixture of celebration and shame, joy and sorrow, exaltation and depression, with which they responded to the brief return to Canada of these rare treasures from far away and long ago. "Overwhelming!" wrote one visitor. "I had no idea of the artistry and creativity that developed in North America before we came." Another wrote along the same lines: "If this display could have been shown every 10 years I'm sure we so-called 'superior' people would have had more respect and compassion for our Native forebears." "The artistic ability of the natives is unbelievable. It is a shame that these artifacts are owned by foreign museums and not the natives themselves. It is their culture," another person observed. An Aboriginal visitor responded similarly: "I was touched, beset, by the wonderful preparations. They were carefully thought out so the people could enjoy it more! I found it most intriguing and exciting to find out more about my ancestors! I had no idea about them and what they did! But now I know. Thank you." For others, the beauty of Aboriginal work inspired guilt or a need to make restitution. "It left me feeling *very sad* for what we have done. I am ashamed to be a non-native Canadian," said one person. "Wonderful!" commented another. "Shows what money can do – *now* let's get on and use some of that money to RIGHT THE WRONGS!!"

There were also, of course, comments that were more critical, both of Aboriginal people and of the museum. "Beautiful Exhibits Wonderfully Done. Took the C-Train down, 4 Indian teens on the platform. Bruised & scraped, reeling drunk. Everyone averts their eyes. Have their spirits ever sung?" And another, sympathetic to opponents of the exhibition, wrote: "I was horrified at the racism embodied in the commentary and in the labeling of exhibits. These accounts represent a falsification of the true nature of the genocide, physical and cultural, imposed by the white invaders. This exhibition represents an extension of this imperialistic attitude, and a justification of the continued presence of whites in Canada."[37]

Viewed historically, the *Spirit Sings* installation must be taken as an honest attempt to renegotiate a modernist museological legacy. The exhibit's unstable oscillation between tropes of art and artifact was a result of its attempt to escape the confinement and representational limitations of a duality that museums have continued to negotiate in the years since. As I will argue elsewhere in this book, we have not yet found a way out of this dilemma. In major long-term exhibitions of recent years, produced by both Aboriginal and non-Aboriginal curators and institutions, the art and artifact paradigms continue to appear, most often in the hybrid forms pioneered by *The Spirit Sings*. When we think of the "futures" to which the *Spirit Sings* controversy pointed, we need to recognize with some humility the degree to which installation as representation has continued to challenge us.

Third Proposition: The Public Relations Wrap

Surprisingly little attention is paid to the ways that exhibitions are publicized and advertised, yet these strategies, too, interact with the other media
through which a show communicates, and they can strengthen or weaken the
coherence and power of that communication. These exhibitionary components are therefore as much deserving of attention from curators and critics
as installation design, label copy, or other kinds of exhibition apparatus. My
third proposition contends that there was a lack of alignment of the messages
transmitted by the curatorial content, graphic branding, and marketing
strategies of *The Spirit Sings* and that the resulting contradictions probably
fed the controversy. In my analysis, the marketing imagery tended to rely on
a common currency of stereotypes, a problem which, as with other components of the exhibition, was not unique to *The Spirit Sings.* Yet the spotlight
shone on the exhibition by the boycott reveals the risks incurred by such a
strategy with particular clarity and allows us to draw some useful lessons.

Carefully constructed public relations campaigns have become crucial elements in the organization of exhibitions. They are made up of posters, brochures, logos, newspaper and magazine advertisements, websites, banners
and graphics applied to the outside of buildings, and souvenirs emblazoned
with museum and exhibition "trademarks." Taken together, these items wrap
exhibitions with a layer of signifying elements – colours, images, and words –
that communicate meanings independently of the exhibition itself.[38] During
the 1980s, as today, museums were under pressure to market exhibitions to
broader publics both because of the democratizing policies of government
funders and because decreasing government support made increased attendance an economic necessity. Good visitor numbers not only add up to
revenue but also strengthen the museum's ability to bring in grants. For all
these reasons, selling an exhibition to the public becomes more important
in proportion to its cost. In the case of a blockbuster like *The Spirit Sings,* at
the time the most expensive temporary exhibition ever mounted in Canada,
marketing was the subject of much discussion and planning.

The title of an exhibition is usually the first element of the public relations
"wrap." It must be determined, at least provisionally, before funds can be
solicited, loans requested, pre-publicity begun, and other venues arranged.
Curators, administrators, and other interested parties struggle to find a sequence of words that is short, memorable, and intriguing and that adequately
represents the concept and content of the show. In the course of its development, *The Spirit Sings* was referred to by three different titles, and these suggest several ways in which the show was being conceptualized by the staff and
the guest curators. In 1983–84, during the initial stages of planning, internal
museum memos refer to the exhibition as the "National Treasures Exhibition" or "World Treasures of the Canadian Inuit and Indian."[39] Although
identified as provisional, the phrase nevertheless points both to the treasures
model favoured by director Duncan Cameron and to the appropriation of In-

digenous heritage to Canada's national identity that had been common since the early twentieth century.[40]

Two years later, in correspondence with potential lenders to the exhibition, Glenbow staff members were referring to the exhibition under the title "Forget Not My World." When this title was announced to the curatorial committee, its members unanimously and vociferously opposed it. On one level, we argued that the notion of forgetting placed Native people and their cultures firmly in the past and implied an existence so fragile that oblivion, the old idea of the vanishing Indian, could be imagined as a real possibility. We also objected to the pleading tone of the phrase, which implied an appeal to strength from weakness – to the dominant settler culture from the imagined Native petitioners. The first-person voice of the pronoun "my" appropriated to the museum a spurious membership in the Native community and the right to speak on its behalf. Finally, the use of "world" in the singular perpetuated the old, false stereotype of a single Native culture, rather than the six distinct regions and numerous individual communities featured in the show. This title had gained the approval of museum administrators because it was judged to be intriguing and catchy. The public of the 1980s, it was alleged, would respond to a nostalgic evocation of the vanishing Indian idea. As the boycott pressures increased, however, it became clear that any such argument would further aggravate matters. As J.G.E. Smith, curator at New York's Museum of the American Indian, wrote in a memo to his director in which he urged that the museum support the boycott: "the title of the exhibit, 'Forget Not My World: Exploring the Canadian Native Heritage,' is an abomination in a province in which the world and heritage of the Canadian Native is forgotten in the best interests of the oil companies."[41] "Forget Not My World" was abandoned only after strenuous objections from the curatorial committee with the critical support of prominent Haida artist Bill Reid, relayed through his wife, Martine, who curated the Northwest Coast section with his collaboration.[42]

Charged with finding a new title, the committee proposed the phrase "the spirit sings," taken from an Inuit poem. Although the new title was adopted with general relief, it can be argued in retrospect that it too conveyed messages that subverted the show's actual content. The exhibition, as has been noted, featured historical works, early Indigenous accommodations of the European presence, and the diversity of Indigenous cultural traditions in the early contact period. Neither historicity nor cultural diversity was, however, reflected in the final title. The tense of the verb "sings" carried the action into the present and suggested contemporaneity, while the singular use of "spirit," like the earlier "world," alluded misleadingly to a unitary Native culture. As an introductory text panel put it, "What is the spirit that sings? It is the spirit of Canada's Native peoples which was heard for centuries before the Europeans came and continues to be heard today. It is also a spirit that will sing to generations to come ... These objects tell of the strength and resilience of cultures which faced the wave of Europeans who came to domin-

THE SPIRIT SINGS
Artistic Traditions of Canada's First Peoples

January 15 — May 1, 1988
A Glenbow Museum exhibition
Shell Canada Limited – exclusive corporate sponsor

2.6 (*see also colour plate 3*) *The Spirit Sings* logo from the cover of the visitor brochure (detail). Reproduced from the author's copy

ate their lands. The spirit which moved Native artisans many years ago to create these works of art continues to sing among Canada's Native peoples."[43] However sincerely intended, such statements sought to finesse the fact that the exhibition – typically for its time – did not include any of those contemporary works of art or direct voices of living Indigenous people that would have made those continuities manifest.

Similar problems emerge even more forcefully from an analysis of the logo, designed by Glenbow staff, that appeared on all advertising and brochures, on a huge disc mounted over the doors of the Lorne Building during the Ottawa venue, and on the T-shirts, key chains, pens, and other souvenirs sold in the gift shop (fig. 2.6). The source for this logo was one of the most sacred objects in the show, a double-headed Anishinaabe drum. This drum had been collected in 1823 by the Italian explorer Gian Costantino Beltrami and bequeathed to the library of his native Bergamo, in northern Italy. It had been largely unknown both to Aboriginal people and to scholars before the exhibition.[44] The Beltrami drum is a rare and exceptionally beautiful expression of Anishinaabe spirituality and visual art. One side displays an image of the sun, an extremely important *manito* (spiritual being) for the Indigenous peoples of the woodlands and plains, while the other side bears the image of a *manito* in anthropomorphic form from whose head and torso project short radiating lines representing a halo of supernatural light. The drum would have been rhythmically beaten by its shaman-owner to induce visionary experience and to summon his helping spirits.

The decision to use the anthropomorphic *manito* as the central element of the logo was based in part on its connection with the word "spirit" in the exhibition's title. There was also agreement, however, that no one work in the exhibition could signify all six culture areas represented in the show. For this reason, the designers simplified the drum's iconography and added new elements to it. Their modifications were explained in a special label placed in the case containing the drum and reprinted in the exhibition leaflet. "In designing the exhibition's logo," it stated, "the Glenbow designers combined the manito's image with bands of bright quillwork, a technique used by the East Coast, Woodlands, Plains and Subarctic groups. A sun image, which is a strong spiritual symbol to many native groups, surrounds the quillwork bands." Although unstated, the specific artistic source of this sun image was the feathered-circle design displayed on Plains painted buffalo robes. In its original context, the design symbolized both the sun and a man's eagle-feather war bonnet. To make this reference clearer in the logo, the circular design was sliced in half and arranged around the *manito*'s head. From any distance, the resulting image reads as a man wearing a feather bonnet, the quintessential and stereotypical image of the Hollywood Indian.[45] Thus, although the logo was constructed of a pastiche of elements drawn from different Indigenous traditions, it conjured up the idea of a single, homogeneous Indian culture in its most popular pan-Indian form. Like the singular "world" or "spirit" in the show's title, it ran counter to the avowed goal of the exhibition to explore diversity and distinctiveness.

The original colours of the Anishinaabe drum were also dramatically altered. The dark red, yellow, and deep blue earth and mineral pigments were replaced by bright red, turquoise, and purple. Colour preferences, in late modern Western consumer culture, are time-specific, and the reason given by the museum's publicity team for this change was that contemporary colours would entice prospective viewers through their association with current fashion. During the mid-1980s, catalogues and decorating magazines were full of products made of glossy-surfaced plastics and other synthetic materials in the same bright hues chosen for the *Spirit Sings* logo. The palette was therefore a clear signifier of contemporaneity, linking the exhibition to the 1980s vogue for high-tech and the machine-made. During the Ottawa showing, huge banners of red, purple, and turquoise also draped the entire facade of the Lorne Building, literally wrapping the exhibition inside in the decade's signifying colours. For the Anishinaabe, in contrast, colours signify far more than consumer fashion. Pigments from the earth are, in their essence, sacred medicines. The new colours of the logo thus altered the meaning of the original drum image as radically as did the added pan-Indian motifs. On the one hand, then, the design of the logo disregarded an important principle of cultural ownership by appropriating an object sacred to a particular Aboriginal nation and transforming it into a secular and anonymous image. On the other, it created unnecessary confusion by preparing viewers for the modern when, in fact, they were to see the historical.

A possible explanation for the contradictions between the show's actual historicity and the wrapping of contemporaneity contributed by this package of title, logo, and colour branding is that the museum administration wanted to convey a general sense of relevance between past and present realities. This is analogous to the "affinity of the tribal and the modern" proposed by the subtitle of the Museum of Modern Art's *"Primitivism"* exhibition. In his penetrating analysis of the controversy raised by that show, James Clifford pointed out that the MoMA exhibit did not, in fact, argue its central allegory of affinity systematically, but that "the allegory is, rather, built into the exhibition's form and featured suggestively in its publicity, left uncontradicted, repetitiously asserted."[46] The parallel between *The Spirit Sings* and the MoMA show was no accident. As artifacts of late modernism, both remained linked to a tradition of appropriating aspects of the "primitive." Both sought a seamless incorporation of aspects of non-Western expressive culture into modernity in order to supply the losses of authenticity, wholeness, and spirituality that modernity was thought to have incurred. Like the juxtapositions of African ritual masks and paintings by Picasso in the MoMA show, the *Spirit Sings* logo sought, in Clifford's phrase to "redeem otherness" by "reconstituting it in its own image."[47]

A museum director once commented to me that the typical wisdom of public relations campaigns is to "start with what they know, and then tell them what you want them to know." What the public "knows" about "Indians" is still, regrettably, the Hollywood stereotypes. By making use of such prior knowledge, however, public relations packaging runs two serious risks. The first is that damaging stereotypes will be reinforced rather than challenged. The second risk, also evidenced by the contradictory installation approaches used in *The Spirit Sings,* is that, by sending conflicting messages, museums may simply produce confusion in the public's mind.[48] Public relations packaging is not, furthermore, encountered only at the entrance to an exhibition, as an initial enticement that can be cancelled by the experience of viewing the show. The images remain fixed after the visit through their repetitious reproduction on souvenirs and posters. Publicity imagery both foreshadows the show and lingers as an afterimage. Like the layered wrappings of texts and images that surround artifacts, the public relations wrap adheres to the total experience of an exhibition.

Ultimately, what these analyses reveal is a profound structural contradiction within the late-modern museum, a crack in the edifice that would continue to widen. In the late twentieth century and still today in many institutions, meaning is created and communicated by two groups of people with separate and sometimes conflicting mandates. The content of exhibitions, catalogue, text panels, and labels are largely left to curators with academic training, orientation, and educational goals usually focused on breaking down simplistic generalizations. The outer wrapping – the packaging, as it is so accurately termed – has often, however, been placed in the hands of marketing experts who, in their efforts to simplify, risk reinscribing the very stereotypes curators try to deconstruct.

An incident that occurred toward the end of the Ottawa showing of *The Spirit Sings* brought this tension into sharp focus. An advertisement, written by the private firm to which the Canadian Museum of Civilization had contracted the advertising for the show, was placed in the *Ottawa Citizen.* It was headed by a line of large type which read, "Going … Going … Go before it's gone!" The ad was brought to me by an Aboriginal student at my university, who had annotated it with a precise diagram of its semiotic referents. He interpreted "Going … going … gone" as referencing the trope of disappearance, and a visitor comment quoted in the advertisement that referred to "a [single] native people" as an appeal to the false generalization of ethnic homogeneity. In his analysis, the second part of the exhibition title, *Artistic Traditions of Canada's First Peoples,* referenced the nation-state's appropriation of Aboriginal people and their land. Finally, the presence of the Shell logo among the other, governmental logos was to him a visual signifier of corporate exploitation. Some of these readings were not lost on museum staff, for whom the advertisement, having been contracted to an outside agency and somehow escaped the normal vetting process, was a great embarrassment. It is nevertheless an important warning of the risks and dangers of the numbers game that modern museums are being compelled to play.

Fourth Proposition: Recovering History

At the heart of *The Spirit Sings* was not only an exhibition but also a very ambitious research project which was intended to bring to light the rich artistic and material heritages of Aboriginal peoples that had remained largely hidden away in museum storerooms around the world. My fourth proposition seeks to recognize both the valuable legacy of scholarship left by *The Spirit Sings* and its contribution to the revival of interest in material culture and museum-based research among both Indigenous and non-Indigenous people. This proposition returns us to the question of the relative weight given to research and exhibitions in museums and who has the power to determine priorities. This question has hovered like a ghost in the background of the other issues that have been discussed in this chapter, for, as we have seen, the exhibition's focus on earlier periods of Indigenous arts and cultures was central to the criticisms that were raised. Boycott organizers asserted that this focus implicitly denied the value and authenticity of contemporary Indigenous cultural expressions and displaced attention from the urgent problems of the present. In addressing my last but perhaps most important proposition, then, I will argue two points that may seem contradictory. First, the recognition that museum representation is always political is, in my view, the single most important legacy of the *Spirit Sings* controversy, for it has led us not only to adopt collaborative methodologies but also to choose topics for representation in terms of contingencies of time and place. Secondly, the controversy has led to a heightened awareness of the way in which this politics is controlled and expressed through the things that are selected, the gestures of display, and the interpretive voices that intervene.

An anecdote from the "Preserving Our Heritage" conference, held in the last days of the exhibition's Ottawa showing (the same occasion on which George Erasmus spoke so movingly), evidences the importance of this aspect of the *Spirit Sings* legacy for Aboriginal as well as non-Aboriginal people. At the opening session of the conference, Ted Montour, the moderator appointed by the Assembly of First Nations, announced that, in recognition of the constructive spirit in which the conference had been organized, the Assembly of First Nations would lift its boycott of the exhibition and the CMC would keep the exhibition open an extra evening especially for the conference participants. I still recall how deftly Montour lightened the tense atmosphere with a well-timed aside that provoked general laughter. "Of course," he said, "like me, you've probably all seen it already, looking both ways before going in to make sure no one saw you." Montour's remark pointed to a desire for connection with the extraordinary array of Aboriginal heritage items that the exhibition had brought together. This desire had manifested itself many times during the exhibition's showings in Calgary and Ottawa, which were attended by many Native community groups and individuals.

As noted, the exhibition's focus on the early contact period had led to the accusation that it reinscribed the modernist proposition that the authenticity of Aboriginal cultures lay in the past. In fact, change, adaptation, and creativity – often in response to situations of great difficulty – were major themes in all sections of *The Spirit Sings*. The Glenbow's strategy for dealing with contemporary life was to complement the exhibition with a full program of performances and demonstrations by contemporary Aboriginal people. Yet it remains an open question whether the times demanded a different focus entirely, one that fostered a more direct engagement with the present.

The lasting legacy of *The Spirit Sings* as a research project has manifested itself in many ways in the years since. In 2007, for example, I spent two weeks at the British Museum and Oxford's Pitt Rivers Museum, researching the two largest ethnographic collections of Great Lakes Aboriginal art and material culture in Britain, collections I had first studied closely in 1984 as part of my research for the exhibition. This time, however, I was not alone but part of a collaborative team made up of researchers based in museums, universities, and Aboriginal communities. As we worked together, references were regularly made to the two volumes of the *Spirit Sings* catalogue, which had first introduced many of those present to the collections we were viewing. With equal frequency, Indigenous members of our research team added critically important observations or information to what had been published in those volumes. Some of these comments reframed the known information from a different disciplinary or cultural angle, and some of them turned long-standing interpretations on their heads. The digital database being developed by the larger collaboration of which we were a part (the Great Lakes Research Alliance for the Study of Aboriginal Arts and Cultures, or GRASAC, discussed in chapter 15) is an ambitious project whose central aims are the "digital repatriation" of Indigenous heritage to members of contemporary Indigenous communities and the development of multivocal and holistic understandings that are more consonant both with Indigenous ways of knowing and with Western academic interdisciplinarity. An important by-product, we hope, will be to provide all researchers with a resource that will allow them to integrate the perspectives of the originating communities with up-to-date scholarly knowledge. Such a project was not, of course, imaginable in these terms in 1988 because the digital technology we have today had not yet been developed. In the mid-1980s, all you could do was to publish books.

The work of GRASAC and of many other parallel projects in progress in Canada and elsewhere illustrate a new, collaborative research model that has emerged since *The Spirit Sings*. These endeavours are, however, also indebted to that troubled project in ways that we do not always recognize. The provision of access to Aboriginal heritage was identified from the beginning as a central goal of *The Spirit Sings*; the curators were provided with the resources to conduct as exhaustive as possible a survey of international collections and to deposit the full results of their findings – not just the selection of items that would be displayed – at both the Glenbow and the Canadian Museum of Civilization, where they could be consulted by all researchers. Because of the definition of expertise and authority that still informed Western academic practices in the mid-1980s and because viable digital imaging capabilities did not yet exist, this aspect of the project could achieve only a very partial level of success. In retrospect, however, I would argue that the problem of the representational scope of the exhibition lay not in its focus on the early contact period but in the lack of direct Aboriginal participation and voice in the research and curatorial processes. Because of this absence, the project could not bridge the cultural divide between Aboriginal and Western systems of knowledge or forge meaningful links between Aboriginal pasts and presents. In consequence, the mood evoked by the exhibition among both Aboriginal and many non-Aboriginal visitors was a confusing mixture of admiration, pride, loss, sadness, and grief. The temporary return of the historical treasures, immured behind glass, seemed to instill a sense of being cut off from the past rather than of being given access to it.

The concept of recovery enunciated today by Aboriginal scholars and researchers – as articulated, for example, in Anishinaabe legal scholar John Borrows's book *Recovering Canada: The Resurgence of Indigenous Law* – focuses closely on earlier periods of history as well as on the essential interconnectedness of art, material culture, language, systems of kinship, land use, and many other phenomena.[49] These must be brought into conjunction with one another, with Indigenous knowledges, and with techniques of knowledge recovery belonging to Western disciplines in order to renew understandings of the systematic nature of Aboriginal intellectual traditions. Since the report of the Task Force on Museums and First Peoples was accepted in 1992, a remarkable array of collaborative research projects involving museum collections as sources for aspects of this knowledge have been initiated, a number of which will be cited in other chapters in this book. *The Spirit Sings* represented a start in this process of recovery, however imperfect, incomplete, and lacking in the critically important elements of Aboriginal perspective, voice, and knowledge that we have since tried to enlist.

After she received her copy of the *Spirit Sings* publication, the late Mi'kmaq poet Rita Joe penned a poem entitled "My Shadow Celebrates," in which she acknowledged the intentions to complement and contribute to the continuity of Indigenous artistic traditions that lay behind *The Spirit Sings* both as an exhibition and as a research project:

Though it was natural for me to create my leather dress
The beads and quill my ornamentation
You call it art
It makes me feel wise with a sense of identity

Though it was necessity I used bone, stone, and wood to
carve my images
You call it art
It makes me feel wise and a seer of beauty

Though I created the mast for mystical purposes
The amulets my ritual objects
You call it art
It makes me feel wise as my spirit flows with love

My sketches have revealed the loneliness of fading away
The message passing the wind into all eternity
You call it art
My shadow celebrates, you have found me.[50]

Rita Joe's poem also, of course, opens up larger questions of the misprision and reframing of Indigenous modes of knowledge and creativity that occur when they enter the exhibitionary spaces of the Western museum. As a critical event, *The Spirit Sings* began to move the Canadian museum world toward the recognition that relations of power and the politics of identity had to be addressed not only outside but also inside the museum. Failing to acknowledge the start that was made in 1988 toward a reflexive consideration of both museum poetics and museum politics can only inhibit the ongoing process of negotiation and change.

3

APEC at the Museum of Anthropology

The Politics of Site and the Poetics of Sight Bite

The central feature of global culture today is the politics of the mutual effort of sameness and difference to cannibalize one another and thereby proclaim their successful hijacking of the twin Enlightenment ideas of the triumphantly universal and the resiliently particular.
– *Arjun Appadurai,* Modernity at Large[1]

Throughout its two-hundred-year history, the public museum has been a powerfully attractive object for appropriative projects. It has been an important agent for the inscription of the universalizing ideology of modernity as well as of imperial hierarchies of Western nations and world cultures. In the early years of a new millennium the museum remains one of the most prestigious of public spaces, a secular sacristy in which are kept the material objects that are most greatly valued and that are held to embody essential evidence of history, culture, nature, science, and art. It is a unique "interspace," mediating the authoritative knowledge produced in the academy and making it accessible to broad publics. To gain control of the museum, therefore, is to take over a prestigious forum from which to propound knowledge and to assert value.[2] In modern multicultural societies, museums also act as important cross-cultural meeting grounds and sites of negotiation. In the politics of postcolonialism they have served as spaces in which knowledges produced within Western disciplinary traditions may be contested by members of Indigenous, immigrant, and diasporic communities, and where discrepant assertions of truth can be symbolically aligned or harmonized.[3] As Sharon Macdonald has put it, "Precisely because [museums] have become global symbols through which status and community are expressed, they are subject to appropriation and the struggle for ownership."[4]

The APEC Meeting: Local/Global Encounters

In this chapter I will examine one such "struggle for ownership," which took place in 1997 at the University of British

Columbia Museum of Anthropology in Vancouver (MoA).[5] On 25 November of that year, at the request of the Canadian government, the university lent the museum as the site of the prime ministerial meeting of Asia-Pacific Economic Cooperation (APEC), an economic union of eighteen Pacific Rim nations, including the United States, China, Japan, Indonesia, Australia, Mexico, and Canada. The meeting provoked large protest demonstrations on the UBC campus – the largest since the 1960s – directed against human rights abuses in member countries and against the negative consequences of economic globalization. Police handling of the protest, which included the forcible removal and detainment of protesters and the use of pepper spray, proved highly controversial and received sustained national press coverage.[6] While the globally oriented protests were going on outside the museum, a second, more locally focused contestatory drama was taking place inside.

The actors in this drama were federal government officials, the prime minister of Canada, and representatives of the Musqueam First Nation, the Indigenous people on whose ancestral land the university and the museum are located. The drama had two acts. In the first, federal officials cancelled scheduled formal speeches of welcome from Musqueam representatives. The Musqueam leaders' remarks would have articulated a postcolonial rhetoric of Native sovereignty and distinct local identity before an audience representing the new transnational rhetoric of economic globalization. In the second act, the federal government used the Museum of Anthropology as a stage for the enactment of a pageant that reinscribed a hoary settler-colonial image of national identity before that same audience.

The confrontation between Musqueam representatives and officials of the Canadian government received less attention than did the protest demonstrations, but it is equally worthy of analysis for what it reveals about the role of anthropology museums today. The episode offers an opportunity to assess the degree to which changing rhetorics of the local and the global signal new relations of power between settler societies and Indigenous peoples. It also raises important questions about the appropriation of the museum as a site for the staging of political and other spectacles – a use to which museums are increasingly lending themselves in the aftermath of cuts in public funding – and the way such appropriations can compromise the role that many museum professionals wish their institutions to play as agents of decolonization. In this chapter I will provide an account of the APEC–First Nations episode and place it within two specific historical contexts from which it acquires resonance. The episode is, on one level, a chapter in a local history that has to do with the evolving relationship between the Indigenous Musqueam community and the Museum of Anthropology, the University of British Columbia, and the metropolitan Vancouver region.[7] On another level, the APEC leaders' meeting can be seen as a recent chapter in a longer history of successive appropriations of Indigenous cultures that have occurred when Canadian governments have been called upon to display national identity before an international audience. As in November 1997, such events have often been organized with the active collaboration of anthropology museums. The loan of the UBC Museum of Anthropology for the APEC leaders' meeting caused these two histories to intersect. Intersections are, of course, places where collisions often occur.

The Musqueam First Nation and the Museum of Anthropology

Anthropology museums in Canada have been especially contested spaces during the past few decades. Products of imperial and colonial constructions of knowledge, official displayers of cultures and cultural hierarchies, repositories of intensely desired objects, they are places where competing claims to ownership, compensation, authority, and interpretation have to be negotiated on an almost daily basis. As discussed in the previous chapter, the boycotts and protests that surrounded exhibitions such as *The Spirit Sings: Artistic Traditions of Canada's First Peoples,* organized for the Calgary Winter Olympics in 1988, and *Into the Heart of Africa*, at the Royal Ontario Museum in Toronto in 1990, not only stimulated a substantial critical literature among academic students of the museum but also catalyzed far-reaching internal changes affecting most areas of museum practice.[8] During the early 1990s, Museum of Anthropology staff and its director, Michael Ames, were actively involved at both the regional and the national levels in the Task Force on Museums and First Peoples, which was organized to address the problems revealed by those two controversies.[9] As at other Canadian museums, the strengthening of partnerships with local First Nations mandated by the task force's report in 1992 became a priority for the museum in the years following the task force meetings.

In November of 1997, while the APEC meetings were being held, two temporary exhibitions were on view at the museum. Both were begun shortly after the task force report was issued as a means of implementing its recommendations. *From under the Delta* featured basketry and weaving, some examples 4,500 years old, retrieved from waterlogged sites in the Vancouver area, including Point Grey, where the university, the museum, and the Musqueam reserve are situated. The second exhibition, *Written in the Earth*, displayed carved amulets, sculpted stone figures, ornaments, and other objects of similar age and provenance.[10] The Museum of Anthropology has long been known as an innovative pioneer in building collaborations with First Nations communities and had worked previously with Musqueam community members on two other exhibitions. *Hands of Our Ancestors* (1986) presented the revival of an ancient weaving tradition at Musqueam and was developed collaboratively with weavers from the community, while *Proud to Be Musqueam* (1988) was a photographic exhibition, curated by community members, about their own history.[11] The process by which the two more-recent exhibitions of archaeological materials were organized had, however, involved the most radical and difficult negotiations of curatorial authority and museological practice in the museum's history. In the course of their development, official agreements were signed with Musqueam and other Lower Mainland First Nations band councils that detailed shared authority over everything from the way objects were to be handled and stored to the label copy and the design of the cases.[12]

The title *Written in the Earth* was contributed by Deborah Sparrow, a well-known Musqueam weaver who has had a long association with the museum. As she has explained,

> During a conference between aboriginal leaders and [Prime Minister] Pierre Trudeau, it was said that the land belonged to Native people and that the creator gave it to us to look after. Trudeau replied, "Why is it yours? I don't see any signs that the land belongs to you. Where is it written that it belongs to you?" I thought to myself, "It is written in the earth. The evidence is everywhere that we have lived in the land. Anywhere that we open the earth so are unveiled the messages from the past ... I think of these objects as a part of me, a part of who we are. A museum is not just an institution: it is a home for these objects and the people they represent.[13]

Sparrow's words provide an essential context within which the issues that arose around the siting of the APEC leaders' meeting at the Museum of Anthropology need to be understood.

The Musqueam are a Coast Salish people, and their arts have historically been less celebrated by Western connoisseurs than have those of other Northwest Coast groups. Following the general pattern, during the 1970s and 1980s the Museum of Anthropology privileged northern and central coastal First Nations in its permanent and temporary exhibitions, and the museum had become particularly identified with displays of Haida and Kwakwaka'wakw (Kwakiutl) artists.[14] *From under the Delta* and *Written in the Earth* built on the relationships established through the development of *Hands of Our Ancestors* and *Proud to Be Musqueam*, as well as other collaborative programs, but they represented the museum's strongest acknowledgments to that date of the special relationship between the Musqueam First Nation and the UBC Museum of Anthropology that arises from their shared occupancy of place.[15] They were also, in another sense, part of a larger project aimed at rebalancing the received hierarchy of Northwest Coast arts that remained embedded in the museum's venerable permanent installations. This hierarchy ultimately derives from modernist primitivism, Western connoisseurship, and early twentieth-century evolutionist anthropological theories of art.[16] While the older hierarchy participates in idealist and universalist constructs of relative cultural value, the new exhibitions were situated in a more recent, flatter, and less fixed system of value formed by the matrix of globalization and localization. They suggest an affirmative answer to the question posed by Arjun Appadurai: "Can the mutually constitutive relationship between anthropology and locality survive in a dramatically delocalized world?"[17]

Shortly after I became director of the Museum of Anthropology in July of 1997, I signed, on behalf of the museum, a general protocol that formalized the relationship between the museum and Musqueam and set out guidelines for future collaborations. The document was the product of many months of discussion and consultation between Michael Ames and Leona Sparrow and Howard Grant, the representatives who had been delegated by the Musqueam Band Council to work with the museum on *From under the Delta* and *Written in the Earth*. Although the present Musqueam reserve borders the University of British Columbia's endowment lands, and although its land claims to a larger area are still being negotiated with the federal and provincial governments, the protocol takes as its point of departure the recognition of Musqueam's traditional ownership of the site occupied by the university on the Point Grey peninsula.

The Politics of Site

It is against this micro-history of Musqueam relations with the university and the museum that the first of the APEC conflicts needs to be understood. By the 1990s it had become accepted practice to follow Indigenous protocol by ensuring that the first greeting to official foreign visitors to UBC or the museum (including representatives of other First Nations) is offered by Musqueam representatives in recognition of the band's traditional ownership of the land. University and museum officials urged the importance of this protocol on federal government officials during the months preceding the APEC meeting. In this spirit, too, Musqueam chief Gail Sparrow wrote to the prime minister on 31 July 1997 "reminding" him that "Musqueam participation should be included in, *but not restricted to,* the opening ceremonies; gala and media opportunities; participation at the leaders [*sic*] meeting; and/ or senior officials meetings" (emphasis mine). She also noted that "history indicates that an Asian Pacific relationship existed prior to and during European contact" – perhaps unwittingly providing the germ of Prime Minister Jean Chrétien's opening remarks at the APEC leaders' meeting. In response to this letter and to representations made by museum and UBC representatives, the Prime Minister's Office scheduled a prayer by Elder Vincent Stogan (Tsimele'nuxw) and a welcome speech by Chief Sparrow at the start of the APEC leaders' meeting. It is clear from documents later released to the Commission for Public Complaints against the RCMP, which looked into the APEC protests, that the Prime Minister's Office always regarded these ceremonies as a harmless form of local colour that could be elided with and used to support established APEC rituals. A memorandum to the prime minister from one of his senior policy advisers states:

The Chief of the Musqueam Indian Band, Gail Sparrow, has written to … request the inclusion of the band in various APEC events.

Recent experience with this band … suggests that their interests will be fully satisfied with a brief ceremonial role during the official welcome ceremony of APEC Leaders, to be held in the Great Hall of the Museum.

APEC officials currently envisage a scenario in which the Musqueam would conduct a demonstration of traditional dance before you and assembled APEC Leaders for approximately five minutes, following which there might be a presentation by the band chief of a Talking Stick, the symbolic implement held by the speaker with the floor during band councils. The presentation may be of a Stick to Prime Minister Mahathir, next year's APEC Chairman or, alternatively, Talking Sticks might be given to each Leader.[18]

On 23 November, two days before the meeting, a rehearsal of the Musqueam prayer and greeting was held in the museum's Great Hall with representatives of the Prime Minister's Office present (fig. 3.1). In the absence of any instructions to the contrary, Vincent Stogan followed his customary practice of asking his auditors to rise and hold hands while he recited the traditional Hunk'umin'um words asking for spiritual blessing. Chief Sparrow's speech, occupying the five minutes she had been allotted, began with a welcome on behalf of the First Nations of British Columbia and Canada to "the ancestral lands of my people – the Musqueam First Nation." It also contained a statement in support of human rights and a plea to the assembled leaders to consider the ordinary working people of which "economies" are made up:

Products and trade: one country selling its products to another country. That's what this is all about. Or is it? When one takes a closer look at this picture one cannot help but see the human element behind the sought-after products. Lately in the news there has been much said concerning human rights. Have we, as leaders, taken the time to hear what the people are saying?

People are the most precious of all resources. Let us quiet the criticisms and replace the cries of the people by honouring the noble objectives of APEC to endeavour to enrich the lives and to improve the standards of living of all citizens on substantial bases. Just as you represent your individual nations, I, too, as chief, represent a nation and the indigenous peoples, the First Nations in British Columbia and Canada. We are nations within a nation. We are traditional peoples struggling for position and inclusion in today's economic arena.

It might interest you to know that this land we are meeting upon was once, and still is, the traditional gathering place of my people. Here we hunted deer, bear, and elk. And, it is here we met with other tribes from up and down this coast to trade: food, clothing, hunting equipment,

furs and medicine. It is fitting that you have assembled here on land owned by this country's first traders – the First Nations people![19]

Chief Sparrow followed this exhortation with an appeal to include within the mandate of APEC the strengthening of the economies of Indigenous communities.

The representatives from the Prime Minister's Office found both Vincent Stogan's prayer and Gail Sparrow's speech unacceptable, and they walked out of the rehearsal before the chief had finished. Sparrow told a newspaper reporter that Robert Vanderloo, the principal APEC organizer, said to her, "Well, chief, that speech has to go ... because there are issues in there that the government doesn't want to be brought up to the officials."[20] It has become clear from other internal documents released to the APEC Public Complaints commission that the Prime Minister's Office was under considerable pressure from some of the APEC members, especially China and the Suharto government in Indonesia, to avoid embarrassing challenges to those countries' human rights records. Although Vanderloo negotiated a much shorter speech with Chief Sparrow from which all controversial remarks had

3.1   Elder Vincent Stogan and Musqueam chief Gail Sparrow rehearsing their speeches in the Great Hall of the Museum of Anthropology. Courtesy of the Museum of Anthropology, University of British Columbia, Vancouver

been omitted, the Prime Minister's Office insisted on cancelling both it and Vincent Stogan's opening prayer. The latter cancellation turned out to have an unexpectedly ironic twist. Government officials reportedly feared that the holding of hands might be contrary to the cultural mores of some of the leaders present. Yet, in the event, the leaders linked arms to stand for the traditional "family photo," which was widely published on television and in the newspapers. In the end, Chief Sparrow's participation was limited to a brief informal greeting to each of the leaders in the museum's lobby prior to the official opening of the meeting. From the museum's point of view, the absence of a formal Musqueam greeting to foreign visitors constituted a breach of the protocol it had only recently signed and offered a serious insult to one of the most respected elders in the region.

In detailing these events, I have already strayed into the intersection between the local and the national that I mentioned in my introduction. In this space the steady movement toward limited recognition of Indigenous sovereignty and of a group's unique relationship to a particular territory crosses a larger, longer-standing, and more powerful history in which a totalizing image of a generic "Indian" population has been appropriated to the national identity. This appropriation requires the narrative positioning of Indigenous people as predecessors to white settlement. Removed from the main story, they become marginal, sources of picturesque detail and local colour who lend distinctiveness to the national self-image, but who cannot be allowed to speak as full members of an international community.

The Poetics of Sight Bite

The process by which the museum had been chosen as the site of the meeting becomes significant in the context of this second macro-history of the internal colonization and marginalization of Indigenous peoples. APEC meetings have usually been held at resorts and conference centres – neutral, commercial spaces that are easy to secure and that lend themselves to commodification. The University of British Columbia is located on a very beautiful peninsula several miles to the west of Vancouver's downtown core. The leaders' meeting, the highlight and last major event of a week-long program, was thus placed at some remove from those of business leaders and lesser government officials, which were held in downtown hotels and convention centres. The Museum of Anthropology, through its displays of monumental Northwest Coast sculpture, its spectacular site, its famous modernist building, and its removal from the realm of ordinary commerce, provided an ideal, distinctively Canadian backdrop for a high-profile international gathering. It is not clear that the choice of the museum over the more usual type of venue was more than serendipitous. A knowledgeable official commented that the suggestion to hold the leaders' meeting at the museum had come from US president Bill Clinton at a meeting with Prime Minister Chrétien held shortly after Vancouver was announced as the site of the APEC meeting. (Clinton

already knew the museum, having met there with Russian president Boris Yeltsin in 1993.) If this was the case – and it rings true, for of all the APEC leaders, only Clinton took an obvious interest in his surroundings, pointing out the sculptures to other leaders and asking to have the gift shop opened at the end of the meeting – then the federal government's subsequent treatment of First Nations representatives and its unprecedentedly violent suppression of protestors assumes a certain logic.

During the three months of intensive preparation that led up to the leaders' meeting, federal officials apparently failed adequately to consider the peculiar characteristics of the university setting they had chosen, particularly the jealousy with which members of the academic community guard their freedom of expression and the seriousness with which many members of the University of British Columbia regarded Aboriginal claims to sovereignty. For the meeting's organizers, the university setting was, I would argue, incidental to that of the museum itself, which was desired because its site, architecture, and displays of monumental Northwest Coast sculpture could be used to project the standard image of Canada. The government spent enormous sums of money to groom the museum's grounds in preparation for the official photo-

3.2 The APEC leaders' meeting in the Great Hall, Museum of Anthropology. Courtesy of the Museum of Anthropology, University of British Columbia, Vancouver

graphs, even hiring the eminent landscape architect Cornelia Oberlander to realize for the first time the landscape of beachfront and pond she had originally designed for the rear of the museum in the 1970s. These efforts to perfect the view through the windows and the area selected for the taking of the leaders' traditional "family photo" were needed to produce the "sight bites" which, together with sound bites, are a principle product of meetings such as this one.

On the morning of 25 November, after Prime Minister Chrétien had led his "guests" into the Great Hall of the museum, a postcard-perfect Canadian scene unfolded. In a fully synchronized sequence reminiscent of an Olympic Games opening ceremony, four Royal Canadian Mounted Police in full dress uniform rode up and stood to attention on the berm outside the floor-to-ceiling glass windows of the Great Hall. To the press invited into the hall for a short briefing at the start of the meeting, the leaders of Australia, China, the United States, and the other fifteen countries appeared seated against a backdrop of totem poles, Mounties, and the distant vista of snow-capped mountains and sea (fig. 3.2). This pageant-like spectacle aligned all the symbols most commonly employed to construct a Canadian identity distinct from that of the United States and to sell Canada as a tourist destination. The semiotic potency of this assemblage has been deconstructed so often in recent years that its sudden appearance that day was shocking in its banality.[21]

Two Origin Stories

Chrétien's opening statement was equally stunning in its disregard for thirty years of postcolonial critique of settler narratives of Canadian history. He began by alluding to the monumental crest poles of the Northwest Coast First Nations that surrounded the leaders in the Great Hall. Chrétien said that they formed an appropriate background for the meeting since the First Nations, having migrated across the Bering Strait into Canada, had been the first Pacific Rim "traders" and had established a precedent for the APEC trade agreement.[22] The prime minister's strategy was transparently appropriative, co-opting ancient Indigenous exchange networks to the globalizing agenda of a late-capitalist free-trade alliance. It employed the well-worn colonialist strategy of selectively narrating Native history as pre-contact precursor of and post-contact contributor to settler nation-building. In Canada these tropes have been actively contested by a generation of revisionist historians, curators, and artists. As we have seen, the first major revisionist coup was staged during the mid-1960s when Native activists within the Department of Indian and Northern Affairs demanded a separate pavilion at the Montreal world's fair, Expo 67, in which Aboriginal people could represent their culture and history and critique the standard narratives. (Prime Minister Chrétien had been minister of Indian and Northern Affairs at that time.) During the thirty years that separated Expo 67 from the APEC meeting, a steadily increasing number of revisionist books, exhibitions, and films had been circulating.[23]

Perhaps most importantly, in its reference to the Bering Strait theory of the migration of Native peoples into the Americas from Asia, the prime minister's speech directly denied First Nations's own stories of their original creation *in* North America. These oral traditions have, of course, been considered to be at odds with scientifically validated archaeological narratives, and museums, as mediators of academic scholarship, had historically either presented Indigenous oral traditions as folktales and myths or ignored them altogether. During the preceding twenty years, however, Canadian museums had made important, though often painful, progress in moving away from such strictly Eurocentric accounts toward acknowledgment of the authority of the First Nations' own accounts of their histories and cultures. Many had developed multivocal strategies to present different narratives evenhandedly. *Written in the Earth*, the exhibit on Musqueam and Coast Salish archaeology discussed above, was guided, as I have noted, by the collaborative and multivocal ethic recommended by the 1992 task force report. One of its major achievements was the integrated presentation of Indigenous oral traditions and archaeological accounts. Hearing the prime minister's opening statement in the Great Hall drove home for the museum staff present the degree to which the museum's authority to represent culture inside its space had been co-opted.

Both the draft of Chief Sparrow's speech and the prime minister's opening remarks at the meeting cited the First Nations as providing an historical precedent for Pacific Rim trade. But where Chrétien used the Bering Straits migration theory to position Indigenous peoples as an early group of immigrants whose journey foreshadowed later immigration and the economic systems introduced by European settlers, Sparrow employed the historical precedent to highlight the coherence of the pre-contact Indigenous world and, at the same time, to assert the importance of human communities over a decontextualized notion of trade. Like other Indigenous leaders who refer to themselves collectively as the First Nations of Canada, she adopted a postcolonial strategy of counter-appropriation and negotiation when she represented the Musqueam (legally defined as a "band") as a nation among nations. At the end of the twentieth century it should not, perhaps, be surprising to discover either the persistence of the colonial attitudes evidenced in Chrétien's speech or its attempt to fold those attitudes into the new global ideology of transnational trade. Postcolonialism describes only the official ending of imperial arrangements of governance, not the final undoing of centuries of social and cultural intervention. Yet the degree to which old official government rhetorics persist in international contexts *is* surprising when placed alongside that same government's domestic policy of fostering new, though limited, forms of Indigenous sovereignty and autonomy. It had been Chrétien's Liberals, after all, who supported the work of the Task Force on Museums and First Nations, the establishment of the Inuit territory of Nunavut in the eastern Arctic, and the Nisga'a land-claims settlement in British Columbia, and who were also continuing to support the repatriation of some museum collections and the development of museums in First Nations communities. It is clear from the events surrounding Musqueam participation that the federal government officials involved did not factor into their plans the possibility that those same initiatives might have created new kinds of relationships between Vancouver-area First Nations and local cultural and educational institutions.

As the artificial pageant was playing inside the museum, thousands of protestors against APEC and the human rights records of several member "economies" were gathering and being forcibly restrained just beyond the sight and hearing of those inside the building. During the year between the announcement of Vancouver as the site of the 1997 meeting (which it was Canada's turn to host) and the choice of the Museum of Anthropology as the venue for the leaders' meeting, student and community groups had been organizing a disciplined and well-planned campaign of protests and parallel meetings. The goals of their activities were to raise public awareness of human rights abuses in a number of member countries and to draw attention to the threats to the well-being of workers, women, Indigenous peoples, and the environment which, they believed, were posed by the corporate agendas of economic unions such as APEC. The federal government helped to fund some of the parallel meetings as part of its commitment to allow the free expression of different points of view.

The elaborate security arrangements put in place for the leaders' meeting included an agreement that the university would surrender its legal jurisdiction over the museum for the day of the meeting, but it had also negotiated a guarantee that the democratic right to protest would be protected. Two days before the event, however, the federal government changed the terms of this agreement to close off a larger precinct around the museum, and it also extended the period of time during which it controlled the area. This shift enabled security and police personnel to move the protest area beyond the line of sight of the leaders attending the meeting in the museum and to remove protest signs from the windows of university buildings along the road travelled by the leaders' limousines. During the days leading up to 25 November, the police also detained and strip-searched protestors camped behind the museum and the Student Union Building.[24]

The culmination of the protest campaign was the demonstration held on the UBC campus on the day of the leaders' meeting. The rally attracted over three thousand students, faculty members, and non-university participants. It was forcefully suppressed by police, who used pepper spray on apparently unresisting protestors, attracting national press coverage and shocking the Canadian public. Fifty-two complaints against the police were lodged with the Commission for Public Complaints created to look into the APEC protests, alleging the illegal suppression of fundamental rights to protest guaranteed in the Canadian constitution and the use of unwarranted force in suppressing the protest. Members of the UBC community also questioned the initial agreement to use a university as the site for such a meeting. In order to understand why the federal government behaved as it did, not only in its suppression of the civil liberties of the protesters but also in its failure to respect established protocols toward Musqueam representatives, it is essential, I would argue, to remember that its choice of venue was dictated by the particular poetics of site provided by the Museum of Anthropology's dramatic framing of landscape and distinctive First Nations displays, and not by a desire to locate the meeting within a university – a point that was lost as the museum became conflated with the university in the press coverage of the protests and their legal aftermath. For example, although the setting seen in TV clips would have been identifiable as the Museum of Anthropology to many local viewers, only UBC and not the museum was named in the vast majority of the broadcasts and articles. Museum staff had initially hoped that one positive by-product of its hosting of the APEC meeting would be a revenue-enhancing raised public profile, but in light of the events that transpired, the unanticipated obscurity was welcome.

Museums, Globalization, and the Production of Public Spectacles

The long-standing historical pattern by which Canada appropriates the First Nations to its national identity before an international audience has already been noted. The Museum of Anthropology served this purpose in 1997, as had, in earlier years, other venues that could be identified with the First Nations. Among the numerous examples are Expo 67's popular Indians of Canada Pavilion, organized in the centennial year of Canadian confederation, its summer season sequel *Man and His World* (1968–81), and the impressive First Nations displays at Vancouver's Expo 86. However, the high visibility accorded to First Nations cultures on these occasions also offered Indigenous activists leverage they could use for their own purposes. At Expo 86 the prominence of First Nations exhibitions and the content of the installations focused attention on the authenticity and renewed vitality of contemporary Native arts and cultural life. The same is true of the Musqueam sculptures and weavings that greet travellers arriving at the Vancouver International Airport, a display that was negotiated as part of the agreement allowing the use of Musqueam land for airport runways.

Museum of Anthropology staff had provided professional expertise and organizational skills to the world's fair exhibits and had also managed the commissioning of the art for the airport. By getting involved in these periodic international displays, the museum gained financial resources that enabled it to further important long-term goals. At the same time, it had also maintained its ethical obligations to First Nations partners by facilitating collaborative processes of representation. All of the previous projects had fostered respect for First Nations voices and authority and/or had foregrounded contemporary First Nations arts and cultures while also making money for the museum that strengthened its ability to carry on its broader educational and curatorial programs. The anticipation that APEC would deliver these kinds of benefits had informed the museum's positive response to the initial suggestion that the leaders' meeting be held at the museum. These benefits were not, of course, realized. What was different this time?

One obvious answer lies in the contrast between the rhetoric of globalization that came to dominate the policies of the Canadian government during the 1990s and the older rhetoric of internationalism that had been pre-eminent after World War II and had informed the earlier collaborations between the federal government and the Museum of Anthropology. In the particular poetics of the global that surround APEC and other free-trade organizations, the term "nation" is replaced by "economy" – APEC is, officially, an association of eighteen economies, not eighteen countries. As Richard Ericson, then principal of UBC's Green College (located along the road leading to the museum and the venue from which police removed protest signs prior to the APEC meeting), has written, "This was not an inter-*national* meeting of strong, sovereign heads of state, but rather a business meeting of heads of state who wished to symbolize that we live in global economies that have no particular respect for national borders, sovereignty and human rights."[25] The commercialized visual culture of the meeting was composed not of national flags but of the logos of the private corporations solicited by the Canadian government as sponsors of the APEC meeting. This corporate visual culture exerted a commodifying pressure on all other visual signifiers, whether they referenced national identity, Indigenous spirituality and sovereignty, or cultural and educational institutions.[26] Appadurai has placed the reductive strategy intrinsic to such visual culture within larger processes of globalization: "National and international mediascapes are exploited by nation-states to pacify separatists or even the potential fissiparousness of all ideas of difference. Typically, contemporary nation states do this by exercising taxonomic control over difference, by creating various kinds of international spectacles to domesticate difference and by seducing small groups with the fantasy of self-display on some sort of global and cosmopolitan stage."[27] The federal government's APEC pageantry – its planned use of Musqueam representatives to perform dances and supply souvenir talking sticks, its foregrounding of totem poles, the Mounties, and a majestic landscape, and its framing of all these images within a prestigious museum – was thus structured to transform politically complex phenomena into stereotypes that could enter, via the media, the same "global flows" as the corporate logos that were so much in evidence on APEC signage. In this analysis economic globalization can be seen to disempower the local, replacing the stratified depth of discrete traditions with a spatially extended network of simultaneity and homogeneity.

The failure of respect signalled by the federal government's cancellation of the welcomes of the Musqueam representatives becomes explicable within this context. But what was the museum's failure? And what can we learn about how a museum should respond when asked to participate in events such as APEC? I would, at this distance in time, draw a number of lessons from our experience. First of all, it is important to recognize that the struggles over the contested representational space of the museum that have taken place during the past thirty years *have* been fruitful, and they have led us to a new moment. We are better equipped to recognize appropriative strategies, to analyze the interests that drive them and the consequences that result. The Museum of Anthropology is, on the one hand, a custodian of collections. Some are held in trust for First Nations communities; others are ones for which the museum has an ethical responsibility to ensure accurate and appropriate representation. When the museum is asked to serve as a venue for the filming of a television show or to rent out its lobby for a corporate dinner, staff members vet each proposal to ensure that nothing in the script or the planned events is disrespectful of the objects we hold or the cultural groups they represent. For a crucial two days in November 1997 the museum lost the power to vet the scenario or enforce its ground rules. Although the formal welcome of foreigners by the traditional Aboriginal owners of the site may have been read in the past as mere local colour, it is incumbent upon museums to point out the new realities that lie behind what may appear to be familiar rituals; they must develop strategies that make clear that these are not mere window dressing or empty gestures but, rather, the visible signs of rearticulated, reassumed, and mutually recognized responsibilities.

Recovering from APEC: A Ritual of Reversal

The very nature of museums as unique spaces of meeting between the academic community and more broadly public communities makes it vital and necessary that they remain "open," that they welcome opportunities to host different groups of people and promote the expression of different points of view. To this end the Museum of Anthropology decided, during the weeks leading up to APEC, to commission two graduate students in the Anthropology Department, Maria Roth and Todd Tubutis, to create for the museum an APEC archive that would document the event as it unfolded in all its complexity. The archive now contains leaflets, posters, protest signs, police tape used to hold back protesters on 25 November, videotapes of parallel conferences, photographs contributed by many individuals, and official texts and statements emanating from the APEC office. Immediately after the meeting, Roth and Tubutis created an installation in the museum's lobby entitled "This Is Not an Exhibition," an interactive display of a selection of the photos and artifacts they had assembled (fig. 3.3). These materials were mounted on panels from a folding screen emblazoned with the APEC logo that had been provided by the federal organizers for use in the museum on the day of the meeting and was then left behind. Viewers to the post-APEC mini-exhibition were invited to post comments or contribute further objects and images to this display.

On 10 February 1998 the museum also lent the Great Hall to the Democracy Street group, representing the plaintiffs in a large lawsuit against the federal government that alleged civil rights violations during the APEC pro-

3.3 (*above*) *This Is Not an Exhibition* (detail), the display of artifacts from the
APEC protest and police suppression in the lobby of the Museum of Anthropol-
ogy. Courtesy of the Museum of Anthropology, University of British Columbia,
Vancouver

3.4 (*below*) The Democracy Street coalition press conference held in the Great
Hall, Museum of Anthropology, to announce lawsuits brought against the
Canadian government, Courtesy of the Museum of Anthropology, University of
British Columbia, Vancouver

tests. The group used the occasion to hold a press conference to announce its lawsuits, but it also had a larger purpose in mind, a "public reclamation" of the museum (fig. 3.4). As a spokesperson for the group wrote, "I believe that the university community needs to take back this public space in an inclusive and non-confrontational manner. This would facilitate the renewal of positive connections amongst the students, faculty and staff, and between the Museum and the rest of UBC. As well, we wish to include the Native community in this reclamation … [and] to include a healing ceremony … and an opportunity to speak on the events of APEC."[28] The Democracy Street theatre group performed a parody of the APEC leaders' meeting in front of the museum using characters modelled on those of the children's television program *Sesame Street*. Inside the lobby the Raging Grannies sang protest songs, and groups such as Students for a Free Tibet, Amnesty International, the Women Opposed to Political Intimidation Group, and the East Timor Alert Network set up booths. After the formal press conference, which was staged in the Great Hall on the spot where the leaders had met, participants wearing outfits mimicking the official Roots leather bomber jackets and cords worn by the APEC leaders restaged the official "family photo" taken on the berm behind the museum (fig. 3.5). When they turned around, large letters attached to their backs spelled out "PEOPLE ARE THE BOTTOM LINE!" (fig. 3.6). Chief Gail Sparrow's message was finally proclaimed on the grounds of the Museum of Anthropology.

We need, however, to go beyond such rituals of reversal to draw an even more profound lesson about the changed relationship between government patronage and the work of museums and other non-profit educational institutions. MoA initially entered into the APEC agreement because it expected to gain specific advantages that would enhance its ability to fulfill its mandated responsibilities. One of the primary gains was expected to be the funding of a "legacy" project, which, museum staff were told, APEC customarily left at the site of each meeting. At the same time that it proceeded to fulfill this normal APEC procedure, however, the federal government also made a public commitment that no taxpayers' money would be used to fund this and other APEC projects, promising that they would be financed by donations solicited from corporations and other private sources. MoA identified as its chosen legacy the construction of a two-part ethnobotanical garden, one part of which would be planted at Musqueam and the other at the museum. This project, which was to feature the native plants used by the Indigenous peoples of the region, would be a valuable educational resource and would enable research on Hunk'umin'um words and traditional Indigenous knowledge about the uses and significance of plants, which had become urgent in light of the age and frailty of the small number of remaining Hunk'umin'um speakers.

Corporate sponsors came forward to fund another legacy project – a glass atrium added to the house of the UBC president, where the APEC leaders had dined – but no corporation expressed interest in the ethnobotanical garden,

3.5 (*above*)   The traditional APEC leaders' meeting "family photo" behind the Museum of Anthropology. Courtesy of the Museum of Anthropology, University of British Columbia, Vancouver

3.6 (*below*)   The Democracy Street coalition and APEC protest group re-enacting the "family photo" behind the UBC Museum of Anthropology. Courtesy of the Museum of Anthropology, University of British Columbia, Vancouver

and the project was not funded. Although the cleaning and landscaping of MoA's building were welcome, the museum did not reap equivalent benefits to those it had gained from participation in such earlier projects as Vancouver's Expo 86. In those earlier ventures, funding was provided directly by government agencies according to a notion of the public interest, rather than by private interests who responded to a corporate and commercial rationality. This seems to be as clear a lesson about the dangers of allowing the agendas of corporate sponsors to govern the activities of public institutions as we are likely to get.

This larger lesson about the way that state patronage had changed during the 1990s should cause members of the museum community to consider with the greatest attentiveness what we stand to gain or lose when, in the future, we are approached to lend our space, our intellectual and cultural prestige, and our skills to government or commercial projects. As with other recent episodes of contestation over museum exhibitions, the manner in which APEC unfolded at UBC was unprecedented, and the consequences of our loss of power over the conduct of events within the museum were unforeseen. But new ideologies and contexts open new spaces of possibility. As I have noted in this chapter, past controversies over museum exhibitions have been the touchstones of the progress I have recounted. The APEC meeting can also be such a touchstone if we examine it well for the auguries it contains of the encounter of late-capitalist global economics with local movements of decolonization and democracy. As Scott Lash and John Urry have argued, the reality of global flows opens up new possibilities even as it shuts down old ones: "The sort of 'economies of signs and space' that became pervasive in the wake of organized capitalism do not just lead to increasing meaninglessness, homogenization, abstraction, anomie and the destruction of the subject. Another set of radically divergent processes is simultaneously taking place. These processes may open up possibilities for the recasting of meaning in work and in leisure, for the reconstitution of community and the particular, for the reconstruction of a transmogrified subjectivity, and for heterogenization and the complexity of space and of everyday life."[29] Museums are as ideally suited to support these "reconstitutions of community and the particular" as they are to be sites for the staging of spectacles.

PART TWO   RE-DISCIPLINING
                  THE MUSEUM

Exclusions and Inclusions: Authenticity, Sacrality, and Possession

Three discursive constructs – authenticity, sacrality, and possession – emerged as key targets of critique and reform out of the boycotts, protests, and debates of the late twentieth century. All three have been fundamental to the operation of the modern museum and especially to its representations of Indigenous arts, cultures, and histories. Because museum practices are ultimately derived from and authorized by academic knowledge formations, the efforts to revise them must be understood in the context of the broader post-structuralist and postcolonial critiques of Western disciplines that were in progress during the last quarter of the twentieth century and particularly in relation to the revisionist projects of "postmodern anthropology" and "new" art history, as they were termed at the time. Museum practices must also, of course, be understood in terms of underlying issues of power.

The first chapter in this section considers the overarching typological tradition of the modern Western museum system. Its aim is to bring into relief the kinds of exclusions and inclusions historically created by the rigid separations and hierarchies of nature and culture and of the West and the rest that this system mandates. Although the chapter was originally written in 1992 during the high tide of the deconstructive critique of museums, its argument remains relevant, for the process of denaturalization it advocates has been less far-reaching than I would have anticipated. As I will argue in later chapters in this book, we are seeing today both a general tendency toward the hybridization of art and artifact paradigms and, in

a smaller number of new institutions, the re-unification of disciplinary museums under a single roof. At Te Papa Tongarewa, the national museum of New Zealand opened in 1998, the removal of the walls (both real and metaphorical) that conventionally separate displays of anthropology, art, history, and natural history when they are housed within a single building has expanded the potential for the more holistic approaches to representation and knowledge advocated by Maori museologists, along with many other Indigenous peoples. A parallel development can be observed in a number of temporary exhibitions on chocolate, pearls, and other commodities that have been mounted in recent years by large American museums motivated both by a perceived need to address environmental concerns from global and comprehensive perspectives and by the trend toward interdisciplinary research in the Western academic world.[1]

The three chapters that follow address attempts to deconstruct essentialist definitions of authenticity and to negotiate conflicts that arise around different cultural traditions of sacredness and ownership. Threaded through all these chapters are three arguments. The first is that the three issues of authenticity, sacrality, and ownership are entangled and must be addressed as interrelated. The second is that the negotiations they have stimulated manifest, in usefully concrete forms, larger social processes that have been at work as Canada's self-image has shifted from the Eurocentric and, in relative terms, culturally homogenous construct of "two founding nations" to the more pluralist notion of multiculturalism.

Thirdly, I argue that the embrace of pluralism regularly defeats reductionist attempts to resolve the conflicts that arise from these three large issues by imposing dichotomous categories and "yes/no" solutions.

Authenticity is a good place to start in order to illustrate the first of these arguments. My discussion in chapter 5, which, like chapter 4, was also first written as a conference paper in 1992, compares the constructs of authenticity that had developed within art history and anthropology during twentieth century and been subjected to critique during the previous decade. Although regularly positioned as a dialectical pair, I argue for their underlying similarities. The modernist and primitivist discourses that governed anthropological research and collecting, for example, assigned the highest value to items produced through the use of pre-contact technologies, artistic styles, and materials – items that were by definition rare and disappearing.[2] The preferences of the promoters of "primitive art," however, also participated in the "rare art" traditions of collecting that, as Joseph Alsop showed, had long governed the institutions of Western art.[3] As I have written elsewhere, this construct has excluded much of what Indigenous people have made during the centuries of contact with settler society, items that blend materials and aesthetic ideas drawn from both Indigenous and Western sources but whose hybrid appearance was long regarded as evidence of loss and contamination.[4] The effect of these exclusions was to devalue the work and creativity of contemporary people and their immediate ancestors, and they have had

a corrosive and debilitating impact on Indigenous identities. As Johannes Fabian has argued, the discipline of anthropology itself was founded on a contradiction, denying the coevalness of its objects of study, even as it relied on a fieldwork methodology posited on direct interaction with people living in a shared modernity.[5]

In search of the authentic and the artistic, Western collectors have tended to privilege things made for traditional ritual and ceremonial use, items that often fall squarely into the Western category of the sacred. From Indigenous perspectives, more accurate renderings of concepts of sacrality may have to do with apprehensions of spiritual presence in varying degrees, or of qualities of personhood, or of deeply felt ancestral resonance. These "things" may thus be thought of as beings or "grandfathers," rather than specimens, objects, artifacts, or works of art. In consequence, some can be appropriately viewed and discussed only at certain times of the year or under particular conditions, or handled only by men, women, members of medicine societies, or people who have acquired particular rights and privileges through dreams or inheritance. The powers inhering in such items may also be dangerous to the general public unless managed by a trained specialist. Such qualities and requirements manifest themselves as a spectrum of powers and presences, rather than as a simple duality of sacred versus secular. As I demonstrate in chapter 6 through a case study of the display of Onkwehonwe (Iroquois) masks, the guidelines and laws established in settler nations in the early 1990s in response to Indigenous objections to the display of empowered objects have tended to be reductive, applying the toggle switch of the Western sacred/secular dichotomy. The imposition of categorical choices can not only distort Indigenous traditions but also inhibit the development of more nuanced, creative, and intermediary solutions.

We have a steadily growing number of examples of the greater success that can be achieved by more nuanced mediations. One of the earliest occurred in the 1989 exhibition *A Time of Gathering*, mounted at the University of Washington's Burke Museum to celebrate the centenary of the state of Washington. The curator, Robin Wright, alerted by the controversy that had arisen the previous year in response to the display of an Onkwehonwe mask in *The Spirit Sings* (discussed in chapters 2 and 6), worked with her Indigenous consultants to find an appropriate way to represent the performances of a Tulalip (Salish) Seowyn ceremony in the exhibition. Sxwaixwe dancers perform in this ceremony, and although the carved masks they wear were long considered a canonical form of Salish art by Western collectors, curators, and scholars, the ceremonies in which they appear are private and Salish people have objected to the public display of these masks. The solution developed by Wright and her advisers was to display a historical photograph of a Seowyn ceremony that included two masked dancers behind a small hole in the wooden slats of the replica Tulalip house built for the exhibition, the typical venue for such ceremonies during the nineteenth century. Visitors were alerted

by the installation mode and signage to the privileged view they were thus being offered and had to *choose* to look. As the installation was mounted low on the wall, the act of looking also required adult viewers to make the extra physical effort of bending down. This example is suggestive of how the category of cultural sensitivity is proving to be a more useful concept with which to think than the dichotomy of sacred/secular.

The issue of ownership can also manifest itself along a spectrum, rather than through a categorical yes or no, but in this area finding creative solutions has been even more challenging. However difficult it may be to change professional museum practices, it is still more difficult to change legal systems that are centuries old and within which property law occupies a central position. The case study of a Mi'kmaq coat that was probably presented as part of a ritual adoption ceremony in the mid-nineteenth century, which I discuss in chapter 7, is intended to focus on the grey areas that occur in the majority of potential repatriation cases. These ambiguous situations often arise, on the one hand, from the lack of provenance documentation for a great many items in museum collections and, on the other, from the difficulties of reconciling Western traditions of ownership grounded in possessive individualism with Indigenous traditions of collective ownership and trans-generational transfer and urgent needs for cultural recovery.[6]

4

How Museums Marginalize

Naming Domains of Inclusion and Exclusion

The contemporary analysis of representational processes has made us aware of the intimate connection between naming and power.[1] In museums this power is exercised at the most fundamental level through the naming of the macro-classifications of the museum system – art, archaeology, ethnology, history, folk culture, natural science, science. This classification scheme is made explicit to museum publics in many forms: it is listed in guidebook rosters of specialist museums and their departments, mapped in visitor floor plans, and indicated in ubiquitous museum signage.

My argument in this chapter can be summarized as a series of propositions, no less urgent for their apparent simplicity. First, the named categories that structure the museum system are a residue of obsolete nineteenth-century ideologies. Second, they create domains of inclusion and exclusion that continue to inscribe colonial attitudes about race, patriarchal ideas about gender, and elitist notions about class. Third, our named categories will, until we change them, continue to have a representational force that overrides and undercuts the revisionist approaches to museum representation in which many academics and museum professionals are engaged. As Aldona Jonaitis has written, "meaning is read in museums, as in other textual representations, through successive, historically accumulated 'wrappings.'"[2]

I will address here only the first of the three areas listed above, the question of how current museological structures and practices marginalize groups of people in terms of race and ethnicity, but I want to stress that this question forms part of a much larger argument. The ways that museums sort objects along ethnic lines have become so naturalized – perhaps because of their very obtrusiveness – that they have been only partially interrogated, even in the current climate of reflexive analysis. Thus far, the main debate, which has centred on the art and artifact paradigms promoted respectively by art and anthropology museums, addresses only one aspect of the problem. The dialectic that the macro-system of museum classification structures between history and the linked categories of ethnology and folk culture is equally problematic.

Like the visitors to the National Museum of American History's *Field to Factory* exhibition, who had to choose to enter either the "white" or "colored" areas of the reconstructed train station,[3] visitors to most general museums in search of African, Native American, or other non-Western displays have to make an either/or choice to enter a space called "history" or one called "ethnology." When a museum assigns certain objects to the domain of history, it identifies the objects' makers as participants in a dynamic, progressive, temporal process; its assignment of other objects to ethnology or folk culture invests them with notions of the traditional, the timeless, and the technologically retrograde. The glow of progressive ideology may be dimmed, but it is still the light that most museum publics see by; the historic remains at the centre, leading inevitably to modernity, while the traditional is relegated to the margins.

While racial distinctions are particularly engaged by the classificatory diad of history and ethnology, hierarchies of gender and class are associated with the distinctions among the categories of fine art, decorative art, applied art, and folk art. As has been argued by many scholars of non-Western arts, the Kantian position that an object's functional specifications or the technical requirements imposed by certain media limit the artist's creative freedom is not shared by many other world art traditions.

Most museum curators are keenly aware of the problems posed by these practices of naming and classification. At three large Canadian museums, curators expressed a degree of ambiguity and confusion when asked to state the collecting mandates for the different departments within each museum, and they pointed to increasing areas of overlap both between divisions and between museums.[4] Thus, although decisions about classification are made daily, no fixed guidelines exist at present. A brief account of three recent curatorial grey areas will indicate current practice better than the citation of rather general institutional mandates.

One curator's office is adorned with a collection of industrially produced popular art, including glass canoes, rubber Indian princess dolls, and Atlanta Braves tomahawks made of styrofoam – all surrounded by an aura of impeccable postmodern irony. Currently private property, the collection was raided for a major exhibition addressing popular stereotypes of Indianness, and the curator is debating whether some or all of the items should be accessioned into the ethnological collection.

Another museum received a complete set of Métis clothing as a donation. The clothes were initially deposited in the registrar's office, and individual curators were expected to claim the items that belonged in their collections. The curator of decorative arts took the silver cuff links, while the curator of costume was interested in the factory-made shirt. The curator of ethnology accessioned the beaded jacket, but she thinks the complete outfit should probably be in her collection.

A third ethnology division bought a set of postcards showing performances by actors dressed in pan-Indian clothing that were staged for tourists at a large Onkwehonwe (Iroquois) reserve during much of this century. The accession of these postcards represents a radical departure from the division's normal collection profile on several counts: as objects manufactured by non-Natives, as representations of commercial activities oriented toward non-Native audiences, and as depictions of "non-authentic" Onkwehonwe dress.

We can gain insight into the consequences of the decisions made in cases like these by examining in detail the museological fate of one rather typical collection originating in the central Great Lakes region. In 1947 Mrs J. Langdon McKee gave a collection to the Public Museum of Grand Rapids, Michigan, that included objects acquired by her grandparents and aunt while they served as missionaries to the Anishinaabe (Ojibwe) at Sault Ste Marie from 1828 to 1855. The collection contains Native-made snowshoes worn by the Reverend Abel Bingham and his wife, as well as the clergyman's dress collar, his black bow tie, and two pairs of his spectacles. It also includes a set of bone alphabet letters used by Mrs Bingham to teach Anishinaabe children, a "papoose cradle" given to her daughter in the 1880s that had "cradled three generations of Indians," several birchbark boxes embroidered with porcupine quills in floral designs, one of which bears the word "Keepsake," a glass letter seal inscribed "Forget me not," a pincushion in a pear-shaped wooden holder (given to the missionary's daughter by an unnamed English visitor in 1835), and several items of "Indian" beadwork bought by the donor at a street fair in Grand Rapids in 1897. Together with these objects, Mrs Langdon McKee gave the museum photographs showing her aunt, the missionary's daughter, with Anishinaabe women at a restaurant in the early 1900s and studio portraits of Anishinaabe participants in the street fair.[5]

For nineteenth-century Anishinaabe objects, this is an unusually full documentation and one that is highly suggestive of the relationships that existed among the makers and users of the objects. The photographs and the gift of the cradleboard to the Reverend Bingham's daughter thirty years after she had left Sault Ste Marie seem to testify to a relationship of enduring trust and friendship. Other objects in the Langdon McKee Collection speak of broader patterns of cultural interaction. Bingham's snowshoes, his spectacles, and the sets of ivory and wooden alphabet letters are the very instruments through which Western ways of seeing and knowing were inscribed in Indigenous Great Lakes populations during the nineteenth century, a material deposit of the role that missionaries such as the Binghams played as agents of Westernization.[6]

The preservation and donation of these mundane objects testify to the value that Victorians ascribed to mass-produced commodities and to their pleasure in the proliferation of household ornaments. This important trend was, in turn, the essential precondition for the large-scale production of tourist commodities that became a critical source of subsistence for the Aboriginal peoples of the Great Lakes during the second half of the nineteenth century as the appropriation of their lands brought about increasing economic marginalization and poverty.

The trade wares produced by Aboriginal people such as the "Keepsake" box were closely modelled on Victorian objects like the "Forget-me-not" paperweight in the Langdon McKee Collection. Indigenous producers also borrowed ideas from the seemingly endless variety of home-crafted items made by Victorian women, such as the pincushion in a pear-shaped wooden holder. Members of settler society read Aboriginal women's production of domestic knick-knacks embellished with suitable floral motifs as evidence of the satisfactory progress that Aboriginal women were making toward "civilization" and their assimilation of Victorian gender roles and ideals of femininity.

The Grand Rapids Street Fair of 1897, which Mrs Langdon McKee lists as the source of a number of pieces of beadwork in her collection, was, like the many other fairs held during the period, an important venue for the sale of Aboriginal trade wares. The photographs in the collections show local Anishinaabe people (both Ojibwe and Odawa), whose everyday clothing in 1897 would have been indistinguishable from that of non-Natives, dressed in the elaborate "Indian" costumes customarily worn to stage an aura of authenticity for the objects they sold.

Enough has been said, I trust, to establish the high degree of interconnectedness of the Euro-American and Aboriginal objects in the Langdon McKee Collection. A collection such as this should be regarded as an assemblage – or, in the language of contemporary art, an *assemblage* – of historically contingent objects. The juxtapositions of the objects in this assemblage yield a range of meanings that speak, first of all, of a critical historical process of interaction and exchange. They reflect the drawing together of Indigenous and non-Indigenous populations in the eastern part of North America during the later nineteenth century into increased physical proximity and economic interdependency. They also suggest the social and psychic tensions arising from forced assimilation, on the one hand, and the internalization of stereotypes of Indianness, on the other.

Like many other donated collections, the Langdon McKee Collection is, to use an analogy from chemistry, a mixture rather than a compound. It is made up of heterogeneous elements, and the objects are linked not by stable bonds but by precarious yet meaningful juxtapositions. The documentation that articulates these interconnections survives more often in smaller museums with a strong local history mandate. In larger, more academically orthodox museums, the fragile webs of interconnectedness have frequently been destroyed by conventional practices of naming and classification, and they can be reconstructed only by painstaking research. When a museum is confronted with the kind of mixture represented by the Langdon McKee Collection, its operation is like that of a centrifuge which separates out the component parts. Objects are sorted according to criteria of homogeneity determined not by historical sensibility but by abstract typologies derived from nineteenth-century discourses of natural history, history, and art history.

The original disposition of the objects at Grand Rapids is typical of general museum practices. The Reverend Bingham's clothing and spectacles went into the collection of Euro-American costume, while the Indian-made snow-shoes he wore and the dressing-table box for keepsakes were assigned to the ethnographic collection. The pincushion and glass letter seal, prototypes of the Ojibwa trade wares in the collection, became part of the decorative arts collection. This treatment had the effect of removing the representation of Ojibwa people from the matrix of history, of denying the process of change and adaptation they were actually accomplishing. In the old Grand Rapids Woodlands Indian exhibition (which has been replaced by one that differs from it radically),[7] some of the street-fair beadwork and objects such as the cradleboard were used to represent a mythic Great Lakes Indian lifestyle lived apart from the mainstream of white society. Mrs Bingham's ivory letters were on view in an adjacent case as markers of the historical interventions of individual white people actively working for change among a passive and "traditional" Indigenous population.

The old forms of museum classification reinforce outdated notions of otherness by denying to objects made or used by Aboriginal people a dia-chronic and historical positioning. Professional anthropological collectors active during the great age of museum collecting at the end of the nineteenth century deliberately rejected objects that demonstrated processes of change and adaptation – the hybrid, the transcultural, and the commodified. They privileged instead items of material culture to which essentialist meanings of cultural difference could be attached and which could be regarded as permanent and unchanging.

In contemporary exhibitions curators are constantly seeking to mediate these false distinctions, to restore historical specificity, to re-establish context and interconnection. The differentiated storage and display spaces of the museum are inhibiting factors, not just because of the bureaucratic barriers they throw up but because of the kinds of objects that fall between the cracks, such as the popular mass-produced art decorating the curator's office in my earlier example. In addition to gaps, increasing areas of overlap are also becoming evident. As James Clifford has pointed out in his foundational discussion, for some years now the same kinds of objects have been collected by and moved among differently named divisions or museums.[8] The inter-penetration of disciplinary spaces is symptomatic of moments when paradigms are changing. Such a blurring can be detected at the boundaries of academic disciplines in the university, manifesting itself in a proliferation of cultural studies and other interdisciplinary programs, in the historicization of anthropology and the anthropologizing of history. In the museum the critique of representation has, however, not yet encompassed the conventions of classification that are embedded in the very institutional structures of the museum establishment and that individual institutions continue to inscribe in their publics.

The success of the Western museum in giving spatial expression and objective, concrete form to abstract schemes for the organization of knowledge has led to a fascination with the museum within the more general critique of representational practices. Yet its very physicality seems at first to render the museum particularly resistant to the kind of renaming I am advocating. Do we have to build new storage rooms or move whole collections around as the cultural politics of the decade dictate? In the age of the computer and digital technologies the work that is required is more conceptual than physical. These tools permit – indeed, promote – overlapping spatial concepts and the assignment of multiple references to an object. To draw out the full semiotic richness of an object, such multi-dimensionality is necessary. The meanings of objects lie as much in who has used them as in who made them. We know that we live in a global economy, that modern technology is used by people everywhere, that we are all "modern." But the naming practices of the museum do not yet reflect this awareness; we need to recognize interconnectedness as well as difference, to rid the object of its aura of essential meaning so that it can travel as freely within the museum as it has in history.

Barbara Kirshenblatt-Gimblett has written eloquently of the fragmentary nature of the ethnographic object: "Objects become ethnographic by virtue of being defined, segmented, detached, and carried away by ethnographers. Such objects are ethnographic not because they were found in a Hungarian peasant household, Kwakiutl village, or Rajasthani market rather than in Buckingham Palace or Michelangelo's studio, but by virtue of the manner in which they have been detached, for disciplines make their objects and in the process make themselves."[9]

I am arguing for acts of renaming that will both recognize already existing shifts in ideology and approach and, at the same time, promote the remaking of our disciplines through the remaking of their objects. If ethnology is to continue as a category, we must, in Michael Ames's phrase, put "white people in the anthropology museum."[10] And we must put them there not just as folk cultures but in their full temporal unfolding up to and including the contemporary moment. Non-Western objects and those of visible minority groups should reside permanently in the art gallery. Installations should represent meetings, conversations, and interconnections where they have occurred in history and where they are occurring today. These museological acts would bring museums into line with changes that have already occurred in academic disciplines such as ethnohistory, postmodern anthropology, and the new art history.

In its role as a classifier the museum participates in processes of analysis and synthesis fundamental to Western habits of thought and scholarship. Since at least the eighteenth century, as Eilean Hooper-Greenhill writes, museum classification has been based on the identification of criteria of difference.[11] I hope it is clear that my advocacy of the bringing into history of ethnographied peoples is not an argument for a simplistic tacking on of colonized groups to universalist linear narratives, of their ghettoization within a Eurocentric historic frame, or of the denial of their differences. The articulation of difference is a cognitive necessity, and there are good reasons for continuing to identify and distinguish discrete traditions that are often urged by the groups of people being represented. But it is important to examine the ways that notions of difference can tend toward hierarchies of value, reinforcing systems of cultural domination. The bases on which discriminations are made need to be periodically rescrutinized in order to ensure that they reflect the thinking about difference and otherness appropriate to a given historical moment. The effective multivocality that most of us value today requires respect for the names people give themselves and for the ways in which they articulate their own historicity and their own concepts of relationship between past and present.

It is important, too, to recognize that although renamings are necessary, they are always part of an open process. The prestige of the art museum in relation to other kinds of museums has led contemporary Canadian Aboriginal artists to initiate a sustained lobbying campaign for inclusion in the country's art galleries, rather than (exclusively) in ethnology museums. They have fought for this inclusion *despite* their clear recognition of the lack of fit of their work with the categories of either art or artifact.[12] Naming something as historical, in a Western schema, is an equivalent "compliment." And, as has happened with art, the opening up of the category of history will inevitably result in important conceptual interventions, just as the interventions of postcolonial subjects have, in their profound effects on the emergence of postmodernism, made possible the intervention I voice in this chapter.

5

Fielding Culture

Dialogues between Art History
and Anthropology

Art history and anthropology are the two fields of scholarship
that treat material objects in their cultural contexts.[1] From
their origins, the two disciplines have operated as a complementary pair. In the late nineteenth century the universe of
human-made things was shared out according to generally
accepted hierarchies of the aesthetic and the cultural. Art, the
achievement of Western fine artists, became the preserve of
art historians, while the arts of other peoples were assigned
to the branch of anthropology called material culture studies.
Since the end of the Victorian era the validity of this division has been called into question at regular intervals, and as
the boundary between the disciplines has shifted, important
cross-fertilizations have occurred.[2]

We are currently in the midst of a renewed phase of mutual
engagement in both the academy and the museum. Evidence
of this engagement can be seen within the study of the Western art tradition, for a key ingredient of the "new" art history,
which began in the 1970s to investigate art in terms of structures of power and social context, has been its incorporation
of anthropological modes of thinking about art and culture.
Debate about the representation of non-Western art was renewed, for example, in the critiques and controversies generated by a number of museum exhibitions mounted during the
1980s and early 1990s, including *"Primitivism" in 20th Century Art*, *The Spirit Sings*, *Into the Heart of Africa*, and *Circa
1492*. These debates can be read as attempts to resolve ambiguities and contradictions inscribed in the original structures of the two disciplines.[3]

There is, however, an important difference between the
interdisciplinary engagements of the beginning and the end

of the twentieth century. Where earlier debates focused on aesthetic issues – on the "art" in art history – the ground contested by late twentieth-century revisionists was that of history and culture. The loss of faith in the possibility of scientific or objective studies caused many art historians, like other scholars, to engage in a far-reaching critique of their representational practices. Unlike in the past, moreover, many of the most vigorous recent attacks on the old hierarchies have come from newly empowered members of formerly colonized groups living both within and outside Western nations. Although the areas of difficulty could be most clearly seen in the borderland regions of non-Western art, the interrogation of the relationship between art history and anthropology has had a broader relevance.[4] In an era when only two of thirty students in a university class on Baroque art can tell the biblical story of the Prodigal Son, the ways in which museums and academies have traditionally contextualized and interpreted Western art are equally relevant to both Western and non-Western art forms.

Spatial metaphors of site, field, terrain, domain, and boundary are frequently invoked in contemporary critiques of disciplinary formations. In reviewing the theorizations of discursive domains put forward by Derrida, Althusser, Foucault, and others, John Tagg identified their critiques as disruptions of linear historical narratives. "What marks the conjunction of space and theory, from the diagrams of structuralism to the active fields of *difference* and power/knowledge," Tagg concludes, "is the displacement of the axis of temporal explanation, unfolding from origin to fulfillment, by the model of a distribution of positions and intersections in a spatial network."[5]

For anthropology and art history the spatial metaphor of the field is a particularly pregnant one. Anthropologists go to and work in the field; art historians work by constructing and surveying a visual field. In both cases the field is used as a metaphor for the construct of culture but with important differences. In a provocative deconstruction, Virginia Dominguez reviewed the fundamental contrast between the ways in which art historians (together with other practitioners of humanistic studies) and anthropologists have constructed the basic concept of culture. Since the turn of the century, she notes, anthropologists have generally followed a holistic and democratic model, put forward by Franz Boas, that was "deliberately antithetical to the old elite German notion of *Kultur*; 'culture' was strategically invoked [by Boas] to wrest it from the elite and make it a property of the masses."[6] Humanistic scholars have continued to utilize the "old German and French notions of *Kultur/Culture* or enclave notions of culture that distinguish between minority populations and dominant populations."[7] Such elitist European notions, imported virtually intact to North America, attribute value to objects according to criteria of aesthetic quality and rarity.

The traditional methodologies used by the two groups of scholars have developed in direct relation to their respective definitions of field and culture. Anthropologists, in pursuit of culture with a small "c," have positioned themselves *in* the field, where they can survey the broad range of economic, social, political, and aesthetic activities in which the object is embedded. The art historian's interest in Culture with a capital "C" has dictated, in contrast, a greater distance from the objects of study made necessary by the goal of reconstructing broad linear sequences of artistic development. The perspective is Olympian rather than worm's-eye, and the raw materials are the more rarefied contents of museums, libraries, and archives.

I would like to illustrate this difference with a personal anecdote against which the developments of the past two decades can be appreciated. In the early 1970s, while I was a doctoral candidate at the School of Oriental and African Studies of the University of London, I was interested in a type of mask worn by Mende women. It happened that I was the first person to propose a dissertation on African art under the university's Board of Studies in the History of Art, rather than in anthropology. The board, which at that time was virtually identical with the senior faculty of the university's most venerable art history unit, the Courtauld Institute, summoned me to make my case at an interview conducted within its dim neoclassical precincts.

Not having fully appreciated the significance of the event, I remember being surprised to find myself in the presence of the eminent art historians Sir Anthony Blunt, Alan Bowness, and John Shearman.[8] Why, they wanted to know, did I think it legitimate to plan art-historical work on a body of material that had such a brief history of collection and was so poorly documented by written texts? The innocence of my unpremeditated answers now seems to me remarkably unreflective. I argued that an important process of change had occurred even within the relatively short century of colonial contact, and that the lack of an archive could be remedied through oral histories recorded in the field. In an ideal world, I went on, one would investigate fifteenth-century Italian art by doing fieldwork in fifteenth-century Florence. While historians of European art have had to resort to documents as second-best, the scholar of African art had the advantage of being able to investigate iconography and style by direct observation and interviews in the field.

My thesis proposal was approved, and I went "to the field." I soon discovered that my notions about the possibilities of fieldwork had been both right and wrong. A process of change *could* be clearly documented, but the nature of that change would not, I suspect, have appeared worthy of the effort to the Courtauld board. During the colonial period, Mende art, like many other traditions around the world, began to display an increased naturalism that was antithetical to the formal qualities most Western art lovers appreciated in African art. The carving preferred by Mende audiences in 1972 had been influenced by Western modes of representation that were journalistic and commercial rather than artistic.[9] I also met Mende carvers in proud possession of recent paperbacks on African art, which they used as source books for replications of sculptural genres from other parts of Africa. The hybrid, in other words, was everywhere to be seen, although – in that pre-postmodern phase of scholarship – it had not yet been "named" or celebrated as a valid form of postcolonial expression.[10]

My investigations of iconography were equally puzzling. The Mende people I interviewed declined to provide the neat equations of motif and meaning I had been led to expect from my studies of medieval historiated capitals and Dutch still-life paintings. Instead, much more polyvalent and associative systems of signification (which I had not yet learned to call semiotic) seemed to be operating. The models of art-historical scholarship available at that time had little to offer in explication of these problems. Like other scholars of non-Western art, I turned instead to theories of symbolism offered by anthropologists such as Victor Turner and Claude Lévi-Strauss.

Although I make no claim to prescience, my ritual trial at the Courtauld and my experience in the field proved prophetic of some movements then about to emerge in mainstream art history, which would both advocate a shift to more holistic contextualizations and employ analytical tools and concepts drawn from various schools of literary and critical theory. For example, Michael Baxandall's and Svetlana Alpers's studies of Italian Renaissance and Dutch Baroque painting can be read as anthropological (or at least ethno-historical) studies in all but their focus on historic visual forms.[11] Baxandall related the style of early Renaissance painting to ordinary activities such as gauging the capacity of barrels or performing popular dances,"[12] and Alpers argued for the need to understand Dutch Baroque art in more culturally specific terms, as a northern art of visual description, rather than an Italianate art of textual narration. In the language of anthropology, both studies contextualized art emically rather than etically, reading it in terms of the aesthetic and cognitive criteria of the producers themselves, rather than those of a distant audience. Significantly, Alpers acknowledged a major debt to Clifford Geertz, the anthropologist most closely identified with the movement of "interpretive anthropology" and a scholar who has had a profound influence on recent work in both history and art history.[13]

In addition to advocating broader and more eclectic contextualizations of art forms, the new art history has also privileged micro-histories of art over metanarratives. Its highly detailed investigations of the embedding of art in social process imply a rejection of what Donald Preziosi, following Foucault, terms the panoptical perspective, according to which meanings are assigned to works by their positioning within progressive linear sequences.[14] Micro-histories, in the new art history, are a means of representing particularity and difference rather than universality. Micro-history, the holistic investigation of culture, and representation of diversity have all been identified as key characteristics of twentieth-century ethnography as well.[15] As George Marcus and Michael Fischer have written, "the main motif that ethnography as a science developed was that of salvaging cultural diversity, threatened with global Westernization, especially during the age of colonialism."[16]

The recent convergence of anthropology and art history has been furthered by the fact that while art historians were democratizing their notion of culture, anthropologists were historicizing their idea of ethnography. Geertzian anthropology, for example, invokes the explanatory utility of micro-history as a complement to synchronic ethnographic description. In so doing, it attends to more recent historical pasts than did earlier, more speculative schools. These historical pasts are not only more accessible to the scholar but also, one could argue, of greater interest to the subjects of the representations. In other words, the Geertzian approach further develops a trend, noticeable in ethnography for the past fifty years, that privileges the colonial experience of "modernization" over the pre-contact era, which had long been considered more "authentic" and scientifically valuable.

The contemporary parallelism of interests between art historians and anthropologists is not without precedent. At many moments in the past, art history and anthropology displayed more similarities than have often been recognized. Both were inscribed during their early phases by the ethos of late nineteenth-century imperialist capitalism, with its dominant paradigm of a scientific knowledge derived from the study of natural history. For example, the materialism and positivism of the Victorian age account for the continued privileging of objects as primary forms of evidence of cognitive experience and for the consequent high value placed on the collection, preservation, and display of the material and visualizable.[17]

Both the formulator of art history's method of connoisseurship, Giovanni Morelli, and such prominent students of material culture as A.C. Haddon were trained as natural scientists, and the modes of describing and classifying objects that they developed were remarkably similar.[18] The same comparative-anatomical approach was applied in both disciplines, a method that wrenched apart form and content with a violence which was to remain highly problematic.[19] The goal of classification systems in both disciplines was to permit the insertion of objects into their proper slots in the grand developmental sequences that illustrated the evolution of world culture.[20] In order to tell the story of humankind's "rise to civilization," scholars of both Western and non-Western art removed the objects of study from their social and historical contexts in equally radical ways – the altarpiece from its chapel and the statue from its procession, as well as the ancestral figure from its shrine and the mask from its costumed dancer.

The racist and hegemonic pretensions of these Victorian approaches soon provoked parallel reactions within both art history and anthropology. By the early twentieth century a resistance to the unrelieved domination by post-Renaissance forms of Western art and culture had developed. The theory of cultural relativism developed by Franz Boas around the turn of the century closely paralleled the aesthetic relativism implied by the concept of the *Kunstwollen* theorized by his contemporary Alois Riegl. Both were stimulated by a much more detailed study of art forms that had been defined as "primitive"– Indigenous Northwest Coast, on the one hand, and early medieval European, on the other – than had been attempted by their predecessors.[21] As theorists who celebrated historical specificity and difference, both Boas and Riegl are ancestral to contemporary trends toward micro-history and pluralistic representation. Their advocacy of relativism, furthermore, prepared the ground in necessary ways for the reclassification of "primitive" artifacts as art which began in the early decades of this century.

The doctrine of cultural evolutionism and the associated positivist and materialist assumptions underlying the nineteenth-century study of natural history have long been rejected within the academy, as has the instrumentality of cultural evolutionism as a justification for political imperialism outside the ivory tower. But in many ways these ideologies continue to determine institutional practices associated with both art history and anthropology. The remaining traces have provoked the current reflexive self-examinations in both disciplines. To this day, for example, only a small number of art history programs in North America teach the arts of Africans, Native North Americans, or the peoples of the Pacific Islands. And the majority of the aesthetic products of these peoples are still held and exhibited by anthropology museums, many located within natural history museums. Until the early 1990s, a visitor using the elevator at Chicago's Field Museum of Natural History was confronted with a floor directory that listed "Indians" and "Dinosaurs" in immediate succession. However sensitively this museum, together with many others, is now approaching issues surrounding representation in ethnographic exhibitions, a basic problem remains.[22] The public's reading of art forms will inevitably be affected by their institutional juxtaposition with displays of dinosaur bones, primate evolution, birds, beasts, rocks, and plants.

The partial reclassification of tribal objects as art, a result of advocacy by modernist artists early in this century, did not (despite its profound effect on the art establishment) result in the transfer of the study of non-Western art from anthropology to art history. To identify oneself as an art historian of "tribal" art is even now considered an oxymoron by many "mainstream" art historians.[23] For despite the general acceptance achieved early in this century of the existence of art in small-scale societies, until recently the producers of tribal art were regarded as existing outside history. The primitivist movement that promoted the artfulness of tribal objects located their greatest authenticity and value in a past uncorrupted by contact with the West.[24]

The discourse of "primitive" art worked upon an object field already divided into two separate and opposed zones, art and artifact. The denial of history, as a denial of change, was instrumental in this dialectical relationship and in maintaining Western art in its position of dominance. Non-Western art forms could continue to occupy the "primitive" slots in the fixed evolutionary schema; the sequential narrative of progress in art history was not disrupted.[25] To put it more sympathetically, the representation of tribal art in a timeless, mythic past, though ultimately damaging, was also the result of a romantic and escapist desire on the part of both art lovers and anthropologists to salvage and celebrate artistic and cultural forms which they saw as having value before they were overwhelmed by Western modernity.

Non-Western objects have always been restless presences in the art gallery. Although Western artists and critics continued to think of their engagement with non-Western art as largely formal, their appropriation of these objects into the gallery space turned out to be subversive in unforeseen ways. The decontextualizations necessitated by their transfer to art institutions, even more radical than the decontextualizations of the ethnographic museum, were inherently provocative. In the mid-1950s, in what remains one of the best discussions of the problem of contextual understanding versus formal appreciation, anthropologist Robert Redfield argued that an exclusively formal-aesthetic experience of works of art is in fact exceedingly rare, and that all viewers, whether inside or outside the producing culture, inevitably bring with them "comparisons and analogies that they have learned about elsewhere, that transcend the object."[26]

If meanings are not already known or supplied by curatorial texts, in other words, they will be invented. The typical art gallery installations of tribal art surrounded these objects with a deafening silence, which had the effect of rendering them intensely mysterious. Initially, this aura invited all kinds of exoticist fantasies, but ultimately it stimulated searching questions, particularly among artists, about alternative concepts of the role of art in social and spiritual process. Artists, and a few interested art historians, had to turn to anthropologists for hard information about these issues.[27] During the middle decades of this century the old relationship of complementarity between art history and anthropology became one of active symbiosis.

The emblematic picture of this symbiosis is the image of Lévi-Strauss and the exiled surrealists pillaging the storerooms of the Museum of the American Indian for *katsina* dolls in the 1940s.[28] The process of exchange was complex; the vision with which anthropologists saw when they went into the field was constructed by their learned, Western ideas about art – ideas that changed as Western art developed, as Goldwater, Rubin, and others have shown.[29] But the anthropologists' preconceived ideas about art were also changed by their field experiences. Fresh recognition of the role of art in social process – in ritual, performance, and politics – was set out for Western readers in the resulting ethnographic texts, mined in turn by artists and art historians. A traffic in concepts of "primitive" art developed that was as important as the traffic in objects. These concepts have been as regularly appropriated by artists as the objects have been by the art market. And the message was not lost that these same social and ritual processes, in which aesthetic objects in other societies are imbricated, must have operated throughout the millennia of Western history in ways not adequately attended to by conventional art history.

The developments of assemblage, installation, and performance art are hard to imagine without the models imported by field anthropologists.[30] All three contemporary art genres are essentially contextualizing projects: they reintroduce magic, ritual, movement, sound, and associative meanings to the gallery spaces from which such distractions had been removed by the decontextualizing impulses of formalism. Although these rhetorics of contextualization emanated first from creative artists, they have increasingly penetrated the representational modes of art critics and art historians. Hans Belting identifies as central to the new art history the convergence of the discourses of artists, art critics, and art historians. Opening his influential little red book on new art history with a detailed description of a performance piece by Hervé Fischer, Belting uses Fischer's artistically expressed insights to interrogate the whole project of art history.[31]

The effect of the dialogues between art history and anthropology during the past century has been incremental, each successive interdisciplinary encounter further displacing the centrality of Western art forms in our thinking about art. The abandonment of universalist Eurocentric narratives of art history is, of course, a sign of a much larger process of decentring in the humanities, a process that must be understood within the context of postmodernism and postcolonialism. In art history, as in other fields of study, the erosion of the centre has opened up a space in which it has finally become possible to seek historical understandings of the aesthetic products of groups of people marginalized by the old art history. Art history, as a historical discipline, suddenly has many more stories to tell, and it has been enormously revitalized and energized as a result.

During my African fieldwork in the early 1970s, I was still complicit in the search for the mythic "authenticity" and "purity" of African art. For me, as for other scholars of non-Western art, it was the experience of fieldwork that began to break down the paradigm. For historians of European art, the expansion in scope of archival research necessitated by feminist art history and other democratizing movements has served the same purpose. An example from my more recent research in Native North American art history illustrates some of the new challenges we face. Nineteenth-century Native North Americans, like twentieth-century Africans, experienced for the first time intense contact with the norms of Western art and commodity culture. Like more recently colonized peoples all over the world, they responded by making art for the market and by an extremely innovative assimilation of Western styles and genres. As "acculturated" or "hybrid" aesthetic forms, however, these objects – which make up the great majority of the art produced by northeastern North American Indigenous peoples from 1850 to 1950 – have been despised as inauthentic, relegated to the category of "tourist art," and rarely displayed in museums or art galleries.[32]

Although there is still resistance to the hybrid, postmodernism has created the conditions in which it can now be much more easily accepted. James Clifford argues that travel and hybridization, normally represented as the prerogative of the people at the centre, are in fact part of the historical experience of all peoples.[33] But the practical problem of investigating this history remains, for the histories of marginalized peoples have not been recorded in the usual places. New art historians have to be enormously inventive and energetic in discovering historical information locked away in diaries, obscure periodicals, ephemeral popular pamphlets, and forgotten storerooms. For the history of non-Western art forms, print media and collecting activity were absent until relatively recently.

Let me give just one of many possible illustrations. We know that Aboriginal people in the northeast annually sold vast quantities of beadwork and other commercial arts at summer agricultural fairs all over the region, where their wares were eagerly bought and preserved. Yet a recent search through fifty years' worth of official programs of the New York State Fair failed to turn up a single mention or photograph of the presence of Indians. How can this art, then, be documented or treated historically? One answer continues to lie in the anthropological fieldwork approach, in collecting oral histories.

The most valuable information I and my co-researcher have found about the organization of this production has come from the oral histories recounted by elderly Mohawk women at Kahnawake, Quebec, in whose memories the pleasures of the fair, its colours and sounds and bustle, are still vivid, and from whom the economic importance and social meanings of the objects can still be learned.[34] More importantly, these women represent themselves, not as an exploited proletariat of commodity producers, but as creative artists who have approached their work with pride and relish.

This example may validate the anthropological fieldwork approach as a means of documenting history, but it still begs the question of art. Are Native North American baskets and beaded purses "art"? Or does such inclusiveness threaten, as many art historians would argue, to deconstruct the whole category? This question flags the big issue hovering over the current invasions of art history's field by practitioners of neighbouring disciplines. If microhistory and ethnographic concepts of culture are penetrating so deeply, what differentiates art history and justifies its continuing existence as a discrete discipline?

One defence of the boundary must come, I believe, from a revitalized definition of the category of art: a pluralizing of the term that recognizes the existence of arts which are differently defined. The words written by Franz Boas to introduce his 1927 classic *Primitive Art* resonate as loudly today as they did then: "All human activities may assume forms that give them aesthetic values."[35] Art history's continuing validity lies in its focus – unique among the academic disciplines – on visual aesthetic forms of human expression. But the enduring relevance of this category lies precisely in its universality. From anthropology, art history can learn to appreciate its own universality. But art history's claim to its territory also lies in the tools of connoisseurship it has developed, which allow practitioners of the discipline to recognize, assess, and appreciate quality in an individual object. The recognition of quality – and of its importance – is probably as universal as aesthetic expression itself, even when specific criteria vary, as Evan Maurer and others have shown.[36] From art historians, anthropologists can learn evaluative practices: the ability to recognize in the playing out of human history the power of aesthetic quality and the energy of artistic creation.

6

Disappearing Acts

Traditions of Exposure, Traditions
of Enclosure, and the Sacrality of
Onkwehonwe Medicine Masks

Smithsonian exploration and
field work has become almost
a tradition among the Six
Nations near Brantford on the
Grand River.
– *William N. Fenton (1941)*[1]

These pieces were not meant
to be taken out of human activity. They're not meant to be
put in vaults, or in metal cases.
They are to be used in our
spiritual practices.
– *Doug M. George (1995)*[2]

One of the most striking changes in ethnographic and art museum representations of Native North American peoples at the turn of the twenty-first century has been the disappearance from public display of object types long celebrated as canonical forms of art and material culture. As the result of carefully orchestrated campaigns by community representatives, Zuni Ahayu:da (or "war gods") have been returned to the Zuni, wampum belts have been repatriated to the care of Onkwehonwe (Iroquois) confederacy chiefs, Coast Salish rattles and masks have been moved to restricted areas of museum storerooms, female museum staff have been asked to stop handling categories of Plains medicine objects specific to men, and research on human remains and associated burial objects has been curtailed.[3] Collectively, these "disappearing acts" represent a grand refusal of key Western traditions for the production and disposition of knowledge. They set limits on classic methods of study – objectification, comprehensiveness, and critical analysis – and they erode the ideal of universal access to knowledge created by technologies of exposure and display in museums, archives, and universities. Contestations such as these engage a wide range of questions around tradition that have both general relevance to the large issues discussed in this book and specific resonance within the history of colonialism and postcolonialism.

In this chapter I discuss one of the most successful and far-reaching of these projects of removal, the Onkwehonwe campaign to stop the public display of the *ga:goh:sah*, or medicine masks (commonly referred to in the literature as "False Face" masks), their reproduction in painted, photographic, or sculptural form, and the academic study of the masks and related cere-monies.[4] It would be easy to interpret such negotiations as battles between censorship and academic freedom or as pressure on the museum, seen as an archetypical Western institution, to yield the ground of its enlightened (but uninterogated) modernity to a reactionary traditionalism. I offer this case study as an opportunity to complicate this kind of interpretation. I will argue that the ethics and politics of pluralism require that museums and aca-demic institutions attend seriously and respectfully to requests that render some objects non-visible. I will also maintain, however, that responses to and resolutions of conflicts must be grounded in accurate understandings of the specific histories of collecting, display, and representation that have led to the current situation, even though the creation of such histories invokes the same Western technologies of exposure that are under attack. Yielding to pres-sures to suppress historical inquiry into the ways that Indigenous traditions have changed over time – and particularly, in this case, in relation to dis-play, representation, and seeing – will ultimately frustrate attempts to reach understanding.

When episodes of museum contestation are examined carefully, the cases, the labels, the lights, the taxonomies, and the security systems of museums come to be seen as integral to traditions that are as culturally specific as are those of the Onkwehonwe. Although privileged under colonial regimes of power, they can no longer be taken for granted. We need to denaturalize the fundamental expository practices of the museum and the academy and to develop more reflexive understandings of the premises that underlie them. At the same time, we need to recognize the organic nature and contempor-ary vitality of Indigenous traditions, even when this entails restrictions on traditions of academic inquiry. The positioning of traditional ritual practi-ces within contemporary multicultural societies is, in other words, a dialogic process involving a continuing negotiation between two systems of know-ledge management.

Finally, my argument will go beyond the museum and the academy as self-contained sites of representation. As interdisciplinary work in visual stud-ies and visual anthropology has shown, the system of exposition and expos-ure to which public museum displays belong extends well beyond its walls. Both museum collecting, display, and academic discourse and contemporary rearticulations of Indigenous traditions are intimately joined to underlying processes of souvenir and art-market commodification, as well as to the mass circulation of mechanically reproduced images and texts in journalism, ad-vertising, film, children's literature, and popular performance. Western and Indigenous traditions for the disposition of knowledge must therefore be analyzed within specific economies of knowledge. Although it has not been acknowledged often enough, postcolonial critiques of museum representa-tion are generated within this broader arena and must therefore be examined systemically and not as isolated incidents of institutional transgression.[5]

Museums, Modernity, and Native North Americans

The case of the Onkwehonwe *ga:goh:sah* masks is representative of the contestations that have taken place in museums around the world as the result of postcolonial activism. As background to the discussion, it will be useful, then, to review briefly the role that museums have played as agents of colonialism in the inscription of modernist ideology. A key aspect of this ideology is its construction of the traditional as oppositional to the modern.[6] For Native North Americans the specific trope that became an article of faith under settler colonialism for non-Natives of all political persuasions is that of the "disappearing Indian."[7] The first challenge that faces Indigenous activists, therefore, is the refutation of this doctrine and the affirmation and demonstration of the survival *within* modernity of Indigenous traditions that have been represented as lost or fragmented. The dialectical construction of tradition and modernity also implies essentialist notions of identity and authenticity, requiring Native North Americans, like other colonized peoples, to argue explicitly for the authenticity of the hybrid and the syncretistic. As the Onkwehonwe case study will show, contestations have regularly been complicated and confused by the disunity and factionalization of Indigenous communities, a situation that is itself a result of colonial policies that encouraged missionization by competing Christian sects, that legally prohibited Indigenous spiritual practices and ceremonies, and that suppressed traditional forms of governance.

As a large and growing literature shows, museums have historically played a central role in the inscription of specific tenets of modernist ideology instrumental to the implementation of such policies. The great period of museum and collection building that began in the mid-nineteenth century coincided almost exactly with the formulation and implementation of official assimilationist policies in the United States and Canada between about 1880 and 1940. Ethnological exhibits organized according to the principles of cultural evolutionism and art museum installations of "primitive art" informed by idealist and formalist theories conveyed to broad publics the racially determined hierarchies of history, culture, and art generated within the academy.[8] Together, these anthropological and aesthetic discourses contributed to a specifically modernist version of primitivism which ascribed interest, value, and beauty within Indigenous cultures exclusively to "traditional" objects, defined in turn as those that appeared to display the minimum of Western influence. Authenticity and value were thus located in an irretrievable precontact past, while the hybrid cultural forms that characterize post-contact and contemporary Indigenous peoples were devalued as contaminated and inauthentic.[9] At the same time, in appropriating the cultural artifacts of Indigenous peoples into their public displays, museums and galleries overwrote their systems of classification and knowledge management with those of the West.

It must be stressed that this rather bald account describes the simplified messages conveyed by public museum exhibitions through their installations and their privileging of certain kinds of objects during much of the twentieth century. It does not refer to the new consultative and collaborative culture that has been developing in many museums during the past two decades,[10] nor to the far more complex and mediated understandings of artistic and cultural process achieved by ethnologists and art historians in their detailed studies and field diaries. But because the exhibition paradigms of art and artifact developed during the first half of the twentieth century have cast such long shadows, lingering on in major urban museums decades after the disciplinary formations that gave them birth were rejected within the academy itself, they have remained legitimate targets for contestation in many places. The taxonomies, life groups, and ethnographic presentism of the early twentieth-century anthropology exhibit remained in place into the twenty-first century at major institutions such as the Smithsonian's National Museum of Natural History,[11] while the connoisseurship-based "rare art tradition" model associated with the modernist construct of Primitive Art, lives on in the Rockefeller Wing of the Metropolitan Museum of Art in New York.

Art-Historical and Ethnological Encounters with Onkwehonwe *Ga:goh:sah*

The appropriation of Native American objects into the Western art system did not occur until the 1930s, late in the sequence of such primitivist redefinitions.[12] This process, like earlier appropriations of "tribal" objects, was driven by the inexorable logic of modernism's universalist presumptions, which predicted the presence of art in all cultures. The inscription of the Western discourse of art on world cultures, furthermore, recapitulated its own hierarchical classification of fine and applied arts. To construct a global art gallery, it was necessary to discover genres that fitted the fine art categories of sculpture and painting.

The specific canon of Native North American art that emerged during the middle decades of the twentieth century was predicated in important ways on a prior process of ethnographic collecting. Virtually every *ga:goh:sah* that has appeared in an art exhibition was temporarily lifted out of an ethnographic collection in order to make its appearance as fine art. (This secondary appropriation is typical of Native American objects in general, few of which were initially acquired by art collectors.) By the 1930s there were well over fifteen hundred wooden medicine masks in ethnological collections in Europe and North America.[13] This is a huge number when one considers that during the late nineteenth and twentieth centuries, when most of the masks were collected, the membership of the Longhouse (whose adherents follow traditional Onkwehonwe beliefs and spiritual practices) was probably not much greater than twice that number.[14] The number of masks collected evidences, on the one hand, a scramble for medicine masks comparable to the competition for Northwest Coast totem poles and other object types regarded as centrepieces of turn-of-the-century museum displays and, on the other, an active Onkwehonwe commercial production of masks for outsiders.[15]

Onkwehonwe *ga:goh:sah* have attracted an inordinate amount of scholarly attention ever since Lewis Henry Morgan's first published account of 1851.[16] No fewer than thirty professional field ethnologists, including J.N.B. Hewitt, M.R. Harrington, Arthur Parker, and Frank Speck, have written about them. The study of the masks and their rituals was central to the long and distinguished scholarly career of William Fenton, the dean of twentieth-century Iroquoianists. He produced over fifteen publications focusing on questions of the ethnohistory, typology, and ritual practices associated with the masks as understood from both non-Native and Onkwehonwe perspectives. His massive 500-page monograph, *The False Faces of the Iroquois*, was published in 1987, fifty years after the appearance of his first article.[17] The question of why, among all things made by Onkwehonwe, carved wooden medicine masks have so consistently been singled out by Western connoisseurs as high art is closely tied to their prominence in ethnographic study and collecting. The importance attributed to these masks by the late nineteenth- and early twentieth-century ethnographers who collected most of what is in museums today exemplifies a tight interdependence between art theory and ethnography that long predates the advent of a modernist discourse of Primitive Art. In both art and anthropological practice the genres and styles of "art" were key diagnostics of the level of civilization attained by a given society. For ethnographers, as for art critics, "true sculpture" – that which is divorced from any functional purpose – was the most highly evolved form of plastic art. Its inclusion was therefore indispensable to any study based on evolutionist principles, and particularly for any ethnographer desirous of displaying "his" people in the most favourable possible light. The entry on sculpture in the Smithsonian Institution's influential *Handbook of American Indians* (1906) states this position clearly: "The sculptural arts in their widest significance may be regarded as including the whole range of the nonplastic shaping arts, their processes and products; but as here considered they relate more especially to the higher phases of the native work, those which rise above the mere utilitarian level into the realm of esthetic expression, thus serving to illustrate the evolution of sculpture into fine art."[18]

The *ga:goh:sah* belong to one of the most important medicine societies of the Onkwehonwe. (That other medicine societies of equivalent ritual importance are not as well known to the general public is undoubtedly due, at least in part, to the fact that they do not make use of carved masks.) The masks represent forest spirits who put their powers at the disposal of human beings for the prevention and curing of illness. They bring healing to individuals and also drive away disease on behalf of the whole community at important annual ceremonies.[19] According to Onkwehonwe origin stories, this great benefit was achieved by the Creator after a contest with *Hadui*, the World Rim Dweller and the most powerful of the medicine beings, who challenged the Creator to a test of their relative powers. In proving his superiority, the Creator caused a mountain to slam into *Hadui*'s face, breaking his nose and twisting his features. The physiognomies of the various types of masks are thus purposeful inversions and exaggerations of anthropomorphic forms. By their deeply grooved wrinkles and shiny metal eyes, the "Common Face" masks are seen to be forest beings, the possessors of other-than-human powers. The mask type that represents *Hadui* himself displays the broken and distorted features that resulted from the great battle.[20]

The intentional and intensely meaningful distortions of the medicine masks have been problematic for most Western observers, who are accustomed to idealized anthropomorphic religious iconographies. In the accounts of Jesuits and other early contact-period travellers who witnessed their public appearances, they are invariably described in terms that denote ugliness, paganism, and the diabolical, such as "hideous" (1687), "clumsy," "antic," and "hobgoblin" (1751), "idolatrous," "frightful," and "awry" (1741), and "ghastly" (1779).[21] Early twentieth-century ethnographic descriptions continued to employ this vocabulary of the grotesque, although rationalized and objectified by means of a new contextualization within mythological narratives.[22] As I have noted, ethnographic collectors enthusiastically collected medicine masks not only because they illustrated Onkwehonwe beliefs and rituals but also because they were pre-eminent examples of "sculpture." But it was not until the primitivist impulse within modern art had reached a certain stage that the *ga:goh:sah* became celebrated as aesthetic creations. The specific history of primitivism in North America was also instrumental. One result of the initial engagement of the turn-of-the-century European modernists with African and Oceanic art had been the assignment of a special prominence to masks as objects that can be easily decontextualized, hung on the wall, and made available for aesthetic contemplation.[23] During the 1930s and 1940s a number of prominent surrealists who spent the war years in temporary exile in New York began to promote genres of Native North American art that seemed to them to embody dream experience, the urges of the unconscious, primal archetypes, and the mythic.[24] During these decades, too, nationalist artistic projects in the United States and Canada drew attention to Indigenous arts as alternatives to European artistic traditions.

Large, anthropomorphic wooden carvings with deeply incised and dramatically distorted features, streaming hair, and shining metal eyes, the *ga:goh:sah* embodied the mid-twentieth-century modernist ideal of Primitive Art far better than other aesthetically elaborated Onkwehonwe objects, which tend to be small and intimate in scale or hybrid in style and made of "craft" materials such as fibres, beads, or hide. It is not surprising to find that carved wooden medicine masks were prominently featured in every book or exhibition catalogue on Native American art published since the 1930s, a convention that has changed only in the last few years.[25] As we have seen, a constellation of apparently disconnected and even, at times, contradictory positions ranging from idealist aesthetics to cultural evolutionism to aesthetic expressionism had combined to make their canonization inevitable.

The earliest publications on Native American art appeared in 1931 and 1941 to accompany the first large exhibitions on the subject, the *Exposition of Indian Tribal Arts* (subtitled the "First exhibition of American Indian art selected entirely with consideration of esthetic value") in 1931 and the Museum of Modern Art's *Indian Art of the United States* in 1941.[26] In both texts the medicine masks are described in terms that remain closely tied to ethnological accounts, despite the self-proclaimed aesthetic orientations of the two exhibitions. In the earlier of these, for example, Oliver LaFarge gave a dramatic account of the *ga:goh:sah* as "awful beings" wearing "grotesque masks" that were "made terrible by great staring eyes."[27]

A recognizably formalist language is more evident in the publications of the 1960s. In the most widely circulated such text, Frederick Dockstadter's *Indian Art in America*, the author noted the "plastic quality of the carving and the dramatic portrayal of the features."[28] In the spate of exhibition catalogues and books on Native American art published in the 1970s, this language is further elaborated. One major survey catalogue describes the *ga:goh:sah* as "among the most virile and spectacular works of art created by the Onkwehonwe."[29] The language of expressive form is perhaps most fully developed in a Denver Art Museum publication of 1979, in which Richard Conn wrote of one mask: "The carver who produced this mask sought to convey the powerful aspects of his subject. Copper rings about the eye holes invoke the searing quality of the spirit's eyes; the vigorous carving of the planes and hollows of the forehead is emphasized by precisely painted red lines that echo the shape and color of the mouth. The dynamic design perfectly embodies the forceful personality and indomitable might of the spirit."[30]

Numerous further examples could be given, including one from my own earlier work.[31] With this kind of close formal reading, curators and writers tried to transpose the experience of Native American art from an object that was to be understood as an illustration of a mythic narrative to one that could be contemplated in more purely aesthetic terms. In doing so, they were promoting the art museum's mandate to act as a special kind of space in which the gaze plays freely over objects. As Svetlana Alpers has noted, "the taste for isolating this kind of attentive looking at crafted objects is as peculiar to our culture as is the museum as the space or institution where the activity takes place."[32]

Medicine Masks and Popular Visual Culture

Onkwehonwe and other Native Americans make little distinction between ethnographic and aesthetic projects of collecting and display. In this sense the distinction between the art and artifact paradigms of the object has been a preoccupation of Western, not Indigenous, writers. The "compliment" that, as Clifford has written, our culture pays to others by recognizing their objects as art has often missed its mark, and both types of museum display have appeared equally invasive to colonized peoples.[33] The Caribbean-Canadian

writer M. Nourbese Philip has expressed the process as a ritual litany –
"identify, describe, catalogue, annotate, appropriate" – whose purpose is ultimately to control "the Other, against which are arrayed the forces of reason,
rationality, logic and knowledge as possessable and certifiable."[34]

I want to add to this list the forces of capital and commerce. The commodification of the *ga:goh:sah* began, as has already been noted, with the production of masks by traditional carvers for ethnologists and private collectors, a production that has continued to the present day, most actively by the
Onkwehonwe-owned Iroqrafts company, located on the Six Nations Reserve
at Oshweken, Ontario. This production supplied needed income for impover-
ished reserve economies. Fenton writes that "by 1930 picking old masks and
carving new ones for collectors was a regular practice, and collecting was
expected behavior of visiting ethnologists. I recall vividly the puzzlement of
persons who showed me old masks and wondered why I simply wanted to
photograph them."[35] During the twentieth century Onkwehonwe artists and
performers have also incorporated the masks into their work. In the 1920s
Esther Deer, or Princess White Deer, a successful dancer from Kahnawake,
used a *ga:goh:sah* in one of her acts at the Ziegfield Follies. A publicity photograph of the time shows her holding the mask next to her face in an image
that very strongly recalls an iconic surrealist photograph, Man Ray's *Noire
et Blanche*, of 1926.[36] During the 1980s and 1990s Joe Jacobs and other noted
contemporary Onkwehonwe sculptors continued to incorporate images of
the masks in their soapstone carvings, for which they were criticized by other
Onkwehonwe community members.

Perhaps the most widely publicized example of this kind of public display
occurred in 1996 during the presentation of the annual National Aboriginal
Achievement Awards, televised across the country by the Canadian Broadcasting Corporation. Native actor Tom Jackson, star of a popular CBC television series, performed an almost identical juxtaposition to Princess White
Deer's, playfully holding a *ga:goh:sah* over his face before making one of the
awards. In one letter of protest, an Onkwehonwe correspondent wrote that
"this misuse of our sacred masks is akin to someone serving sacramental
wine and consecrated hosts at a cocktail party."[37] John Kim Bell, the founder
of the Canadian Native Arts Foundation, which organizes the awards and
the ceremony, and himself a Mohawk from Kahnawake, defended the show
by affirming a distinction between active masks, carved according to correct
ritual procedures, and the masks used on the program, which he described
as "tourist replica knock-offs, which are made and sold by the hundreds
by Iroquoian people."[38] This debate, which has been conducted in terms of
conflicting interpretations of Onkwehonwe tradition and an assumed dichotomy between the sacred and the secular, needs also to be understood
against the background of a much more extensive twentieth-century history
of the mechanical reproduction of images of *ga:goh:sah*. The 1996 telecast was
only the most recent of these but, thanks to the power of television, the most
widely seen. I would like now to fill in several chapters of that history.

Since the nineteenth century the primary mandate of the public museum has been the education (and, as Bennett and Duncan argue, socialization) of an audience defined in ever broader and more democratic terms.[39] In addition to the representations they produce in-house, museum ethnologists have regularly collaborated in commercial projects such as world's fairs and publications. During the twentieth century, then, medicine masks and their images have been inserted into commercial circulation through the entrepreneurial activities of Onkwehonwe themselves, through authorized public-private collaborations with museum curators, and through other, unauthorized appropriations. Most of these projects have left only ephemeral traces. The following examples do not, therefore, represent a systematic sampling, but they serve to rough in a commercial context of popular visual culture essential to the understanding of contemporary contestations.[40]

One of the largest early twentieth-century non-museum displays of Native North American objects was installed in the grill room of the Hotel Astor in New York City, named the American Indian Hall.[41] The printed guidebook to the hall, illustrated with photographs of the installations and museum-like catalogue entries for the artifacts, clearly states the combination of nationalist, sentimental, and commercial motives behind the hall's creation. It also foregrounds the professional museological authorization for the artifact displays (which, like those of the museums, were bought from a trading company). "Leading officers of the American Museum of Natural History and the Ethnological Bureau in Washington," it states, supplied busts of Indians taken from life casts as well as ethnographic photographs, which served as an attraction to foreigners and other visitors at the same time that they commemorated "the noble red man." As the guidebook notes, "Being deeply interested in the history of our country, the creation of an American style of decoration appealed to [the owner] strongly."

The hall was divided into eight sections that roughly followed the standard ethnographic culture-area map, one of which was dedicated solely to the "Iroquois," identified in the guidebook as "the most famous of all groups of Indian tribes." Guests entered through a foyer decorated with artifacts of the early settler era of old New York and then, "having so far examined the relics of the white men who drove the Indian back from the shores of the Atlantic to the desert fastnesses of the far west, one passes to the room where historical relics of vanished or fast-vanishing tribes have been made the sole attraction." The hall was intended as a *lieu de mémoire* in Nora's sense; here in the midst of bustling urban life, people could "pause to remember at times that the wigwam of the Indian once stood on the very ground now occupied by our great cities." Like the museum, it was also intended to serve as the locus of the displaced authenticity of Indigenous people, since on the reservation "the progress of civilization has stripped him of his most attractive characteristics."[42]

In the middle of the hall, in the section devoted to the Iroquois, seven *ga:goh:sah* were prominently displayed (fig. 6.1). As in the other sections, life

THE IROQUOIS

THE sixth section is given to the Iroquois, the most famous of all groups of Indian tribes. Once their territory included parts of Canada, New York, Pennsylvania, Ohio and Michigan, but it was surrounded everywhere by land of the Algonquin stock.

To the Iroquois belong the Wyandots or Hurons, Cherokees, Eries, Nottawas, and the tribes which made up the celebrated "League of the Six Nations": the Mohawks, Onondagas, Oneidas, Senecas, Cayugas and Tuscaroras.

At present the Iroquois number about 44,000. To a greater extent than all other Indians, they became agriculturists, live in permanent villages and have adopted the ways of the whites.

Two busts, the one of a Cayuga and the other that of a Mohawk Indian, give the characteristic features of the Iroquois.

As in time past the moose was frequently found in the forests of the Iroquois, a fine head of this formidable animal has been placed among the implements, which, by good fortune, have come down to our days. The most familiar objects in the group to the left are a pair of

MOHAWK
INDIAN

snow-shoes, by the use of which the hunter was able to follow game when the snow was too deep to travel with moccasins.

Beneath the snow-shoes hangs a war-shield, with the rough outlines of a bear and a bison painted on its front. A tobacco pouch and a pair of moccasins dangle at its sides. Moreover, there are a pipe of peace, war-clubs, a rattle and a sword-like implement of war. The most peculiar objects are two hideous masks beset with hair and smeared with red and black paint. They belong to the outfit of medicine-men, who, up to the present day, prey upon their kinsmen by pretending to have power over the many demons and witches which threaten the life of the Iroquois.

Opposite the moose head, hanging on the balcony, are several other masks, one of which is fearfully distorted. To the right of the moose we see a pair of snow-shoes, intended for the feet of pack animals. Partly covered by these shoes hangs a hunter's pouch, finely done in bead-work. Other hunting implements, as bow and arrows, a powder-flask, another pouch of

6.1   The trophy display in the Hotel Astor's American Indian Hall, incorporating Onkwehonwe medicine masks, as illustrated in the souvenir guide published for the hotel. Private collection

busts (wearing Plains feather bonnets) were mounted on pedestals, and framed photographs were set into the wainscoting – although most showed feather-bonneted Plains Indians, it having proved impossible (the guidebook explains) to find more than two "authentic" images of Iroquois life. The ethnographic objects were arranged in the trophy formation used in world's fairs and other expositions. Amongst the moose head, snowshoes, bags, ladles, and other objects that made up the Iroquois trophy, three *ga:goh:sah* were suspended like captured shrunken heads. The special interest associated with these masks is suggested by the second grouping of five masks displayed on an adjacent wall. The masks are glossed in the guidebook as follows: "The most peculiar objects are two hideous masks beset with hair and smeared with red and black paint. They belong to the outfit of medicine men, who, up to the present day, prey upon their kinsmen by pretending to have power over the many demons and witches which threaten the life of the Iroquois. Opposite the moose head, hanging on the balcony, are several other masks, one of which is fearfully distorted."[43] In this passage, despite the careful academic and museological framing of the American Indian Hall, a revealing slippage has occurred. The standard anthropological account has given way to the untrammelled popular imagination, and older tropes of the primitive and the savage have surfaced, demonizing the Onkwehonwe medicine society in a language that harks back to the *Jesuit Relations*.

Other examples can be given of anthropologically authorized popularizations of the *ga:goh:sah* that also diverge, though in different ways, from the representations of the museum or academic ethnologist. For example, the text of *Indians of America*, a children's book published in 1935, reflects the more liberal attitudes toward Indians that began with the Roosevelt administration and its commissioner of Indian affairs, John Collier. The book credits "well known anthropologists at the Heye Foundation in New York" for their help.[44] Its stated aim is to counter the "bloodthirsty" and warlike image of the Indian by emphasizing an understanding of "their life before these troubles began." "The famous benevolent society of the Iroquois," the child readers are told, "was known as the Ja-di-gon-sa meaning 'False Face Society.' Members wore carved false faces, some of which were extremely hideous, with large noses and twisted mouths. They believed these faces gave them power to do good, the deed being of greater benefit if the benefactor was masked and unknown."[45] While this account does not demonize the masks in the manner of the Hotel Astor publication, the language of the grotesque with which the masks are described and its desire to "arouse your interest in a vanishing race" remain fixed within familiar aesthetic and temporal boundaries.[46]

The appropriation of images of medicine masks, among other objects, to the interests of private corporate enterprise is even more comprehensively realized in a 1956 publication, issued by the Canadian Pulp and Paper Association, entitled *National Asset – Native Design*. The twenty-page, large-format paperback is lavishly illustrated with examples of Canadian Aboriginal art and French-Canadian folk art.[47] The National Museum of Canada and some of the most authoritative and respected figures in the Canadian cultural world are prominently credited as collaborators in its production, including Canada's premier ethnologist, Marius Barbeau, his son-in-law, artist Arthur Price, and the well-known painter A.J. Casson, who designed the publication.[48] Effectively, the booklet presents two parallel texts, one written and the other visual. The written text is a history of and a paean to the pulp and paper industry, while the visual text is comprised of photographic and painted images of Canadian Indigenous and folk art that fill the margins of the pages. The two texts are connected only in the opening passage, entitled "Native Design": "This book, which concerns a great national asset, is illustrated with native Canadian folk designs," it begins. "The Indigenous art used herein is an adornment well suited to the story of a great native enterprise that enriches the life of every Canadian whether in the vast hinterland, in the teeming cities, or in the pleasant countryside." Since "Indians of the forests" made many of the objects, they can serve as "reminders" of the even greater importance of the forest to the modern nation. And just as the Indigenous objects served as tools, historical records, or "means of expression and communication," "the products of Canada's leading industrial enterprise fulfil much the same purpose as these designs served some hundreds of years ago: for Canada is a world leader in the manufacture of pulp and paper, the currency of civilization and the handmaid of commerce." The final paragraph sounds again the note of appropriated indigeneity: "primitive design and folk art have ever served to lend character to national culture and to national art. So, perhaps, the illustrations herein may help to widen the adaptation of native art to architecture, to furniture, to textiles, to metals, to industrial design, to fine art, and to wherever craftsmanship can add distinction and value to the products of Canada." The four *ga:goh:sah* that appear midway through the book are, then, completely divorced from any specific ethnographic context. Rather, they are positioned as a prelude to the progressivist and assimilationist settler narrative of Canadian history, in which the dynamic, industrial Anglo-Canadian economy is asserted to be the natural successor to the primitive Aboriginal (and French-Canadian) economies that preceded it. Their arts, like their lands, become a resource to be legitimately exploited by the newcomers.

When we turn to the many unsanctioned commercial appropriations of medicine masks, we find that the attachment of romantic, derogatory, or opportunistic significations to the *ga:goh:sah* was accomplished with even greater disregard for ethnographic or Indigenous meanings than in the previous examples. A *ga:goh:sah* appears in one of the plates of *Le plus bel album du monde pour les industries de luxe*, a portfolio advertising a French art deco jewellery design firm published during the late 1920s.[49] The tag attached to a made-in-Japan souvenir doll representing a *ga:goh:sah* states: "GOOD LUCK / MEDICINE MAN / INDIAN DOLL/ Protects You Against All Evil Spirits/ While Driving – At Work – At Play." The reverse side reads: "An interesting American Indian custom was the wearing of hideous masks by their Medicine men. They believed that by wearing the face of a particular animal or one representing an evil spirit they could prevent bad luck"[50] (fig. 6.2).

During the 1970s or 1980s Nabisco Canada distributed a series of cards about North American Indians in boxes of Shreddies cereal. As in baseball cards, one side bore an image and the other a set of vital statistics. One of the cards shows a *ga:goh:sah* with a particularly twisted face and the terse caption

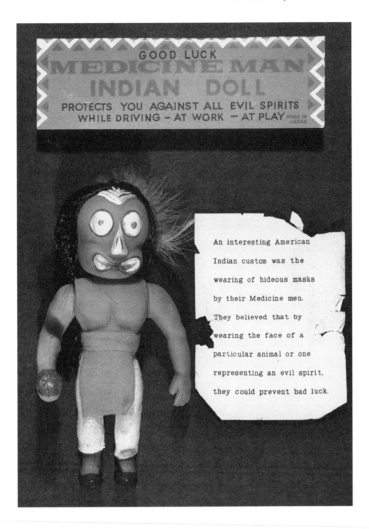

6.2   A doll for an automobile windscreen made in the form of a caricatured Onkwehonwe medicine masker, c. 1920–30. Private collection. Photo courtesy of the Royal Ontario Museum, Toronto

"Seneca Indian Mask (Northeast United States)." On the reverse is a map locating the Seneca within North America and the text "This mask made by the Seneca Indians represents a spirit of the forest whose face became twisted out of shape as a punishment for boasting. Thus, a warning for both children and adults." The format of the card conveys a bogus ethnographic authority through its museum-like map and label, while the format of the set miniaturizes, infantilizes, and trivializes Indigenous people by creating the illusion of their collectability. (The top corner of the map side, which bears the admonition "Punch hole here / Collect all twenty cards," appeals directly to the obsessive psychology of the collector as described by Baudrillard.)[51] Most seriously, the interpretive text distorts out of all recognition the meanings the masks have for the Onkwehonwe.

Numerous other such unmediated commercial appropriations have occurred, but let me end with one particularly blatant example. In a 1952 issue
of the *National Geographic* a full-page advertisement for The Travelers insurance company appeared featuring a large, highly naturalistic drawing of
a masked *ga:goh:sah* shown in a ritual posture crawling toward the viewer,
turtle-shell rattle in hand. It was headed "Iroquois scare-devil," and the text
below read:

> Iroquois medicine men wearing horrible masks like this crawled into
> the tribe's lodges twice a year – jumping and moaning and rattling
> their turtle-shell noisemakers.
>
> As a part of the ceremony, they scattered ashes on the floor. And that
> particular Iroquois dwelling was supposed to become a safe place in
> which to live.
>
> A wonderful idea – chasing out evil spirits that might later harm you
> and your family. But it won't work for you any better than it did for the
> old-time Iroquois.
>
> But mishaps around the house, or personal injury accidents any-
> where, needn't be a heavy burden on your pocketbook, Just call in
> your Travelers agent and let him tell you about Travelers Accident
> Insurance.[52]

As in the Nabisco Indian baseball cards, the fragmentation of the narrative
results in disinformation. Not only has the *ga:goh:sah* become completely
detached from the significations attached to it as an ethnographic artifact,
but the context in which the ad occurs – a magazine whose readers could be
presumed to take a sympathetic interest in cultural differences – makes its
sarcastic and scornful tone particularly shocking.[53]

Commercial exploitations of this sort and museum installations are at opposite ends of what I would term a "spectrum of responsibility" to originating communities. Although museums also decontextualize ethnographic
artifacts in order to reinsert them into non-Native narratives, the new significations assigned to them have been controlled by processes of research
that connected them, through fieldwork and, more recently, a range of collaborative strategies, to Indigenous systems of meaning. Commercial commodification loosens these controls to differing degrees. During the twentieth century, as the power of mechanical reproduction and consumerist
commodification grew to reach ever-expanding audiences, Onkwehonwe activists increasingly identified the museum as the site where the initial gesture
of display and interpretation occurs and therefore as the originating point of
the semiotic chain that ends in such offensive and uncontrolled examples of
commercial exploitation. It is one of the many contradictory features of this
history, however, that once images become disseminated in popular visual
culture, it is virtually impossible to call them back. Paradoxically, it may be
museums – both the older institutions and the newer Native-run centres –

that can most effectively respond to and critique the fictions and fantasies of popular culture.

Debating Removal, Replication, and Reproduction

In the mid-1970s and 1980s, as part of a renewed political activism in Native North American communities, Onkwehonwe groups in the United States and Canada began to create written policies on medicine mask display and to approach museums with formal requests for changes to public exhibits. In a longer historical perspective, the "disappearing" of the *ga:go:sah* masks that resulted can be seen as one of a series of strategic removals from and insertions into spaces of display that articulate successive proto-colonial, colonial, and emergent postcolonial phases in Onkwehonwe relations with Euro–North Americans. As numerous accounts make clear, during the early years of contact the public appearances of the *ga:goh:sah* in Onkwehonwe villages could be viewed by any outsiders who happened to be present. One effect of the destabilization of Onkwehonwe life that followed upon the political defeats, population losses, and land appropriations of the early nineteenth century was the division of communities into traditionalists, or Longhouse followers, and a variety of Christian sects.[54] As a result, the ritual appearances of the medicine masks, which had once been public and communal, gradually became private and sectarian. During the first half of the twentieth century, as we have also seen, anthropologists were able to observe ceremonies, interview faith keepers, and gain the collaboration of Onkwehonwe who believed that salvage anthropology offered a valuable means of preserving a record of their historical cultures. In recent decades, however, the resurgence of traditional practice and belief and a determination to control unauthorized and exploitative uses of the masks have combined to close off access for researchers and other outsiders to all ceremonies of the Society of Faces and the Longhouse.

For many traditional Onkwehonwe the making available of *ga:goh:sah* to spectatorial scrutiny and pleasure, which is the museum's central mandate, had always been a potentially dangerous activity and, to some extent, a contravention of ritual correctness. For them, masks that have been properly prepared are alive and full of power. They must be ritually fed with corn mush and offered tobacco. Viewing must be restricted and carefully managed by specialists, for without proper treatment the masks can cause illness and trouble the dreams of those who come in contact with them, including museum visitors. During the twentieth century Onkwehonwe consultants pointed out to the ethnologists with whom they worked the need to care for masks in museums, and some museums made arrangements for faith keepers to come at intervals to perform necessary rituals. William Fenton reported that "if the mask is going to a museum, *diyekdo?tha?*, 'a place where people pass in and out to look,' the maker tells it: 'lots of people will be coming in to see you … You shall go back with him to the museum, and don't create any disturbance there, for you shall remain there forever from now on.'"[55] This passage suggests both how unnatural museum display is from an Onkwehonwe point of view and also that the viewing of the masks was not, per se, forbidden.

Part of the confusion in the museum world results from variations in the policies and requests brought forward by different Onkwehonwe organizations and communities. The National Museum of Canada (now the Canadian Museum of Civilization) was one of the first to be approached. "In various visits we have had from Longhouse Iroquois leaders," wrote the Iroquoian ethnologist at the National Museum of Canada to his director in 1975, "the point has been quietly though forcefully made that we should not be displaying 'living' false face masks in the Iroquois Hall … The Iroquois consider the masks highly sacred and even 'dangerous' objects that should be on view only at the time of curing rituals. The issue has come up from time to time, and I think we ought now to give serious consideration to the possibility of substituting replicas."[56] Five years later, in 1980, the masks were removed and replaced with fibreglass casts.[57] The use of replicas, however, was explicitly rejected in a statement developed in the early 1980s by the Haudenosaunee Grand Council of Chiefs, which represents most of the Onkwehonwe communities in New York state.[58] Its current policy statement identifies the masks as "essential to the spiritual and emotional well-being of the Haudenosaunee communities" and says that any interference with them is a violation of religious freedom. It denies that any distinction exists between ritually and commercially carved masks and forbids the public exhibition of all masks. It also forbids all forms of reproduction or the distribution of any kind of information. The language is explicit:

> The exhibition of masks by museums does not serve to enlighten the public regarding the culture of the Haudenosaunee, as such an exhibition violates the intended purpose of the mask and contributes to the desecration of the sacred image. In addition, information regarding medicine societies is not meant for general distribution.
>
> The non-Indian public does not have a right to examine, interpret nor present the beliefs, functions and duties of the secret medicine societies of the Haudenosaunee. The sovereign responsibility of the Haudenosaunee over their spiritual duties must be respected by the removal of all medicine masks from exhibition and from access to non Indians …
>
> The Council of Chiefs find that there is no proper way to explain, interpret, or present the significance of the medicine masks and therefore ask that no attempt to be made by museums to do other than to explain the wishes of the Haudenosaunee in this matter.[59]

Finally, the statement requests the return of all masks to the "proper caretakers among the Haudenosaunee" because "it is only through these actions that the traditional culture will remain strong and peace be restored to our communities."

A number of large American museums, notably the Smithsonian's Native-run National Museum of the American Indian, are guided by this statement. The NMAI has made special provision for the closed storage of its masks. The Mohawk community at Kahnawake, though not formally part of the Grand Council, has taken a similar position. During the showing of the controversial exhibition *The Spirit Sings: Artistic Traditions of Canada's First Peoples* in 1988, the Kahnawake Mohawk brought an unsuccessful lawsuit against the Glenbow Museum to remove a medicine mask on loan from the Royal Ontario Museum (see chapter 2). Although the courts did not uphold the request, the mask was voluntarily removed before the show's second venue, the Canadian Museum of Civilization, and replaced with a replica made by the late Chief Jacob Thomas. As a result of these and other actions, over the past fifteen years or so, the *ga:goh:sah* have been removed from most of the major museums in North America.[60]

The question of replication and the closely related question of commercial art-market production remain, however, subjects of debate within the Onkwehonwe community, confusing museum officials in their efforts to respect Aboriginal views on the display of sacred objects.[61] Both the ethnographic literature and interviews with modern-day faith keepers establish quite clearly a distinction between active and inactive masks which, in the view of some Onkwehonwe ritual specialists, would permit the viewing of replicas and reproductions. The initial solution adopted by the National Museum of Canada to replace masks with replicas was posited on this distinction. The museum of the Woodlands Cultural Centre on the Six Nations Reserve has removed from view all of its live masks, but it displays a medicine mask still attached to a tree trunk because, as an incomplete carving, it is not yet alive. In 1995 the museum's director, Tom Hill, wrote that "we do believe, however, that it remains important to discuss their creation which can successfully be conveyed without putting the mask on display."[62] Similarly, the museum's Policy on Sacred and Sensitive Material states: "Only images of masks which have not been 'blessed' or have not been used in any ceremonial function will be presented in any Centre sponsored display. Such a display will be approved by the appropriate traditionalists." And, further, "Mask classifications will not be based on ethnographic or museological standards but standards which are appropriate to the traditional community."

This policy conforms with the teaching of Chief Jacob Thomas, who was both a faith keeper of the *ga:goh:sah* society at Six Nations and a member of a prominent family of mask carvers. In a CBC television documentary in 1982 he was filmed as he carved masks on a living tree and in his studio. He explained: "My grandfather was also a carver and there were many carvers in those days ... It took me time before I did get to know the art of it ... Now I do carving most of the time and I have a lot of standing orders. It's mostly for commercial, but we don't bless the mask for commercial purposes."[63] The narrator further explains, "The full ritual which gives a medicine mask its powers and the annual feeding of the mask to sustain these powers could never be shown to outsiders. But part of the ritual can be shown, the physical carving of a mask in the old way, from a living tree." The reproduction of images and the publication of ethnographic information also remain controversial. The National Museum of the American Indian refused my request to reproduce a painting of *ga:goh:sah* ceremonies in its collection made in the 1930s by Seneca artist Ernest Smith. The work had been produced during a project sponsored by the Works Progress Administration which was designed to strengthen traditional material culture and was overseen by Seneca ethnologist Arthur Parker. Similarly, my request for a copy of the guidebook to the Hotel Astor's American Indian Hall from the University of Virginia's Bayly Museum, which now owns the masks that were displayed there, was reviewed in relation to the Grand Council's policy. Yet during the same period at Kahnawake, where community leaders have categorically opposed the publication of photographs or information about the masks, images were to be found painted on the walls of a local tourist village and reproduced in advertisements published in the annual powwow program.

The suppression of reproduction hits most directly at the principle of freedom of inquiry and the secular system of knowledge management that are at the heart of post-Enlightenment Western academic traditions. The two positions, representing secular and religious modes of control over knowledge, were taken by two different reviewers of William Fenton's encyclopedic 1987 monograph, which was published just as the debates summarized here were becoming public and heated. Both of the reviewers, ethnohistorian Bruce Trigger and Six Nations Mohawk writer Joel Montour, were well-informed and sensitive to the complexities of the issues. Trigger praised Fenton for his success in accomplishing "the anthropological task of presenting Iroquois culture on its own terms" and offering "as complete insight as it is possible for outsiders to acquire into Iroquois beliefs and rituals and how these have survived and adapted to changing conditions."[64] Montour took the opposite view, arguing that the information, gathered decades earlier, contributed to the picture of a culture frozen in time. Where Trigger praised the book for transcending stereotypes and offering a respectful historical record useful to Onkwehonwe and outsider alike, Montour argued the need to acknowledge the shifting of meaning over time and the importance of representing "living expression and individual application."[65] Montour's objections were not based so much on his opposition to breaches of ritual secrecy – he states that he did not grow up in the Longhouse – but, rather, on the anthropologist's use of what Carlo Ginsburg calls the "evidential paradigm." "The emphasis on material culture as *sine qua non*," Montour remarked, "negates individual interpretation and style ... the reality is that we seek to understand other cultures by their material presence ... but it is still the view of outsiders looking through a window fogged by their own breath."[66] For Montour, Fenton's material culture methods and ethnohistorical perspective weakened the vitality of contemporary practices, which he wanted to privilege, while Trigger's allegiance to Western academic traditions led him to affirm the value of historical understandings and the generalizable insights into cultural process produced by anthropological work.

Disappearing Acts as Postcolonial Strategy

Anthony Grafton has remarked that a museum is a place where you put things behind glass to protect them from people, where once people had to be protected from them.[67] On one level, the motivations behind the disappearing acts performed by the Onkwehonwe and other Indigenous people can be read as efforts to protect people from certain objects whose power has been denied by the premises of secular modernity. That is, they can be read as attempts to return to earlier traditions that are not, after all, lost. In this sense Onkwehonwe goals are diametrically opposite to those of modernist and postmodernist artists who celebrate mechanical reproduction, following Walter Benjamin, as a means of destroying the art object's aura and with it a precinct of class privilege. For Onkwehonwe and other Aboriginal people, it is precisely the destruction of aura, understood as essence or power, that needs to be prevented. Onkwehonwe efforts to limit access to the *ga:goh:sah* are directed at the preservation and restoration of those ineffable qualities and inherent powers that technologies of scientific and formal exposition and analysis, as well as of mechanical reproduction, seek to render transparent. Furthermore, as a large body of work by anthropologists and art historians has clearly established, very few non-Western peoples have developed a discourse of the visual art object as autonomous and commodifiable parallel to that of the West. In most world cultures the aesthetic has traditionally been located among a range of patterned behaviours that can be kinetic, auditory, olfactory, gestural, performative, and/or visual. Visual aesthetic production, furthermore, has often been incidental to the work of the ritualist, the healer, the hunter, or the maker of clothing. The expressive and cognitive tradition related to the treatment of objects being invoked by Onkwehonwe activists is, then, holistic and spiritual, rather than specialized and secular.

When, in contrast, Onkwehonwe activists attempt to suppress the reproduction of texts and images, they are trying to find solutions for modern realities for which there can be no appeal to historical traditions. Their goal here is to terminate the long history of colonial surveillance of Onkwehonwe society and to throw off the still-lingering, inquiring gaze of the outsider. Disappearing acts are intended to disable the axis of knowledge and power that was activated during the colonial period, through academic and popular projects of representation.[68] It would be naive to think that in the early twenty-first century any people on the face of the earth can avoid the necessity of negotiating the Western "art-culture" system, as Clifford terms it, that has been inscribed by centuries of colonial rule, economic integration, and global mass communication.[69] At the same time, however, the incomplete and partial nature of the Western inscription is becoming increasingly apparent.

In 1992, when I was preparing the lecture that eventually turned into this chapter, I had the opportunity to ask Mohawk elder Ernest Benedict's advice about whether or not I should show slides of the *ga:goh:sah*. He replied that the matter was difficult and still unresolved within the Onkwehonwe community. Then he told me a story. "I heard about a carver," Benedict said, "who gave permission to some people who wanted to photograph masks, because, as the carver said, 'The masks can take care of themselves.' When the pictures were developed," the punchline went, "they came out black."[70] Benedict's story, I think, is more than an assertion of the living power of the *ga:goh:sah*. It is also a metaphor for the ultimate inadequacy of the "pictures" made by outsiders, be they ethnographic texts or formalist descriptions, to capture the reality of the masks as understood by cultural insiders.

I began this chapter by remarking on how Onkwehonwe protests usefully reveal the traditions of knowledge management that operate in the academy and the museum. In 1992 I decided not to show any slides when giving my lecture. I have now come to a different decision. Although I do not illustrate ritually active masks, I do display some of the secondary representations of the masks because of their importance to the postcolonial scholarly project. The very power and centrality of the visual in the Western tradition makes the critique of visual images a necessary part of the work that scholars need to perform in order to develop critical understandings of the histories of representation and misrepresentation that are colonialism's legacy.[71] In her book *Double Exposures* Mieke Bal has powerfully analyzed the need to perform such acts of critique with discretion, judgment, and sensitivity to framing so that we do not end up reinscribing that which we are attempting to critique.[72]

Traditional Onkwehonwe, like other Native Americans, regard the whole universe as animated by powers that must be respected. All kinds of objects – and images – can potentially share in these powers. My own attempt to separate the issue of sacred power from that of resistance to surveillance remains an example of Western analytical practice. In order to write this chapter I have had to use Fenton's book. Nor will the issue of reproduction be resolved by individual acts of intervention in the museum. As I was working on an earlier draft of this chapter, someone taped to my office door a xeroxed *New York Times* article describing an attempt by Seneca leaders to stop the sale of *ga:goh:sah* at a Sotheby's auction.[73] The article was illustrated with five clear photographic reproductions. Indigenous people will, no doubt, continue to confront us with other ways of thinking about the issue. The Saulteaux-Ojibwa artist Robert Houle did this, for example, in his 1992 installation *Mohawk Summer 1990* when he painted on one wall, in reverse lettering, the words "sovereign," "longhouse," "landclaim," and "falseface." Houle has said that this work – dissonant, oppositional, and expressive of an almost perversely inverted reality – is a metaphor "of contemporary Mohawk life." His elegant conceptual piece and punning use of language ties the false face to a fully integrated notion of Onkwehonwe social life and insists that culture cannot be divorced from larger political concerns about power and self-government. But Houle's artistic statement is made in an art gallery, suggesting, with equal urgency, the indispensability of the museum as a secular space within which the competing traditions co-present in the contemporary world can continue to be negotiated.

A Repatriation Update

A new chapter was added to the ongoing negotiations over the fate of medicine masks in museum collections in 2009 when Harvard University's Peabody Museum of Archaeology and Ethnology published a Federal Register notice repatriating ten of its Onkwehonwe masks to representatives of the Onondaga near Syracuse, New York.[74] Two are wooden *ga:goh:sah* and show signs of use, although they are not documented to a specific Onkwehonwe nation. Four other wooden masks, which have solid backs that have not been hollowed out for wear, bear labels identifying them as having been made for sale by the Iroqrafts company based on the Six Nations Reserve at Oshweken, Ontario. The remaining four are corn husk masks.

Onkwehonwe representatives had learned of the Peabody's holdings during the late 1990s when, in a pioneering move, the museum put its collections online, and in 1998 and 2002 members of the Onkwehonwe Standing Committee on Burial Rules and Regulations visited the museum to view the masks. They discussed the masks in the collection that were documented to specific Onkwehonwe tribes in the United States and could therefore be considered sacred objects according to the provisions of the Native American Graves Protection and Repatriation Act (NAGPRA). Specific care and handling requests were made, which the museum then carried out.

More recently, Onondaga representatives have taken responsibility for the care of Onkwehonwe masks not documented to specific communities, and they requested the return of the Peabody's ten undocumented masks. Consultations between the Onondaga representatives and museum staff regarding the history of commercial mask production, along with information regarding plans by Onkwehonwe people to revitalize masks originally made for commercial sale, led the museum to agree to categorize the Iroqrafts masks as "sacred objects" under NAGPRA. The notice of intent to repatriate was published in the Federal Register on 1 March 2010, which enables repatriation after a thirty-day waiting period. At this writing, the museum is waiting for the community to complete the process of return.

7

The Global Travels of a Mi'kmaq Coat

Colonial Legacies, Repatriation, and the New Cosmopolitanism

Since the late nineteenth century, one of the most important collections of Mi'kmaq and Huron-Wendat art from what are now New Brunswick and Quebec has lain largely unregarded in a large urban museum on the opposite side of the globe from its communities of origin. Consummate examples of Native North American textile and sculptural art, the clothing, textiles, wampums, and carved pipes in the collection accompanied the aspiring young Canadian writer and amateur ethnologist Samuel Douglass Smith Huyghue in 1852 when he emigrated to Australia to take up work as a government clerk in the Ballarat gold mines. Huyghue never returned to Canada, and he bequeathed his collection to the National Gallery of Victoria (now Museum Victoria) through his friend the Reverend R.E. Johns, a man with whom he shared an absorbing interest in world cultures and ethnography.[4]

Today, more than a century and a half after the collection was assembled, modern-day Mi'kmaq from the Millbrook First Nation in Nova Scotia have requested the return of the chief's outfit that forms the centrepiece of the Huyghue collection (fig. 7.1). This request invokes neither illegality nor sacredness nor the rubric of "cultural property," the criteria established during the early 1990s in Canada, Australia, and the United States for the repatriation of Indigenous artifacts. As we will see, it is highly likely that Mi'kmaq leaders from a different community in New Brunswick presented the chief's outfit to Huyghue or to a Euro-Canadian acquaintance as a component of one of the ceremonies of ritual adoption that had long constituted a key strategy of Indigenous diplomacy. Furthermore, because Huyghue was not only a collector of

In many communities, few cultural materials remain; the very word "museum" is often a reminder of what has been lost to Aboriginal people, not what has been preserved for their use.
– *Report of the Royal Commission on Aboriginal Peoples (1996)*[1]

Only after being appropriated by outsiders or by establishment (or even dissenting) insiders does cultural property disclose its field of force. Its positive existence has a dialectical relation to deprivation, and its significance cannot be clear except in the experience of alienation.
– *Elazar Barkan and Ronald Bush (2002)*[2]

I have beheld [the Indian] in each phase of his simple life, and discovered how many elements of good are implanted in the natural heart, independently of culture or creed; not that he is devoid of either, for to me he ever appeared less a *savage* than a high-souled and religious being.
– *S.D.S. Huyghue (1850)*[3]

7.1 (*also colour plate 4*)
Mi'kmaq chief's coat
(back), cloth orna-
mented with appliquéd
cloth, silk ribbon,
and bead embroidery;
collected by S.D.S.
Huyghue before 1848.
M V X 8938. Photo by R.
Start, 2003; reproduced
courtesy of Museum
Victoria, Melbourne,
Australia

artifacts but also a writer and an amateur ethnologist, his legacy includes a body of texts that can be used to investigate both his motivations and those of the Indigenous people from whom the chief's outfit and other items were acquired. These texts reveal Huyghue to have been a liberal and something of a freethinker, and his collecting was informed by a sympathetic and respectful interest in Indigenous cultures. At the same time, however, as a man of his age, he was also motivated by a preservationist impulse posited on the belief that Indigenous material and cultural traditions could not survive in the modern world. Similarly, although his reading notes and papers testify to a global breadth and a comparative analytical framework that seem strangely contemporary, his universalism and his precocious cultural relativism are inevitably coloured by an evolutionist tinge.

Both the anomalous nature of the repatriation request and the survival of these contextual materials make the Huyghue chief's outfit particularly revealing as a case study that brings into relief the grey areas and unresolved issues which trouble repatriation processes two decades after they were formally initiated by museums and governments in Canada, Australia, and the United States. In this chapter I will develop the case study in detail in order to argue that the material legacies of the past impose upon us a complex set of responsibilities to different consituencies, both living and dead. In many cases, they cannot be addressed through categorical laws or rules, however much we might desire the simplicity these promise. Rather, repatriation requires a complex balancing of sometimes competing needs, desires, and rights. On one hand, the series of human rights declarations and conventions ratified by international bodies during the past fifty years has affirmed a universal right of access to cultural property. These conventions impose a particular obligation to support the efforts of formerly colonized Indigenous peoples to recover the cultural knowledge and traditions that have been weakened or lost through the policies of directed assimilation to which they have been subjected.

Taken to its logical extreme, however, the right to cultural property has led a number of repatriation advocates to argue that all Indigenous artifacts now in museums – even those that were made specifically for sale or that are clearly documented as gifts and presentations – cannot be considered to have been voluntarily surrendered because of the coercive conditions (such as poverty and religious conversion) in which Indigenous people lived under colonial regimes.[5] According to such arguments, the letters, affidavits, and receipts now in museum archives that document commercial transactions with Indigenous intermediaries and affirm their belief that the museum offered the safest place then available for the preservation of Native heritage are simply evidence of colonial brainwashing.[6] I will argue here not only that such arguments are dangerously ahistorical but that they also ignore both the legitimate rights of the dead and the contemporary needs of other members of the complex and pluralist societies in which we all live today. Artifacts that have survived into the present because they were given, commissioned, or purchased "put down roots" in their new places. As illustrated by a recent study of the social networks formed in, around, and through the collections in Oxford's Pitt Rivers Museum, for example, once established in museums, collections come to interact with and become sedimented into other cultural heritages and human communities.[7] Not only do such museum communities have legitimate rights and interests of their own, but important social benefits can flow to the general public from access to diverse cultural heritages. Artifacts that evidence the aesthetic, social, and intellectual traditions of others offer highly effective sites for fostering the understanding and respect for diversity that is needed today, perhaps more than ever before. Because we are material beings inhabiting a material world, artifacts can uniquely serve as trans-temporal and trans-spatial witnesses to alternative modes of cross-cultural historical interaction. By testifying to both the worst and the best of historical human achievement and experience, they can expand our horizons and help us to imagine ways out of contemporary quandaries.

Closely related to the need to consider these rights and needs is our responsibility to respect the intentions of the historical actors – both Indigenous and non-Indigenous – whose transactions ensured that those legacies would come down to us. These different rights, needs, desires, and responsibilities may, of course, compete with one another. It is often easier and cleaner to apply guidelines that are categorical, comprehensive, and absolute than to weigh and balance these various factors through a nuanced case-by-case approach. Yet the Huyghue example suggests how such a careful case-specific approach might, in the end, work to the greater advantage of all the interested parties.

Repatriation since the 1990s

Before I embark on a detailed exploration of the Huyghue case, it will be helpful to summarize in a little more detail the frameworks that currently exist for the repatriation of Indigenous cultural property in the settler nation-states of Australia, Canada, and the United States. In the early 1990s both Canada and Australia established processes by which Indigenous people could request the return of certain categories of cultural property. The report of Canada's Task Force on Museums and First Peoples (1992) is cited as a source for Australia's *Previous Possessions, New Obligations: Policies for Museums in Australia and Aboriginal and Torres Strait Islander Peoples* (1993, revised in 2005), and both documents build on some of the key concepts articulated in the United States' Native American Graves Protection and Repatriation Act (NAGPRA) of 1990.[8] All three mandate museums to return items that were illegally acquired or that can be defined as "sacred" or as objects of "cultural patrimony."[9] Although their precise definitions differ in the three documents (or are left only generally defined), the three categories have been applied in remarkably similar ways. All distinguish for repatriation forms of cultural property that could not properly have been alienated by individuals because (like the contents of a church sacristy or the entailed property of a European aristocratic family) they can be considered to be collectively owned or to serve trans-generational purposes and/or they are required for continuing religious observance. In Canada the reopening of a treaty process in the early 1990s created a further channel through which communities pursuing land claims can negotiate for ethnographic collections held by provincial and federal museums alongside land, money, and resource rights.[10]

The recognition of the authority of Indigenous religious practices and concepts of property that inform these three repatriation documents testifies to a notable shift in public consciousness and emergent postcolonial power relations during the late twentieth century. In particular, they signal the rejection of the belief, widely held for more than two centuries, in the inevitable assimilation of Indigenous people and their disappearance as culturally distinct groups. Both this momentous change and the resumption of land-claims negotiations were achieved through campaigns that had been directed at local, national, and international bodies by Indigenous people and their supporters for many decades.[11] At the level of international law, these efforts have resulted in the ratification of global conventions for the protection of cultural property that are based on universal principles of human rights.[12]

A number of recent assessments have, however, revealed the slippages and the unexpected barriers that have also emerged as repatriation requests are made and protocols applied. Assessing problems that have arisen in the United States, anthropologist Michael F. Fisher and Abenaki repatriation specialist Margaret M. Bruchac note that by giving museums the power to assign poorly documented collections to specific tribes, NAGPRA can create inter-tribal conflict. They also point out the arbitrary exclusion of unrecognized Native American communities from the repatriation process, and they argue that the terms that tribes must use to make arguments for repatriation under NAGPRA can have the effect of freezing notions of "culture" and "tradition" in ways that are out of step with contemporary anthropological thinking.[13]

In both Canada and the United States, furthermore, the categories of illegality, sacrality, and cultural patrimony have been defined in ways that many Indigenous people find either restrictive in relation to their own cultural traditions or inadequate because they are not comprehensive. Ann Tweedie, who studied the efforts of the Makah of Washington state to repatriate cultural property, notes that "NAGPRA as written does not allow for individual ownership of communally significant objects."[14] Because the criterion of "collective ownership" does not fit Makah traditions, she observes, "the struggle by Makah tribal members to resolve the problem seems to be simultaneously taking two different approaches. On the one hand, they are presenting alternative readings of past practices to fit their material culture into NAGPRA definitions. On the other, they are trying to reinterpret NAGPRA definitions to incorporate their significant material culture."[15] Despite such difficulties, Indigenous claimants in Canada who have found the process of repatriation frustratingly slow and the number of returned objects disappointingly small, look enviously at the legal tools that NAGPRA has given to US tribes. Yet here again, comparisons based on speed or quantity can be misleading. In my reading of David Hurst Thomas's analysis of three highly contentious claims for control of North American Indigenous human remains, the Canadian process of negotiation is shown to be the more capable of arriving at a harmonious compromise that satisfied the largest number of goals of both the Indigenous claimants and the archaeological researchers.[16]

The largest grey areas in contemporary repatriation processes arise, however, around the many items in ethnographic collections that are neither sacred nor objects of cultural patrimony nor illegally acquired, but are no less precious and desirable to contemporary Indigenous people. Some of these items were made for sale in the commodity trade that has existed almost since the beginning of contact, while a great many others are simply undocumented, making it impossible to identify the specific community of origin that is entitled to reclaim them. Many such pieces today stand as rare examples of extraordinary artistry and skill or as evidence of technologies and artistic styles that are no longer practised. As embodiments of Indigenous knowledge, they can enable that knowledge to be recovered so that old artistic traditions can be revived or they can simply help to re-establish a community's sense of its historical and social continuity.

Both Canadian and Australian repatriation policies recommend that museums use a case-by-case approach to enable the return of or create access to items that fall outside the established categories. The processes of dialogue and negotiation that have taken place have often yielded highly innovative solutions, such as co-ownership and co-management agreements, long-term loans to cultural centres, or short-term loans to individuals of items needed for ceremonies. Other solutions have involved collaborative projects of research and restoration and have led to the recovery of lost techniques and the enrichment of artists' skills. The Canadian Museum of Civilization (CMC) and the Gwich'in Cultural Centre, for example, worked together to recover the knowledge needed to make a nineteenth-century type of man's summer outfit that is no longer in use, while the Smithsonian Museum of Natural History's collaboration with contemporary Tuscarora beadworkers resulted in the restoration of a nineteenth-century tablecloth richly ornamented with floral beadwork.[17] In both cases, the museum items concerned had probably been made for sale and have not been requested for repatriation.[18]

In the Gwich'in project, Indigenous seamstresses and elders brought essential knowledge of hide tanning and sewing, and as Gwich'in fashion designer and seamstress Karen Wright Fraser recounts, their reconnection with the historical examples in the museum recalled long-disused knowledge of locations where ochres, silver berries, and other traditional materials could be found and the technologies used in their preparation.[19] The museum made available the patterns that Judy Thompson and the late textile specialist Dorothy Burnham had recovered from their study of historical clothing in the

CMC's collection. The result was the replication, in four Gwich'in communities, of a style of nineteenth-century summer clothing worn by Dene men that had not been made for more than a century and of which no examples existed in the Northwest Territories.[20] In another project in which the CMC participated, a museum in Ireland sent to Canada a rare example of a nineteenth-century Maliseet canoe for repair by expert Maliseet craftsmen. In this case, however, the renewed contact with an ancestral artifact, renamed the "Grandfather Akwiten canoe," resulted in an impassioned and successful campaign to keep the canoe permanently in the New Brunswick Museum, close to the Maliseet community.[21]

There are good reasons why museums are guided by the principle that restitution can be made only to members of the originating community and/or descendants of the original owners or makers. Aside from the fundamental ethic involved, failure to do so can result in legal challenges from competing claimants. In one notorious case, a decision made by a curator at the University of Winnipeg's anthropology museum to return sacred materials to a group of Anishinaabe claimants unrelated to the originating community was soon shown to have contravened the expressed desires of the direct descendants of the Anishinaabe people who had decided to place their items in the museum. The incident led to a formal inquiry by the office of the auditor general of Manitoba.[22] But there are also good reasons why, even when the absence of definitive information about provenance makes a transfer of ownership risky, other kinds of solutions are needed to ensure the desired access. The Huyghue chief's outfit falls into this grey area in terms of both the circumstances in which it was probably alienated and the lack of specific provenance information. In the context of current repatriation policies, how might its fate be decided? As full an account as possible of the context in which Huyghe acquired his collection is, I would urge, the essential first step in seeking a resolution.

Huyghue the Collector and Man of Letters: Antiquarianism and Advocacy

S.D.S. Huyghue was born on Prince Edward Island in 1816, the son of a British army officer who had settled in Canada after the War of 1812.[23] We know little about his early life, but his later achievements make clear that he received a standard classical education, including instruction in drawing. By 1840, when he was twenty-four, he was launched on a literary career, and his poems, fiction, and essays on natural history were beginning to appear in local periodicals and newspapers. Most important among Huyghue's literary endeavours were his novels *Argimou: A Legend of the Micmac*, which was published in serial instalments in a New Brunswick periodical between 1841 and 1843, and *The Nomades of the West; or, Ellen Clayton*, published in England in 1850.[24] The opening pages of *Argimou* evidence Huyghue's deep sympathy with the plight of Mi'kmaq and other Aboriginal peoples of the Maritimes, who, evicted by settlers from most of their ancestral hunting lands and fisheries, were experiencing poverty, deprivation, and cultural trauma. "We are the sole and only cause of their overwhelming misery, their gradual extinction," he wrote.

> Directly, by lawless appropriation of their hunting grounds, to utter violation of every principle of justice, human or divine, which is supposed to influence the conduct of a christian [*sic*] people; indirectly, through the propagation of disease in its most harrowing forms, and the blighting introduction of that direst of all plagues, the accursed "fire-water," which metaphorical designation is most strongly illustrative of its destructive effects … Every tree that bows its proud head beneath the axe of the settler is a death-knell to their vanishing tribes. Driven back as exiles from their country, and sacrificed at the shrine of an inhuman policy, with numbers fearfully diminished, the unflinching heroism of their ancestors burns brightly still within their hearts.[25]

Huyghue turned this meditation into a direct plea for government action: "O ye Legislators and Philanthropists! Who yearly expend large means upon projects of speculative utility, if you come forward even in the last hour with generous determination to lighten in some respect the dark shadow that sullies the vaunted integrity of the national character, incalculable misery may be averted, and blessings, instead of bitter curses, your reward."[26]

Yet, more typically for his time, Huyghue was convinced of the inevitable and tragic fate that awaited Aboriginal cultural traditions and ways of life: "Alas! poor remnants of a once mighty nation – ye are like the few remaining leaves on a tree from whence their companions have withered; a little while and the blast will moan a lonely dirge through the naked boughs – the voice of nature will sigh her last farewell."[27] Like other antiquarian collectors, Huyghue undoubtedly regarded the Aboriginal curiosities he acquired as "relics," to be preserved as a record of a noble people and a simple but wholesome way of life that were doomed to disappear.

Huyghue's views on Aboriginal people were probably influenced by those of Moses Perley, the Indian commissioner for New Brunswick during these years and an activist who worked to protect reserve lands and provide health and educational services to Aboriginal people. In the early 1840s Perley conducted a census of New Brunswick Indians, assisted by Captain Henry O'Halloran. In November 1841, in recognition of their efforts, Perley and O'Halloran were adopted as chiefs of the Miramichi and Restigouche Mi'kmaq. During the eighteenth and nineteenth centuries, Aboriginal peoples throughout eastern North America used such ritual adoption as a form of strategic alliance-making to establish ties of fictive kinship with sympathetic and critically placed non-Aboriginal people. The ceremony involved the presentation of new clothes to the person being adopted, and when he or she was a person of importance, the clothing provided could be particularly splendid.

The outfit given to Captain O'Halloran is the best documented of those presented by nineteenth-century Mi'kmaq. In recent years the Canadian Museum of Civilization, which now owns the outfit, has placed it on loan in the Nova Scotia Museum in Halifax for extended periods to make it more accessible to people in its region of origin. The CMC's purchase included the scroll that O'Halloran had made to commemorate the occasion, written in English, Mi'kmaq transliteration, and Mi'kmaq "hieroglyphics" and adorned with portraits of some of the Mi'kmaq people who were present at the ceremony.[28] The chief's outfit presented to Perley in 1841 has not been identified, nor has either of the other two outfits that were probably presented when he was adopted by the Maliseet in 1839 and when Mi'kmaq leaders elevated him to the rank of "Wunjeet Sagamore" in 1842. That he did have and valued at least one Mi'kmaq chief's coat is well documented, however, for he regularly wore one when addressing Aboriginal gatherings as well as on the occasion of his presentation to Queen Victoria in later years.[29]

The O'Halloran and Huyghue outfits are among the greatest extant examples of nineteenth-century Mi'kmaq textile art – similar in style but still more elaborately ornamented than those worn by Mi'kmaq chiefs in surviving paintings and photographs.[30] Both coats are enriched with elegant silk ribbon appliqué and an array of complex, lacy beaded motifs. As with other northern Woodlands graphic art, the Mi'kmaq design vocabulary is characterized by sun images and by curvilinear motifs that have been interpreted as having significations associated with plant and animal growth, regeneration, and power.[31] In the early twentieth century Frank Speck, the leading ethnographic researcher among northeastern peoples during the first half of the twentieth century, wrote a classic essay on the "double curve motif" displayed on Mi'kmaq chief's coats and other textiles and graphic arts.[32] He also documented specific associations between this motif and political leadership among the Penobscot of Maine, who are closely related culturally and politically to the Mi'kmaq.[33]

Since the eighteenth century, Mi'kmaq people had translated their ancient graphic traditions, once executed in paint and porcupine quill embroidery on animal hides tanned to a velvet suppleness, into the new media and value system represented by European trade cloth and light-reflective glass beads, sequins, and silk ribbon.[34] These textile arts reached their greatest development during the mid-nineteenth century, and although women who excelled in these arts were known and acclaimed in their own day, it is not yet possible to attribute with certainty any but a few of the examples in museum collections to named individuals. Stephen Augustine, curator of Maritime Ethnography at the Canadian Museum of Civilization and a Mi'kmaq elder knowledgeable in oral tradition, suggests a possible attribution of the O'Halloran coat to Annie Ganace (Ginnish), wife of New Brunswick Mi'kmaq chief Peter Joseph Augustine. Another possibility is famed artist Christina Morris. Stylistically, the Huyghue outfit appears to be by a different hand, but our present state of knowledge is inadequate, and further and more rigorous comparative study is needed in order to establish such attributions more securely.[35]

In addition to carrying out his many government commissions, Moses Perley was also a man of letters who read widely and wrote books on government policy, natural history, and Indian legends.[36] In 1841 he founded a Mechanics' Institute in Saint John, the antecedent of the New Brunswick Museum, and he lectured there regularly on Indian cultures and other topics. In 1842 a Saint John newspaper reported that Huyghue, described as "a young gentleman of much taste," was assisting Perley in arranging an exhibition of Aboriginal material to be displayed in the institute.[37] It seems highly likely that one or more of the chiefs' outfits that had been presented to Perley and O'Halloran in 1839 and 1841 would have been included in the exhibition. Augustine has suggested that the Huyghue chief's outfit could very well be the one presented to Perley on the Miramichi in 1841, a suggestion made all the more plausible by Perley's probable investiture with another fine outfit when he was raised to the rank of "chief over all" during the year of the exhibition.[38] That Huyghue was very familiar with these outfits and their role in such ceremonies is clear from his description of the creation of Argimou as a chief in his eponymous novel of 1847. "The young warrior," he wrote, was "invested with a dress of costly material, heavy with minute embroidery, and leggings of scarlet cloth, beaded and fringed, were in succession delivered into [his] keeping."[39] Huyghue remained in New Brunswick for another few years, finding employment in 1843 as a member of the commission appointed to fix the boundary dividing the United States from Canada along the upper Saint John River. He would later describe his experiences of wintering over in the woods in essays published during his London sojourn.[40]

In 1846 Huyghue was near Quebec City visiting the Huron-Wendat community of Wendake, where he interviewed the wampum keeper at the Wendat council house about the history and uses of the archive of historic belts made of shell wampum beads.[41] "The venerable Indian who kept the records of the council house of the Hurons," he later wrote, showed him the "large bag containing wampum belts, some very ancient, and differing both in size, the color of the ground work, and in the figures with which they were wrought."[42] The notes he took and the examples he collected continued to occupy his mind, for his papers contain two copies of a nine-page handwritten manuscript entitled "Some Account of Wampum." The earlier of these is dated 1860, fifteen years after Huyghue left Canada, and was written while he was working at the Ballarat gold mines. This document makes evident the evolutionist intellectual framework within which he sought to make sense of his observations of Canadian Aboriginal social, political, economic, and material traditions. That he, like Garrick Mallery and other nineteenth-century students of pictography, saw wampum as a primitive form of communication and writing is implied in his comment "Possessed with few exceptions ... of no superior means of communicating their ideas at a distance, they adopted a number of signs, generally understood to express their meaning and desires."[43] Equally, Huyghue's understanding of cultural evolution as a universal process that required a comparative method of study is evident in his account of the use of strings of wampum: "In a single string, wampum was also used as a letter … conveyed by a messenger between tribes and families, and was so employed by individuals to send intelligence to distant friends and in this form it assimilated to the knotted cords of the Peruvians and early Chinese, and the rosaries and chaplets of the Buddhists, Roman Catholics and many oriental peoples."[44]

A passage in which Huyghue emphasizes his difficulty in acquiring examples of wampum attests to the "salvage" model of preservation and commemoration that informed his collecting. "The use of wampum as an ornament has now become extremely rare, and it was with great difficulty that in the year 1846, at Lorette, the Huron village near Quebec City, I procured a few specimens, the remains of necklaces, which had become in some instances, flat on the surface from the constant abrasion for a period of fifty years or more, during which they had never been removed from the neck of the wearer. The art of making the beads having been long lost, it was seldom now that they are to be met with except in the council lodges, where, as wampum belts, they are carefully preserved as the archives of the tribe."[45] Huyghue may also be providing a glimpse of the strong persuasion he may have used to induce the old wampum keeper to part with the examples in his collection. These include not only strings but also some examples of apparently early shell wampum belts, one of which is made into an ornament and the other into a European-style belt, while a third is made of the glass imitation wampum beads popular in northeastern North America during the late eighteenth century.

This passage is also significant in light of the larger question about repatriation that I have asked. Wampum is one of the categories of Aboriginal material culture that has been defined by our recent repatriation policies as collective property, and belts or strings that signified agreements could not therefore have "legally" been sold in the past by individuals. In the last three decades, important collections of wampum have been returned to Aboriginal claimants by major North American museums, including the Royal Ontario Museum and the Canadian Museum of Civilization.[46] One of the wampum items in the Huyghue collection is now fitted with a belt buckle, and while this feature does not preclude a continuing ceremonial and ritual significance, it suggests that by the mid-nineteenth century its use may have become personalized. In either case, Huyghue's rationale for collecting such historically resonant items was typical of the emergent nineteenth-century anthropological project. He took as given the need to preserve records of Indigenous societies already in the process of modernization, and his meticulous drawings and carefully recorded historical identifications of now-lost belts that were in the Huron council house in 1846 do in fact constitute valuable historical documentation[47] (fig. 7.2). Finally, Huyghue's decision to make his Canadian col-

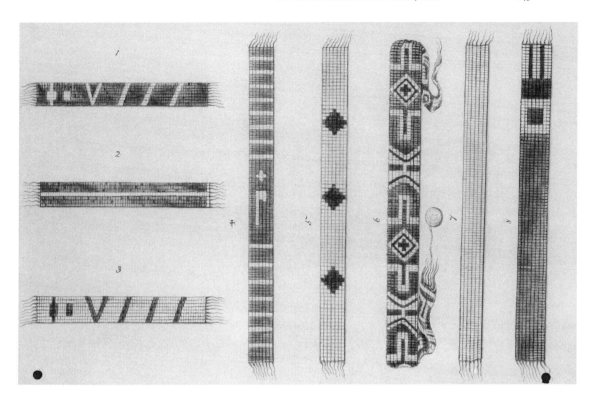

7.2   S.D.S. Huyghue,
Drawing of wampum belts
kept in the council house at
Wendake, Quebec. MV XM
1495. Reproduced courtesy
of Museum Victoria, Mel-
bourne, Australia

lections available to the people of Melbourne testifies, on the one hand, to the imperial form of nineteenth-century global consciousness in which he shared and, on the other, to his acceptance of the doctrines of universal human evolution that he thought such a gift would help to demonstrate.

In addition to the few examples of wampum that Huyghue acquired, he also bought moccasins, mitts, and leggings displaying the exquisite embroidery made by Huron-Wendat women in dyed moosehair on hide and cloth. Among his curiosities is a beaver tail mounted on a board with a moosehair embroidered handle, a unique object that may have been intended to be used as a staff or a fan (fig. 7.3). During the middle decades of the nineteenth century Wendat women made such items in quantity for sale to appreciative Euro-American curiosity buyers. Their embroideries on cloth and bark, like the porcupine-quilled bark boxes made by Mi'kmaq women and the finely carved pipes made by Mi'kmaq men, were part of a dedicated art-commodity trade marketed in speciality stores in the cities and resorts of the northeast[48] (fig. 7.4). In Huyghue's romantic imagination such items continued to figure as authentic: in his 1850 novel he has the heroic Abenaki character Saleixis light "a short pipe of dark stone, beautifully

7.3 (*above*)   Huron-Wendat beaver tail mounted on a wood form with handle made of hide embroidered with moosehair; collected by S.D.S. Huyghue, probably at Wendake, Quebec, in 1846. MV X 8916. Photo by J. Augier, 2010; reproduced courtesy of Museum Victoria, Melbourne, Australia

7.4 (*below*)   Mi'kmaq stone pipe bowl with quill-wrapped wooden stem; collected by S.D.S. Huyghue before 1848. MV X 8919. Photo by R. Start, 2007; reproduced courtesy of Museum Victoria, Melbourne, Australia

plates 1 and 2 Northern Woodlands section (*above*) and Northwest Coast installation (*below*) of *The Spirit Sings*. Photo © Glenbow Museum, Calgary

THE SPIRIT SINGS
Artistic Traditions of Canada's First Peoples

January 15 — May 1, 1988

A Glenbow Museum exhibition
Shell Canada Limited – exclusive corporate sponsor

plate 3   *The Spirit Sings* logo from the cover of the visitor brochure (detail).
Reproduced from the author's copy

plate 4 (*opposite*)   Mi'kmaq chief's coat (back), cloth ornamented with appliquéd
cloth, silk ribbon, and bead embroidery; collected by S.D.S. Huyghue before 1848.
MV X 8938. Photo by R. Start, 2003; reproduced courtesy of Museum Victoria,
Melbourne, Australia

THIS IS MY HISTORY
IN THE BEGINNING THERE WERE
NATIVE PEOPLES ACROSS THE
LAND. WHEN NEW PEOPLE CAME
THEY SHARED WITH THEM THEIR
KNOWLEDGE AND GOODS AND THE
NEW PEOPLE TOOK WHAT THEY WANTED
THEY SHARED THEIR THINGS: THEIR
VALUES THEIR RELIGION, THEIR LANGUAGES
AND THEIR LAWS THEN THEY TOOK, TOOK
TOOK AND THE NATIVE PEOPLE WERE
TAKEN FROM. THEY GAVE THEM NEW

THINGS: VALUES, RELIGION, LANGUAGE
AND LAWS. THEY GAVE THEM NEW
LAND IN FENCED OFF AREAS. THEY
GAVE THEIR CHILDREN NEW PARENTS
WHO TAUGHT THEM NEW WAYS...
BUT WHEN THEY VENTURED OUT
INTO SOCIETY THEY WERE TREATED
DIFFERENTLY THAN THE NEW PEOPLE

ETHICS INTEGRITY RESPONSIBILITY

THERE WERE DIFFERENT RULES,
LAWS, VALUES FOR NATIVE PEOPLE
THE NATIVE PEOPLES KNEW THIS WAS
WRONG BUT SINCE THEIR PHILOSOPHY IS
LIVE AND LET LIVE THEY TURNED THE
OTHER CHEEK AND FOUND SANCTUARY IN
THEIR BELIEFS AND TRADITIONS. BUT
SOME COULD NOT OVERLOOK THESE
GROSS INJUSTICES AND SOUGHT
RELIEF BY ANESTHETIZING
THEIR RAGE WITH DRUGS AND
ALCOHOL. SOME MOVED INTO CITIES
AND BECAME LOST PEOPLE. IN 1945
A CREE CHIEF ROBERT SMALLBOY AND
A BLACKFOOT NAMED NELSON SMALLBOY
DID MUCH TO CREATE A RENAISSANCE
AMONG CANADIAN NATIVE PEOPLE BUT
TRUE TO A 100 YEAR OLD PREDICTION IT
WAS THE ARTISTS: MORRISSEAU, STUMP
ODJIG, REID, MARTIN, JANVIER
WHO GAVE MY PEOPLE THEIR SPIRITS BACK

PLANNING FOR THE FUTURE

VER   NELSON RIVER   SAGUENAY RIVER   ATIKONAK RIVE   MISTASSINI   SANDY   SIMCOE   DAUPHIN   SIPIWESK   FERGUSON   TATAMAK

GOV'T ISSUE

plate 5 (*opposite*)   Joane Cardinal-Schubert, *Preservation of a Species: DECONSTRUCTIVISTS,* from the exhibition *Indigena,* 1992. Reproduced by permission of the artist's heirs; photo © Canadian Museum of Civilization

plate 6 (*above*)   Rebecca Belmore, *Mawu-che-hitoowin: A Gathering of People for Any Purpose,* installation: audio recordings, headsets, chairs, plywood, linoleum, and wood stain. In *Land, Spirit, Power: First Nations at the National Gallery,* 1992. Reproduced with the permission of the artist; photo © National Gallery of Canada, Ottawa

plate 7 (*opposite, above*)   The first room of Gerald McMaster's *Savage Graces*. Photo by Tim Wickens; reproduced with the permission of the artist and the Ottawa Art Gallery

plate 8 (*opposite, below*)   "(Im)Polite Gazes" section of Gerald McMaster's *Savage Grace*s. Photo by Tim Wickens; reproduced with the permission of the artist and the Ottawa Art Gallery

plate 9 (*above*)   Traditional Blackfoot teepee and simulated landscape in *Niitsitapiisinni: Our Way of Life*. Photo © Glenbow Museum, Calgary

plate 10   The contemporary beadwork display from *Across Borders: Beadwork in Iroquois Life*, a travelling exhibition organized collaboratively by Indigenous and non-Indigenous museums, cultural centres, and curators, 1999–2003. Photo courtesy of the McCord Museum of Canadian History, Montreal

carved," a description that matches the Mi'kmaq pipe in his collection.[49] Yet in terms of today's repatriation processes, these made-for-market curiosities constitute a category distinct from diplomatic gifts such as chiefs' outfits and communal cultural property such as wampum.

That Huyghue's antiquarian interests, collecting habits, and taste for curiosities were typical of their time is evidenced by a brief comparison with two much more famous men who were actively documenting Great Lakes Indigenous arts and cultures in exactly the same years. In 1846, the year that Huyghue visited Wendake, Henry Rowe Schoolcraft, an explorer, geologist, writer, and – like Huyghue – former member of a boundary commission, was commissioned by the US Congress to gather data for a comprehensive account of the "Indian Tribes of the United States."[50] Also during the 1840s Lewis Henry Morgan, the "father of American anthropology," was working with his Seneca collaborator Ely S. Parker to collect for the New York state cabinet and to document the customs, material culture, and beliefs of the Onkwehonwe (Hodenosaunee or Iroquois), material that would be published in his reports to the regents of the state of New York in the late 1840s and in his classic work *The League of the Iroquois* in 1851. Both of these men were, like Huyghue, amateurs: Schoolcraft was a former Indian agent who had married an Anishinaabe woman, and Morgan was a Rochester, New York, lawyer who in his youth had become interested in the local Onkwehonwe as a source for the rituals of the men's literary and philosophical association to which he belonged.[51] Both also collected and apparently valued made-for-sale curiosities.[52] In North America the 1840s were thus both a key decade in the gestation of anthropology as a discipline and one in which the activities of amateur ethnographers and collectors such as Huyghue were foundational. Although a belief in progress informed much of the writing of these men, it would not be until the publication of Darwin's *On the Origin of the Species* in 1859 and *The Descent of Man* in 1871 that a formal doctrine of evolution and a fixed hierarchy of cultures would come to inform the story of human social and intellectual development.[53]

It must have been almost immediately after Huyghue's trip to Wendake that he left Canada to pursue his literary ambitions in London. By the late 1840s he was publishing memoirs of his life among Aboriginal people in Canada in the British periodical *Bentley's Miscellany*. In 1850 Bentley also published his second Indian-themed novel, *The Nomades of the West; or, Ellen Clayton*, which contained a preface reiterating its author's support for the redress of the condition of Indians. The novel's failure to make money was probably a key factor in his decision to emigrate to Australia, where he arrived in 1852. Hired as a government clerk in the Ballarat gold mines, he witnessed the historic miners' uprising that occurred two years later. In Australian history and art Huyghue figures as the author of an eyewitness account of this event and the creator of several drawings of the Ballarat stockade. He continued to work in the Ballarat region until 1876, when he transferred to the Department of Mines in Melbourne. He retired two years later and died in 1891, having arranged through his friend the Reverend R.E. Johns to leave his Canadian collections and scholarly papers to the National Gallery of Victoria, which had been founded in 1854.

Huyghue the Intellectual: Nineteenth-Century Cultural Relativism and Contemporary Global Ideology

In addition to the Canadian artifacts and the manuscript on wampum, Huyghue's papers contain notes that testify to his wide-ranging reading. He commented on books about the Hindu religion, Rosicrucianism, the Pueblo peoples of the American Southwest, and South Asian archaeology and copied some of the illustrations. The novel *Nomades of the West* demonstrates that he had also read widely on pre-Columbian civilizations of Meso-America. The Victorian edifice of human cultural evolution that the writers and readers of these books constructed has been carefully dismantled by postcolonial critical theorists and students of the history of anthropology.[54] Tony Bennett has argued compellingly for the social utility of museums (and the academic disciplines that grew up alongside them) to governments anxious to discipline their growing urban publics to particular political ideologies and ideals of citizenship, whether in Melbourne, Australia; Saint John, New Brunswick; or London, England. "History and natural science museums, dioramas and panoramas, national and, later, international exhibitions," he writes, "served as linked sites for the development and circulation of new disciplines (history, biology, art history, anthropology) and their discursive formations (the past, evolution, aesthetics, man)."[55]

The development of art history, like that of the museum, was informed by a Eurocentric project of artistic development that sought to arrange world arts in evolutionary cultural hierarchies. Both participated in a common, universalist intellectual project. Yet while I subscribe to Bennett's analysis and to the critique of evolutionary and progressivist theories that it accomplishes, I do not think that the deconstructivist project exhausts the problem of universalism. For among Huyghue's papers, there is an unfinished essay, entitled "Christ a Myth," that suggests the extent of the cultural relativism to which his eclectic reading had led him. "It must be admitted," he wrote,

> that there is a certain internal evidence in the New Testament to justify the belief in the once existence of an exceptionally Goodman in Judea who is called Christ ... but as far as the supernatural and theological is concerned he cannot but be considered a myth by those who sufficiently investigate the question. If the story of Christ as related by the Apostles be true, how happens it that the incidents of his birth, career and death are identical with those of Bacchus and Mithra, the impersonations of the God Sun among the Romans and ancient Persians? Euripedes calls Bacchus "the son of God and intelligence of God." The

historic parallel between Bacchus and Christ is too exact to be mere coincidence.[56]

What is suggested by this passage – startling in its freethinking rejection of the normal late nineteenth-century Christian pieties – is how the opportunity to see and study the plenitude of human creativity and thought can combat xenophobic tendencies and promote openness to difference. This, too, is a point to flag in light of our contemporary battles against ethnocentricities and fundamentalisms.

I have not been able to confirm whether Huyghue's collection was exhibited publicly in the years following its donation to the National Gallery of Victoria, but it has certainly not been on regular view for many years.[57] If you visit the museum today, you will find wonderful and moving exhibits about Australian Aboriginal peoples, just as, in most Canadian museums, permanent exhibitions focus exclusively on Canadian Aboriginal peoples. The direction of museology since the late twentieth century, particularly in settler societies and outside our largest cities, has been inward-looking, focused on national and local histories. While this movement responds in the first instance to settler nationalism, it also creates a site from which Aboriginal peoples can begin to reclaim both voice and authority in the interpretation of their histories, cultures, and contemporary realities.

Yet a loss is also entailed in this course of events. The removal from sight and mind of exhibitions that make available the diversity of human creativity robs audiences of the opportunity to appreciate not only the uniqueness of what people have invented and dreamt and understood and survived and celebrated, but also the shared experiences that make translation across cultures possible. As Kwame Anthony Appiah puts it in his book *Cosmopolitanism: Ethics in a World of Strangers*, "the challenge ... is to take minds and hearts formed over the long millennia of living in local troops and equip them with ideas and institutions that will allow us to live together as the global tribe we have become."[58] Appiah also comments on efforts to legislate absolute forms of control over cultural property and the risk that the "movement to confer the gleaming, new protections of intellectual property on such traditional practices would damage, irreparably, the nature of what it seeks to protect. For protection, here, involves partition, making countless mine-and-thine distinctions. And given the inevitably mongrel, hybrid nature of living cultures, it's doubtful that such an attempt could go very far."[59]

During the past twenty years or so, globalization has steadily gained prominence in cultural studies and the humanities. As we come to understand its profound effects on cultural production in the present, we have also refocused our studies of past historical eras on earlier global circulations of people and objects, particularly as stimulated by colonialism and imperialism. Transnational approaches are promoted through curricula and conferences, while the term "world" is increasingly inserted in front of "history," "literature," and "art history" in order to move disciplines away, as the World

History Association's mission statement puts it, "from a sole emphasis on national and regional histories toward broader cross-cultural, comparative, and global approaches."[60] In his exploratory discussion of the renewed interest in world art history, James Elkins implies the need for access both to a broad range of works of art and to the scholarly literature about them. "If world art studies deserves the name," he writes, "then an art historian working in Estonia, for example, should not be able to afford to ignore what is being written by art historians in Argentina, Peru, or China: not because the Estonian art historian needs to know about Argentine modernism, Peruvian Moche pottery, or Chinese tomb reliefs, but because the Estonian art historian may need to know about the new interpretive methods and senses of history that are being tried on those very different kinds of objects."[61] The gradual expansion of curricula in university art history departments to include Asian, African, Latin American, and Indigenous arts is perhaps the most significant evidence of the pressure that is being put on older constructs by demographic diversity and what Charles Taylor calls the "politics of recognition."[62] Yet postcolonial critics such as Chika Okeke-Agulu make powerful arguments that these "new" inclusivities can also constitute neo-colonial projects whose goal is to maintain the West and its knowledge systems as the essential reference points for all other cultural traditions.[63]

In museums, especially in Europe and the United States, the move to a more global scope is continuous with colonial practices, since many of the larger institutions became universal in scope during the nineteenth century as a result of and in the service of imperial conquest and governance. As they have come under increasing pressure to decentre the West and to incorporate the perspectives of the rest, revisionist efforts focused more on the problem of perspective than on the issue of global scope. The less hierarchical modes of representation required today are also leading to a much more fluid relationship between the anthropological museum – long the home of the arts of Indigenous and non-Western peoples – and the art gallery – traditionally the preserve of the arts produced by "great civilizations." In settler societies such as Canada, Australia, and New Zealand, which have been both colonies and colonizers, museums and art galleries were, for much of the twentieth century, absorbed in projects of nationalist identity-construction. Yet today, as they come to lead the world in demographic diversity, their museums are also having to reinvent themselves as postcolonial, multicultural, and pluralist institutions. In Canada these efforts are manifested by the National Gallery's creation of a new curatorial division of Indigenous arts; by the new or expanded exhibits not only of Canadian Indigenous arts but also of Asian, African, Pacific, and Philippine arts and cultures that the Royal Ontario Museum opened during the first decade of the twenty-first century; and by the Art Gallery of Ontario's even more radical move (in relation to its previous Eurocentric mandate) to include not only Canadian Indigenous but also African and Australian Aboriginal arts in the newly expanded building it opened in 2008.

Twenty-First-Century Mi'kmaq and Nineteenth-Century Legacies

With these accounts of colonial loss, contemporary cultural renewal, and global consciousness in mind, I will now return to the repatriation request of the Mi'kmaq Millbrook First Nation. Although the chief's coat in the Huyghue collection was included in the exhibition and publications of *The Spirit Sings*, which brought it back to Calgary and Ottawa briefly in 1988, members of the Millbrook Mi'kmaq first became aware of the outfit's existence in the 1990s, possibly from its publication in *The Spirit Sings* book and catalogue volume.[64] Two community members subsequently travelled to Melbourne to see it, leaving offerings of tobacco, now carefully bagged and placed in the storage drawer.[65]

In 2007 the Millbrook First Nation opened its Glooscap Heritage Centre, the first Mi'kmaq facility built to modern museum standards. Its mission is to "communicate to the public the history of the Mi'kmaq nation in Atlantic Canada, from the Mi'kmaq perspective … combined with a commitment to authenticity and accuracy, and in so doing, making the Centre the pre-eminent Aboriginal tourism counseling and orientation facility in Atlantic Canada for the Mi'kmaq heritage."[66] Named after the great Mi'kmaq trickster and culture hero, the building is strategically located on a major highway near Truro, Nova Scotia, an hour's drive from Halifax. Its displays are introduced by an impressive video presentation, which contextualizes them within Mi'kmaq oral tradition, pre-colonial and postcolonial history, and contemporary concerns. Artfully rendered wrought iron images from the Kejimakujik petroglyphs are placed against the high white walls, while large text panels displaying historical and contemporary photographs recount the community's history and contemporary concerns. The band worked with consultant Ruth Holmes Whitehead, a leading expert on Mi'kmaq visual culture and a former curator at the Nova Scotia Museum, to create displays of historic Mi'kmaq material culture, arranged in glass cases according to standard categories such as "Early Clothing," "Early Basketry," "Quillwork and Beadwork," "Made from Wood," and "Made from Birchbark." Language is a focus of the exhibits, and all texts are in both English and Mi'kmaq.

Another case, entitled "Ceremonial Clothing," was prepared for the chief's outfit acquired by Huyghue. Mi'kmaq cultural worker Deborah Ginnish has stated that the community's request to Museum Victoria was for a loan, possibly leading to a more permanent transfer. Nova Scotia Museum curator David Christianson has affirmed that the request for the return of the outfit is based on its value for modern-day Mi'kmaq, who lack access to the artistic achievements of their forebears. "The [Australians] own it," he stated. "They own it legally, and as far as we know, they own it ethically. It's not as if something was stolen."[67] When I visited the Glooscap Cultural Centre in the summer of 2008, I was startled to see the outfit already installed in its case – until, on closer inspection, I realized that I was looking at a remarkably lifelike set of full-sized, dry-mounted colour photographic reproductions

7.5   Display case with
dry-mounted photographs
of Mi'kmaq garments from
the Huyghue collection
in the Glooscap Cultural
Centre, Truro, Nova Scotia.
Photo by Ruth Phillips, July
2008

(fig. 7.5). That these anticipate a return which the Mi'kmaq
confidently expect is made clear in the case label:

> This elaborate Mi'kmaw man's ceremonial costume was
> purchased in central Nova Scotia in the early 1840s by
> Samuel Huyghue.
>
> Fortunately the Melbourne Museum has a policy
> whereby artifacts that are not directly related to Aus-
> tralian cultures are repatriated. For repatriation to
> take place, ownership of the cultural property must be
> clearly established. In the case of the items displayed
> here, ownership has been vested in the Mi'kmaq As-
> sociation of Cultural Studies, whose Directors are all
> of the Mi'kmaq Chiefs of Nova Scotia. Now on loan to
> Millbrook First Nation from the Association, the cos-
> tume has come full circle, home to its place of creation
> after an absence of more than 150 years.
>
> The costume may have been created to enter for com-
> petition at a Nova Scotian Provincial Exhibition, or it

may have been commissioned by Samuel Huyghue. If, however, this coat was sewn for a specific person, that man may have been Louis-Benjamin Peminuit Paul, Chief at Shubenacadie from 1814 until his death in 1843.[68]

The provenance information on which the Millbrook claim is based differs, as we have seen, from the historical information that has resulted thus far from Stephen Augustine's and my research. It may well be that we will never find hard documentary evidence that can resolve the discrepancy, leaving open the question of what should be done in its absence.

At this juncture, it is helpful to remind ourselves of the role that material objects have historically played in cross-cultural communication and also that Aboriginal activism involving material culture has a long history. Like other Indigenous peoples, the Mi'kmaq have never given up their fight for justice. In 1841, the year in which the New Brunswick Mi'kmaq of Restigouche and the Miramichi adopted Moses Perley and Captain O'Halloran and presented them with their magnificent outfits, another Mi'kmaq leader from Nova Scotia, Chief Louis-Benjamin Peminuit Paul, wrote to Queen Victoria to ask her to intervene on behalf of his people. The letter employs the rhetorical convention adopted by many Woodlands peoples when petitioning a more powerful being, whether human or supernatural:

> I cannot cross the great Lake to talk to you for my Canoe is too small, and I am old and weak. I cannot look upon you for my eyes not see so far. You cannot hear my voice across the Great Waters. I therefore send this Wampum and Paper talk to tell the Queen I am in trouble … My people are in trouble. I have seen upwards of a Thousand Moons. When I was young I had plenty: now I am old, poor and sickly too. My people are poor. No Hunting Grounds – No Beaver – no Otter – no nothing. Indians poor – poor for ever. No Store – no Chest – no Clothes. All these Woods once ours. Our Fathers possessed them all. Now we cannot cut a Tree to warm our Wigwam in the Winter unless the White Man please.[69]

It was an integral part of Mi'kmaq rhetoric to petition in the voice of someone reduced to a pitiable state, just as it was proper for a leader to wear fine chief's clothing when he made such representations. Equally, the presentation of clothing in ritual adoption ceremonies recognized political alliances, as was probable in the case of the Huyghue outfit. Such garments are thus material embodiments of diplomatic exchanges that have continuing relevance for contemporary Indigenous communities.

The conditions that motivated Chief Peminuit Paul's speech were not ameliorated during the nineteenth century, and they were aggravated still further during the first half of the twentieth century by the imposition of the system of residential schooling that has come to epitomize the suffering and the losses inflicted by the government of Canada's assimilationist policies.[70] In 2008 the persistence of Aboriginal people finally succeeded in forcing the government to release the "hundreds and thousands" of dollars Huyghue had urged the government to make available to relieve the sufferings he witnessed. The money was given as part of the settlement and apology made to compensate the victims of residential schooling. The woman credited with launching this campaign was Mi'kmaq elder Nora Bernard. In January 2008, only a few months before the apology was delivered, Nora Bernard was murdered; the police charged her own grandson, a man known to be addicted to drugs, with the crime. It would be hard to find more moving evidence than that presented by this double tragedy of the ongoing suffering and want that caused Huyghue's outcry a century and a half earlier or of the continuing need for repair and reparation. Aboriginal people have identified the recovery of cultural knowledge as vital to the healing process, and as we have seen, access to traditional forms of material culture such as the Huyghue chief's outfit can play an important role in this process.[71]

The other set of concerns I outlined at the beginning of this chapter has to do with the legitimate interests of broader museum audiences. In 2007, when I had the opportunity to conduct research on Canadian Aboriginal materials in Australia, a curator in a Sydney museum discussed with me the parallel desire of Australian Aboriginal people to repatriate their ancestral property now held by foreign museums. I found this wish striking in light of a conversation I had had a few years earlier with a curator in a major Canadian art gallery. His institution had recently begun to include Canadian Indigenous arts in its permanent installations, which had previously displayed only Euro-Canadian arts, and he was also beginning to plan for the inclusion of African and Australian Indigenous arts. In this context, he was considering the purchase of a collection of historic Australian Aboriginal art. Would these be the kind of things that Australians would now want to have returned? Here again is the dilemma. Indigenous groups need access to ancestral heritage now scattered widely as a result of colonial collecting projects, many of which were conducted during a period when the ability of Indigenous peoples to continue normal cycles of artistic creativity and cultural renewal was placed under threat by official assimilationist programs. Yet just at the moment when these Indigenous communities are acquiring the resources to take action, the world is going global and universalist again.

In this context it is helpful to recall that the Huyghue outfit was probably originally made to serve a kind of ambassadorial function. Like the wampum that Chief Peminuit Paul sent to Queen Victoria, it extended the material presence of Mi'kmaq to distant places, carrying messages that could bind outsiders to Mi'kmaq interests. In this sense, respect for the intentions of the original makers would require that ways be found to allow the outfit to continue to move between cultures, stimulating people in both Australia and Canada to want to learn more about each other's historical experience and contemporary concerns and providing a site for dialogue. Hidden away in its

Melbourne storeroom, it has not been able to perform this function, just as the refocusing of museums in Canada on exclusively national concerns has deprived Canadians of opportunities to learn about Australia and other parts of the world. The spotlight that has been shone on the outfit as a result of the Mi'kmaq repatriation request thus provides an opportunity to renew cross-cultural travel, not only for items of material culture but also for the living representatives of those cultures. An open ticket will thus be a better solution than a one-way return, if it can provide the occasion for the resumption of cultural exchange.

The final set of considerations I have urged involves our responsibility to honour the intentions of collectors and donors in earlier periods, whether Indigenous or non-Indigenous. In the case of Huyghue's legacy this is probably the easiest issue to resolve, for the evidence of his writing leaves little doubt that if he were alive today, he would be gladdened by the knowledge that Mi'kmaq culture and identity have not disappeared as predicted, and he would want his chief's outfit to support contemporary Mi'kmaq projects of cultural recovery.

Taken together, then, the weight of these different considerations tends toward a return of the outfit to Canada, but not to a permanent transfer of ownership. It is likely that Museum Victoria will make a long-term loan. Although such a resolution would not satisfy the kinds of categorical claims for repatriation made on the basis of absolute doctrines of human rights, it would address a strong moral obligation and avoid the possibility of a return to the wrong community of origin. It would also hold open the possibility that the outfit can continue to travel, providing people in both Canada and Australia with the opportunity to come to know the Mi'kmaq through their creative achievements.

At the heart of this chapter is the question of whether we can pursue cosmopolitan values and comparative projects of study at the same time as we respond to the postcolonial demands of Indigenous and other colonized peoples. As John Merryman has written, the rights-based arguments for comprehensive repatriation are "carried on at a level of abstraction and generality that washes over important factual and logical distinctions." As he also remarks, "no thoughtful person would seriously argue that everything should be returned or that everything should be retained, but there is little agreement on the criteria for deciding whether a particular object ... should be returned or kept or whether some other disposition of the object is desirable."[72] In comparison with the comprehensive-claim approach, the case-by-case method can accommodate historical perspectives as well as contemporary ethics and needs. Yet, as a number of recent essays make clear, it is important to remain attentive to the ways in which both arguments grounded in specific historical contexts and the revived ethos of cosmopolitanism with which they are often paired can serve as neo-imperial attempts to defend the current holdings of museums.[73] In this context, the example of the Huyghue collection usefully complicates the politics of repatriation by illustrating the layered historical interactions that often lie beneath the diasporic travels of cultural property. It illuminates the difference between nineteenth-century universalism and contemporary global consciousness and perhaps also reminds us that many of the "new" thoughts we are thinking today have also been thought by earlier generations.

As I was completing this chapter, an email arrived from a staff member at the Glooscap Cultural Centre informing me that Museum Victoria had agreed to a loan and that the coat acquired by S.D.S. Huyghue would return to the lands of the Mi'kmaq for the first time in more than 150 years. Although the timing of the loan has not yet been resolved, the dry-mounted images will be replaced, at least for a time.

PART THREE   WORKING IT OUT

INTRODUCTION TO PART THREE

Indigenizing Exhibitions:
Experiments and Practices

Critical writing on museums during the past two decades has produced a widely accepted understanding of the ways in which nation-states have historically used these institutions to educate their publics to desired forms of social behaviour and citizenship. The compelling arguments for the instrumentality of the museum in producing citizens for modern democracies made by Tony Bennett, Carol Duncan, and others are cited repeatedly in this volume. The chapters in this section explore what could be considered a corollary argument that has developed out of the late twentieth-century political contestations and disciplinary reflexivity discussed in the previous two sections. If museums, as educational institutions that embody and inscribe official ideologies, are key examples of what Louis Althusser has termed ideological state apparatuses (ISAs), then, logically, changes in state ideology will be reflected in their practices, and all the more so when these changes have been officially mandated. In Canada such shifts have been announced both by the passage of the federal Act for the Preservation and Enhancement of Multiculturalism in Canada in 1985 and by the report of the Task Force on Museums and First Peoples in 1992, as well as by the numerous federal, provincial, and local policies and programs designed to implement them.

Althusser also theorizes a tight relationship between ideology and practice. "An ideology always exists in an apparatus, and its practice, or practices," he states. "This existence is material."[1] We can therefore expect to see ideological changes manifest themselves through the emergence of new ways of doing museum work. The case studies in this section describe the new collaborative practices explored and devised in Canadian museums during the decade following the ratification of the task force report in 1992 in order to implement the partnership model it recommended. I first drafted these texts between 1992 and 2005, and they therefore testify to the speed with which the new forms of museum work gained widespread acceptance during the decade or so that followed that report's ratification by the Canadian Museums Association and the Assembly of First Nations. Collaborative methods have not only come to characterize Canadian museology but, as noted in the introduction to this book, have also had important impacts on international practices.

Inevitably, however, the question of the broader impact of socially activist museum practices arises. How do they map onto the wider social and political world outside the museum? One view, articulated in relation to the official multicultural policies that have been allied with Indigenous reforms of museums, is that these policies have constituted a strategy for the containment of difference, rather than effectively altering Canada's traditionally Eurocentric cultural and political dominance.[2] For these critics, multiculturalism reinscribes and continues to essentialize identity, and it thus works to ghettoize and marginalize diversity. Other critics have characterized the power-sharing partnership model recommended by the task force report as a cosmetic cover-up that distracts attention from the underlying structures of power and capital, which remain undisturbed. Robyn Gillam, for example, describes the task force report as "cultural tokenism" that "looks convincing enough to the public to excite charges of partisanship and political correctness, ensuring that groups such as Natives don't get too much sympathy, particularly in times of shrinking economies and cutbacks in social spending."[3]

The weight of the critical museological literature, however, has tended to regard collaborative models of museum work as examples of the ways in which museums can serve not just as sites of official ideological inscription but also of contestation. In Althusser's formulation, "The Ideological State Apparatuses may be not only the stake, but also the site of class struggle, and often of bitter forms of class struggle. The class (or class alliance) in power cannot lay down the law in the ISAs as easily as it can in the (repressive) State apparatus, not only because the former ruling classes are able to retain strong positions there for a long time, but also because the resistance of the exploited classes is able to find means and occasions to express itself there, either by the utilization of their contradictions or by conquering combat positions in them in struggle."[4] Such a perspective is reflected in the comment of British critical museologist Eilean Hooper-Greenhill, for example, when she writes that "visual culture within the museum is a technology of power. This power can be used to further democratic possibilities, or it can be used to uphold exclusionary values."[5]

I subscribe to this belief in the positive potential of museums to play activist social roles that, over time, can exert a transformative force on the deeper socio-political structures of wider communities. As I have written elsewhere, during the past two decades museums have many times served as spaces for the *rehearsal* of modes of social action not yet possible in wider political arenas, and they have thus prepared the ground for effective lobbying of schools, governments, cultural funding agencies, and even courts of law.[6] Work with museums, for example, has helped to strengthen the capacity of communities to fight larger battles by providing a "safe" space in which factionalized groups can come together, where they can identify common goals, collaborate on a common project, forge bonds based on mutual respect and trust, and form effective networks. Museums can also help to strengthen communities by supporting the work of recovering traditions of expressive culture that have been silenced by official policies of assimilationism and marginalization. It is important to stress, however, that such outcomes are a potential, rather than a given, of collaborative work: Althusser, as we saw, wrote that institutions such as museums "*may* be not only the stake, but also the site of class struggle" (emphasis added).

For museum staff, true collaborations are also transformative. Curator Carol Mayer writes of the tremendous effort they require of all concerned. After the close of the 2001–2 exhibition *The Spirit of Islam: Experiencing Islam through Calligraphy*, she describes experiencing the "need to recover, to rediscover a sense of normality, to move back into a more comfortable and predictable space – only to discover that the space was no longer the same. By working on *The Spirit of Islam*, we had changed our trajectory and could no longer do things in the ways that we had."[7] Most museum professionals can point to both failures and successes of collaborative museology. My own faith in the potential of these new practices is based on my experiences both as an observer and as a participant in collaborative projects in recent years. I will here give just two brief examples.

The exhibition of which Mayer wrote, *The Spirit of Islam*, was held at the University of British Columbia's Museum of Anthropology during my term as director there. (I also discuss it further in the last section of chapter 11.) It adapted the collaborative model the museum had developed through its pioneering collaborative work with First Nations communities to a new context of global diasporic community life. The exhibition process brought together representatives of the major Islamic sects and diasporic communities in the Lower Mainland area of British Columbia, groups who had never before come together to work on a common project.[8] It created a basis of mutual understanding upon which they have since been able to build.[9] Arguably, the demands of the collaborative process itself were a factor in forging among these communities a sense of common purpose, for as curator Mayer has explained, she did not take the normal "singular" curatorial role but was "guided by a collaborative process

wherein the community would be the 'curator.'"[10] Following the bombing of the World Trade Center a month before the exhibition was scheduled to open, it also acquired urgency and relevance that could not have been predicted. In Vancouver, as in other North American cities, the Muslim population became vulnerable to various kinds of harassment, and the museum also worried about possible threats to the security of its visitors, the building, and the borrowed art. As one of the community representatives on the advisory committee memorably and movingly put it at the meeting called to decide if the exhibit should open as planned, "God put it in our minds to organize this exhibition, for if we hadn't had it ready we would have had to begin organizing it now."

The value of community consultation and collaboration in identifying topics that are timely not only in terms of social integration and cohesion but also in terms of healing and cultural regeneration was also brought home to me by an exhibition I worked on as a guest curator in the mid-1990s, *Across Borders: Beadwork in Iroquois Life*.[11] This exhibit was organized by the McCord Museum of Canadian History in Montreal in collaboration with the Castellani Museum of Niagara University near Buffalo, New York, the Kanien'kehaka Raotitiohkwa Cultural Centre at Kahnawake, Quebec, and the Tuscarora Nation near Buffalo.[12] It was begun in the years following the Oka crisis and the related confrontation with Kahnawake Mohawk activists, who had barricaded one of Montreal's key bridges in support of the Oka protestors. A few years earlier, Kahnawake Mohawk had also brought the lawsuit against the Glenbow Museum for the exhibit of Onkewhonwe medicine masks deemed sacred and inappropriate for display (see chapter 6). The collaborative structure made it possible to re-present beadwork, an art form that had been devalued as inauthentic and commercial for much of the twentieth century, from the perspectives of community members and in light of new academic research on its stylistic sources, intercultural contexts of production and sale, and historical development. It also made possible a museological presence for Onkwehonwe through displays of material culture that do not transgress boundaries of the sacred and that emphasize Onkwehonwe entrepreneurial and artistic agency within modernity. As well, it has supported the continuing production of beadwork by providing new contexts for its aesthetic and cultural appreciation.

What is evident from these two examples and from the other collaborative projects discussed in the following chapters is their experimental nature. In 1992 Canadian museologists and community partners were given only general recommendations and principles in the task force report. The practices had to be invented, and as these and other case studies suggest, a multitude of specific solutions have been introduced, often emanating as much from partner communities and individual artists as from museum professionals. In their edited volume *Exhibition Experiments*, Sharon Macdonald and Paul Basu urge that we think about museums not only through the

dichotomy of the temple and the forum suggested over three decades earlier by Duncan Cameron but also as a form of experimental laboratory for trying out new arrangements of the social.[13] Such museum experiments, they write, "must be understood as sites of cultural mediation; and mediation, furthermore, must be understood as a process that partly constructs that which it mediates."[14] Such experimentalism, they further argue, is "intended to be troubling. Experimentalism is not just a matter of style or novel forms of presentation. Rather, it is a risky process of assembling people and things with the intention of producing differences that make a difference. In their production of something new, experiments seek to unsettle accepted knowledge or the status quo."[15]

The first two short chapters in this third section of *Museum Pieces* describe early experiments in collaboration and intervention involving contemporary Indigenous artists as curators or exhibitors. Two of these exhibitions – *Indigena* and *Land, Spirit, Power* – were mounted during the year of the Columbus quincentennial, and the third – *Savage Graces*, organized by artist-curator Gerald McMaster and the late Rosa Ho – was mounted and toured during the next two years. The following two chapters discuss collaborative experiments staged by anthropology museums. Chapter 10 reviews *Threads of the Land*, a project organized by curators in the ethnology division of the Canadian Museum of Civilization and Inuit, Dene, and Nlaka'pamux makers of clothing. I originally wrote chapter 11, "Toward a Dialogic Paradigm: Developing New Models

of Collaborative Curatorial Practice," as
an introduction to a group of case studies
on collaboratively organized exhibitions
in Laura Peers and Alison K. Brown's important 2003 edited volume, *Museums and
Source Communities*. It offers a typology
of the spectrum of collaborative models
that evolved during the first decade of experimentation. I refer readers to Peers and
Brown's collection for more detailed discussions of the case studies to which I refer.
Chapter 12, the last and most recent piece in
this section, compares the two largest and
most ambitious museological projects that
have been mounted by national museums
in the United States and Canada in recent
years: the First Peoples Hall of the Canadian
Museum of Civilization and the Smithsonian Institution's National Museum of the
American Indian. As I argue, the two have
in common a number of themes that testify
to a shared paradigmatic shift, but they also
differ in ways that, in my view, can be traced
to the different identity politics and histories
of the two countries.

8

Making Space

First Nations Artists, the National Museums,
and the Columbus Quincentennial (1992)

Making space is a key image in cultural politics today.* We
map with metaphor a cultural landscape that has discern-
ible topographical features – a centre, margins, a mainstream
running through it. Charting a way through this terrain is
by definition difficult for artists from marginalized communities. How to enter the mainstream while simultaneously
swimming against its current? How to negotiate the gravita-
tional pull of the centre while maintaining the separateness
needed to define, preserve, and celebrate distinctive identities
that have been put at risk?

For those comfortably occupying the mainstream, making
space means moving over, getting out of the way, decentring.
During recent months, two remarkable exhibitions in Ottawa
brought the tensions of margin and centre squarely into the
country's most official spaces for artistic and cultural display:
the Canadian Museum of Civilization and the National Gallery of Canada. Both shows have begun national tours. And
both demonstrate that even large, established, influential institutions can achieve major cultural repositionings.

The first to open was *Indigena: Contemporary Native Perspectives on Five Hundred Years*, organized for the Canadian
Museum of Civilization by its curator of Contemporary Indian Art, Gerald McMaster, and his associate Lee-Ann Martin.[1] The show brings together paintings, sculptures, and installations, many of them commissioned, that address the
meaning for Indigenous peoples of the five hundred years
since Columbus's arrival. An important landmark in Canadian museum history, the show is the first to be mounted
by a major institution in which all the key participants – the

* This review was first
published in the *Canadian
Forum* 71, no. 816 (January/
February 1993): 18–22. It
appears here with only minor
changes.

curators, artists, and writers who contributed essays and poems to the catalogue – are members of the Aboriginal community. *Indigena*'s openly political stance diverges sharply from the broad, "objective" academic surveys usually favoured by large museums.

The second exhibition, *Land, Spirit, Power: First Nations at the National Gallery of Canada*, is less tied to the specific historical moment.[2] It was conceived and organized by Diana Nemiroff, the gallery's curator of Contemporary Canadian Art, in collaboration with Saulteaux artist and curator Robert Houle and anthropologist and art critic Charlotte Townsend-Gault. In one sense, the exhibition is a celebratory response to the sustained lobbying of the Society of Canadian Artists of Native Ancestry for inclusion in the gallery's permanent collections and exhibition spaces. But in a larger sense, *Land, Spirit, Power* is simply a show whose time has come. It presents a broad range of contemporary visual art from Canada and the United States made by an artistic community that has achieved maturity. The curators have selected and arranged the works with sensitivity in a sequence revealing interwoven themes that are both aesthetic and political.

Despite the commonalities of style and conceptual approach among the artists in the two shows (three artists – Carl Beam, Lawrence Paul Yuxweluptun, and Domingo Cisneros – are included in both), the exhibitions complement, rather than parallel, each other. Last fall, during the two months that they faced each other across the Ottawa River, viewers could see contrasts between the shows as marked as the contrasting architecture of their sponsoring institutions. For several years, both the museum and the gallery have been collecting and displaying contemporary Native art, an overlap that reflects its ambiguous place in our cultural landscape. In these recent installations, however, they have been true to their complementary mandates. *Indigena* mounts a powerful lesson about history and cultural survival. *Land, Spirit, Power*, while not eschewing the political, is first of all about art.

A Change of Venues

At the same time, the two shows also invert the conventional practices of ethnographic museums and art galleries. This time it is the gallery that shows "artifacts" among the easel paintings and sculptures – masks and dance blankets made not only for display but also to be worn in important ceremonials. The museum, however, includes only works that fit Western "fine art'" genres. This is a refreshing reversal; it clears the air of the endless and often circular critiques of art and artifact (both Western concepts arbitrarily imposed on the aesthetic products of non-Western peoples) and opens the way for an appreciation of the multiplicity of purposes for which the aesthetic can be used – for ritual, for persuasion, for cultural representation, for pleasure.

The contemporary art gallery at the Canadian Museum of Civilization is a relatively small space, subdivided into rectangular rooms. The works in *Indigena* were closely hung and installed, and the resulting atmosphere was dense, sombre, and confining. *Land, Spirit, Power* was mounted in the National Gallery's large, airy temporary exhibition rooms, with their beautiful views of Parliament Hill and the Ottawa River, and the show had a spacious and open feeling. In a seminar I taught this fall on the two shows, there was much debate about whether the marked tonal contrast between the two exhibitions resulted from the very different spaces available to their curators. Although the architectural givens of the installations undoubtedly influenced their messages, the contrast must ultimately be attributed to the very different agendas of the exhibitions.

Indigena is, by intent, a profoundly didactic exhibition. It confronts the visitor with the retelling of history from a Native point of view. So radical and revisionist a critique has rarely found expression in national institutions dedicated, almost by definition, to reinforcing an official and consensual federalist politics. The last such full-scale, taxpayer-supported Native initiative, it is interesting to note, took place a full twenty-five years ago, in the Indians of Canada Pavilion at Expo 67.

In *Land, Spirit, Power*, the National Gallery also took up the challenge of accommodating pluralism, and in this sense its project is no less radical. It is a generous and inclusive exhibition; in addition to the "traditional" pieces, it presents some works that do not fit the unforgiving criteria of contemporary connoisseurship, works in which message is privileged over medium, and in which authenticity is located as much in sincerity and urgency as in form and technique. *Land, Spirit, Power* relies, however, on the rhetoric not of confrontation but of seduction. It first beckons to the visitor with works that display relatively familiar kinds of formal beauty: the pure, seemingly minimalist shapes of Faye HeavyShield's sculptures and the elegant formline designs of Robert Davidson's mask and Dorothy Grant's textile works. Only afterwards is the visitor brought up against the compressed pain and threat contained in Domingo Cisneros's juxtapositions of shamanistic imagery with the mass-produced detritus of confinement and destruction. The history that is implicit in Cisneros's work is made explicit in other, more text-based works, such as Hachivi Edgar Heap-of-Birds' paintings and Jimmie Durham's installation of poetry and sculpture.

The chorus of voices in *Land, Spirit, Power* sounds many different notes. There is the punning, ironic wit of James Luna's supermarket of racial harmony, a consumer-oriented multiculturalism structured by ancient symmetries and numerologies. There are also many images of the land, ranging from the lyrical grace of Truman Lowe's majestic monumental sculpture *Ottawa* to the mystical Turneresque beauty of James Lavadour's landscape paintings, the more densely featured symbologies of Kay Walkingstick's images, and the surrealist eco-scapes of Lawrence Paul Yuxweluptun. Yuxweluptun's paintings, derived in equal parts from Salvador Dali and from Indigenous Northwest Coast graphic traditions, embody a fierce environmental and cultural politics that is given an alternative expression in his highly popular virtual-reality installation.

The show ends almost where it began, with a group of "traditional" works by Tlingit artist Dempsey Bob. Like Davidson's and Grant's pieces, these carvings push the formal traditions of Indigenous Northwest Coast art into the present moment. The last piece is one of Bob's carved relief panels. Its black-painted image of a whale is a reference to the *Exxon Valdez* disaster. Leaving the exhibition, the visitor sees this image, juxtaposed with her own, in a mirror placed at right angles to the panel. With this master stroke, we see that the path through the exhibition has been a spiral, not a circle; we are *not* at the same place where we began. *Land, Spirit, Power* reveals the two imperatives to which contemporary Native artists are responding: the demand of our moment in history for cultural and political intervention and the eternal lure of aesthetic play.

History Retold

Indigena illuminates the nature of this historical moment. It confronts us with reflections on the past five hundred years ranging from the first moments of Native-European contact to the present. By his acts of regilding and framing the lithic spheres found in the graves of the Taino Indians first contacted by Columbus – objects whose meaning is not known – Lance Belanger constructs a meditation on the immense loss the world has suffered through the extinction of peoples and their knowledge. The companion piece to this work, together with pieces in the show by Bob Boyer, Luke Simon, and others, reworks the form of the crucifix: Belanger covers his with the false coin of Spanish gold; Boyer's crosses bleed into the ground of the trade blankets on which he paints; and Simon's cross, surmounted by a skull, merges with the phallic form of the Peace Tower.

From such works as these, it is easy to see why *Indigena* upset many people, including some strong supporters of Aboriginal empowerment in the museum community. The exhibition is permeated with the signs and symbols of death; yet it is hard to see how it could have been otherwise. Annihilation, biological and cultural, *is*, irrefutably, the primary legacy to Aboriginal people of the arrival of Europeans in the Americas. This is the history lesson that has not been taught in our institutions, and the long silence could not have been broken without anger, lamentation, and mourning.

Survival, the refusal of death, is also an insistent theme in *Indigena*. In Jane Ash Poitras's signature painting *Shamans Never Die V: Indigena*, the artist actively resists the idea of extinction. She inscribes petroglyph faces, medicine wheels, and cosmic crosses over the photographs and newspaper clippings that document past and present tragedies. Poitras's layerings are rich and deep. The collage elements and the chalky markings, drawn in a graphic style that is at once graffito, petroglyph, and child's drawing, appear against a screen of memory that is also a blackboard. By an act of artistic will, Poitras reverses history: for the blackboard is the emblem of a repressive educational system that tried to overwrite aboriginal languages and belief systems with Western credos and ways of knowing.

Works from Carl Beam's *Burying the Ruler* series (one of which is also in the gallery show) engage the same theme, but they seem to argue the possibility that an equilibrium can yet be achieved between these two competing systems of understanding. Beam's works possess a reductive elegance that is the result of a decade's worth of artistic investigation. The ruler is his symbol of Western scientific knowledge; in the self-portrait that occupies the central panel of his triptych, he holds a ruler tight against his body. The image is the analogue of the adjacent abstract panel in which a triangle, emblem of mathematical rationalism, is placed in balanced tension with a feathered circle that represents Aboriginal spiritual empowerment. The third panel, in which Beam partially obscures the ruler with a wash of paint, is a declaration of the power of art itself. The uncompromising contemporaneity of his blue-jeaned self-portrait represents another theme that runs through the show: the deconstruction of romanticized stereotypes of Indianness. The everyday banality that is all too often the mask of the tragic, especially in Native communities, is evoked by Jim Logan's pop-art snapshots of a snowbound northern community of television-watching, hockey-playing – and alcohol-ravaged – Aboriginal people. The loss of identity that is the very essence of the banal is also signalled by Edward Poitras's enigmatic *The Big Picture*. The large cibachrome photograph of the multiracial patrons of Poitras's favourite Regina café is a companion piece, in its way, to James Luna's photographic works in *Land, Spirit, Power*.

A Study in Contrasts

Successful exhibitions cause us to read works in the light of their framing contexts. The context of *Indigena* renders ominous the subtle ironies of Edward Poitras's work, while James Luna's equally serious and ironic images take on a lightness and playfulness within the context of *Land, Spirit, Power*. The contrasting intentions and atmospheres of the two shows are most clearly revealed, however, in the two major works – both of them large and complex installations around which each exhibition revolves, physically and, I would argue, conceptually. These are Joane Cardinal-Schubert's *Preservation of a Species:* DECONSTRUCTIVISTS *(This is the House that Joe built)* in *Indigena* (fig. 8.1) and Rebecca Belmore's *Mawu-che-hitoowin: A Gathering of People for Any Purpose* in *Land, Spirit, Power* (fig. 8.2). DECONSTRUCTIVISTS is a summary work that brings together images Cardinal-Schubert has been working with for many years. Landscapes remembered from childhood, the haunting suicide of an Aboriginal boy, ancient prairie petroglyphs, and family photographs line the walls. An altar to lost souls and a peep show that engages the visitor in a process of racist visualization furnish the room; it is peopled by a fenced-in reserve inhabited by kerchiefed stick figures recalling

8.1 (*above and colour plate 5*)   Joane Cardinal-Schubert, *Preservation of a Species: DECONSTRUCTIVISTS*, from the exhibition *Indigena*, 1992. Reproduced by permission of the artist's heirs; photo © Canadian Museum of Civilization

8.2 (*below and colour plate 6*)   Rebecca Belmore, *Mawu-che-hitoowin: A Gathering of People for Any Purpose*, installation: audio recordings, headsets, chairs, plywood, linoleum, and wood stain. In *Land, Spirit, Power: First Nations at the National Gallery*, 1992. Reproduced with the permission of the artist; photo © National Gallery of Canada, Ottawa

both sacred offerings and rural poverty. The black-painted walls close in on the visitor; they are densely scrawled over with text, a whole history book that lectures an audience constructed by the artist as cultural other.

Beside this noisy, imagistic profusion, Belmore's work looks very different. It is spare, quiet, and minimalist. On a floor painted with flowers that suggest both old linoleum and the flitting shadows on a forest floor, Belmore has arranged a circle of chairs taken from her own kitchen and the living spaces of the women closest to her. The work issues a tacit invitation to sit down, to put on the earphones dangling over each chair back, and to listen to the voices of the artists' community talking about the lives they have lived as Aboriginal women in Canada, their struggles, their joys, and the sources of their strength. The invitation is accepted; on many days at the gallery people waited patiently for a free chair so that they could join this circle, glancing at each other, smiling briefly.

Both Cardinal-Schubert's and Belmore's works are at once broadly conceived and intensely personal. Both speak of stereotyping, racism, and the toll paid by the victims of these evils. Both are, furthermore, interactive installations and rely on words as much as on visual images. But here lies the difference. Cardinal-Schubert wants to destroy the equilibrium of her viewers, to make us uncomfortable. She addresses us through our own medium, the written word, and turns our modernist strategies of Dadaist subversion and our post-structuralist arsenal back against us. There is nothing hidden about Cardinal-Schubert's approach. Near her Duchampian peep show, the artist has written: "It is uncomfortable to peek through the little holes of this site. You miss some of the picture. What's more, it is an uncomfortable and unsettling experience. Good! Now you know how I have felt for most of my life." Belmore, in contrast, uses the testimony of human voices, of the oral tradition, of common discourse. She welcomes us into the circle of the Aboriginal community and exploits traditional Aboriginal tactics for reaching understanding: listening to elders, talking in council. Another tricksterish reversal of convention has occurred. Make space for Native artists and what do you get? Deconstruction in the museum and ethnography in the gallery.

The two shows are not, however, in opposition to each other. Anger must precede reconciliation, and there can be no healing without the acknowledgment of injury. These two exhibitions illustrate that art can be both sword and balm. As Jimmie Durham writes in his contribution to *Land, Spirit, Power*, "If we do not let our memories fail us / The dead can sing and be with us. / They want us to remember them, / And they can make festivals in our struggles." In *Indigena* the dead are mourned with an angry grief too long pent up, too long denied the dignity of public commemoration. In *Land, Spirit, Power* they are celebrated at the same time as their pain is remembered. Both kinds of artistic – and curatorial – acts are necessary in this moment.

9

Cancelling White Noise

Gerald McMaster's *Savage Graces* (1994)

Deconstruction and Risk

In 1994 the *New York Times* carried an article about the booming market in African-American popular kitsch.* Over half the buyers, it reported, were African Americans who bought these mammy dolls, Aunt Jemima salt shakers, and little black jockey figures. They did so for several quite different reasons.[1] Some acquired them in order to destroy them, others put them on display as reminders of a history of racism that must never be forgotten, while still others confessed to buying them because they evoked feelings of nostalgia. These three reactions, it seems to me, neatly capture the range of responses stimulated by recent museum exhibitions that re-assemble the visual detritus of racial stereotyping.

Public exhibitions, of course, carry risks not incurred by private collectors. The automatic expectation of most people upon entering the space of the museum exhibition is that they will be presented with authentic objects and authoritative truths, and the presentation of racist images in order to sub-vert them can cause confusion. This danger was illustrated by the clamorous boycott, protests, and accusations of racism that engulfed the Royal Ontario Museum's *Into the Heart of Africa* in 1989, despite the exhibition's explicitly anti-colonial text panels and object labels.[2] As critics argued, the use of irony in those texts proved too weak a weapon to undercut the power of the material artifacts of colonial-era racism fea-tured in the exhibition.[3]

Norman Bryson has drawn on semiotic theory to explicate the representational mechanisms that are at work in such

* This is a slightly expanded version of a paper presented on 3 February 1994 at a roundtable discussion held at the Ottawa Art Gallery during its showing of *Savage Graces*. I have updated references only in cases where a relevant publication appeared during the run of the exhibition.

visual systems. He points in particular to Roland Barthes's theorization of the pleasure that viewers take from the recognition of signs that are already known: "The pleasures of viewing will accordingly be those of repetition; the image will not interrupt; or break with the comfortable familiarity of the already-known; it will belong to the same kind of vague, urbane, disengaged interest that is reserved for people, performances, clothes, books one finds 'up to standard' … it will quote, consolingly, the familiar spatial and temporal order of the world."[4] Bryson also argues, however, that the artist's labour has the potential to interrupt the closed semiotic system through the transformative power of "aesthetic disruption": "We might speak of the *other* space of the image where the principle of repetition is unsettled, the homogeneity of the viewing subject dissolved in 'the collision of signifiers cancelling one another out'; and we might propose, like Barthes's *Leçon*, a mode of painting that not only repeats, but turns, and overturns, the discourses, fixing and privileging none of them."[5]

Gerald McMaster's one-man exhibition *Savage Graces* focuses on stereotypes of Indianness whose history is as old as European contact. In their capacity to evoke the romanticism, nostalgia, and desire not only of the settler viewer but also, on occasion, of the Indigenous person herself, these images of noble savages, Indian warriors, and princesses must surely be among the most intransigent and resistant of all colonial image systems. Indian stereotypes have come to pervade international high art and popular culture at all levels and in virtually all genres. Furthermore, because they are systematically inscribed through childhood activities ranging from the recreational to the educational – from toys and games to summer camps, holiday resorts, television shows, movies, novels, and school textbooks – they are also intimately associated with feelings of pleasure and nostalgia. In an era when the African-American kitsch mentioned earlier could not easily be publicly exhibited, we need look no further than the long-lived and stubborn refusal of the Washington Redskins, the Atlanta Braves, and the University of Illinois "fighting Illini" to abandon their names, war cries, and half-time warrior-chief performances for evidence of the extraordinarily resistant nature of Indian stereotypes.

In its deconstructive intent, *Savage Graces* shares in the broader postcolonial and deconstructive project represented by a number of other roughly contemporary Canadian and American exhibitions, including not only *Into the Heart of Africa* (1989) but also the Center for African Art's *Art/Artifact: African Art in Anthropology Collections* (1988) and Fred Wilson's *Mining the Museum* (1992–93).[6] In its specific subject matter *Savage Graces* is closest to the Woodland Cultural Centre Museum's 1988 exhibition *Fluffs and Feathers: An Exhibit on the Symbols of Indianness,* whose showing at the Canadian Museum of Civilization overlapped the OAG showing of *Savage Graces*, providing a historical and ethnographic analogue to McMaster's project of "aesthetic disruption." As we now know, the success of such exhibitions is not guaranteed, however pure the curatorial intentions, and the controversies

they so easily spark remind us of how much we still need to learn if we are
to acquire the capacity to create exhibitions that break, rather than recon-
firm, the semiotic circle of the stereotype. Even *Fluffs and Feathers,* produced
by Hodenosaunee curators and historians, was accused of losing some of its
critical edge when it was remounted as a touring exhibition in partnership
with the Royal Ontario Museum, because, in the process, it was transformed
into the more high-design, elegant, and spacious exhibit typical of a large
urban museum with more resources and a wider range of professional expertise at its disposal.[7]

I have long thought that visual artists are best equipped to find solutions
to these difficult problems, for they are by profession experts in exploiting
the theatrical and narrative potential of the gallery space, in evoking aesthetic responses that compel viewer attention, and in choreographing the
viewer's relationship to space, text, and image. In this context, *Savage Graces*
has presented us with a curatorial tour de force that successfully draws on
McMaster's dual identity as both a contemporary Indigenous artist and a
professional curator. (He developed *Savage Graces* while serving as curator of
Contemporary Indian Art at the Canadian Museum of Civilization.)

In his introductory text, mounted at the entrance to the exhibition, Mc-
Master writes that his subject is the historic theft of identity, and he poses the
question of whether it is possible to take back stolen images, to reappropriate
and efface bogus representations, to repossess the "Indian as sign." Walking into the exhibition after reading this text, the visitor enters a series of
spaces filled with images that the artist has remade and re-presented in order
to test whether such reversals of history and such discursive deconstructions
are possible. These acts of reappropriation require the artist to conjure up the
phantasmagoria of racial stereotypes and make them again available to the
visitor's gaze. I will focus my discussion of *Savage Graces* on the strategies of
re-presentation that McMaster has devised to counter, rather than reinscribe,
these images in order to draw out the lessons his exhibition offers for future
deconstructive projects.

The first such strategy, I would argue, is McMaster's conception of *Savage
Graces* as a *Gesamtkunstwerk,* a total multi-dimensional and multi-media installation that encompasses in its critique not only the discrete objects and
depictions that carry stereotypical imagery but also the museum system that
has contributed to the perpetuation of this imagistic system. McMaster developed *Savage Graces* together with Rosa Ho, curator of Contemporary Art
at the University of British Columbia's Museum of Anthropology (MoA),
and it was first mounted at MoA in 1992. Integral to the curatorial concept,
however, is the exhibition's ability to adapt to and take on a local coloura-
tion at each new venue. At the Ottawa Art Gallery, McMaster has taken over
the full suite of temporary exhibition rooms in order to recreate the multidisciplinary museum system on a miniaturized scale. The sequence of galleries replicates in turn the installations of the contemporary art gallery, the
ethnographic museum, the traditional art gallery, and the historical archive.

The reframing of a museum history specific to the local context is accomplished in several ways; Group of Seven and other historical Canadian art from the OAG's Firestone Collection are incorporated into the fine art installations, and the artifacts of pop culture are displayed in mahogany and glass specimen cases that once furnished the National Museum of Canada's anthropology halls in the Victoria Memorial Museum.[8]

McMaster's fundamental strategy for avoiding the voyeuristic trap – for preventing, in Mieke Bal's words, his "critique of the colonial visual practice" from becoming "a secondary reaction which in fact legitimizes [the] gaze" – is to begin by revealing the characteristic Western technologies of representation and display that have been used by colonial regimes to silence the authentic voices of its colonized Others.[9] His two specific targets are the post-Renaissance mode of picture making based on monocular perspective and the "scientific" objectification of the early modernist museum display. Their conjunction in his exhibition is designed to demonstrate that, despite the illusion we retain of an oppositionality between art and science, their representational strategies are grounded in a common fiction of objectification designed to render the Other available to the surveillance of the gaze.

A Walk through *Savage Graces*

The visit to *Savage Graces* begins in a large room re-created as a kind of studio space or contemporary art gallery, the space in which McMaster's own artistic practice can be located. He has washed the walls in black paint – a colour that keys, perhaps, the deadly seriousness of the project – and marked its corners with the four basic colours that refer at once to the elements of painting and to the Aboriginal practice of centring the self in relation to the four cardinal directions. His canvases are stretched directly on the wall with drawing pins, perhaps in reference to their exploratory status as works in progress. This "studio" is also a kind of anteroom and orientation chamber, revealing the codes with which we are to deconstruct the installations that follow.

The pictures in this first room confront the viewer with paintings and texts that reassemble the signs of Indianness as a semiotic field, revealing the constitutive elements with which we have all been taught to think about the Indigenous nations of North America. Here are the monstrous beings with faces in their chests dreamed by early European explorers. Here, too, are the eroticized Indian princesses splayed on decals across the hoods of cars and fantasized in popular culture. And here we also find the most powerful of all Indian signs, the feather-bonneted warrior romanticized by eighteenth-century novelists, nineteenth-century painters, and twentieth-century Hollywood films. McMaster paints this figure on the centre wall of the room in the infantilized guise of a kewpie doll Indian boy, top-heavy with the weight of his large headdress (fig. 9.1). He transforms the feathers of this headdress into a contestatory litany, each lettered with a question: "Do Native people have to be dead to be in museums?" "Are you threatened by others? Why do

9.1 (*see also colour plate 7*)
The first room of Gerald
McMaster's *Savage Graces*.
Photo by Tim Wickens;
reproduced with the per-
mission of the artist and
the Ottawa Art Gallery

you call us Indians?" "Is there a universalizing intelligence?
Does Western knowledge control the framework of relevant
evidence?" "Do we represent only the past to you?" On one
level, this figure points to the special toxicity of stereotypes
directed at children. On another level, McMaster seems to be
pointing to his own young self. The tag that occurs on one
of the central feathers – "I never knew I was an Indian until
somebody told me" – recalls an anecdote he has told of his
own moment of childhood revelation and loss of innocence
through schoolyard taunts levelled at him when he left his
reserve to attend school in the neighbouring town of North
Battleford, Saskatchewan.[10]

This introductory gallery is designed to foreground the
postmodern and postcolonial project of contemporary art.
It also introduces McMaster's concern with the way that all
Western modes of visual representation – popular, commercial, and high art – have worked together to objectify the
Other and to the contingent need to deploy multiple strategies of disruption. The imagery set out by his suite of paintings in this first room thus refers to three representational
modes that have done the work of stereotyping: traditions of
pictorial representation that go back to the early contact period, museum displays, and mass commodification. The paintings take on all three registers of representation, assert their

interconnectedness, mix them up, and deal them out again. The canvas *HyperPhotogenics* is particularly important. Held to the wall by a grid of wires, its images confined and multiplied by its superimposed pattern of rigid squares, this piece recalls the one-point perspective invented in the Renaissance that constituted the organizing principle of the Western pictorial tradition. McMaster's work is a painterly equivalent of Bryson's comment that "what we are really observing, in this first geological age of perspective, the epoch of the vanishing point, is the transformation of the subject into object: like the camera, the painting of perspective clears away the diffuse, non-localised nebula of imaginary definitions and substitutes a definition from the outside."[11]

As we enter the next rooms, thematically sign-posted with the phrase "(Im)polite Gazes," we are transported into another kind of museum space that is overtly didactic. In it McMaster lays out the means through which the colonial social formation, particularly in its more recent phases, has defined identities (fig. 9.2). It presents us with the artifacts that this system of representation has produced in all their myriad forms, from the painted portraits of Indians by Yvonne Housser and the picturesque drawings of Northwest Coast villages by A.Y. Jackson, to postcards showing early paintings of Indigenous peoples of the Amazon, to public sculp-

9.2 (*see also colour plate 8*) "(Im)Polite Gazes" section of Gerald McMaster's *Savage Graces*. Photo by Tim Wickens; reproduced with the permission of the artist and the Ottawa Art Gallery

And here's the Vanishing Race, which symbolizes my whole work.
Edward S. Curtis, photographer.

"Kill the 'Indian,' save the man.
Unknown.

9.3 The third section of Gerald McMaster's *Savage Graces*. Photo by Tim Wickens; reproduced with the permission of the artist and the Ottawa Art Gallery

tures of Massaquoit and Samuel Champlain's nameless guide. We are made to witness the ways in which mass production and mechanical reproduction have vulgarized and endlessly multiplied the signs of Indianness, allowing them to seep into every corner of life from the food cupboard to the toy chest.

Repetition made of the signs of Indianness a kind of ever-present white noise, rendering "invisible" images that McMaster wants to make us see and hear. He does this by miming the ethnographic museum's formats for public scrutiny and display. The museum, like the picture gallery, is an institution structured to invite the gaze; as Svetlana Alpers has argued, both inscribe "a way of seeing."[12] The museum, too, forces us to see things through artificial schema of typology and ethnicity that are physically manifested by the grid-like arrangements of its squared-off display cases. Very well, says McMaster, I will play the game. His artifacts are arranged in pristine taxonomies – food and food containers, clothing and dress, toys and amusements – relentlessly subverted by the witty inversions of his labels and captions. A lucite case containing sewing patterns, Indian-themed fabric, and paper dolls is entitled "Covered Pagans" on one side and

"Sweet Dreams" on the other; another, filled with children's books, bears the label "Captured by Indians / Copyright Invalid"; while a third, filled with food packages for Land o' Lakes butter, corn chips, and Indian salt and pepper shakers, is labelled "Food for Thought / Absolutely No Preservatives." In the old National Museum cases we find displays of sheet music for a version of "Ten Little Indians," a children's game of Wa-Hoo decorated with grotesque Indian faces, and seemingly endless variations of these images printed on comic books, toy weapons, children's clothing, bubble gum wrappers, tobacco tins, soft drink cans, and motor-oil containers.

On the walls of the final section of *Savage Graces* are lettered the words "'Kill the Indian, Save the Man' – Unknown" (fig. 9.3). The documentary archive that papers these walls under lucite panels is densely packed with images of men, women, and children – historical and contemporary, Aboriginal and not – ranging from portraits to informal beach scenes to photographs of official delegations to Washington or Ottawa. The professional performers of Indianness and the re-enactors are also there, as are pages from dime-store novels, comic books, and other artifacts of print culture that have alternately romanticized, barbarized, and carried the propaganda of the vanishing Indian. The repetitive nature of this material is so overwhelming and so relentless that it ceases to provide the pleasurable sensation of comfort and familiarity identified by Barthes. Here McMaster's simple but effective strategy is to use repetition against itself, exhausting the viewer's ability to attend and evacuating the images of meaning. In an even more insistent way, the drone of repetition turns these white representations into white noise whose individual components can no longer be distinguished.

After we have passed through these three different museum environments, each conveying the same visual stew of stereotypes served up in a different format, we come to one last case, standing apart in the hallway leading to the exit. It is filled with a jumble of miscellaneous objects, each bearing a flattened stereotypical image of Indianness. The case label is headed "Cultural Amnesty (stereotypes hurt)," and the text reads: "Collected from public contributions. Objects deposited in this display are voluntary contributions to Cultural Amnesty, a work in progress by Gerald McMaster. All donated works will be used in the future development of this piece. Thank you for your contributions." The case beckons to the visitor and offers the opportunity to transform the passive act of viewing that she has experienced into an active gesture of refusal of all that she has seen. The Cultural Amnesty box drives home one of the key propositions of *Savage Graces* as a *travelling* exhibition by pointing to the ubiquity of the stereotypes of Indianness. We realize that it could be mounted virtually anywhere in the Western world, that any art museum could offer up its share of nineteenth- and twentieth-century primitivist fantasies of Indianness, and that any environment will be able to supply abundant popular and commercial kitsch. The exhibition's own protean and chameleon-like adaptability is thus essential to its message.

Exchanging Looks in the Counter-Museum

Mieke Bal writes in "The Politics of Citation" that successful postcolonial critiques require of the viewer that "you ... put yourself in the exact same situation as the person you are looking at so that looking becomes an exchange of looks."[13] She also stresses the need to achieve an effective balance of text and image, recommending "a thoughtful, sparse use of visual material where every image is provided with an immediately accessible critique that justifies its use with specificity."[14] The calibration, variation, tone, and placement of the texts in *Savage Graces* in relation to its images are, in Bal's sense, also at the heart of McMaster's strategic achievement. The textual interpellations painted directly on the walls, the captions for the artifacts and paintings, and the texts inscribed on McMaster's own paintings are alternately punning, ironic, biting, and bluntly questioning. They subject the images to a constant critical tension, interrupting their references to childhood games, vacation treats, or other remembered delights and refusing the viewer's pleasure of recognition. They constitute a reclamation of voice, the turning of the back onto the viewer, the transformation of "looking into an exchange of looks."

The clarity and formal elegance of the three-part structure McMaster uses in *Savage Graces*, which moves from the art gallery/studio to the artifactual and historical museum to the didactic format of the bulletin board, constitutes another kind of artistic strategy. It produces a compelling sense of simplicity, maintains a sharp critical edge, and avoids ambiguity despite the exhibition's comprehensive scope and complex layering. By coming at the problem of the stereotype from three different directions, McMaster undercuts the truth claims of the individual images and objects and flattens the hierarchies of medium and genre that can distract critics from the apprehension of the systemic nature of oppressive discourses. This quality of comprehensiveness is, perhaps, the reason that the exhibition is able to avoid the weaknesses that have dogged other such projects. Its counter-appropriation of museum space and the Western representational system leaves no room in which their defenders can take refuge. On this level of meta-critique *Savage Graces* should perhaps be compared, not to the exhibitions that have already been mentioned, but to the *Museum of Jurassic Technology*, opened by David Wilson in 1989 in Los Angeles, an art installation in the form of a museum and a meditation on the Western system of knowledge as laid out in museum space.[15]

I would like to end this discussion of the exhibition with what I take as evidence of the way in which this process of critique and rejection may enact the sort of real therapeutic work that leads to healing. For some years now, we have watched Gerald McMaster work with one particular image, a three-quarters figure with an armless torso and the head turned to the side. The figure bears a resemblance to sacred carvings used by Plains and Woodlands peoples, yet it is not identical to any particular example. The artist has painted and sculpted this form many times and in many guises, sometimes inscrib-

ing the face with generalized features, but most often leaving it blank. It has seemed to resist individuation, to remain a template awaiting definition. The last image in the documentary installation that precedes the Cultural Amnesty box in *Savage Graces* is a small painting displaying one of these figures, but for the first time a specific face appears within the form of the head: it is the artist's own, derived from a photographic self-portrait (fig. 9.4). The placement of this piece at the end of the exhibition was new in the Ottawa venue. I read a deep meaning into its positioning at the end of the long sequence of exposition and deconstruction enacted in *Savage Graces*. It seems to me to be evidence of the exhibition's success on a deep psychological level, as a process that moves viewers to replace generalized stereotypes with individualized images. The intention of the exhibition, as manifested in the Cultural Amnesty box, is not merely to analyze the historic sources of stereotypes or the damage they have done by assembling a static montage of examples but, rather, to do real transformative work in real time and space. McMaster wants visitors to abandon false images so that they can see

9.4 Gerald McMaster, Self-portrait, in *Savage Graces*, third section. Photo by Tim Wickens; reproduced with the permission of the artist and the Ottawa Art Gallery

more clearly the modern Aboriginal identities that have been obscured by the masks of the stereotype.

The new placement of McMaster's self-portrait seems to me evidence that the exhibition has worked on the artist as well and that it has served him as something of a self-liberating project. The representation of a powerful spiritual being bearing the artist's adult face at the end of the exhibition answers back to the kewpie doll boy in the war bonnet whose feathers are inscribed with falsehoods, doubts, and questions with which the exhibition opens. On his adult self-portrait McMaster has written the Latin word used by the Western old masters when signing their paintings: *fecit*, "he made it." The word signals closure; it is the sign of a singular achievement brought to a state of completion, appropriate to the moment when identity is declared and authorship claimed.

10

Threads of the Land at the Canadian Museum of Civilization (1995)

On the day that I visited *Threads of the Land: Clothing Traditions from Three Indigenous Cultures*, at the Canadian Museum of Civilization (CMC) to make notes for this review,* the European Community voted to introduce a ban on the importation of furs caught with leghold traps. This ban, long opposed by the Canadian government and Aboriginal organizations such as the Assembly of First Nations, puts in jeopardy both the economic well-being and the cultural survival of many Aboriginal people in Canada. The irony of my timing – and, more importantly, the timeliness of the show – became immediately evident as soon as I entered the exhibition, for the commonly taken visitor path begins in the Dene section with what must be one of the most graphic didactic displays on hide-tanning ever mounted. Practically the first thing the visitor sees is a display of caribou hides in successive stages of preparation, preserved by some alchemy of the conservator's art with their flesh, blood, and fur intact (fig. 10.1). The consummate technical mastery of Aboriginal tanners is demonstrated across the narrow corridor, where samples of the finished products – fox, beaver, caribou, arctic hare – irresistibly draw visitors of all ages and both sexes to stop and stroke their seductively silky and soft textures.

The text panels and photographs in this introductory section make the connection to the theme of the exhibition: the way in which Aboriginal people affirm and express, with beauty and clarity in the design and embellishment of their clothing, their intimate interdependence with the land and all its life forms. "From the land," as George Blondin is quoted as saying in one of the panels, "came our religion ... from the

* This review was originally published in *Archivaria: The Journal of the Association of Canadian Archivists* 40 (Fall 1995): 243–5. It is reproduced as written with only minor changes and the addition of an account of the solution arrived at for the display of the girl's beaded puberty regalia, which I learned of after the review was published. *Threads of the Land* was shown at the CMC from 3 February 1995 to 14 September 1997 and did not travel.

10.1   Installation on hide-
tanning techniques in
Threads of the Land. Photo
© Canadian Museum of
Civilization, s96-26604

land came our life … from the land came our powerful medicine … from the land came our way of life."

Threads of the Land is,· in fact, three exhibitions in one,
each of which is the fruit of years of research by staff curators
on the rich collections of the CMC and related objects in other
institutions. "From the Land," curated by Judy Thompson, focuses on Dene clothing traditions of the Northwest Territories; "Earth Line and Morning Star," curated by Leslie Tepper,
presents Nlaka'pamux (Thompson River) clothing from the
Plateau area of British Columbia; and "Sanatujut, Pride in
Women's Work," curated by Judy Hall, is about Copper and
Caribou Inuit clothing. On the level of archival and historical
research, each of the exhibitions and its accompanying catalogue makes a major contribution to scholarly knowledge. The
generous number of high-quality illustrations and the clearly
written, well-organized texts make this knowledge uniquely
accessible to the general public, both Aboriginal and non-
Aboriginal. A great deal of new information about historic
and contemporary clothing is brought to light from unpublished archival sources, collated from often obscure works of

ethnography, or revealed in little-known museum collections. The publications, which closely follow and faithfully record the material presented in the exhibitions, are bound to become standard reference works.

On the whole, the parallel presentation of the three regional clothing traditions and the common format adopted by their publications add to the impact of each of the individual components. By providing opportunities for comparison, they invite an appreciation of the inventiveness and seemingly endless variation that human beings devise in response to the eternal problems of protection, warmth, and self-presentation. They also reveal the culturally specific ways in which members of different societies express the components of individual identity, such as gender, stage of life, personal achievement, aesthetic sensibility, and taste. These comparative resonances are, however, left largely up to the individual viewer or reader to draw out. An introductory video or other enhancement to the exhibition might have made some of the comparisons clearer to the general public. Such an addition might also have commented more reflexively on the differences in historical depth and interpretive ethnographic information that are available for each of the three areas as a result of different histories of contact and collecting. Both the Dene and the Inuit, for example, have been in contact with Westerners since the eighteenth century, and their cultural artifacts have been collected by many different people throughout this period. The Nlaka'pamux, in contrast, have been less widely written about, and museum goers are almost exclusively dependent on the early twentieth-century collections made by James Teit for knowledge of their material and artistic traditions. Teit, having married Lucy Antko, an Nlaka'pamux woman, was well positioned to collect; he was enlisted by Franz Boas to aid in Boas's comprehensive project of salvage ethnography, and he engaged in the common practices of the time, including the re-creation of objects no longer in common use. A comparison of both the limitations and the unusual resources offered by such a historically specific collection with the more extensive Inuit and Dene collections could have been more fully developed.

The three exhibitions are models of the collaborative museological practice urged by the report of the Task Force on Museums and First Peoples in 1992. All the curators worked closely with community experts on clothing, and the knowledge, insights, and perspectives of these consultants are well and respectfully integrated with the historical research (fig. 10.2). The exhibitions are also rich in displays of contemporary clothing (fig. 10.3). In this respect, the difference between *Threads of the Land* and earlier exhibitions on similar topics is subtle but significant. Although past exhibition projects have certainly included contemporary examples, the presence of the contemporary is much more vivid and its authenticity asserted much more successfully than has been common in the past, even when the new examples of clothing present a dramatic contrast with those of the past.

Both for museum curators and for contemporary seamstresses, one of the most valuable legacies of the exhibition project is the recovery of knowledge

10.2 (*above*)   CMC curator Judy Thompson (left) discussing the *Threads of the Land* exhibition with Dene and Inuit consultants: (left to right) Debra Evaluajuk, Sally Qimmiu'naaq Webster, and Jane Dragon. Photo © Canadian Museum of Civilization, IMG2011-0018-0023Dm

10.3 (*below*)   Exhibit on contemporary Dene sewing in *Threads of the Land*. Photo © Canadian Museum of Civilization, S96-26599

about historical clothing. All three curators acknowledge a debt to Dorothy Burnham, curator emerita of textiles from the Royal Ontario Museum and research associate at the CMC, who put her unique knowledge of garment construction at the service of the project, analyzing lost techniques of construction and drawing out patterns for older types of garments that have long gone out of use and memory. Here too, however, the expertise available from contemporary consultants varied from area to area in relation to the different histories of contact and white settlement. The early establishment of the fur trade with the Dene made for the longest history of contact and for the most gradual process of change in clothing styles and materials. Among the Nlaka'pamux such changes have been no less profound, but they happened much more rapidly during the late nineteenth century; while in the Arctic, of course, similar changes are still within living memory. Inuit consultants, in consequence, are thus able to provide much more detailed information about the reasons for the use of particular materials and types of construction and about the symbolic meanings of particular images and forms than can modern Dene or Nlaka'pamux about their historic clothing traditions.

Threads of the Land is a rich and multifaceted exhibition that will reward repeat visits – indeed, it is impossible to see it properly in a single trip. It is also the first major exhibition of historic materials produced by the ethnology division since its move to the Canadian Museum of Civilization's new building, designed by Douglas Cardinal and opened in 1989. It is a shame, therefore, that the museum was not able to provide it with a more spacious layout. It is hard to see how the designer could have done much else with the small space that he was allotted than to present us with the rather cramped and sometimes confusing winding corridors that house the exhibition. (The lack of ceilings overhead adds to the discomfort – the experience is rather like walking through an Elizabethan maze placed inside an airplane hangar.) Yet this maze-like arrangement also fortuitously provided the opportunity for a highly innovative solution to a dilemma that faced the curator of the Nlaka'pamux exhibit and her community consultants. In the past, one of the most beautiful and elaborate articles of Nlaka'pamux ritual art was a long beaded "puberty veil" with which girls covered their mouths during their ritual seclusion at the time of their first menses. The power inherent in such articles makes them culturally sensitive and potentially unsuited to public display. The museum staff initially suggested placing one such veil in their collection in a case that directly faced visitors as they entered one of the exhibition sections. Community consultants found this position too exposed. They might have requested that the veil not be shown at all, and the museum would have respected their decision. Instead, however, they suggested that it be placed in a corner of the same room, where visitors would come upon it gradually and in the course of a careful perusal of the contextualizing display, rather than potentially by accident.[1] Although visitors will not be aware of this backstory to the exhibition, it is worth noting as an example of the gains to be had from the careful and respectful community collaboration that has become established practice in most Canadian museums during the past few years.

The ethnology division at the CMC is currently at work on the museum's new First Peoples Hall. *Threads of the Land* has set a high standard of scholarship, research, clarity of content, and collaborative interpretation. If more attention is paid to a successful spatial realization of the curatorial content in the new installations, it will surely provoke equivalent words of praise to those spoken at the *Threads of the Land* opening. Inuit Tapiritsat director Rosemary Kuptana explained that the Inuit section relays "many untold stories of the people." Chief David Walkem of the Cook's Ferry Band of Nlaka'pamux said, "Going in [to the show] was a very powerful experience," and he welcomed it particularly as a way of transmitting knowledge and traditions to the young. And surely no praise could be greater than the words of Jane Dragon, one of the consultants for the Dene section, who said simply, "I wouldn't change one thing in the show."

11

Toward a Dialogic Paradigm

New Models of Collaborative Curatorial Practice

There is no intelligibility that is not at the same time communication and intercommunication, and that is not grounded in dialogue.
– *Paolo Freire (1998)*[1]

Visual culture within the museum is a technology of power. This power can be used to further democratic possibilities, or it can be used to uphold exclusionary values. Once this is acknowledged, and the museum is understood as a form of cultural politics, the post-museum will develop its identity.
– *Eilean Hooper-Greenhill (2002)*[2]

Exhibits are the reason most people go to museums.[3] They are the museum's premier product, designed to address the public directly through a unique language configured of visual, textual, and spatial elements. Through the creation of exhibits, museum professionals seek to render more intelligible and accessible knowledge that is specialized, esoteric, and complex. Through their selective sponsorship of exhibits, governments and private interest groups hope to educate and shape public opinion. Critical museological literature has identified exhibitions as a key area of cultural production with important agency in the inscription of constructs of nation, citizenship, race, and gender. It demonstrates how, historically, exhibits have contributed to the formation of the universalist ideologies and nationalist power structures that inform modern societies.[4] In collaboratively organized exhibits the intellectual, social, and political dynamics of these processes change in fundamental ways. On the one hand, the communities that choose to partner with museums have often been marginalized and/or exoticized by the museum's traditional state and private sponsors. On the other, by validating knowledge produced according to diverse cultural traditions, museums contribute to the erosion of the modernist universal values in which these sponsors have been invested. The paradigmatic shift being introduced through collaborative exhibit development thus raises fundamental questions not only about the ways that contemporary museums are repositioning themselves as they respond to the powerful currents of cultural pluralism, decolonization, and globalization but also about the changing relationship between museums and the societies within which they operate.

The Opening

If the museum's messages are most concentrated in its public displays, its sponsoring social and political network is most clearly visible when a new exhibition is inaugurated. Museum openings are highly ritualized events. Typically, speeches are made by the director, the curator, the chairman of the board, artists, community representatives, and the officers of corporate sponsors and funding agencies. People dress a little more formally, wine is drunk from stemmed glasses, canapés are nibbled. The members, volunteers, "friends," professional colleagues, critics, and others in attendance make up what Herbert Gans has termed a "taste culture" and which, in turn forms part of the "art world" – as defined by Howard Becker – to which the museum or gallery belongs.[5] In Pierre Bourdieu's terms, the players on the "field of cultural production" become, for an evening, visible within the museum's walls.[6]

I begin, therefore, with an opening, one that occurred on 23 April 2002 at my own institution, the University of British Columbia Museum of Anthropology, to mark the Vancouver showing of *Kaxlaya Gvilas: The Ones Who Uphold the Laws of Our Ancestors*. This exhibit was the first to display the historical and contemporary art of the Heiltsuk people of British Columbia's central coast, and the opening ceremony was a particularly splendid example of the kinds of performances staged to mark the collaboratively organized exhibits discussed in this section.[7] The contrast it presented to conventional museum openings is emblematic of the ways in which collaboratively organized exhibitions differ from those that preceded them.

Over seven hundred guests, many of them Heiltsuk, filled to overflowing the museum's Great Hall. Sixteen hereditary chiefs, community members, artists, and dancers from both the urban and reserve Heiltsuk communities, dressed in ceremonial button blankets, carved frontlets, and other regalia, entered the hall to begin the evening's ceremonies.[8] In accordance with First Nations protocol, they requested permission to enter Musqueam territory and share their culture from the chief of the Musqueam First Nation, on whose traditional lands the museum and the university are located. The Heiltsuk guests then became the evening's hosts, and for a night, the museum's foyer and major exhibition gallery (generically, as Carol Duncan has shown, already a ritual and ceremonial space) effectively became a Heiltsuk "big house."[9] The speaker formally announced the names and titles of the chiefs, displayed the inherited privileges of important families through song, dance, and masked performance, and publicly recognized the contributions made by different individuals through the presentation of gifts. The hosts then offered a feast of wild salmon and home baking to all the guests, whose collective witnessing of the proceedings had conferred on them essential validation. The ritual performance translated the basic principles and components of the potlatch of the Northwest Coast First Nations into the language of a museum opening – or vice versa – and the brief speeches by museum, university, and sponsors' representatives which normally provide the substance of a museum opening were decentred and became enfolded within an Indigenous Heiltsuk ceremonial event.

The bringing together of so many people, many of whom had made a long and expensive journey to Vancouver from the Heiltsuk community at Bella Bella on the central BC coast, with all the ingredients of celebration, was the result of months of careful planning and a huge expenditure of time, energy, and money.[10] As Victor Turner has taught us, "a celebratory performance rejoices in the key values and virtues of the society that produces it."[11] The communal values, unique traditions, and knowledge of the Heiltsuk people that were being affirmed that evening reflected the success of a collaborative process which had not only effected the trans-generational reunion of the historical objects with the descendants of their original makers and owners but also accurately expressed the community's contemporary understanding of itself. The contributions of the curator, Pam Brown, and the associate curator, Martha Black, model the collaboration that lay behind this success. Brown is a member of the Heiltsuk First Nation, while Black is an art historian whose doctoral research on the collection of objects made by a medical missionary at the height of the colonial era provided an essential research base for the project. To create the exhibit, Brown took that research back to the community, amplified it with further levels of community interpretation, added a substantial contemporary art component, and worked with community members to identify the themes and issues that Heiltsuk people wanted to communicate both to the roughly half of their members who live in Vancouver and to broader southern Canadian publics.

The Emergence of Collaborative Exhibitions in the 1990s

The approach to exhibition development that informed the production of *Kaxlaya Gvilas* has established itself with remarkable rapidity during the past two decades, initially in the settler societies of North America, Australia, and New Zealand and more recently in the former centres of European empire.[12] In this chapter I discuss five articles that appeared together in Laura Peers and Alison Brown's *Museums and Source Communities* (2003). They present case studies of important collaborative exhibitions organized in North America and Great Britain.[13] As a group, the five articles offer a micro-history of the development of the new paradigm. Work on the earliest of the projects considered here, the two pioneering archaeological exhibits described by Michael Ames, began in the early 1990s. *Written in the Earth* and *From under the Delta* were developed by Coast Salish communities and the Museum of Anthropology at UBC in direct response to the challenge to develop new and equal forms of partnership that was issued to Canadian museums and Indigenous peoples by the report of the Task Force on Museums and First Peoples in 1992.[14] Anita Herle's article on the Cambridge University Museum of Archaeology and Anthropology's *Torres Strait Islanders: An Exhibition to Mark the Centenary of the 1898 Anthropological Expedition*, discusses a temporary exhibit opened in 1998 to commemorate a formative episode in the history of anthropology – and equally, as she shows us, in the history of the Torres Straits Islanders. Anthony Shelton's documents the curatorial process adopted by London's Horniman Museum for the new installation of its African collections, designed to replace a typical mid-twentieth-century ethnographic exhibit; entitled *African Worlds*, the installation opened in 1999. A second Canadian example, also a long-term installation, is discussed by Gerald Conaty: the Glenbow Museum's *Niitsitapiisinni: Our Way of Life* was organized with Blackfoot community members and opened in Calgary in 2000. The most recent of these collaborative exhibit projects was still in development when the article about it was being written. As described by Stephanie Moser and her colleagues, it brought together archaeologists from the University of Southampton with the Quseir Heritage Preservation Society to conduct archaeological research on the ancient Roman harbour of Myos Hormos and to co-develop exhibits based on this research for a new museum or heritage centre at Quseir al-Qadim, Egypt.

As all the examples make clear, the collaborative paradigm of exhibition production involves a new form of power-sharing in which museum and community partners co-manage a broad range of the activities that lead to the final product. These usually include the initial identification of themes, the design of the research methodology, the object selection, and the writing of text panels. It can also involve the integration of training and capacity building for community members and community input into other activities, such as conservation, the design of the installation, and the selection of gift shop products and poster images. Community consultants and advisory committees have long been features of exhibition development in anthropology museums, but collective decision making in this broader array of activities, which are normally controlled by museum professionals with specialized training, requires a much more radical shift within the institution. It amounts to what Michael Ames calls "a realignment of power, achieved through a redistribution of authority."[15]

In the remainder of this chapter I will discuss several key features of collaborative exhibitions that are revealed by the case studies as a group. These include the articulation of a postcolonial museum ethic, a shift in emphasis from product to process, and a renewed affirmation of the museum as a research site. I will also seek to problematize two aspects of collaborative exhibits that seem to me to require deeper analysis at this stage in the development of a dialogic paradigm. First, I will argue that this representative group of case studies reveals that there is no one single model of collaboration in exhibition development, as writing on the topic often seems to imply. Rather, a spectrum of models has emerged bracketed by two distinct types that I will term the community-based exhibit and the multivocal exhibit. Each of these models prescribes particular authorities, responsibilities, and forms of public recognition for the community and museum participants. I will further argue that clarity in identifying the model to be used in a given collaborative exhibit project greatly enhances not only its chances of success but also the long-term viability of the new paradigm. Finally, I will raise the theoretical question of the role that museums play in processes of social change. Put simply, does the growing popularity of collaborative exhibits signal a new era of social agency for museums, or does it make the museum a space where symbolic restitution is made for the injustices of the colonial era in lieu of more concrete forms of social, economic, and political redress?

The Ethics of Collaborative Exhibits: From Postmodernism to Human Rights

The case studies demonstrate that the move to collaborative curatorial practice in anthropology museums is rooted in two important intellectual and moral developments that have steadily grown in power during the past half-century. First, the reflexivity in the humanities and social sciences associated with postmodernism has raised awareness among museum anthropologists of the ways in which earlier, objectifying traditions of material culture display have supported colonial and neo-colonial power relations. Second, the evolving discourse of human rights has, in the years since its first broad codification in the United Nations' Universal Declaration of Human Rights in 1948, been vigorously argued to extend to cultural property and the protection of traditional indigenous knowledge.[16]

Postmodern anthropology and rights-based arguments are reflected in the language used by the authors of the articles under discussion. All begin by situating their projects in relation to the prior history of anthropological exhibits. Shelton, for example, refers to the "old neo-colonial paradigm" in which people are represented "through the voices of their foreign interpreters."[17] Similarly, the Quseir team affirms the legitimacy of community interest in the development of exhibits about their own histories and ways of life because these exhibits play an important role in the construction of the identities by which their members become "known" to museum visitors. All the authors affirm either implicitly or explicitly the need to repair the psychological damage that has been done in the past to individuals forced to negotiate negative stereotypes by creating new exhibits that disseminate more accurate (and usually positive) images of contemporary ways of life.

The five exhibits under discussion adopted a number of specific strategies to counter the stereotypes and dehumanization that have been produced by the scientific objectification of earlier ethnographic exhibits. The "African Voices" component of the Horniman's *African Worlds* foregrounded the photographic portraits and words of contemporary Africans and members of African diasporic communities in order to effect a "conscious purge of some of the more familiar and perhaps comfortable illusions about Africa in the popular conscience."[18] In *Torres Strait Islanders*, Herle countered the historical legacy of objectification by meticulously attributing information, quotations, and objects to named individuals and by personalizing and considering as historical subjects both the Islanders and the Western academic investigators. A concept of knowledge as property also underlies these discussions. All of the authors point to past asymmetries of power in the treatment of intellectual property – justified, as Ames notes, by an uninterrogated notion of academic freedom – and all sought to rectify this imbalance through collaborative approaches. While the knowledge taken from communities has historically been used to create museum exhibits that advance the careers and status of anthropologists and curators, those who shared this knowledge and their descendants usually have not benefited. Rather, they have often suffered from the loss of cultural property and from the uses made of the knowledge taken away. A point of departure for Ames's discussion is, thus, the need to acknowledge Indigenous people's right to own their own histories. Moser and her group state that "it is no longer acceptable for archaeologists to reap the material and intellectual benefits of another society's heritage,"[19] and Conaty expresses similar principles through concepts of profit and appropriation.

A key ethical principle of collaborative exhibition projects is, then, that *both* sides should be able to define and gain the benefits they deem appropriate. Ames notes that his museum's innovative collaboration with Coast Salish communities illustrates the importance of the Canadian requirement, after 1992, for museums to provide letters of support from the First Nations communities being represented when applying for government grants. His insight that community partners thus assumed the rights of sponsors already defined in research ethics policies is crucial. As a result, he writes, the Salish communities had the power to insist that they "become the primary audience because their histories and cultures constitute the subject matter."[20] Similarly, Conaty points out that "the Blackfoot made it clear that they were not participating just to help Glenbow create an exhibit … They saw this project as an opportunity to develop an educational place where future generations of Blackfoot youth can learn the fundamentals of their own culture."[21] The multiple components of the Community Archaeology Project at Quseir were designed to confer an array of economic and educational benefits even before the exhibit came into being. While the Horniman and Cambridge projects could not so directly serve the educational needs of community partners thousands of miles away, Shelton and Herle found innovative ways to return research materials and information to them, and Herle was able to arrange for a version of the Cambridge exhibit to travel to Australia, where Islanders could more easily see it.

The flip side of the identification of benefits is the need to avoid harm. In addition to the damage caused by stereotyping, Conaty points out the harm that can be done to a cultural tradition when its system of knowledge management is not respected by outside scholars and when information whose circulation is restricted because of its sacred or proprietary nature is made generally accessible through display or publication. In both Herle's and Conaty's projects decisions were made not to put on display certain kinds of objects or information. As Herle relates, while the changes and omissions that were requested by community members seemed relatively minor to the museum, from the Islanders' point of view they were critical to the exhibit's success.

Michael Ames points out the parallels between the ethics that inform collaborative exhibition projects and the democratizing, activist research process known as participatory action research (PAR) developed by social scientists, medical researchers, and others during the past few decades.[22] "In essence," as Joan Ryan and Michael Robinson have written, "PAR addresses the perceived and felt needs in a community to reclaim knowledge, power, and decision making from the colonizers and/or oppressors, and the desire to have local knowledge accepted as equally valid and scientific as western knowledge." The overall purpose of PAR projects, as they state, is change, and it is achieved through an involvement of the whole community "in the definition of goals, in the research process, and in the verification of data."[23] Equally important, training for community members is built in at all stages of the project. Collaborative museum exhibition projects are controlled by principles nearly identical to those of PAR, and they are proving to have similar impacts on community development in the areas of education, cultural preservation, and the tourist industry.

"To-ing and Fro-ing": The Primacy of Process

Both Ames and Shelton refer to the characteristic movement of collaborative processes as "to-ing and fro-ing," although they use this evocative phrase in different ways. For Ames it is "the extended process of negotiation and consultation,"[24] while for Shelton it is the "to-ing and fro-ing between a collection and a suitable discourse" that "eventually gives rise to a coherent system which embraces both objects and narrative into a rationalised order."[25] All the authors stress the extended negotiations that collaborative museum projects require and provide examples of the back-and-forth process. Herle demonstrates that the need for negotiation can be just as demanding within the partnering community as between it and the museum. As her examples illustrate, the historical legacy of colonialism is a Pandora's box, which, when opened, releases into the space of the museum unresolved conflicts or tensions among individuals, families, or communities with which the communities must deal before the project can proceed. In many collaborative exhibition projects the museum is serving as a useful "neutral space" where such conflicts can be provisionally or even permanently resolved.

Conaty emphasizes the need to give time to relationship building, pointing out that before the Glenbow exhibit project could be initiated, trust had to be built between Blackfoot communities and the museum. Not only are anthropology museums often categorically associated with the institutional machinery of state surveillance and oppression, but they also serve as repositories for human remains and cultural objects requested for repatriation. All the authors whose articles I discuss here agree, however, that while a collaborative project takes longer to develop than a conventional exhibition, the added investment of time allows the project to become a much more effective site for research, education, and innovation. In collaborative exhibits, the extended development process is, therefore, becoming as important as the physical exhibit itself. The emphasis on process is also a reflection of a fundamental insight of reflexive museology that the messages of an exhibit are carried not just by objects, texts, and design but also by many other aspects of its realization.[26] As Ames recounts, in collaborative projects all the phases of exhibit preparation and object handling need to be discussed and agreed upon, and a wide range of museum professionals must therefore become involved in the negotiation of their practices. Throughout the ensuing discussions both they and the community participants are called upon to articulate their reasons for procedures and requirements that may appear natural or unnatural, depending on the participant's subject position. The subject/object relationships constructed by collaborative exhibitions thus move away from the monologism of the past and toward a dialogic structure.

The emphasis on process in collaborative projects leads, then, to the redefinition of the scope of an exhibit, which is increasingly understood not just as a physical arrangement of objects and interpretive materials in a gallery but as an interrelated set of activities that takes place before the show opens, during its public display, and after it closes. These projects often encompass an array of educational initiatives that can include training opportunities and internships for community members, performances and public programs, the sharing of research and resources, and the building of an ongoing partnership that can lead to social and political advocacy. Eilean Hooper-Greenhill has discussed the museum's redefinition of its scope and mission in terms of a break with modernism. "Where the modernist museum was (and is) imagined as a building," she writes, "the museum in the future may be imagined as a process or an experience … it moves as a set of processes into the spaces, the concerns and the ambitions of communities."[27] Her use of the term "post-museum" for this enlarged and politicized scope and mission conveys the same sense of rupture with historical traditions of museology as my notion of paradigm shift. As this shift continues, the museum becomes a participant in the community as much as the community becomes a participant in the museum. Museums are just beginning to address the implications of their commitment to building long-term relationships with communities. As collaborative projects become normative and as museums engage serially with different communities, innovative solutions will have to be found to the increased demands on staff and community members' time. It seems probable that new electronic media will play a major role in sustaining these relationships.

The Development of New Knowledge and the Mutuality of Education

The authors of the case studies I examine here also argue that through collaborative exhibits the museum is being revived as a site for the production of new knowledge. Anthropology museums were founded as active research sites during the late nineteenth and early twentieth centuries, but this function has been in abeyance during much of the past century as the discipline of anthropology turned away from material culture study. As Indigenous communities engage with museums, however, the power of museum objects to stimulate memories suppressed by the pressures of assimilationism and modernization becomes ever more apparent. Aldona Jonaitis and James Clifford, for example, have offered compelling examples of the new kinds of research questions that are being investigated in the course of collaborative exhibit development. As Jonaitis wrote of the landmark Northwest Coast exhibition *Chiefly Feasts* at the American Museum of Natural History in 1992, the collaborative research process on which the exhibition was based took participants beyond relatively straightforward problems of ethnographic and art-historical documentation and yielded new understandings of colonialism and historical process. She observed that the "continuity, vividly disclosed as the full significance of the Siwidi material came to light, has served as an enlightening example of the enduring nature of many Kwakiutl traditions," and she pointed to the value of such research for the understanding of our shared postcolonial condition.[28] Clifford has also stressed the value of community-museum collaborations in illuminating not just standard ethnography but also the intercultural social relationships that have been constructed by colonial histories. "In the contact zone of the Portland Museum's basement, the meanings addressed to white interlocutors were primarily relational: 'This is what the objects inspire us to say in response to our shared history, the goals of ongoing responsibility and reciprocity we differently embrace.'"[29]

The five case studies discussed here provide further examples of how collaborative research for museum exhibitions is yielding critical understandings about the workings of history and memory. The two archaeological exhibits are particularly interesting in this regard. Although contemporary people have traditionally been thought to have little if any "hard" data to offer that can help to explicate materials dating back centuries or millennia, in both British Columbia and Egypt new data and new understandings did result from collaboration between community members and archaeologists. The Quseir team learned not only of the locations of new sites and the uses of unfamiliar objects but also about "how the past is experienced."[30] Similarly, Herle's work with Torres Straits Islanders produced new facts and also a more nuanced understanding of the capacity of anthropological research both to disrupt and to contribute to the preservation of traditional Indigenous life. Shelton's African and Caribbean co-curators articulated African ways of categorizing cultural knowledge as well as their perspectives on such sensitive topics as the continued holding of confiscated Benin brasses in British museums.[31]

The authors of these essays also reflect on the value of collaborative processes as sites for mutual learning and education, even when initial meetings and discussions prove to be difficult. Conaty notes the surprise of Glenbow designers when some of their "good ideas" could not be used because they breached cultural sensitivities. Yet, he says, as the partners continued to work together, not only did the museum staff come to understand Blackfoot perspectives, but the Blackfoot also developed a better understanding of museum process. In this sense the development of a collaborative exhibit fosters a bilateral version of the radical pedagogy advocated by Paolo Freire. His anti-authoritarian, democratic practice insists on the recognition that both teachers *and* students have important knowledge and that, for education to occur, their different subject positions have to be respected and rendered mutually intelligible. "Through dialogue," he has written, "grassroots groups can be challenged to process their social-historical experience as the experience that is formative for them individually and collectively. And through such dialogue the necessity of going beyond certain types of explanations of the 'facts' will become obvious."[32] The educational process invoked by collaborative exhibits is even more egalitarian and two-directional. In it both community and museum partners are simultaneously "teachers" and "grassroots" participants, experienced in their own worlds and inexperienced in the others'. When collaborative exhibit projects are successful, both museum and community partners come to new understandings through mutually respectful dialogue and exchange.

Members of the public regard museums, like the universities to which they have historically been linked, as sources of authoritative knowledge. The new methods of knowledge production and dissemination fostered by collaborative exhibits thus have the potential radically to change the very definition of the educational mission that the museum shares with other institutions. Because the partners are aware that the narratives and formulations they present will be publicly accessible to and vetted by community, academic, and general audiences, collaborative exhibits come under particular pressure from the multiple sources of authority. When successful, they can convey the situated nature of knowledge even more effectively than can "purer" formats of museum research. As the case studies show, these exhibits are serving as experimental sites where constructivist, pluralist, and multivocal theories of communication and representation are finding a practice.

A Typology of Collaboration: Community-Based Exhibits and Multivocal Exhibits

Although we are accustomed to speak as if there were a single process for collaborative exhibition work, I would like to argue that these case studies reveal a tendency for individual projects to cluster around two distinct models, which I term the community-based exhibit and the multivocal exhibit. The identification of the specific model being used in a given exhibition project is not just an analytical exercise but, rather, a practical necessity for both museum practitioners and viewers. Clarity among museum and community participants about the approach chosen will avoid unnecessary confusion, conflict, and frustration, while the disclosure to viewers of the model being used will provide them with the tools they need to assess the new pluralization of knowledge that collaborative exhibits foster. I will now turn to a more detailed discussion of each of these two models and the characteristic problems each encounters.

In community-based exhibits the role of the professional museum curator or staff member is defined as that of a facilitator who puts his or her disciplinary and museological expertise at the service of community members so that their messages can be disseminated as clearly and as effectively as possible. The community is the final arbiter of content, text, and other key components, and the museum becomes an extension of its space, a place in which the community's own images of its members' lifestyles, values, and concerns are projected. On one level, then, the community-based exhibit serves as a kind of semiotic repair kit that attaches new meanings to objects which museum visitors have become accustomed to see exclusively through the lenses of Western disciplines.[33] Furthermore, as Conaty's discussion shows, the decentring of objects in favour of narratives, stories, and performances is often a result of such processes.[34]

Kaxlaya Gvilas, the Heiltsuk exhibit whose opening I described at the beginning of this chapter, was a classic community-based installation. It resisted the standard presentation of ethnographic information about the functions, ceremonial uses, and meanings of the displayed objects. Instead, it focused on the lineage histories, names, and identities of the artists-ancestors who had made them and on contemporary issues of importance to the community. Although shown in southern Canadian cities, the exhibit was clearly intended to make sense, in the first instance, to Heiltsuk people and to serve their political ends. The privileging of community ways of knowing and the identification of community members as a primary audience – two hallmarks of the community-based exhibit – are also immediately recognizable in key decisions made in the Salish, Blackfoot, and Quseir exhibit projects. In *Written in the Earth* and *From under the Delta*, 4,000-year-old archaeological objects were juxtaposed with images and narratives of contemporary Salish people (fig. 11.1). In *Niitsitapiisinni* visitor attention is focused on stories and on holistic environments, contexts of meaning of primary importance for the Blackfoot, while the iconic Plains feather bonnets and painted shirts that have long fascinated museum visitors recede into the background (figs. 11.2 and 11.3). And at Quseir the artifacts recovered from a Roman harbour city that can be assumed to interest Euro-American tourists will be presented against the context of the subsequent Arab and Egyptian history of the region.

Torres Straits Islanders and *African Worlds* differ from these three exhibits in important ways that typify the multivocal exhibit. In both, museum staff and community consultants worked to find a space of coexistence for multiple perspectives. Both were characterized by a reflexive historicization of the earlier traditions of museum anthropology against which the curators were working, and both sought to share this reflexive awareness with visitors. In the case of *African Worlds*, this was done in two ways. The first strategy was the development of an intentionally dissonant installation design that aimed, as Shelton explains, "to convey a sense of alienation in the gallery: alienation

11.1 (*above*)   *Written in the Earth* at the Museum of Anthropology, University of British Columbia. Photo by David Cunningham

11.2 (*opposite, above*) Exhibit about traditional Blackfoot botanical knowledge in *Niitsitapiisinni: Our Way of Life*. Photo © Glenbow Museum, Calgary

11.3 (*opposite, below, and colour plate 9*) Traditional Blackfoot teepee and simulated landscape in *Niitsitapiisinni: Our Way of Life*. Photo © Glenbow Museum, Calgary

in the sense that these objects were displaced, far removed from the conditions of their usage and original signification"[35] (fig. 11.4). The second strategy was the use of four levels of text for each of the objects on display. These foregrounded the voice of a living community member, but also acknowledged Western ways of understanding the object's identities, functions, and meanings. Herle, too, used strategies of juxtaposition rather than harmonization in *Torres Straits Islanders* in order to create an exhibit that displayed, rather than elided, the multiple meanings attributed to objects and events by anthropologists and Islanders, past and present. She exploited the ironic resonances that resulted from the fact that the commemorative exhibit was installed within the early twentieth-century architecture and cases contemporary with the anthopological project she was re-presenting. The goal of both exhibits was to encourage visitors to consider their own historical positions in relation to colonial anthropology and the displacement of objects it achieved and to maintain an awareness of the dialogic tension between European and community partners' points of view.

11.4   Installation of the long-term exhibition *African Worlds* at the Horniman Museum, London. © Heini Schneebeli

This typological distinction between the community-based and multivocal approaches is, of course, ideal rather than real, and neither model can be applied in a pure form. In the case of community-based exhibits, the ideal role of facilitator prescribed for the museum professional would, if taken literally, constitute a kind of museological ghostwriting. Yet professional museum staff can never "only" facilitate, because community-based exhibits, like multivocal ones, are always built on top of layers of information, interpretation, and museological conventions that have accumulated over time. This point can be most clearly illustrated by collaborative exhibit projects involving archaeologists, perhaps because of the scientific methods and tools they use to develop basic data. The two archaeological case studies considered here demonstrate the ways in which a cognitive separation continues to be maintained within the model of the community-based exhibit project. In both examples the communities decide which objects are displayed and what is said about them. At the same time, however, much of the "what" is arrived at through the scientific methods of Western archaeology and is presented in specified registers of the exhibition text. And through the publication of articles in professional journals, site reports, and academic conference presentations, professional archaeology continues to constitute the authoritative basis for representation.

The new interpretations and knowledge that are brought forward in collaborative exhibits do not, in fact, erase Western traditions of discourse and display; rather, they intervene in them to a greater or lesser extent. The characteristic process of the collaborative exhibit, whether community-based or multivocal, is one of selection and supplementation. Discipline-based interpretation is always present, but certain elements are silenced, overlaid, or challenged in order to make room for new information and perspectives. The problem of acknowledging this occlusion – and of adequately presenting the grounds on which archivally or scientifically verifiable forms of knowledge are omitted – is particularly marked in community-based exhibits. As a result, they run the risk producing only a partial intelligibility by ignoring the needs of one set of viewers in favour of those of another. During the initial showing of *Kaxlaya Gvilas* at Toronto's Royal Ontario Museum, for example, the non-Heiltsuk visitors, who were in the vast majority, were frustrated because the lack of standard ethnographic information made it difficult for them to learn what the objects were used for and what the imagery "meant."[36]

In community-based exhibits there is a double danger, then, that legitimate modes of explanation will be dismissed along with oppressive constructs – that one set of exclusionary practices, in other words, will be traded for another. In their desire to atone for the historical legacy of colonialism, museums as institutions and their staff members as individuals often seem to seek a degree of self-effacement that borders on the deceptive.[37] Curiously, for example, the names and photographs of the Glenbow staff who served over several years as full partners and collaborators in the development of *Niitsitapiisini* are not included in the credit panel that occupies a large wall as the visitor leaves the exhibition. This omission is in accordance with a general Glenbow policy not to name individual staff members in exhibition credit panels. Unfortunately, however, by crediting only the Blackfoot consultants, the museum leaves the impression that, having pulled off a superb, fully collaborative exhibit, the Glenbow wanted to silence its own role out of some misconceived belief that the inclusion of the non-Aboriginal museum staff who contributed ethnographic and museological knowledge that was accepted by all the collaborators somehow undercut the exhibit's authenticity as truly Blackfoot.[38] The Glenbow example represents a more general tendency. At the Royal Ontario Museum the text panel identifying the original collector of the objects displayed in *Kaxlaya Gvilas* and crediting the extensive research conducted by associate curator Martha Black was placed facing a wall at the far end of the gallery, denying visitors an important point of orientation and inadequately crediting her work. As noted earlier, the collaborative paradigm is founded on a need to deconstruct the singular, distanced, and depersonalized authority of the modernist museum, but the deconstruction remains incomplete when museums fail to disclose their processes fully. Furthermore, if the contributions of both museum and community partners are not accurately and adequately credited, there is a real risk that either one or the other group will eventually turn to other forms of professional or community production in which their individual and collective voices can be heard clearly. I would urge, then, that the collaborative paradigm carries with it a particular need for museums to disclose the plural authorities behind the narratives they present so that visitors are left free to evaluate new and possibly discrepant contents and interpretations for themselves. If the actual processes of research, exchange, and negotiation are not made clear, the exhibit will end up occluding its own constructive pluralism and will sabotage the public's ability to appreciate its dialogic achievement. Indeed, since collaborative exhibits model an ideal that the partners would usually like the public to take home and apply in other social interactions, such silences are, in the end, self-defeating.

Multivocal exhibits also carry their own characteristic dangers. Most viewers are conditioned to find clarity, simplicity, inspiration, and/or pleasure in museums, yet these exhibits endeavour to make complexity and contradiction comprehensible and stimulating. If they are too successful in reconciling and aligning factual and perspectival differences that emerge from the contributions of community and museum partners, they can end up transmitting a falsely harmonious representation of conflicts not yet resolved in the world outside the museum. Successful efforts to maintain multiple perspectives even-handedly, however, can risk confusing and frustrating visitors. Exhibits that attempt to denaturalize the presence of foreign objects in Western museums can, furthermore, fail to provide adequately respectful contexts of display for these objects or, alternatively, obscure the legitimate ways in which some were obtained. To use Stephen Greenblatt's terms, while multivocal exhibits are more successful at conveying the historical and intercultural "resonance" of museum objects, community-based exhibits are usually more successful in creating the sense of "wonder" that most compellingly engages visitors and can most immediately instill in them the respect and admiration for the makers and their descendants that community partners typically desire.[39]

In light of this analysis the collaborative exhibit becomes recognizable as a typical hybrid product of the postcolonial era. It has been made both possible and necessary by processes of mixing and mutual education that have been going on for centuries. The Indigenous community member and the academically trained museum professional (the two, of course, are often found in one body) are hybrid beings, and the decision to engage in collaborative projects only intensifies this process of hybridization by promoting new dialogic exchanges. As Robert Young has noted, colonial hybridity was never a process of cultural fusion but, rather, one that maintained a tension among discrepant elements – a tension out of which critical insights can be generated. His statement that "in its more radical guise of disarticulating authority hybridity has also increasingly come to stand for the interrogative languages of minority cultures" can be taken as a gloss on collaborative exhibit projects.[40] In these terms, the difference between the community-based and the multivocal exhibition resides in the degree to which each seeks to explore its own dialogic tensions by giving voice to coexistent and multiple points of view and by revealing its own hybridity to visitors.

It is also useful to think about collaborative museum processes as negotiations of the new languages through which the colonized have been forced to speak. Simon During has termed the two sides to contemporary negotiations of the colonial legacy as the "post-colonized," who "identify with the culture destroyed by imperialism," and the "post-colonizers," who, "if they do not identify with imperialism, at least cannot jettison the culture and tongues of the imperialist nations."[41] The museum exhibit, like other European languages imposed by colonialism, is a Western expressive format which, while inevitably changing local meanings through processes of translation, also possesses a communicative power whose transnational reach is irresistible. What collaborative exhibits seek, in contrast to those they replace, are more accurate translations. In Shelton's words, "Representation of the 'other' is … a constant decolonisation and recolonisation of the imagination where truth is measurable only by the persuasive quality of the coherence and intelligibility of the discourse and its moral authority."[42]

Sitting Well with Each Other: The Museum in the Community

We may logically ask, then, to what degree we can read the changes we have been examining as evidence of broader social and political shifts *outside* the museum and to what degree they represent a new kind of agency *for* the museum. It has become a commonplace of the literature on museums to read earlier exhibits as expressions of a calculated and strategic program of enculturation to modernist notions of nation, empire, and colony. Yet today collaborative exhibits that directly challenge aspects of the status quo are being funded and even mandated by both liberal and conservative governments. They are being organized, furthermore, not only in smaller and more local museums but also by large, national institutions such as the Smithsonian, the Canadian Museum of Civilization, and New Zealand's Te Papa. Is the increasing acceptance of the collaborative paradigm by this last group, then, evidence that a pluralistic postcolonial ethos has established itself as ideology? Or, alternatively, do collaboratively produced exhibits present museum audiences with celebrations of diversity and dreams of social harmony that cannot be realized in the real world of legal rights, property, land, and money? Conaty's discussion of the difficulty of finding corporate sponsorship for *Niitsitapiisinni* and the disappointing initial visitor numbers suggests this last possibility.

Hooper-Greenhill has urged us to understand museum display as a technology generative of new forms of social interaction and as "a form of cultural politics."[43] Her faith is justified by the demonstrable power of the lengthy dialogic interaction required by collaborative exhibits to effect permanent changes in both community and museum participants. Collaborative exhibits lead the participants to ask new questions and to identify new kinds of

11.5 (*see also colour plate 10*)
The contemporary bead-
work display from *Across
Borders: Beadwork in
Iroquois Life*, a travelling
exhibition organized col-
laboratively by Indigenous
and non-Indigenous mu-
seums, cultural centres, and
curators, 1999–2003. Photo
courtesy of the McCord
Museum of Canadian
History, Montreal

problems; they reorient professional and institutional activities and change priorities; they stimulate the reformulation
of policies and procedures. I call these changes paradigmatic
precisely because they are so pervasive, affecting and transforming a comprehensive range of museum practices. As yet,
however, we have less evidence of the impact of these exhibits
on audiences. Museum exhibits do not do their work in a moment, and the creator of an exhibit usually finds out only years
later, if ever, about the new perspectives that were suddenly
glimpsed by a local visitor, a tourist, or a schoolchild during a
visit to the exhibit, of the curiosity that was whetted, or of the
small epiphanies that were sparked. Yet this accumulation of
small impacts may well, over a long period of time, constitute the most lasting impact of any exhibit project. Museums
pursue collaborative exhibits in the hope of multiplying these
small impacts and because of their faith that the directness
of voice they privilege will remove distorting lenses and correct mistranslations, enabling rather than obstructing authentic communication across the boundaries of difference.
The proponents of collaborative exhibits have, in the words of
Anthony Shelton and his African and British collaborators,
"embraced the vision of museums as places of dialogue where
members of different cultures can 'sit well with each other'"[44]
(fig. 11.5).

A Closing

A month after the opening with which I began this chapter, the UBC Museum of Anthropology hosted another formal event. On that evening the monumental totem poles that ring its Great Hall witnessed, not the singing of the First Nations, but the melodic chanting of verses of the Qur'an. The evening's ceremonies marked not the opening but the closing of a collaboratively organized exhibition, *The Spirit of Islam: Experiencing Islam through Calligraphy*. Closings, unlike openings, are not common museum rituals, and this ceremony had been improvised in response to a need, felt strongly by all the partners, for a communal, ceremonial marking of an extraordinary experience which had taken over their lives during the previous three years of development and public exhibition. The decision to begin the project had initially been taken at the behest of Muslim communities in the Vancouver area, who wanted to find ways to create a better understanding of Islam and to combat pervasive and inaccurate stereotypes of Muslims. It thus arose, not from a desire to present and interpret an available collection of objects, but from a felt need to educate and to change public perceptions. The masterpieces of the Islamic art of calligraphy that were on display had been borrowed in order to provide an appropriate "hook" for the educational project.

When the exhibit opened in October of 2001, the terrorist attacks on New York City and Washington of the previous September lent the project an even greater urgency. For the museum staff and the more than seventy community volunteers, however, during the more than two years of intensive collaborative work, the world had already changed in positive ways that had prepared them to meet the unanticipated challenge. Museum staff had discovered in their city a geography of previously unknown Muslim schools, mosques, and cultural centres. They had attended numerous community functions, celebrated Muslim holidays with new friends, and begun to learn a previously unfamiliar history of calligraphy, art, and belief. The community volunteers had raised hundreds of thousands of dollars through donations large and small. Perhaps most remarkably, the museum had proved to be an effective meeting place for the highly diverse Muslim communities who, although they had established themselves in the same metropolitan area, had not previously worked together on a common project. It provided a site from which a highly diverse assemblage of linguistic, diasporic, and religious groups could constructively articulate its own differences, identify a common ground of shared belief and experience, and find a unified voice with which to speak to non-Muslims.

The need for a closing was also born of a collective desire to ensure that the end of the exhibition did not mean the end of the collaboration between the museum and the Muslim communities. It was an occasion both for self-assessment and for the affirmation of a joint commitment to continue to work together. Although the gallery space had to be cleared for a new project and the loans of embroidered textiles, illuminated manuscripts, and inlaid furniture returned to their owners, a path of future collaboration was also being opened not only between the museum and the communities but amongst the communities themselves. The closing was a public testimonial of the transformative social power that can be generated by collaborative exhibit projects, when diverse communities with different intellectual, cultural, and social orientations come together in a museum as equals, in determined and patient search for a language of common understanding.

12

Inside-Out and Outside-In

Re-presenting Native North America at the
Canadian Museum of Civilization and the
National Museum of the American Indian
(2003–2004)

For Native North Americans, the new millennium started
with a big museological bang when national museums in
both the United States and Canada inaugurated new and radically revised exhibitions about the Indigenous peoples of the
Americas.[1] The First Peoples Hall of the Canadian Museum of
Civilization (CMC), which opened in February 2003, occupies
almost 35,000 square feet in Canada's national museum of
history and anthropology in Gatineau, Quebec. The Smithsonian Institution's National Museum of the American Indian
(NMAI), which opened in September 2004, is an even larger
project, occupying a new four-storey building on the Mall in
Washington, DC. From the outside, the structures that house
the new installations are close cousins. Both were designed
in the signature style of Douglas Cardinal, a Canadian architect of Blackfoot ancestry. Cardinal's organic forms reflect his
deep conviction of the integral bonds linking humans to the
natural world and the topographies of land.[2] On the banks of
the Ottawa River (fig. 12.1) as on the Mall in Washington (fig.
12.2), the undulating strata of his buildings and the warmth of
their gold-hued stone stand out against the rectilinearity and
grey historicism of nearby government buildings.

The choice of Cardinal's design over other entries in the
international architectural competition for the design of the
new national museum of Canada held in 1982 signalled the
transformation that had occurred in the country's sense of
national identity since 1905, when the government commissioned its predecessor, the Victoria Memorial Museum, to
be built in the neo-Gothic Scottish baronial style typical of
nineteenth-century British imperial architecture. Cardinal's

12.1   View of the Canadian Museum of Civilization, Gatineau, Quebec, showing the Parliament Buildings on the Ontario side of the Ottawa River. Photo courtesy of Ottawa Tourism

12.2   The National Museum of the American Indian in Washington, DC, from the back, looking toward the adjacent Capitol building. Photo © Getty Images

architecture for the NMAI represents an analogous break with the Greco-Roman and republican references of the older Smithsonian museums of art and natural history that face it across the Mall, as well as with its neoclassical predecessor, the Museum of the American Indian in New York.[3] In keeping with the guidelines provided by the NMAI's Native American advisers, it was designed to be "welcoming … open to the sky, warm in color and tone, and facing the East."

Inside, however, the new exhibitions display as many differences as similarities. On the one hand, there are a number of striking convergences in the themes and display approaches adopted for the two exhibitions. These similarities, I will argue, testify to the epochal changes in the power relations between Indigenous peoples and settler institutions that took place inside and outside both museums during the last two decades of the twentieth century. These changes were part of a global movement toward a postcolonial museology powered by the anti-colonial activism of Indigenous peoples in informal alliance with academic post-structuralist critics of museum representation.[4] The contrasts between the new exhibitions, on the other hand, point to historically contingent differences in the relationships between Indigenous peoples and the institutions and governments of Canada and the United States. These result from more local and idiosyncratic processes of decolonization that have been shaped by distinctive national and institutional histories. To explore both the global and the local resonances of the new exhibitions, I will ask two kinds of questions. The first has to do with power. What are the structural problems inherent in mounting revisionist exhibitions within national museums, and to what degree can Indigenous peoples who have been marginalized within modern nation-states use such museums as effective sites for political contestation? The second, related question has to do with poetics. In what ways do contestatory politics intervene in the modernist display paradigms of art and artifact which, as we will see, have been compromised by their historical deployment in colonial museology? I will not, of course, be able to explore either of these questions exhaustively in a single chapter. Rather, by looking briefly at the historical contexts of both exhibitions and by comparing their thematic structures and several specific installations, I hope to provide a fruitful analytical framework for thinking about Native North American museum representation, not only in Washington and Ottawa but also elsewhere.

Contexts: Institutional, Personal, Political

Museum exhibitions begin with abstract conceptual plans, but they are realized by individuals who must negotiate particular institutional histories, who bring to the table their prior experiences of exhibition development, and who are ultimately answerable to external sponsors and government agencies. It will, therefore, be useful to position the First Peoples Hall and the NMAI's long-term displays in relation to the modernist twentieth-century exhibitions that preceded them, to several critical events that had formative impacts on key individuals who worked on the new exhibitions, and to the late twentieth-century identity politics that shaped the expectations of external sponsors.

Although the older permanent installations replaced by the new exhibitions differed in numerous details, both were informed by the assumptions about universal progress and cultural evolution that were fundamental to twentieth-century modernist museum anthropology. The Museum of the American Indian and the National Museum of Canada's previous installations were organized according to a standardized system of culture areas that was closely associated with environmental determinism, and they employed a taxonomic approach to artifacts derived from natural history classification that objectified and dehumanized Aboriginal people and their cultures. Their exhibits located Native North Americans in an idealized and fictive past prior to contact with the West and, whether overtly or implicitly, conveyed the message that Aboriginal people had lost their authenticity and that their traditions were incompatible with modernity and were fated to disappear.[5] The crowded cases of the Museum of the American Indian seemed to epitomize the greed of Western collectors, their fetishization of rare and old objects, and – through their public displays of human remains and sacred objects – their disrespect for Indigenous beliefs and sensitivities.

The almost exclusive reliance of these typical twentieth-century installations on displays of historical material objects has been analyzed by Tony
Bennett in his searching discussion of the connections that link evolutionist
museum narratives, colonialism, and the "new liberal" political agendas of
Victorian Britain and its colonies: "The museum's task was, so to speak, to
batten down a new order of things by reassembling the objects comprising
the artefactual domain (bones, fossils, minerals, tools, pottery, etc.) in gradual and continuous lines of evolutionary development. This comprised the
central exhibition rhetoric through which the 'evolutionary showmen' sought
to display the orders of nature and culture, and the relations between them
in ways that would regulate progress by providing a template for its smooth
and uninterrupted advance."[6] Although Bennett's focus in this passage is on
museums at the turn of the twentieth century, the reliance on objects and
texts that he describes and the "orders of nature and culture" they charted
remained largely undisturbed for most of that century. When opportunities
arose in the United States and Canada to build new national museums, however, the link between material culture display and oppressive colonial discourses of race, history, and time, long naturalized by modernist museum
displays, would become a key site for reformist attacks.

The active development of both the CMC's and the NMAI's exhibits began
during the period of heightened Native North American cultural activism of
the late 1980s and early 1990s. In both countries, change in museum representation had been identified by Aboriginal leaders as a visible and immediately
obtainable goal useful to broader, long-term political agendas. In Canada the
Aboriginal boycott and national controversy over *The Spirit Sings: Artistic
Traditions of Canada's First Peoples*, a high profile "super show" of Native
art and culture organized for the 1988 Winter Olympics in Calgary, provided
the catalyst for the creation of a national Task Force on Museums and First
Peoples. The central recommendation of its report, issued in 1992, was that
partnerships between museums and First Nations be established to guide all
future projects related to Aboriginal peoples, including exhibitions, research,
and the care of collections.[7] During the same period, Indigenous activism in
the United States resulted in the creation of a legal instrument for repatriation rather than a more general policy, when the Native American Graves
Protection and Repatriation Act (NAGPRA) was passed by the US Congress
in 1990. NAGPRA requires the disclosure of museum holdings and the return
of human remains, sacred objects, and objects of cultural patrimony to appropriate Native American tribes and descendants. Despite these different
points of departure, during the past fifteen years museums in both countries have moved in similar directions; in US museums, collaboration with
Native American communities or curators is increasingly normative, while
in Canada repatriation has proceeded both under the guidelines included in
the task force report and as part of the treaty and land-claims negotiations
that were renewed in the early 1990s.[8]

A third important event that lies in the background of the new exhibitions was the Columbus quincentenary in 1992, which provided occasions for Native American contestations of settler historical narratives. Special exhibitions that were perceived as presenting triumphalist settler narratives became sites of protest, while other, Native-curated exhibitions presented works by contemporary Indigenous artists that powerfully conveyed revisionist perspectives on colonial history. These protests and curatorial initiatives succeeded in shifting initial plans for public celebration to more sombre forms of commemoration and mourning.[9] In retrospect, several specific projects can be seen as opening salvoes in the reformist campaigns that resulted in the First Peoples Hall and the NMAI's exhibits. These include *Indigena: Contemporary Aboriginal Perspectives*, co-curated for the CMC by Gerald McMaster (Plains Cree) and Lee-Ann Martin (Mohawk); *The Submuloc Show/Columbus Wohs*, organized by ATLATL-National Native Arts Network; and the National Gallery of Canada's *Land, Spirit, Power: First Nations at the National Gallery,* co-developed by a team of Aboriginal and non-Aboriginal curators. Together, the art works, installations, and texts stimulated by the Columbus quincentennary comprised a powerful corpus of revisionist historical work which, in Canada, was situated inside the space of two national museums.[10]

The 1992 exhibitions were important formative experiences for several Aboriginal artists and curators who would go on to play key roles in conceptualizing the new CMC and NMAI exhibitions. McMaster, for example, served as the initial co-chair of the First Peoples Hall and then as special assistant to the director for Mall Exhibitions at the NMAI, while Tuscarora artist, curator, and academic Jolene Rickard, who contributed artwork to several 1992 exhibitions, such as *Partial Recall*, curated by Lucy Lippard, would co-curate two of the NMAI's three permanent exhibitions, *Our Lives* and *Our Peoples.*[11] The experience gained in 1992 helped to shape a sense of common cause among Indigenous cultural producers, as well as an understanding of how contemporary art and installation could be used as effective rhetorical strategies for political contestation and historical revisionism.

New Museums and New Opportunities

The occasion for a comprehensive rethinking of the CMC's installations arose in the early 1980s, when the government of Prime Minister Pierre Trudeau allocated long-awaited funds to create new buildings for the National Museum of Man and the National Gallery on the Quebec and Ontario sides of the Ottawa River, adjacent to Parliament Hill. The initial program of permanent exhibitions developed for the new national museum, renamed the Canadian Museum of Civilization,[12] was informed by the vision of its director, Dr George MacDonald, a specialist in Northwest Coast archaeology, and it reflects his passionate admiration for the arts and cultures of that region and the populist communication theory of his early mentor, Marshall McLuhan.

The two major exhibitions that were installed for the museum's official opening in 1989 were, accordingly, a Grand Hall devoted to Northwest Coast arts
and cultures and a Canada Hall devoted to settler history that was modelled
on the streetscape environments of the Milwaukee Public Museum, the Royal
British Columbia Museum, and the Epcot Center at Disneyworld.

The Canada Hall is conceptualized as a journey across the country from
the east to the west coast. The visitor follows a winding path that is not only
geographically but also chronologically directive. The sequence of small, enclosed, and realistic environments moves from seventeenth-century Basque
whalers on the Atlantic coast to the Wildcat Café in modern-day Yellowknife,
Northwest Territories. Aboriginal people make a few brief appearances along
the way – we meet Métis buffalo hunters on the prairies and Nisga'a fishermen in British Columbia – but their presence is overwhelmed by the bustle
of settler commerce and industry. The Canada Hall's additive and sequential
structure contrasts with the unity and simultaneity of the Grand Hall pan-
orama. Where the former evokes travel, modernity, and progress, the latter
conveys stability and timelessness.

The elongated oval of the Grand Hall is the museum's most prestigious
space, and its windowed outer wall provides spectacular views of Parliament
Hill. Along the opposite wall and facing out over the expanse of a polished
stone floor designed to suggest the surface of water, MacDonald and curator
Andrea Laforet installed the museum's outstanding collection of totem poles
and a line of Northwest Coast house fronts. These fronts were commissioned
from contemporary Aboriginal artists in the traditional styles of six different
coastal peoples. The historicism and the fictive unity of these houses seems at
first to evoke the frozen time of the "ethnographic present" that has been deconstructed by Johannes Fabian and others. Yet, arguably, in the Grand Hall
this impression of timelessness converges with an important goal of the First
Nations artists and experts who collaborated in its creation and who have insisted that museums represent their cultures as *both* traditional *and* living. It
could be argued that important aspects of the Grand Hall were accomplished
through partnership models *avant la lettre*.

Early in the CMC's planning process, a huge space behind the Grand Hall
was allocated for a First Peoples Hall that would present exhibits on Indigenous peoples outside the Northwest Coast. Initially, the exhibits were envisioned as a set of standard culture-area displays using dioramas and sci-
entific/ethnographic information focused primarily on historical lifestyles
and traditional subsistence patterns (fig. 12.3). During the 1980s the museum's
non-Native ethnology and archaeology curators completed detailed plans
for the exhibits, but implementation was put on hold so that the museum
could devote its resources to completing the Grand Hall and the Canada Hall
in time for the 1989 opening. By the time the museum returned to the First
Peoples Hall project in the early 1990s, the boycott of *The Spirit Sings* and
the task force report had radically altered the familiar modernist terrain of
Canadian museum anthropology. Three of the CMC's curators – Andrea La-

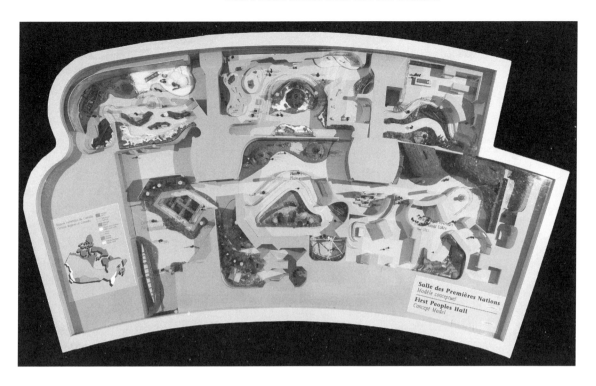

foret, Gerald McMaster, and Robert McGhee – were members of the task force and had helped to develop the new model of partnership between Aboriginal communities and museums. The CMC board endorsed the task force report just as the museum was resuming work on the First Peoples Hall, and in accordance with its recommendations, the museum appointed an Aboriginal advisory committee to work with the team of museum curators in the development of the new hall. Although the CMC had worked with many Aboriginal consultants on previous exhibits, this process marked a defining break with the traditional academic and disciplinary structures of curatorial authority because it fundamentally altered the power relations embedded in earlier consultative processes.[13]

The power relationships that were put into place for the development of the NMAI's Mall building involved an even more radical shift than occurred at the CMC. When the US Congress agreed to transfer the collections amassed by George Heye to a new National Museum of the American Indian created within the Smithsonian Institution, it entrusted the project to a Native American–dominated directorate and board, who created a curatorial process that inverted the power relationships characteristic of modernist museum anthropology.

12.3   Model showing the initial late-1980s plan for the Canadian Museum of Civilization's First Peoples Hall. The culture-area map is visible on the left. Photo © Canadian Museum of Civilization, IMG2011-0038-0001Dm.

In contrast to the past, when the Native "informants" consulted by professional ethnologists in the course of fieldwork or exhibition development had
no authority over the end product, the NMAI set up a series of vetting sessions during which a range of Aboriginal and non-Aboriginal experts were
invited to Washington to critique the storylines being developed by the museum's Aboriginal-led curatorial team.[14] Whereas the CMC's First Peoples
Hall took shape as the result of a process of negotiation and compromise, at
the NMAI ultimate decision-making power was unambiguously in the hands
of senior Native American staff. As we will see, these contrasting curatorial
structures and power relations have resulted in different narrative structures
and modes of display.

Power structures operate not only intra- but also inter-institutionally, especially in national museums. In establishing the NMAI, Congress had followed
the precedent set earlier by the Smithsonian's National Museum of African
Art and the United States Holocaust Memorial Museum, both of which accommodate the representational needs of ethnic minorities through separate
institutions operating under the Smithsonian umbrella. As would be the case
with the NMAI, the National Museum of African Art had come into being
when Congress accessioned the collection of a private museum with chronic
funding problems and empowered a new, African-American–led institution
to display as works of art objects very similar to those already being displayed
as ethnographic artifacts by the anthropology division of the Smithsonian's
National Museum of Natural History.[15] The United States Holocaust Memorial Museum has a historical and commemorative mandate, rather than an
ethnographic focus, and it is governed by members of the American-Jewish
community it represents. The system of special-interest museums is accompanied by its own politics. The Canadian model of collaboration requires negotiation, whether among staff belonging to different professional and ethnic
communities working within a single institution or between the institution
and outside cultural communities. In contrast, the system of separate museums dedicated to particular cultural interests that has been developing
within the Smithsonian Institution must also negotiate the space between the
more homogeneous subject positions of their staff members and the majori-
tarian views and ideologies promoted by the governing institution. In part,
the difference between the museum structures developed in Canada and the
United States in response to late twentieth-century identity politics must be a
result of Canada's much smaller population and resources. But, arguably, it is
also likely that the Canadian reliance on internal negotiation within a single
institution reflects the country's different political history and the national
culture of negotiation that has developed in response to unresolved issues of
federal-provincial, French-English, and Aboriginal–Euro-Canadian power
and sovereignty.

Timothy Luke has addressed questions of power in the museum in his
book *Museum Politics: Power Plays at the Exhibition*.[16] He underscores the
importance of looking at both the macro- and the micro-levels of exhibition-

ary events – at both the larger issues of power they engage and the individual choices and decisions through which their intents are realized. Successful exhibitions, he argues, "are always already shows of force that articulate new plays of political power in their presentations of 'culture,' 'history,' 'nature,' or 'technology' for the museum. Which images and objects are mobilized, how they are displayed, where they are situated, and why they are chosen all constitute powerful rhetorical strategies for governmentalizing maneuvers, especially at those sites, like the Smithsonian Institution … where the authoritative pretense is maintained that these sites are where 'the nation tells its story.'"[17] Revisionist exhibitions can backfire, as Luke demonstrates in his analyses of two widely publicized controversies that developed at the Smithsonian around the National Museum of American Art's 1991 exhibit *The West as America* and the National Air and Space Museum's planned *Enola Gay* exhibit in 1995. Both provoked conservative reactions inside and outside Congress, revealing the limits of institutional tolerance for historical revisionism during the 1990s, just as the planning process for the NMAI was beginning.

National museums, funded by national governments and directed by their appointees, have no choice but to navigate official ideologies and politics. The framing strategies of the Smithsonian's minority-interest museums can be detected in specific elements of their installations. One of the first installations that visitors encounter at the United States Holocaust Memorial Museum, for example, is comprised of the flags of American battalions that liberated concentration camps, an exhibitionary gesture that links the European story told inside the building to US history. Native American histories are, of course, by definition indigenous to the country, but the NMAI evidently saw a need to make visible contemporary alliances with dominant political forces to counterbalance the revisionist thrusts of the museum's historical narratives. It could be argued that the prominence of US senator Ben Nighthorse Campbell, a Native American and a Republican, at the museum's opening ceremonies and the inclusion of his work as a jeweller among its opening exhibitions served a similar purpose to the flags at the Holocaust museum.

The First Peoples Hall was begun in the midst of what political scientist Alan Cairns has referred to as a "revolution" in Aboriginal peoples' relationships with Canada. This revolution has been advanced through a series of contestations, political negotiations, and legal decisions, including the federal government's withdrawal of its 1969 White Paper on Indian policy, which, as Cairns argues, finally ended the century-old official policy of directed assimilation.[18] Among the landmark settlements and negotiated agreements that followed were the enshrinement of Aboriginal sovereignty in the Canadian constitution in 1982; the re-establishment in the early 1990s of a federal-provincial treaty process for the negotiation of land claims after a hiatus of nearly a century; the institutionalization of new forms of territorial sovereignty and self-government with the Nisga'a agreement of 1997 and the establishment of the eastern Arctic territory of Nunavut in 1999; and the federal government's formal apology in 2008 for the damage wrought by the residential school system. The past few decades have also witnessed violent confrontations between Natives and non-Natives, most notably at Oka, Quebec, in 1990, when Mohawk residents and their supporters opposed plans to build a golf course on a traditional burial ground, and at Burnt Church, New Brunswick, in 1999 and 2000, when Mi'kmaq exercised treaty rights to fish commercially as well as for their own use, upheld by a recent Supreme Court of Canada decision. Direct references to many of these events are found inside the First Peoples Hall.

The legal and political issues facing Native Americans during this period have been somewhat different. On the one hand, title to major tracts of unceded Indian land in the United States had been settled with California tribes after World War II and in Alaska in the 1970s. Arguably, however, endemic problems of racism, poverty, and stereotyping faced by Aboriginal people have had a relatively low profile in the United States, where Native American issues must compete for attention with those of numerically larger African-American and Hispanic-American minorities. During the last decades of the twentieth century, two federal initiatives intended to clarify issues of Indian identity under the law have, instead, according to many Native Americans, exacerbated existing ambiguities and injustices. The federal recognition process established by the Bureau of Indian Affairs in 1978 to enable unrecognized tribes to claim legal status as Indians has proved controversial, and it is widely regarded as overly stringent in its requirements and political in its implementation.[19] The Indian Arts and Crafts Act of 1990, which was intended to prevent appropriation and false advertising by authorizing only enrolled members of recognized tribes to exhibit or sell work as Native American, is also regarded as having made matters worse.[20] Thus, while land claims dominate the agenda of Aboriginal people in Canada, issues of identity have particular prominence among Indigenous people in the United States.

The First Peoples Hall at the Canadian Museum of Civilization

It is not surprising to find that the issue of land claims confronts the visitor at the entrance to the First Peoples Hall. Visitors come first to a billboard-sized panel bearing words of welcome. In conformity with a protocol that had become widely established in Canadian museums during the preceding decade, this welcome is issued not by the museum or its sponsor, the government of Canada, but by the Kitigan Zibi Circle of Elders, the representatives of the First Nation recognized as the traditional owner of the land on which the museum sits (fig. 12.4). It is inscribed over a mural-sized picture which seamlessly combines an early nineteenth-century watercolour with a contemporary photograph of the same site.[21] Through the use of digital wizardry, the image proposes an impossible fiction that collapses time and allows two bodies to occupy the same space. In the lower half of the panel, a group of Aboriginal people dressed in the clothing of the early nineteenth

Pijashin • Bienvenue • Welcome

12.4   Welcome panel (first version) for the First Peoples Hall, Canadian Museum of Civilization. Photo © Canadian Museum of Civilization, D2004-06125

century stand on the bank of a river looking across at the opposite shore. We, the museum visitors, are positioned behind these figures in the space of the gallery, and as our eyes follow the direction of their gazes, we become aware of two things in quick succession. First, these nineteenth-century Algonkians are standing on the site of the museum, where we now stand, and, second, the upper half of the image is filled with something that they could not have seen, the neo-Gothic buildings of the Canadian Parliament. These buildings, constructed between 1860 and 1922, symbolize the historical process by which Aboriginal peoples' sovereignty was supplanted and their lands appropriated. We realize that these Aboriginal figures stand before us not only in pictorial space but also temporally, and their priorization begins to open the questions of other claims to priority – to land, power, and voice – that will be affirmed in the exhibits of the First Peoples Hall.

The advisory committee established four themes for the introductory zone of the hall: "We are diverse," "We are still here," "We contribute," and "We have an ancient relationship with the land." The themes are articulated through a series of individual text panels and through visual materials that focus on the achievements of prominent contemporary Aboriginal people. Repeatedly, the headers tie the themes to the issue of land: "We celebrate our long history in this land"; "We celebrate our work, our creativity, our creations"; "We celebrate

12.5 (*see also colour plate 11*)   Introductory section, "An Aboriginal Presence,"
in the First Peoples Hall, Canadian Museum of Civilization. Photo © Canadian
Museum of Civilization, D2003-13058

our differences, our similarities, and our survival as Aboriginal people"; "We
have not forgotten the land …"; "We have an Ancient Bond with the Land";
"Our bond with the land is forged in knowledge"; "Our bond with the land
is forged in centuries of hard work"; "Our bond with the land is forged in the
prayers, offerings, and dances that hold our connections with other living
beings of the earth"; "We speak of our bond with the land in the things we
make, in the memories of our Elders and in the voices of our own experience." This is the only section of the exhibition that foregrounds the beautifully crafted and artistically elaborated objects that are today featured not
only by anthropology museums but also by art galleries. However, instead
of the hushed quietude typical of the poetics of the art installation, which is
intended to foster an appreciation of aesthetic singularity, or the typological
groupings of earlier ethnological displays that promoted the kind of analytical clarity characteristic of the earlier exhibits described by Tony Bennett,
the First Peoples Hall presents us with a party – cheerful, noisy, and crowded
(fig. 12.5). Along one curving side of the visitor path, a thematically structured installation spells out the advisory committee's key messages through
a sequence of text panels, images, art, and material culture that focus on the
achievements of contemporary individuals. The theme of diversity is illustrated by a jumble of objects from different times and places that jostle each
other in purposeful but chaotic confusion, leaving an impression of colour,
variation, and vitality, but denying the possibility of isolated scrutiny of individual pieces.

    In the next section of the exhibition, "Ways of Knowing," these affirma-
tions and assertions are addressed in more depth and through a strategy of

calculated juxtaposition with the findings of Western ethnology and archaeology. The key themes continue to echo – literally as well as figuratively. As
we walk through the space, we can hear in the background the audio track
of a video entitled "Relationship to the Land" – "The land owns us, we don't
own land"; "Until land claims are settled, we're trespassers ... in our own
way of life"; and "We are the memory of the land." The central message of
this section is the equivalent authority of traditional Indigenous knowledge,
particularly as articulated through oral traditions and stories, to Western scientific knowledge. It is conveyed by inverting the usual proportion of space
devoted to traditional Indigenous knowledge and Western anthropological
and archaeological knowledge. The First Peoples Hall's main archaeological
installation is surrounded by an array of Indigenous storytelling forms centring on Norval Morrisseau's painted account of Ojibwa cosmology, *A Separate Reality*, and Shelley Niro's sculpture of the Hodenosaunee creation story,
Skywoman. Also prominent are a storytelling booth and a large theatre in
which CMC curator and Mi'kmaq elder Stephen Augustine narrates parts of
the Glooscap trickster-hero cycle.

The archaeological exhibit is also theatrical. Through glass floor panels we
see and walk over the recreated artifactual deposits that museum archaeologists have found at the Bluefish Caves in the Yukon Territory, a 25,000-year-
old site containing the oldest deposits of human-made tools in Canada. Adjacent text panels describe the excavations and research, as well as the scientific
arguments for climate changes thought to have controlled the movements of
people into North America across the Bering Straits from Asia. In "Ways of
Knowing," then, the visitor is presented with two different kinds of stories
that account for the human habitation of North America, but no attempt is
made to resolve their discrepancies. Rather, they are presented side by side
as coexistent, alternative, and competing forms of explanation – two bodies
occupying the same space.

When we enter the third section of the First Peoples Hall, "An Ancient Bond
with the Land," we could be forgiven for thinking that the initial 1980s plan
for the First Peoples Hall had survived after all. As the introductory panel in-
forms us, its six large semicircular bays "explore the role of whaling, fishing,
communal hunting, farming and trading in supporting Aboriginal societies
across the northern half of North America." Structured according to classical
anthropological frameworks, it purports to explain the traditional lifestyles
of regional Aboriginal groups in terms of the interdependence of ecology,
Indigenous subsistence systems, technologies, and material culture. Large
scrims evoking the natural environment form the backdrops for tableaux of
pre-contact types of tools, hunting and fishing equipment, and dwellings. On
closer inspection, however, we find a number of strategically placed interventions and negotiations of these standard ethnographic tropes. In the "People
of the Longhouse" bay devoted to the Onkwehonwe (Iroquois), for example,
the focus is on the role of women in Onkwehonwe society, a revisionist stress
that intervenes in the dominant patriarchal discourse of colonial anthropol-

12.6 The "Contemporary Issues" booth adjacent to the "People of the Long-house" bay with video and artifacts related to the Oka confrontation of 1990, in the First Peoples Hall, Canadian Museum of Civilization. Photo by Ruth B. Phillips

ogy. But the juxtapositions are often uneasy. A text discussing "Changing human-plant relationships" and the importation of corn from Mexico seven thousand years ago is followed by others identifying the earth as Turtle Island and discussing "Clans and Clan Mothers" and "Women's Influence on the Men's World."

Adjacent to each bay, furthermore, is a small booth containing a video, texts, and artifacts that address contemporary issues. The booth adjacent to "People of the Longhouse" focuses on the 1990 Oka crisis and shows modern-day clan mothers assuming traditional leadership roles (fig. 12.6). Its artifact label reads: "Razor wire / 1990 / Used at Kahna-wake (near Montreal) by the Canadian Armed Forces during the Oka Crisis / steel / Loan from the Kanien'kehaka On-kwawen:na Raotithohkwa." This standard "tombstone" label verges on postcolonial mimicry in its terse reference to the violent history associated with the object. Similarly, the booth adjacent to the "People of the Maritimes" bay focuses on the confrontations between Aboriginal and non-Aboriginal fishermen at Burnt Church that followed the Supreme Court's Donald Marshall decision.

This video so well illustrates the complex negotiations of tradition and innovation, history and politics, and memory and modernity that characterize the First Peoples Hall that it is worth looking at in detail. As the video opens, the voice of a young man begins to tell a story from the Glooscap cycle about the lobster and the eel. The voice of an elder takes it up, explaining how the two sea creatures at first tried to inhabit the same river but found in the end that each had to find its own seasonal habitation in order for them to coexist in harmony. While we listen, we watch children in a modern-day Mi'kmaq school making enormous full-body masks, with which they will enact the story for an annual festival. We then hear about the Donald Marshall case and watch familiar though still shocking newsreel footage of the tense confrontations and boat rammings that occurred during the summer of 2000, when angry non-Aboriginal fisherman found they had to compete with Aboriginal fishermen on new terms for dwindling Atlantic fish stocks. The narrator concludes: "Today the Mi'kmaq are still waging political battles. Today the lobster and the eel continue to avoid each other, returning to the river at different times of the year." The solution being offered here to the two-body problem is, then, that of spatial separation and parallelism, which is, as Cairns notes, the favoured option of many contemporary Aboriginal political leaders.

The final section of the hall is devoted to "The Arrival of Strangers" and the enormous changes that have been enforced on Aboriginal people in the course of five centuries of contact with settler society. In installation terms, the displays in this section adopt conventional didactic forms, such as text panels and a rich array of artifacts, images, and documents shown behind glass and on the walls, all organized along a linear path subdivided according to a succession of thematic topics. Yet these themes reflect, summarize, and reduce to digestible proportions a generation of revisionist historical and ethnographic research, not only about the fur trade, the explorers, and the retention of traditional beliefs but also about conversion, residential schools, high steel workers, canneries, gambling, the adoption of Western farming, legislation, rodeos, and veterans. Although created by ten different curators, Native and non-Native, the installation speaks to the visitor in the singular, anonymous voice of the modernist museum.

The First Peoples Hall closes with a display on Aboriginal humour, complete with a video of stand-up comedians and a montage of cartoons, and with an installation of contemporary paintings and sculptures that are presented as an important site of Indigenous resistance and discourse. The words of Aboriginal elder statesman George Erasmus are mounted at the exit of the hall: "The history of our people needs to be told. We need to present accurately what happened in the past, so that we can deal with it in the future. I don't like what has happened over the last 500 years. We can't do much about that. But what are we going to do about the next 500 years? What are we going to do about the next ten years?" His eloquent, authoritative words issue a challenge to the viewer to use the experience of a visit to the First Peoples Hall to carry forward the process of change that has linked the hall's varied and heterogeneous installations both as counterpoint and as a continuing thematic.

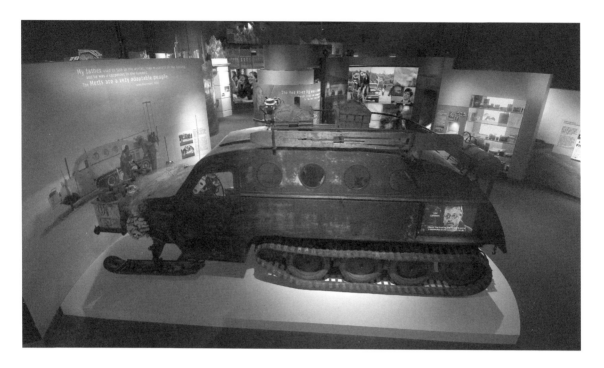

12.7   Module curated by the Saint-Laurent Métis of Manitoba featuring a Bombardier ice-fishing vehicle, from the "Our Lives: Contemporary Identities" section of the National Museum of the American Indian. Photo by Walter Larrimore; courtesy of the National Museum of the American Indian

The NMAI's Exhibits

The NMAI's long-term exhibits are divided into three large thematic sections: *Our Universe* focuses on Indigenous cosmologies and belief systems, *Our Lives* explores issues of lifestyle and identity, and *Our Peoples* addresses the heavy legacy of history since European contact. In each of the three areas there is a central installation created by named NMAI curators that explicates the general theme. A series of smaller modular exhibits, planned to rotate over time, open off this core. Each is created by a group of non-professional curators from a different Aboriginal community. In the opening round of exhibits the communities represented ranged from Chile to the Canadian Arctic. As at the CMC, one of the main messages of the exhibits, taken as a whole, is diversity. Not only recognized tribes are included but also the unrecognized Pamunkey of Virginia, a Métis community from Manitoba, and an ethnically diverse urban Indian community in Chicago (fig. 12.7). And also as in the First Peoples Hall, the theme of contemporaneity is everywhere. Despite the unparalleled richness of the NMAI's collections, the large majority of the objects that serve as adjuncts to the busy, didactic photo murals and the text panels that feature the faces and voices of contemporary community members are from the second half of the twentieth century, a period that had been excluded from most exhibitions by the modernist paradigm of authenticity.

These two emphases can be illustrated by looking more closely at the exhibit curated by a team from the Mohawk community of Kahnawake as part of the *Our Lives* section. It is particularly useful to the comparative thrust of this chapter because one of the team members, Kanatakta, also served as a member of the advisory committee for the First Peoples Hall and contributed to the "People of the Longhouse" exhibit discussed above. The differences and similarities between these two modules illuminate the larger patterns that emerge from a comparison of the two exhibitions. Invited to contribute to the *Our Lives* section, the Kahnawake curatorial group chose to highlight their history as ironworkers, and large steel girders provide the visual focus of their exhibit. Kahnawake men have worked on skyscrapers in major cities in the United States and Canada – they helped both to put up and take down the World Trade Centre, for example – and this focus allows them to emphasize their integration into modernity. A counterbalancing stress is also placed on the role of Mohawk women in protecting traditional ways of life and in starting the Kahnawake survival school for their children. One text reads:

> Women and men in our community have always had different but complementary roles. In the early years, men ventured away from the village to hunt and trade. Women stayed in the village as heads of households, raising children, and managing community affairs.
>
> These roles are still carried out in Kahnawake, but we're going through a period of change where women's and men's roles are becoming more intertwined. While men still work outside Kahnawake – mainly as ironworkers – a greater number are staying in the community and have become more involved in child rearing and community decisions.
>
> Women remain active in community and home affairs, though full time jobs have changed their responsibilities, too.

At CMC, similar points about women's roles were made in the highly politicized context of a display about Oka, but the major emphasis was on premodern Iroquoian lifestyles and women's former roles in traditional agriculture. Strikingly, the objects on display in the Kahnawake module at the NMAI do not present any of the museum's rich collections of historical beadwork, cradleboards, or other traditional objects. Rather, what we see are the artifacts of contemporary industrial and urban life. Plans on file in the CMC archives show that, except for the "Contemporary Issues" display on the Oka crisis, the "People of the Longhouse" exhibit is very similar to the installation designed by the museum's non-Native ethnologists and archaeologists in the 1980s, before the collaborative process was introduced. The contrast between the NMAI, where the community curators had a free hand, and the CMC, where they had to negotiate the museum's modernist traditions of museum anthropology, illustrates the different end products produced by the multi-vocal and community-curated models of collaboration.[22]

The central thematic area of *Our Lives* elucidates the problematics of identity and contemporaneity. The visitor first walks through a corridor onto whose walls are projected images of contemporary Native people walking by on city streets. "Anywhere in the Americas, you could be walking with a twenty-first century Native American," the text panel states. The long, curving "Faces Wall" in the centre of the space was designed by curator Jolene Rickard, who is both an academic and a noted contemporary photographic and installation artist (fig. 12.8). The elements of her installation underscore the opening message: you cannot tell a Native American by his or her physiognomy; contemporary Native American identities are complex but authentic. The face in one image is adorned with traditional face painting that divides it into four quadrants. Another face is broken up by digital video into a mosaic of separate squares; when these fragments resolve into the unified image of a single woman, she smiles.

The use of techniques from contemporary art and installation is even more in evidence in the large, introductory thematic exhibits created one floor above for the *Our Peoples* section. It is here that history is confronted. No attempt at a linear chronology is attempted, nor, more surprisingly, does the exhibit provide a narrative of the pre-contact civilizations of the Americas. Rather, the aims of the installations are to deconstruct the histories that visitors already "know" and to provide a site for commemoration and mourning. It is in *Our Peoples* that the influence of the Holocaust Memorial Museum is most fully felt. On the frosted glass wall through which the visitor enters, the word "EVIDENCE" is etched in large letters in a classic typeface. A series of installations are mounted in long curving glass cases that spiral off to the right. The first is filled with ceramic figurines from archaeological sites throughout the Americas. None is individually identified within the cases, for their primary purpose is not to invite aesthetic contemplation or to convey specific historical facts but, rather, to evoke in a more general way the populous pre-contact and pre-epidemic vitality of the Americas. "They aren't 'Indians,'" the text panel tells us. "They have never heard of 'America.' The figures standing before you knew this world. Many spent centuries underground until farmers, tomb raiders, road builders, and archaeologists brought them to light. Like their human descendants they are survivors of a buried past." Similar arrays occupy the next cases, filled in turn with objects made of gold, guns, Bibles, treaties, and legal documents – artifactual "evidence" that comes from the interspaces of colonial contact, not from hermetically sealed-off "native cultures." The power of these installations derives from the additive strategy of the curators and the cumulative weight of the objects as evidence. They recall the haunting displays of the shoes and hair of Holocaust victims that visitors pass as they enter the exhibits at the Holocaust museum.

Facing these installations another historical legacy is exposed, that of the romanticization of the American Indian through stereotypes embedded

12.8 (*above and colour plate 12*) The "Faces Wall" introducing the "Our Lives: Contemporary Identities" section in the National Museum of the American Indian. Photo by Walter Larrimore; courtesy of the National Museum of the American Indian

12. 9 (*below*) Installation of George Catlin's Indian Gallery, incorporating a video presentation on stereotypes of Indianness by Floyd Favel, in the "Our Peoples: Giving Voice to Our Histories" section of the National Museum of the American Indian. Photo by Ruth B. Phillips

in art, film, and museum displays. The focus here is a recreation of George Catlin's mid-nineteenth-century Indian Gallery (fig. 12.9). Video screens the same size as the framed portraits are interspersed. On them the stereotypical images flicker, accompanied by the commentary of Plains Cree playwright Floyd Favel. "This gallery is about history and the past – two different things. What they all have in common – they were not created by Native Americans." In classic trickster fashion an adjacent text panel issues a warning: "We are left then with this paradox. For all our visibility we have been rendered invisible. And silent. A history-loving people, stripped of their own history. This Gallery is making history. And like all other makers of history it has a point of view, an agenda. What is found here is our way of looking at the Native American experience. So view what is offered with respect, but also with scepticism." The installation thus reproduces the nineteenth-century hang of Catlin's Indian Gallery, only to intervene in and disrupt its historical integrity. In so doing, it ventures even more aggressively into the revisionist terrain of *The West as America*. Yet, in marked contrast to the controversy that greeted that exhibition in 1991, the NMAI's critique of a well-loved and iconic corpus of nineteenth-century American art went relatively unremarked – a barometer, I would argue, of a sea change that occurred during the late 1990s. At the beginning of the twenty-first century there appears to be a wider acceptance of postcolonial perspectives and of the role played by the Smithsonian's special-interest museums as sites where alternative viewpoints can be presented.

Conclusions

The aspects of the NMAI's exhibitions that have met with criticism are, rather, its refusal of the standard modernist rhetorical strategies of art and artifact display. The reviewers from major newspapers who attended the museum's opening fully expected to see more of its famous collections used as anchors for its narratives about history, art, and culture. As Paul Richard wrote in the *Washington Post*, "The museum owns 800,000 Indian objects. Where are they? Mostly absent. Mostly absent, too, is the brain food one expects from good museums."[23] "The eye should have been offered a feast of many courses," he lamented, "Instead it's served a stew."[24] Edward Rothstein of the *New York Times* agreed. Citing one of the community-curated exhibits, he complained, "One does not learn what daily life is like or even what the tribe's religious ceremonies consist of … The notion that tribal voices should 'be heard' becomes a problem when the selected voices have so little to say."[25]

The lacks these reviewers felt are the result of deliberate choices made by the NMAI staff. While non-Native art and anthropology curators have wrangled over the relative merits of the art and artifact paradigms, many Native North Americans have found both approaches fetishizing and appropriative because they involve radical decontextualizations and disruptions of holistic Aboriginal expressive cultures. In numerous talks the NMAI director, Richard West Jr, gave about his museum project during its development, he insisted that its exhibits would not be an object-driven.[26] Similarly, one of the principles adopted by the CMC's Aboriginal advisory committee states: "In developing the exhibits, we are working with ideas. While we recognize and treasure the skill, knowledge and aesthetic quality represented in the objects in the collections, in exhibits the role of objects will be to illustrate ideas. The shape of the collection will not determine or limit, the character of exhibits."[27] As we saw, in the sections of the First Peoples Hall most closely overseen by the advisory committee, cultural artifacts are grouped in ways that disrupt both standard anthropological taxonomies and modes of aesthetic appreciation. At the NMAI contemporary objects are much more prominent than in the installations that preceded it. In his assessment of the Mall museum, historian Steven Conn argues that the NMAI lost an opportunity by failing to exploit the natural relationship between object display and the fundamental rhetorical strategy available to museums: "Objects are simply not at the center of what visitors experience. That's too bad, and not only because the Heye Collection is such an extraordinary resource. Museums have always tried to tell stories with objects. We might and should argue over which stories get told and how, but the notion that original objects can convey an immediacy and a 'realness' to a narrative is at the very heart of what a museum is. Nowhere at NMAI are we asked to pause to consider an object, to study it, to admire it, ask questions of it. Apparently the curators at the NMAI have little faith in the power of objects to convey meaning."[28] As Bennett's historical study also demonstrates, the evolutionary installations that so demeaned and dehumanized Indigenous peoples were highly constructed, produced by attaching certain texts and meanings to items of material culture that were, in and of themselves, innocent. From this perspective, both art and artifact paradigms can be understood as technologies that can be used to convey many different kinds of messages. By the late twentieth century, however, they had become guilty by association with colonial ideologies of nation, race, citizenship, and property promoted to serve the needs of Western nation-states.

In Althusserian terms, museums, like other government-supported educational institutions, are ideological state apparatuses (ISAs), and as such, they reflect and inscribe governing ideologies.[29] Althusser, however, also observes that ISAs can serve not only as institutions for the dissemination of official state ideologies but also as sites of struggle, available for appropriation by disempowered groups within the state. A productive contradiction is exposed: the sponsoring of a new representation by a national government can only happen if the representation is seen to serve its current ideological needs, and when national museums allow *new* stories to be told, as has happened at both the NMAI and the CMC, we need to ask how the new representations align themselves with the evolving constructs of nationhood of their sponsors. Yet at the same time, Althusser's model suggests that the space of the museum lends itself to the contestation of established ideologies, inviting our consideration of the ways that choices of narrative structure and rhetorical mode can reveal or silence contradictions, ambiguities, and ambivalences.

Both the First Peoples Hall and the NMAI demonstrate the linked processes of ideological inscription and contestation. As Charles Taylor has argued, one of the dominant developments of the second half of the twentieth century in Western democracies was a new "politics of recognition" which grew out of an older Western discourse of rights.[30] These politics have become part of contemporary national ideology in both the United States and Canada, supported by the multicultural policies that are now fostered by the national museums. Aboriginal curators and advisers working with both museums have taken advantage of the inherent tension between these policies and the state's desire to create a national citizenry with a shared sense of history and values. The new multicultural and postcolonial ideologies authorize exhibits that break down homogenizing stereotypes and insist on the diversity and the authenticity of contemporary Aboriginal lifestyles. Political theorist Andrew Barry has commented on the relationship between the neoliberal agenda and the new, less directive, and more interactive poetics that characterize many contemporary exhibits, making the visitor "a more creative, participative or active subject without the imposition of a direct form of control or the judgment of an expert authority."[31]

But the different histories of Aboriginal people in Canada and the United States have also led to contrasting emphases in the new exhibitions. Each has used the potential of the museum to serve as a site of struggle from which to advance its local agendas. In Canada, as we have seen, the large and unresolved issue of land claims provides the thematic spine of the First Peoples Hall. I would argue that the relative lack of attention given to Native American issues and past histories of oppression in the United States in comparison with those of larger visible minorities has resulted in the NMAI's relatively greater stress on problems of identity and stereotyping, on the one hand, and the need for public commemoration, on the other. The historic shift in power that has allowed both of these new representations to take the material form of exhibitions is the hard-won achievement of activist movements of resistance. Positioned close to the symbolic centres of governmental power – the NMAI next to the Capitol building and the Canadian Museum of Civilization across from the Parliament Buildings – the new exhibitions are landmarks in the ongoing Aboriginal and Native North American struggle against the legacy of five centuries of death, loss, and compromised identity. Yet the critics of the exhibitions also have valid points. The two museums can only gain in rhetorical power as they combine Indigenous perspectives with a renewed deployment of historical materials – objects, texts, and traditional Indigenous knowledge – more fully in the service of their new goals.

PART FOUR   THE SECOND
                   MUSEUM AGE

Working with Hybridity

If a time traveller from the first museum age, the critical period of museum building that was at its height between the 1840s and the 1890s, were today to visit the Royal Ontario Museum, the Canadian Museum of Civilization, or another of the institutions that owes its foundation to that era, she would probably experience both recognition and confusion.[1] The large galleries, the hushed atmosphere, the guards, the glass cases filled with artifacts, and the ordered ranks of pictures would mark the space unmistakably as a museum, understood as a site where education and pleasure can be expected to merge to produce a heightened state of consciousness. However, our time traveller would also probably find many of the exhibitions on view surprising and disconcerting. In place of the familiar linear chronologies of human history and the grand narratives that chart the progress of humankind and the triumph of the West, she would find local histories, unknown historical actors, evocations of personal memory and experience, and multiple perspectives on major historical events.

As this imagined scenario suggests, the museum world of today is not as different from its nineteenth-century predecessors as the revisionist museum activists of the early 1990s might have expected. In those pioneering years of critical museology, many projects were framed within the various modes of "post" thinking – postmodernism, postcolonialism, post-racialism, and post-industrialism – that predicted the imminent demise of many familiar conventions of representation, including those of

museums. In the event, we have experienced few clear breaks with modernist ideologies and traditions. Rather, we continue to operate – at best – within a hyperconscious state of reflexivity, ever mindful that we may still be caught in one of the discursive, representational, and political traps that perpetuate discredited regimes of power, thought, and art.

The changes that have been advanced by critical museology are not, however, negligible, and they are slowly moving our institutions toward alternative modes of representation. The four chapters that follow this brief introduction explore early twenty-first-century innovations in exhibitions and museum-based research. Each responds in its own way to the critical museological thinking that developed during the last decades of the twentieth century. Each demonstrates possibilities for change as well as parameters of limitation. The specific examples that they present seem to me to indicate potential future directions of museum activity.

Chapter 13 describes plans for a new national museum that has not (yet) come into being, the Portrait Gallery of Canada. It analyses the tensions that arise from attempts to provide an account of Indigenous perspectives and ways of thinking about history within an overarching narrative of settler nation building. The next chapter discusses two projects that deploy electronic technologies as strategies for decolonization and digital repatriation in anthropology museums, while also supporting collaborative research on museum collections in virtual space. Chapter 15 considers the pioneering efforts of Canada's two largest art museums to extend the definition of Canadian art to include Indigenous arts. Each of these discussions both illustrates the innovations made possible by new museological practices designed to make museums more inclusive and also identifies limiting forces exerted by resilient modernist traditions and constructs – the nation-state, Eurocentric hierarchies of fine art and craft, and anthropological typologies of culture. In the last chapter I draw on the work of Bruno Latour and other actor-network theorists to seek a strong way forward for the second museum age we appear to be entering. I urge the need to think about the changes we have seen as positive outcomes of controversies, which, as Latour argues, have provided valuable opportunities for the re-creation of museums and other modernist institutions as components of effective networks. This history, in my view, points to the need for museums to embrace debate and to continue to take curatorial risks. I endorse the value of thinking of exhibitions and other museum projects as experiments that, whether they succeed or fail (and perhaps especially when they fail), usefully enhance the social agency of the museum.

Recent museology, I argue, has embraced hybridity in several different senses. One of the most noticeable manifestations is the merging of distinctive paradigms of display and interpretation that used to be specific to museums of art, anthropology, history, and science respectively. The cross-borrowings that James Clifford so perceptively identi-

fied more than twenty years ago in his foundational essay "On Collecting Art and Culture" today appear not as anomalies but as normal and desirable.[2] They are in evidence everywhere, bringing oral traditions into the archaeology exhibition, art into the history museum, environmental science into the art museum, and all of these into the anthropology museum. On another level, hybridization results from the mutual acculturation of museum insiders and (former) outsiders to each other's ways, an inevitable product of successful collaboration. A virtue of actor-network theory is its validation of such heterogeneity as a means of recognizing the interdependent networks of politics, nature, science, and art whose effective combination, as Latour urges, is necessary to our very survival.

One of the clear achievements of Canadian museology since the 1980s has been the establishment of a culture of shared authority and power, both in cross-cultural and cross-professional contexts. The widespread entrenchment of this new museum culture not only in Canada but also in other countries was evidenced by a remarkable conference that took place in Ottawa in 2007. "Preserving Aboriginal Heritage: Technical and Traditional Approaches" was organized by the Canadian Conservation Institute (CCI) to explore the new alignments that have been developing between that most scientific of museum professions, conservation, and the knowledge traditions of Indigenous societies. The conference attracted 385 international participants, 145 of them Aboriginal. During a five-day period a long list of speakers presented a dazzling array of case studies describing projects in which conservators and other museum professionals had worked respectfully and productively with Aboriginal collaborators to create models of conservation and cultural preservation that combined Western and Aboriginal concepts and technologies.

As director Jeanne Inch wrote in her preface to the "Preserving Aboriginal Heritage" proceedings, the genesis of the conference lay in the CCI's recognition of a problem: "Aboriginal people in Canada are concerned about the preservation of their material culture, but their preservation requirements are not yet adequately met." A carefully constructed Aboriginal consultation process began, and as Inch noted, it produced an immediate awareness that in both design and content the conference "would have to focus on more than just the technical and scientific issues. To be successful, it would have to incorporate the values and perspectives of Aboriginal people in Canada."[3] In his message, written on behalf of the advisory committee, Anishinaabe member Gilbert Whiteduck was unequivocal in his praise for the fully collaborative planning process that lay behind the success of the conference: "The symposium demonstrated what can be accomplished when aboriginal peoples and government agencies listen to each other and are willing to find compromise. The CCI symposium planning approach is a model to be replicated as a first step for meaningful changes."[4]

The larger societal agency that museums and museological activities can have is

implied in these words. Unusually for an organization of its kind, the CCI had positioned the conference in what Latour would understand as a network of heterogeneous activities – scientific, political, and spiritual. Such a positioning carried with it the need to accommodate and respect a plurality of knowledges, a position that, although stated in principle in Canada's various multiculturalism acts and policies since the 1970s, has not always been realized in practice. As Whiteduck noted, the planning of a conservation conference involving staff from museums and Aboriginal cultural centres created a process with much wider potential applications. It demonstrated the capacity of the museum or cultural organization to serve as an experimental laboratory out of which can come models of respectful dialogue involving *listening* as a precondition for the development of mutual understanding and power-sharing. Such models, translated into larger social and political arenas, may be one of the most important contributions of the second museum age.

13

From Harmony to Antiphony

The Indigenous Presence in a (Future) Portrait Gallery of Canada

The Museum as Political Football

In 2001 the Liberal government of Jean Chrétien announced the development of a new museum, the Portrait Gallery of Canada.[1] It was to be created as a separate branch within Library and Archives Canada (LAC) and would draw primarily on that institution's rich collections of photographs, documentary art, film, and television and audio recordings. The gallery would be housed in the classic beaux arts building built in 1931–32 by American architect Cass Gilbert as the United States embassy. Located at 100 Wellington Street, directly across the street from the centre block of Parliament, this building provided an ideal location for a national portrait gallery (fig. 13.1). The new national museum would narrate Canada's history through the images of its people and would complement the episodic social history narrative conveyed through the streetscape installations of the Canadian Museum of Civilization's History Hall. Dr Lilly Koltun, appointed as the gallery's interim director in 2001, explained the genesis of the project on its website: "Over the years, many Canadians had written to newspapers … pointing out our unsung heroes and how valuable it would be for Canada to recognize its own achievers. Recently, Canadians have shown they want to know more about their own history, their own roots. So it all came together – the idea, the place, the rare hidden collection, the strong desire of Canadians to see the faces and hear the stories of those who have contributed to the building of Canada, and those helping to build our country today."[2]

13.1   Aerial view of the Parliament Buildings, Ottawa, showing the site proposed for the Portrait Gallery of Canada by the Liberal government of Jean Chrétien in the former US embassy (upper right-hand corner). Photo by Duke Aerial Photography, Mississauga

During the next five years, Koltun and her staff were engaged in developing a full curatorial program encompassing long-term, temporary, and travelling exhibits and in the architectural planning needed to adapt a heritage office building for use as a museum. Late in 2005, however, a Conservative minority government led by Prime Minister Stephen Harper came to power, and in April 2006 it halted work on the gallery. In 2009, after an abortive process involving a competition whose purpose seemed to be the relocation of the gallery outside Ottawa, the Harper government folded the Portrait Gallery into the programs branch of Library and Archives Canada (LAC). This decision eliminated the positions of Koltun and, ultimately, a number of her senior staff. After negative public reaction to the change, the government retained the Portrait Gallery name for a small group in the LAC programs branch. In effect, however, the new national portrait gallery, as a museum, had been cancelled.

During its first five years of existence, however, the Portrait Gallery of Canada achieved a vibrant existence on paper, through off-site exhibitions, and as a virtual gallery. It brought to completion a detailed curatorial program for its opening installations, worked with the Department of Public Works to commission an elegant and functional architectural

design, and conceptualized travelling exhibitions and educational programs (fig. 13.2). By the time work on the Wellington Street site was stopped, the thematic structure of the
exhibits had been established, the portraits had been selected
and conservation work begun, the captions and text panels
had been written, and exhibit design and interpretive programs were in development. This curatorial program and related activities has never been released to the general public
and does not even seem to have been known to the government officials who engineered its cancellation. Yet it constitutes an innovative and distinctively Canadian reinterpreta-
tion of the national portrait gallery as a twenty-first-century
museum genre. In particular, it reimagines the national historical narrative in relation to the particular forms of inclusivity that settler nations, and Canada in particular, require:
highlighting its bicultural French and British settler history,
the rapid and profound changes in its population brought
about by the growth of diasporic communities from around
the world, and the processes of decolonization being pursued
by Indigenous peoples.

On a more practical level, the development of the building and the plans for its exhibits represent a monetary investment by Canadian taxpayers of more than eleven million dollars. To allow the curatorial program of the Portrait Gallery
of Canada to languish in obscurity on the shelves of the archives would, it seems to me, compound the appalling waste-
fulness caused by the years of partisan political wrangling.
Even in its unrealized state, the conceptual work that was
accomplished can contribute to the ways in which Canadian
museums think about inclusivity. The plans also lay a foundation for the eventual realization of a national portrait gallery when, as will surely happen, a future government revives
the project. The detailed narrative structure for the long-term
installations was the achievement of Curator of Exhibitions
Johanna Mizgala, and during the years of the Portrait Gallery's development she, Koltun, and other staff presented aspects of the project in numerous public talks. The curatorial
program has also been drawn on to enrich the Portrait Gallery's current website.

In this chapter I will focus on one component of these plans
which, I would argue, is representative of the kind of inclusivity envisioned by the project as a whole. As guest curator for
the Aboriginal component of the gallery's long-term installations, I was asked to develop an approach to its representation
of the Indigenous presence in Canadian history through por-

13.2 (*see also colour plate 13*)
Computer simulation of the
design for the Portrait Gallery of Canada by Dixon
Jones architects, winners of
the 2005 architectural competition. Photo courtesy of
Dixon Jones, London

traiture, considered in its broadest sense as a mode of representing identity. This assignment usefully illuminated for me both the possibilities and the continuing tensions that arise from our attempts to achieve inclusivity within Western museum traditions that remain rooted in Western hierarchies of the arts and the senses. Because these representational conventions are also grounded in Eurocentric concepts of spectatorship and constructs of subject/object relationships, they limit the degree to which other aesthetic and intellectual traditions – and Indigenous portraiture, in particular – can be accommodated. The assignment also, however, allowed me to explore, together with Portrait Gallery staff and my colleague Norman Vorano, installation strategies that can move us closer to true inclusivity.

Multiculturalism and the Trope of Harmony

Polls regularly show that Canadians increasingly regard multiculturalism as a core aspect of their national identity. There is, however, an inherent tension between an ideal model of pluralism and the singularity of the construct of nation. In the Departmental Performance Report for the Department of Canadian Heritage, written as the Portrait Gallery was in full development, Minister Sheila Copps wrote, for example: "Canadians have entered the 21st century with a vibrant culture comprising many distinct voices. Brought together through accommodation and not assimilation, Canadians are becoming increasingly aware of the distinctiveness of their cultural model and the enormous opportunity it represents … That distinct model is based simultaneously on the reality of our diversity and values of mutual responsibility and respect. Today, Canadians embrace a multiplicity of cultures and a broad spectrum of creative diversity from the perspective of a set of common values and a sense of shared purpose."[3] Critics of official multiculturalism policies point out that although these policies reject a singular relationship between national origin and citizenship, they reinscribe the nation (and race) as the fundamental unit of identity, rather than constructing an alternative understanding of the multiple and fluid identities in which an individual can participate.[4] In so doing, the argument goes, they continue to ghettoize minority groups and maintain them as marginal.[5] Nathan Glazer, for example, has pointed to the production of a "benign neglect" which, while guaranteeing tolerance, consigns difference to a hidden and private realm of social activity.[6] In Canada, the Department of Canadian Heritage, the ministry responsible for national museums, libraries, and archives, is also charged with monitoring compliance with the Canadian Multiculturalism Act. In its programs and policies, Canadian Heritage often invokes an ideal of harmony as a means of resolving this tension. This ideal was performed with startling literalness in 2003 when, at the Minister's Forum on Diversity and Culture, a large national conference organized by Minister Copps, the several hundred invited bureaucrats and cultural workers were presented with a series of spectacles in which Canadians with origins in different parts of the world came together in seamlessly coordinated ensembles. Among these was a performance by a multi-ethnic ensemble of musicians playing violins, zithers, Japanese taiko drums, and other instruments belonging to different traditions of world music.[7]

A similar pull toward the trope of harmony is strongly felt in museums, where modernist historical narratives of the nation, traditional architectures, and paradigms of art or artifact installation exercise a controlling force over the exhibition of diversity. Although the hierarchical system of continents, nations, and peoples that informed modern imperial and colonial narratives of art and history has been subjected to thoroughgoing deconstruction in the academy over the past few decades, art galleries and museums have generally appeared conservative, if not actively reactionary, relative to these new understandings, at least on the surface. Although we know that we all live in "old countries" and share in multiple and increasingly global art traditions, we continue to struggle to find ways to reconfigure our inherited historical narratives to reflect this awareness. I have come to think that a postcolonial museology demands, not the kind of unified chorus implied by the notion of harmony – which, as a musical term, is defined as the "combination or adaptation of parts, elements, or related things, so as to form a consistent and orderly whole; agreement, accord, congruity"[8] – but, rather, the autonomy of voices signified by the notion of "antiphony" – defined as "1. Opposition of sound; or harmony thereby produced, or 2. A musical response; a responsive musical utterance, the answer made by one voice or choir to another."[9] True inclusivity in museological practice, in other words, may require that we disrupt classical structures of display to express not just historical convergences and contemporary commonalities but also past divergences and contemporary differences.

Though modelled on national portrait galleries in Great Britain and the United States, Mizgala's overall plan for the long-term exhibits of the Portrait Gallery of Canada seeks to accommodate a particularly Canadian politics of identity. It addresses both the pre-existing construct of the nation as a bicultural mixture of French and British traditions and the more recent public consciousness of Canada as a multicultural nation. In the early twenty-first century, however, the positioning of Aboriginal portraits is not entirely containable within either of these constructs. Since the 1960s, Aboriginal peoples in Canada have succeeded in repositioning themselves as the First Nations, whose historical precedence in North America has not been erased, either legally or symbolically, by settlement, colonization, or recent immigration. Aboriginal people have advanced these claims through the renewed political activism that began after World War II, and they have achieved a number of landmark changes that led to the entrenchment of Aboriginal sovereignty in the newly patriated Canadian constitution in 1982. In the early 1990s a federal-provincial treaty process was reinstated to negotiate a large number of outstanding land claims, and new forms of self-government have been established through the settlement of the Nisga'a land claim in British Columbia in 1997 and the establishment of Nunavut in the eastern Arctic in 1999. The federal government also offered financial compensation and in 2008 made a formal apology for its oppressive residential school system.[10] As such arrangements demonstrate, Aboriginal people in Canada are recognized as having unique political, social, and moral relationships to the development of the Canadian nation: they are positioned both as part of the multicultural rainbow and outside it. In this context it was undoubtedly not accidental that at the 2003 Diversity and Culture conference, the two masters of ceremonies were the eminent French-Canadian broadcaster and senator Laurier Lapierre and the equally eminent Aboriginal filmmaker Alanis Obamsawin. Together, they performed the mediating role between the Anglo-Canadian majority, which metaphorically stood in the background, and the new diasporic communities, whose entrance into Canadian society was being heralded and validated.

As Lilly Koltun's website statement also makes clear, in a national institution such as a portrait gallery, all such inclusions are inevitably framed within a dominant settler narrative of nation and nation building. In considering the Aboriginal component of the gallery, then, two questions arose: First, to what degree could a national museum allow dominant narratives of history to be challenged? And, second, how far could the Western genre of portraiture be stretched, through design and installation, to accommodate culturally different expressive traditions? Before turning to a more detailed discussion of the answers we suggested and the specific proposals we devised to accommodate the Aboriginal presence in the Portrait Gallery of Canada, I would like to cite one further argument that has informed my thinking about the representation of diversity in public institutions.

In his influential 1991 essay "The Politics of Recognition" McGill University philosopher Charles Taylor provided an argument for an important evolution in thinking about human rights that has resulted in, among other things, the moral and ethical imperatives that have come to inform contemporary museum practice in Canada.[11] He maintains that one of the major achievements of identity politics during the second half of the twentieth century was the broadening of the understanding of human rights to encompass the right to "recognize" oneself and one's cultural identity in the public representations current in the society in which one lives. Taylor refers to this as a right to be acknowledged as authentic in one's own way of life. "In the case of the politics of difference," he writes, "we might also say that a universal potential is at its basis, namely, the potential for forming and defining one's own identity, as an individual, and also as a culture."[12] He points out the hurt and the potentially paralyzing psychic damage that can result when one's inner sense of identity does not register with the images reflected back from media such as films, advertising, school textbooks, and museums. This right to recognition has important implications for museum representations in light of the accumulated critiques of recent decades that expose the imperialist, racist, classist, and sexist bases for stereotypes circulated by these media and institutions.

In Canada, Australia, and many other countries, we have had abundant evidence of how, more specifically, stereotypes of Indigenous peoples can result in dysfunctionality leading to poverty, high suicide rates, and other evils. Collaborative models of curatorial process are one way in which museums are endeavouring to redress this situation by ensuring that exhibits will be accurate, authentic, and "recognizable" to Aboriginal people in Taylor's sense. As we work in such partnerships, we are learning, not surprisingly, not only about the factual information that needs to be corrected but also about the silences and gaps in archives and museum collections – about the unwritten histories and the unpictured people – that need to be addressed in order to achieve greater accuracy and self-recognition. One of the most challenging issues arising from such collaborative work has been the realization that the primacy accorded to the display of visual images and material objects in Western museums may contribute to slippages in recognition. In many Aboriginal traditions other expressive media, such as dance, song, or story, may be the most important media through which to portray personal and cultural identity.

Facing the Other

One of the first steps we took in designing the Aboriginal component of the Portrait Gallery of Canada was to invite about twenty Aboriginal professionals from across the country who have expertise in historical and cultural matters to meet in Ottawa to identify parameters and provide feedback on the curatorial program. I also invited Norman Vorano (now curator of Contemporary Inuit Art at the Canadian Museum of Civilization) to work with me on the project. The Portrait Gallery's main charge to us was to develop an introductory room that would present early encounters between Europeans and Aboriginal peoples through both Indigenous and Euro-Canadian genres of portraiture. A second obligation was to recommend images of Aboriginal people to be included in the subsequent thematic and chronological sections of the long-term installations. A central message we were asked to convey was that when Europeans arrived in what is now Canada, they encountered highly diverse, complex, and sophisticated societies with their own traditions of portraiture. One of the first modifications of this task we suggested was to broaden the generically specific notion of portraiture to "representations of identity," an enlarged category that can better accommodate Aboriginal traditions which are conceptually very different from conventional Western understandings of portraiture.

We entitled this first room "Facing the Other" to signal the dialogic nature of early encounters between Aboriginal people and Europeans. The title also references the historical imposition of a Western emphasis on the naturalistic depiction of the face in representing individual human identities. Although renderings of anthropomorphic heads and faces do occur in Aboriginal art, these are generally not intended as likenesses of specific individuals. Rather, for many Aboriginal peoples in Canada, the most significant Indigenous

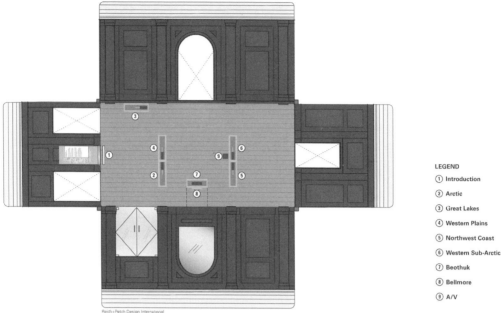

LEGEND
① Introduction
② Arctic
③ Great Lakes
④ Western Plains
⑤ Northwest Coast
⑥ Western Sub-Arctic
⑦ Beothuk
⑧ Bellmore
⑨ A/V

Reich+Petch Design International

13.3   Floor plan for the "Facing the Other" gallery in the Portrait Gallery of Canada. Photo courtesy of Reich and Petch Design International; © Government of Canada; reproduced with the permission of the Minister of Public Works and Government Services Canada (2011). Library and Archives Canada, DWG 54-2, Gallery Four – Concept One

visual renderings take non-human forms, most often animal. These images also usually refer not to individuals but to collectivities and may represent the trans-generational identities of clans that are also carried in inherited names, titles, songs, and narratives. A second difficulty of translating the Western notion of a portrait into Aboriginal expressive traditions is that the visual images and material objects that stand for these clans and kin groups are not usually autonomous graphic or plastic representations. Rather, they acquire meaning when presented together with the oral narratives, songs, and dances in which identity is *primarily* embedded.

In order to explore these contrasting concepts of portraiture and identity, we decided to design the initial installation of "the Other" as a series of dialogically structured groupings representing six different cultural/geographical regions or peoples: the Inuit, the Great Lakes, the Prairies, the Northwest Coast, the Western Subarctic, and the now extinct Beothuk of Newfoundland (fig. 13.3). In each grouping we juxtaposed an early European portrayal of an Aboriginal person from the region with a traditional Indigenous way of representing identity from the same area. The specific groupings were intended to be changed regularly in order to provide opportunities to explore, over time, a wide range of different Aboriginal traditions and to rotate drawings, watercolours,

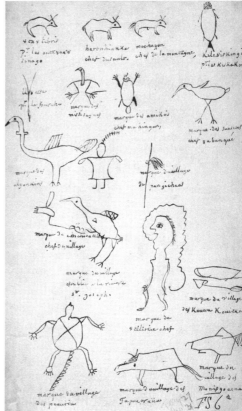

and other items that can be damaged by too much exposure to light. The account that follows, therefore, describes our selection for the opening installations.

To represent the Great Lakes region we proposed to juxtapose pages from the earliest European compilation of images of Great Lakes peoples, the *Codex Canadiensis,* drawn in the 1670s by Jesuit missionary Louis Nicolas (fig. 13.4), with Indigenous representations of identity inscribed on a key treaty document of 1701 (fig. 13.5). The *Codex Canadiensis* is the earliest comprehensive visual record of the plants, animals, and Aboriginal peoples of New France. Drawn from life by a man who spent years living among Great Lakes Native peoples, it is a rich source of information about Aboriginal technologies, ways of life, and languages of the period. Typically for the European tradition, the portraits focus on the details of body decoration and appearance that seemed most exotic. The written texts, although brief, state the French interest in these people as allies and trading partners. The treaty, known as the Great Peace of Montreal, records the historic agree-

13.4   Louis Nicolas, Portrait of an Onkwehonwe man from the village of Gannachiouave, in *Codex Canadiensis* (1675–80), ink on paper. The turtle on his left leg, probably tattooed, would have identified the man as a member of the turtle clan. Courtesy of the Gilcrease Museum, Tulsa, Oklahoma

13.5   Dodem signatures on the 1701 treaty known as the Great Peace of Montreal. From the official copy in the Archives nationales de France; courtesy of Library and Archives Canada

ment reached by French colonial officials and representatives of the major Indigenous nations of the eastern Great Lakes and adjacent regions in 1701.[13] The written document to which French and Aboriginal leaders affixed their signatures is the only material evidence of a complex ritual exchange that involved formal oratory and the presentation to both parties of belts of woven shell wampum beads whose mnemonic designs symbolized the nature of the agreements that had been reached.

The Indigenous signatures on the document, however, are key evidence of the ways in which Indigenous peoples in many parts of North America traditionally depicted their identities. Each of the thirty-nine First Nations leaders drew his *dodem*, or totem, a graphic motif representing the animal, plant, or anthropomorphic being from whose body had emerged the primeval ancestor of his clan. *Nindoodemag* (plural of *dodem*) are the keys to a system of kinship that ties Indigenous nations to specific originary territories.[14] The most important and essential aspect of a person's identity was thus not made visible through a naturalistic likeness tied to a specific moment in time but, rather, through an iconic image associated with a narrative that was carried across generations, connecting the dead, the living, and the as yet unborn. A true portrait, from this Aboriginal perspective, is both trans-temporal and collective. In his lecture *Comparing Mythologies* northern Cree writer Tomson Highway has expressed this way of thinking about time, space, and the individual as simultaneously spatial and temporal: "Existence in the universe is merely one endless circle of birth and life and death and re-birth and life and death and re-birth and life and death so that those who lived in times before us – our mothers, our grandmothers, our great-great-grandmothers, those children of ours who have died, those loved ones – they live here with us, still, today, in the very air we breathe, in the shimmer of a leaf on that old oak tree, in that slant of sunlight that falls in through your window and lands on your wrist. They are here."[15] When one of the signatories to the Great Peace of Montreal inscribed his dodem on paper or displayed it in woven, engraved, or painted form, he was not so much denying the importance of his individual identity or lifespan as asserting the greater priority and relevance of collective and continuous forms of identity.

The impulse of European portraiture of this period is the opposite, as is demonstrated not only by the *Codex Canadiensis* but also by the portraits commissioned by Queen Anne of the Hodenosaunee and Mahican leaders known as the Four Indian Kings.[16] These portraits are a highlight of the Library and Archives Canada collection, and plans were made to feature them in the thematic section "Tangled Garden," which would follow immediately after "Facing the Other." I will turn to them briefly here because of their relationship to the early Great Lakes images I have been discussing. Painted in London by John Verelst in 1710, nine years after the signing of the Great Peace of Montreal, these portraits display not only European but also Onkwehonwe concepts of identity. They bear out Shearer West's comment that such European portraits "are not merely likenesses, but engage with ideas of identity …

plate 11 Introductory section, "An Aboriginal Presence," in the First Peoples Hall, Canadian Museum of Civilization. Photo © Canadian Museum of Civilization, D2003-13058

plate 12   The "Faces Wall" introducing the "Our Lives: Contemporary Identities" section in the National Museum of the American Indian. Photo by Walter Larrimore; courtesy of the National Museum of the American Indian

plate 13
Computer simulation of
the design for the Portrait
Gallery of Canada by Dixon
Jones architects, winners
of the 2005 architectural
competition. Photo
courtesy of Dixon Jones,
London

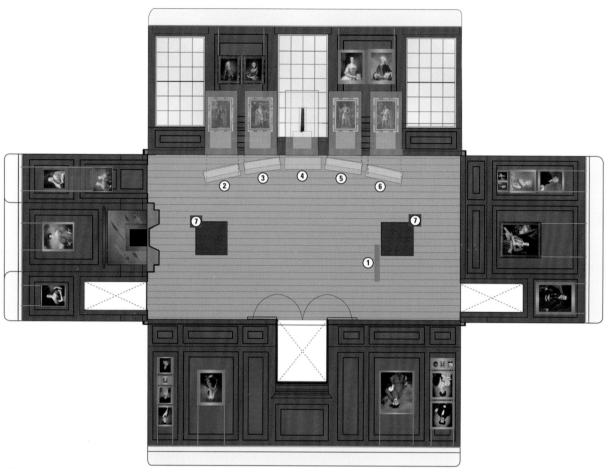

plate 14 (*above*)   Floor plan of the installation of the portraits of the Four Indian Kings designed for the Portrait Gallery of Canada. Photo courtesy of Reich and Petch Design International. © Government of Canada; reproduced with the permission of the Minister of Public Works and Government Services Canada (2011). Library and Archives Canada, DWG 54-9, Gallery Seven – Concept One

plate 15 (*opposite, above*)   The Rideau Chapel with sculpture of an angel attributed to Tsimshian carver Frederick Alexcie (on loan from the University of British Columbia Museum of Anthropology) in *Art of This Land*. Photo © National Gallery of Canada, Ottawa

plate 16 (*opposite, below*)   Kent Monkman's *The Academy* (2008) anchors one of the galleries of the "Power" section of the Canadian galleries. Photo © Art Gallery of Ontario, Toronto

plate 17 (*opposite, above*)   The Multiversity Galleries at the Museum of
Anthropology, University of British Columbia, opened January 2010. Photo by Bill
McLennan

plate 18 (*opposite, below*)   Installation of mask and photographs by Douglas Curran
in *The Village Is Tilting: Dancing AIDS in Malawi* (2007), Museum of Anthropology,
University of British Columbia, Vancouver. Photo by Ruth B. Phillips

plate 19 (*above*)   Terrance Houle, *Aakaisttsiiksiinaakii: Many Snake Woman:
"The Daughters after Me"* (2008), video; shown in *Tracing History: Presenting the
Unpresentable*, 2008. Reproduced with permission of the artist; photo © Glenbow
Museum, Calgary

plate 20 Tanya Harnett, *Skull Mountainettes* (2008), digital photographic prints mounted on Plexiglas, shown in *Tracing History: Presenting the Unpresentable*, 2008. Reproduced with permission of the artist; photo © Glenbow Museum, Calgary

[which] can encompass the character, personality, social standing, relation-ships, profession, age, and gender of the portrait subject."[17] Verelst reprodu-ces not only the facial features and elaborate tattooing of his subjects but also the fine clothing presented by the queen, the exotic accessories that indicate their wealth and status, and the wampum belts, tomahawks, and guns that identify their roles as foreign diplomats, warriors, and military allies. In these terms, the portraits record both specific and unique individual features and the more generic identities conferred by their duties and responsibilities. Yet other images incorporated into the portraits also express Onkwehonwe con-cepts of collective and trans-generational identity. In the lower background of each portrait the clan animal of the sitter appears – wolf, turtle, and bear. The clumsiness of Verelst's renderings strongly suggests that they were painted from verbal descriptions rather than known prototypes; I would argue that the crude execution is evidence that these clan animals were included at the express request of the sitters, for whom they would have been essential mark-ers of identity. Such traces evidence both the agency of Indigenous portrait sitters and the hybrid genesis of Indigenous portraiture.

A second grouping in the "Facing the Other" gallery was chosen to dem-onstrate the longevity of these Indigenous traditions. In 1881 the Marquess of Lorne made an official trip to the Canadian prairies as governor general. In his party was Sydney Prior Hall, a professional artist employed by the London illustrated weeklies. Hall's drawings of the chiefs who addressed the governor general in Manitoba include a portrait of the Saulteaux leader Osoop (fig. 13.6). In the lower right-hand corner of this portrait is the drawing of a cow moose and, in Hall's writing, "Osoop (Back Fat) His Mark." On the back of the sketch Hall further notes that Osoop was "their best speaker and dis-tinguished himself by an eloquent speech … his cape of beaver with the tail hanging down the neck, he gave to his Excellency. The outline intended for a moose drawn with much difficulty by himself is his totem." In conjunction with Osoop's portrait, made by another European artist a century and a half after Verelst painted the Four Indian Kings, we also planned to display the magnificent beaver-trimmed shirt that Osoop presented to the Marquess of Lorne, now in the British Museum. Its prominent beaded disc represents the sun, the supreme power of the Anishnaabe cosmos and the source of physical and spiritual illumination. Aboriginal men historically portrayed their status as leaders by displaying images of the sun in tattooing and shell ornaments and, after contact, by wearing shining silver chief's medals and fine beaded clothing. Osoop's shirt can be considered a portrayal of the qualities of moral and intellectual enlightenment appropriate to a leader that made it not only expressive of his own identity but also a fitting gift from a chief to the queen's representative.

We selected the other groupings in "Facing the Other" to reveal similar conceptual disjunctures and parallels with Western portraiture. The images from the Arctic juxtapose a 1567 German woodcut of a Labrador Inuit woman and child with archaeologically found portrayals from the Dorset and Thule

13.6   Sydney Prior Hall,
*Chief Osoop (Back Fat), a
Saulteaux Indian*, 18 August
1881. Courtesy of Library
and Archives Canada,
1984-45-145

cultures. The woodcut is one of the earliest European images
of Aboriginal people from Canada. Little is known of the two
unnamed captives, who were taken to Antwerp in 1566, possibly by Basque fishermen, but the print was probably copied
from an original drawing made from life. Although it records
clothing and details of visual appearance with a fair degree of
accuracy, the accompanying text spins fantasies of "savage"
life. The Dorset-period wand and the Thule-period figure to
be juxtaposed with this image illustrate different contexts in
which mimetic representations of faces and bodies occur in
ancestral Inuit traditions, as well as the difficulty of knowing exactly what such images represent. The Dorset faces may

depict spirits or people or both and reflect shamanistic belief systems, while the Thule figure, wearing a long European robe and bearing a small cross on the middle of the chest, may represent a Norse priest. If so, this image demonstrates an Inuit impulse to portray the exotic other that was shared with early European visitors to Canada, although the figurine may also have had ritual uses of which we are now ignorant.

For the Northwest Coast region we planned to feature a drawing of a high-born Nuu-chah-nulth man made in 1788 by John Webber during Captain Cook's third voyage. Cook's month-long stay at Yuquot, on the west coast of Vancouver Island, brought about the first sustained contact between Europeans and Nuu-chah-nulth people. Webber's sensitive, naturalistic portraits of men and women participate in the Enlightenment project of scientific description, and this portrait faithfully records the face-painting designs that were part of rituals of hunting and gathering and the hairstyle and finely woven cedar-bark cape worn at the time of contact by high-born Nuu-chah-nulth people. Our plan was to display this drawing next to a Nuu-chah-nulth whaler's hat collected around the time of the Cook expedition. Among the Nuu-chah-nulth, whaling was a highly ritualized activity that was important to the Indigenous economy. It was reserved for chiefs, whose privileges included the wearing of hats that signified to the community their high rank and status. Made of double layers of finely woven cedar bark and spruce root and ornamented with onion-shaped knobs and pictorial scenes of the whale hunt, these hats appear in many of Webber's portraits and represent an Aboriginal way of displaying inherited privilege, status, and identity.

Nuu-chah-nulth artist and anthropologist Ki-Ke-In, whose English name is Ron Hamilton, has pointed, however, to Western collecting practices that focus on material objects and visual images and to the partial nature of the cultural representations that result: "They brought along John Webber and his sort to make representations, to draw, to etch, to paint what the Natives were doing, and to exhibit again just how far away from civilization the visitors had been. So that the first collecting of these things … represents a need to have a souvenir, some material, portable proof of having been where the devil still reigns, and to be able to bring that back to the civilized, the clean, the white, the Christian." As Ki-Ke-In's remark indicates, the Aboriginal material expressions on display were not, in their origins, intended to be freestanding modes of communication. The art or history museum, however, can suggest this broader performative context only with difficulty, not only because the museum is, traditionally, as Svetlana Alpers has argued, a "way of seeing,"[18] but also because of the great historical losses of contextual information and Indigenous knowledge that have resulted from colonization and modernization. Many contemporary collaborative museological projects require extensive research on the part of Indigenous partners not only to identify traditional practices interrupted during the colonial era but also to invent ways to adapt them to contexts of museum display that did not exist historically.

13.7   George Back, *Egheechololle, a Tlicho man, December 1825 – March 1826,* watercolour over pencil. Courtesy of Library and Archives Canada, 1955-102-52, C-005559

13.8   The Tlicho Tea Dance, still photograph from a film made by anthropologist June Helm during the 1950s. Courtesy of the Northwest Territories Archives

We designed the module focusing on Dene traditions to suggest these missing components. It pairs George Back's sketch of a Tlicho (Dogrib) man named Egheechololle, made in 1825–26 (fig. 13.7), with a twenty-first-century video recording of the Tlicho Tea Dance, a consummate expression of the Tlicho as a community which has historically been performed at moments of unity and celebration (figs. 13.8 and 13.9). In this grouping we also planned to display a suit of fine clothing made for a high-ranking person by a Dene woman of the Tuchone nation from the southern Yukon. The bold beaded designs that by the late nineteenth century had replaced the earlier porcupine quillwork are expressive of the wearer's personal well-being and success and in this sense constitute a portrayal of character, identity, and status.

On one level, the display of the portrait and outfit would seem to convey a reasonable dialogic pairing of European and Dene modes of portraying identity. George Back was a topographical artist who accompanied Lieutenant John Franklin on his first two overland expeditions to explore the northern coast of North America. His sketchbooks contain not only the first careful maps and views of the landscape but also the earliest European portraits of Dene people from what is now the Northwest Territories. Like earlier European artists, Back was interested in faces and in Indigenous styles of clothing,

but, more unusually, he also recorded the names of his subjects. His watercolours suggest the consummate skill of Dene women in tanning hides and furs and making exquisite ornaments of dyed porcupine quills and seeds for trade as well as for their families.

Yet discussions with Dene people in the Northwest Territories made clear that, on their own, neither fine clothing nor early portrait drawings are adequate or "authentic" portrayals of identity in Charles Taylor's terms. Consultants stressed that Dene expressions of identity privilege communal values and relationships with the land and are most directly expressed through story, song, and dance. This very different expressive hierarchy was clearly articulated when, during research for the Portrait Gallery selection in the Tlicho community at Rae, Northwest Territories, we asked Tlicho elder Elizabeth Mackenzie to examine and comment on a colour reproduction of the Back drawing. Her comment was, in Tlicho: "That person dressed in good hide clothing, that person is shown as a young man. When he hears the drum and when he sees the people dancing that person is going to want to dance. He's not going to think of the way he's dressed, the way that he appears, or the bad times. He is going to dance."[19] In its fullest sense, in other words, Dene identity is communicated

13.9   Tlicho representatives performing the Tea Dance in the Senate lobby, Parliament Buildings, Ottawa, following third reading of the Tlicho land-claim bill, February 2005. Courtesy of Indian and Northern Affairs Canada

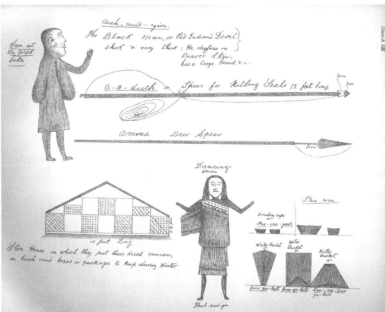

through performance that incorporates material objects and not through the visual record of an outer appearance alone.

The space of a museum, however, is designed for directed, processual walking, and in practical terms it is difficult to stop visitors long enough to use storytelling, dance, or song as a primary expression of identity. With the agreement of Dene advisers, we decided to place in dialogue with the Tuchone beaded hide clothing and the George Back sketch a video of the Tea Dance that was performed by Tlicho representatives in the foyer of the Senate chamber on 15 February 2005 after their land-claim agreement had received third reading in the Senate, the final legislative stage prior to royal assent and the transformation of the bill into law. Installed at 100 Wellington Street, this video footage would have resonated powerfully with the view of the Parliament Buildings, clearly visible from the "Facing the Other" gallery through the large front windows of the adjacent room. The a cappella singing accompanying the dance would have filled the whole gallery, animating not only the Dene module but also the groupings from other regions of Canada.

The last module planned for the introductory gallery presented two portraits of the last surviving members of the Beothuk of Newfoundland, a First Nation driven to extinction in the early nineteenth century. The LAC collection includes a famous 1819 miniature of Demasduit painted on ivory in St John's by Lady Hamilton, wife of the governor (fig. 13.10). Demasduit was captured by members of an expedition sent to stop Beothuk thefts of equipment left in fishing camps during the winter freeze-up. Her gentle and demure expression seems to reflect the sympathy she evoked among the settlers, but it can also be read as the sign of the disorientation and numbing grief of a woman who had lost her only child, been removed from her community, and

13.10   Lady Henrietta Martha Hamilton, Portrait miniature of Demasduit (Mary March), 1819, watercolour on ivory. Courtesy of Library and Archives Canada, 1977-14-1, C-087697

13.11   Shawnadithit (1801–29), Drawings of a dancing woman (lower centre) and other aspects of Beothuk life, with annotations by W.E. Cormack; redrawn from the original pencil sketch for publication in James P. Howley *The Beothucks or Red Indians* (Cambridge, 1915). As Howley noted, Shawnadithit's portrait suggests the movement of dance: "From under the right arm, a portion of the dress ... is seen flying loose, as if extended by the action of circling round while dancing." Photo courtesy of Dr Hans Rollman

13.12   Rebecca Belmore, *Shawnadithit*, 2001, Ultracal 30 gypsum cement, paint, human hair, wood shelf, and paper. Private collection. Reproduced by permission of the artist. Photo © Vancouver Art Gallery

seen her husband killed before her eyes through one of the tragic misunderstandings typical of Beothuk-settler relations during the early nineteenth century.[20] Adjacent to the miniature we planned to place a portrayal of a "dancing woman" made by Demasduit's niece, Shawnadithit, the last surviving Beothuk (fig. 13.11). The image is part of the visual record of Beothuk life made at the behest of the Newfoundland intellectual William Cormack, who was anxious to preserve a record of Beothuk culture. Although Shawnadithit's images and the words are too fragmentary to form a clear concept of Beothuk beliefs or customs, her portrait of a woman is an indication of the primacy of dance as a cultural expression among the Beothuk, as among other Aboriginal peoples. As such, it stands as a tragic double to the contemporary Tlicho Tea Dance.

For many Aboriginal people in Canada, the extinction of the Beothuk has become emblematic of the cumulative historical tragedies they have suffered during the past four hundred years. In order to acknowledge and respect the emotion that Beothuk images evoke and to create a space for commemoration and mourning, we placed the Beothuk images apart from the other modules. We also planned to introduce here a contemporary sculpture by Anishinaabe artist Rebecca Belmore that addresses the Beothuk tragedy. Her piece, *Shawnadithit* (2001), is composed of casts of the artist's feet and hands positioned in an ambiguous position that could be read as a posture either of bondage or of prayer. The space where the body should be is empty (fig. 13.12).

In the overall curatorial plan, the "Facing the Other" gallery was to be followed by five chronological and thematic sections that extended over two floors and narrated the history of Canada from the perspective of the settler population. They were "Tangled Gardens" (the seventeenth century to the 1830s), "Becoming Canadians" (1830s to 1914), "Changing Tides" (1900 to 1940s), "Rising Voices "(1950s–1970s), and "In the Here and Now" (1980s to the present).[21] The exercise of choosing Aboriginal images to include in these galleries brought home even more forcibly the need to establish the antiphonal relationships of Aboriginal-to-settler historical roles, for, contrary to conventional accounts, these have more often involved struggle and resistance than harmonious relationships with settler society and the "contributions" to the creation of Canada so often stressed in the textbooks.

The selection of images was, however, only the first step in communicating such messages, for the final test of any curatorial concept is the success with which design and installation can convey curatorial concepts. How could the notion of dialogic relationships be expressed in "Facing the Other" and antiphony in the subsequent sections? The spaces assigned to the first two sections presented particular opportunities and challenges. "Facing the Other" was planned for the elegant, rectangular wood-panelled, and neoclassically ornamented rooms formerly used as the ambassador's anteroom. Working with the Toronto design firm Reich and Petch Design International, we provided for five modular groupings that would be separated in the space of the gallery to indicate cultural traditions that were independent of each other in time and space. The Beothuk installation, as noted, would be displayed apart, allowing space for commemoration and contemplation.

The installation of the Four Kings was planned as the centrepiece of the "Tangled Gardens" section situated in the former ambassador's office, whose large windows look directly out onto the centre block of the Parliament Buildings (fig. 13.13). The theme of this section was European efforts to reproduce the Old World in the New from the seventeenth through the early nineteenth century. We recommended that the portraits be mounted inside four separate tall cases standing on the floor rather than hung on the walls, where they would have been contained and constrained by the neoclassical architectural ornament. The four cases would describe an arc suggestive of the circle that is the ideal model of the Onkwehonwe confederacy (fig. 13.14).

13.13 (*right*) John Verelst, *Portrait of Sa Ga Yeath Qua Pieth Tow (Christianized Brant)*, 1710, one of the Four Indian Kings; oil on canvas. The animal on the lower right identifies the Mohawk leader as a member of the bear clan. Courtesy of Library and Archives Canada, 1977-35-2, C-092418.

13.14 (*below and colour plate 14*) Floor plan of the installation of the portraits of the Four Indian Kings designed for the Portrait Gallery of Canada. Photo courtesy of Reich and Petch Design International. © Government of Canada; reproduced with the permission of the Minister of Public Works and Government Services Canada (2011). Library and Archives Canada, DWG 54-9, Gallery Seven – Concept One

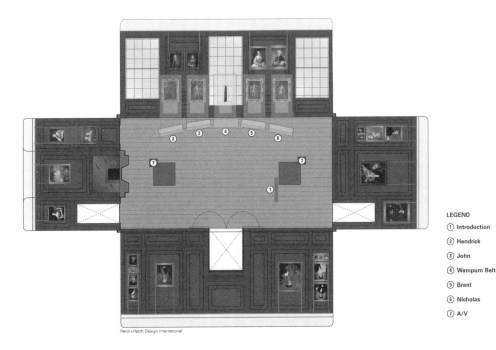

LEGEND
1 Introduction
2 Hendrick
3 John
4 Wampum Belt
5 Brant
6 Nicholas
7 A/V

Reich+Petch Design International

We sent this proposal to the confederacy chiefs at the Six Nations Reserve in Ontario and asked if they would deem it appropriate to exhibit a wampum belt. The response was positive, and the suggestion was made that a replica of a historic wampum such as the Covenant Chain belt be commissioned and presented to the Portrait Gallery. Such a replica would constitute a renewal of the agreement of mutual respect and support made in the early contact period by the Onkwehonwe and the British. Here too the direct view of the Parliament Buildings through the facing windows would powerfully convey the historical continuities being invoked.

Conclusion

During the past three decades of heightened Indigenous political activism, many Aboriginal leaders have cited the symbolic meaning of one wampum belt that has particular resonance today. First exchanged in confirmation of an agreement between the Dutch and the Hodenosaunee in the seventeenth century, the Guswenta, or Two-Row Belt, is woven of white shell wampum beads, which form a rectangular field divided by two parallel rows of purple beads. These purple rows are interpreted as representing Europeans and Aboriginal people paddling their canoes down the river separately but in parallel, a reading that can be understood as supporting the isolation of Aboriginal and settler communities from each other. Yet for many people today, both Aboriginal and non-Aboriginal, such a reading needs to be extended to acknowledge the complex historical interconnectedness that has evolved in the course of four hundred years of shared habitation of the lands we call Canada. The tension and stability of this coexistent relationship has recently been explored in a video work entitled *Two Row II* by Onkwehonwe artist Alan Michelson, now part of the collection of the National Gallery of Canada. Michelson videoed the two opposite shorelines of the Grand River, which separates the lands of the Six Nations Reserve from those of the settler communities on the other side. These shoreline videos are tinted purple and projected on a wide rectangular white screen as two parallel bands of video images. In Michelson's Guswenta the two bands stream in opposite directions, creating both a tension and a sense of indissoluble interlinkage – as two shores of the same river, they are forever joined, yet they are also expressed as currents that pull against each other. The viewer is thus initially made aware of Aboriginal-settler relations in Canada as taut and tense, but as the mingled and overlapping voices of the people who inhabit the two sides of the river are heard, speaking mostly English but also, still, in Iroquoian languages, the numerous references to histories that are both separate and shared create a further awareness that the construct of separation, too, is an illusion.

Michelson's *Two Row II* captures the kind of antiphonal tension that was the goal of our curatorial strategy for the Aboriginal presence in the galleries that followed "Facing the Other." In such installations much depends, as has already been noted, on success in fine-tuning details of the installation and exhibition texts in such a way that visitors do not interpret the groupings and spatial arrangements in terms of familiar tropes of Aboriginal peoples' "contributions" to the founding of the settler nation and their subsequent "disappearance." Success in this project often depends on subtle details of installation, involving not only the careful selection of images and wording of texts but also the relative scale and spacing of the exhibition components; even the size of the fonts that are used and the proportional relationships of texts and images can be critically instrumental.

For example, a similar installation to what we proposed is now on view in the recently renewed and reopened US National Portrait Gallery in Washington, DC. Mezzotints of two of Verelst's portraits of the Four Indian Kings have been placed adjacent to a wampum belt, but because this installation is contained within a section of the gallery's historical narrative entitled "American Origins, 1600–1900," it is inevitably subordinated to a teleological account of American continental expansion and dominance, leaving no space for an antiphonal expression of continuing Native American claims to sovereign status. The label for the wampum belt states: "William Penn's Lenape Wampum Belt / Lenape tribal leaders presented this belt to William Penn, the founder of Pennsylvania. This belt was not intended to be worn, but instead served as a token of the covenant between the Lenape and Penn. The meandering pattern may refer abstractly to terms of the agreement reached with Penn and his Quaker followers." Although this text explains the significance of wampum belts in early diplomatic exchanges, the distanced and objectifying curatorial voice does not allow for any intrusion of living and continuing Indigenous agency. Dialogue has been silenced.

An important aim of postcolonial art history is the recovery not only of the dialogic but also of the contestatory relationships produced through contact, conquest, colonization, and decolonization. As I hope I have been able to suggest, the traces of these relationships often exist, uniquely, in portraits and other works of visual art. But I have also pointed out what has been lost from these visual traces. We can no longer hear Osoop's eloquent oration, just as the chains of memory and narrative carried by many of the wampum belts given at the Great Peace of Montreal or extended in the painted hand of one of the Four Kings have been broken. Yet, even if such specific art histories are unrecoverable, the concepts that informed them have, as we have seen, survived and are currently being strengthened, revived, and reinvented. The Canadian Multiculturalism Act enjoins the federal government to "encourage and assist the social, cultural, economic and political institutions of Canada to be both respectful and inclusive of Canada's multicultural character." Museums in Canada today have a major role to play in aiding this process by publicly explaining, validating, and communicating the identities of the diverse communities that make up the nation in ways that accord with those communities' own traditions and self-understandings.

14

Modes of Inclusion

Indigenous Art at the National Gallery of Canada and the Art Gallery of Ontario

This book began with an analysis of the Indians of Canada Pavilion at Expo 67, a project whose popular success and anticolonial politics can be seen as auguries of the major changes that have subsequently come to Canadian anthropology and history museums. In this chapter I focus on modes of inclusion in the art gallery, and I begin it with a discussion of a second major exhibition that was in development during the same years as the pavilion. *Masterpieces of Indian and Eskimo Art from Canada* was shown in Paris and Ottawa in 1969 and 1970. It was the first major exhibition at the National Gallery of Canada (NGC) to focus exclusively on Aboriginal arts from across Canada and the first to fully adopt the modernist installation style associated with the Western appreciation of Primitive Art.[1]

Although its curatorial process and its politics contrasted sharply with those of the Indians of Canada Pavilion, *Masterpieces* was also a landmark exhibition which, like the pavilion, foreshadowed more permanent movements toward inclusivity. Three decades later, Canada's two largest art museums began to plan the integration of Indigenous arts into longterm installations of Canadian art that had previously focused exclusively on settler arts. The National Gallery of Canada's *Art of This Land* opened on 21 June, National Aboriginal Day, in 2003, and the Art Gallery of Ontario's new Canadian galleries were launched in November 2008, when that institution reopened after its major expansion and redesign. While both represent historic decisions to broaden the category of "Canadian art," each approaches the challenge of inclusivity differently. At the National Gallery, Indigenous art forms

The history of Canadian Art begins with the indigenous peoples who have occupied the vast territories now known as Canada. Transformed over time through interaction with other cultures and evolving according to their own needs, the arts of the Aboriginal peoples have remained vital components of the many art histories of this country.
– *Introductory text panel*, Art of This Land, *National Gallery of Canada*

Relationships of power are complex and dynamic. They are at play in our institutions and governments, as well as in our social and cultural groups. These dynamics are often documented through art, while art has frequently been used to promote the values of those in power.
– *Introductory text panel, "Art and Power," Canadian galleries, Art Gallery of Ontario*

14.1   Installation of Northwest Coast art and paintings by Emily Carr in the National Gallery of Canada's *Exhibition of Canadian West Coast Art, Native and Modern*, in 1927. Photo © National Gallery of Canada, Ottawa

have been incorporated throughout its classic modernist chronological survey; at the Art Gallery of Ontario (AGO) a new thematic organization invokes postmodern and postcolonial critiques of the twentieth-century art museum installation. The high modernist display paradigm manifested in the *Masterpieces* exhibition in 1969 makes it a useful point of departure for a discussion of these twenty-first-century initiatives and also provides a ground line against which to assess their relative merits.

Import/Export: The National Gallery and *Masterpieces of Indian and Eskimo Art from Canada*

The first exhibition that brought Aboriginal carvings, textiles, and paintings into the National Gallery was *Exhibition of Canadian West Coast Art, Native and Modern* in 1927, a show that displayed the paintings of Emily Carr and other settler artists alongside historic Northwest Coast Indigenous carvings, textiles, and paintings (fig. 14.1). This exhibition has been much discussed in the critical museological writing of Diana Nemiroff, Lynda Jessup, Leslie Dawn, and others, and its teleological structure has been laid bare. The exhibition positioned Indigenous arts as the prelude to a history of Canadian art that reached its culmination with the advent of the modernist settler painting of Emily Carr and the Group of

Seven. Indian artists set the stage for this development and then disappear, leaving behind a treasure of historical art that can continue to inspire new and distinctively Canadian art forms.[2] This narrative was made explicit by the National Gallery's director, Eric Brown, in his forward to the small exhibition catalogue. He lamented the disappearance of traditional arts, urged the need to preserve what remained, and ended with an affirmation of the natural pattern of succession as he saw it: "enough … remains of the old arts to provide an invaluable mine of decorative design which is available to the student for a host of different purposes and possessing for the Canadian artist in particular the unique quality of being entirely national in its origin and character."[3]

Between 1927 and 1969 the National Gallery displayed historical Aboriginal arts in four other exhibitions.[4] Two of these, *A Century of Fine Crafts* (1957) and *Canadian Fine Crafts* (1963), appropriated Indigenous art forms into the hierarchical Western classification of fine and decorative arts, implicitly identifying them with the lower category of "applied" art. The other two exhibitions, *Arts of French Canada, 1613–1870* (1947) and the centenary installation *Three Hundred Years of Canadian Art* (1967), were broad chronological surveys in which Indigenous arts continued to be presented as precursors of the more highly evolved settler traditions. The advent of a contemporary and commoditized production of Eskimo (Inuit) stone carvings after 1949 created pressure on the NGC from collectors and government agencies to exhibit the new art.[5] Yet early NGC exhibitions continued to present Inuit sculptures in a continuum with "craft" genres such as baskets, garments, and dolls. Norman Vorano and Judy Hall have shown that the first exhibition to present contemporary Inuit sculpture in the Primitive Art/fine art mode was held, not in Canada, but in London in 1953 at the Gimpel Fils Gallery.[6]

The inspiration for *Masterpieces of Indian and Eskimo Art from Canada* also came from Europe. The project was initiated in Paris in the mid-1960s, when representatives of the Societé des amis du Musée de l'Homme, the friends organization of the French national anthropology museum, approached the Canadian consulate with an idea for an exhibition that would showcase outstanding Native historical arts from Canadian collections.[7] The consulate arranged for the society's president, Marcel Evrard, to go to Ottawa with his colleague Alix de Rothschild in order to meet with Dr William Taylor, the director of the National Museum of Man (NMM). Evrard, commissioner of exhibitions at the Musée de l'Homme, was a collector and a curator who had run a bookstore in Belgium during the 1950s which showed both modern art and those of Africa and the Pacific. He was a consummate representative of the tradition of appreciation for Primitive Art which had been tightly linked to the development of artistic modernism since the early twentieth century and which had become deeply embedded in the European art world by the 1960s.[8] Evrard and his associates had already organized an exhibition called *Primitive Art from Artists' Studios,* as well as other "masterpieces" exhibitions of African and Oceanic art that drew on the Musée de l'Homme's collections.[9]

William Taylor, an archaeologist specializing in the Arctic, was the obvious liaison in Ottawa for Evrard's project, not only because expertise in Indigenous arts and cultures was concentrated in his museum but also because
he was himself an early champion of contemporary Canadian Indigenous art.
Under his directorship, the NMM had begun collecting this art, although it
was still considered to be of questionable authenticity by other institutions.[10]
His museum also had a history of collaborating with the National Gallery
going back to 1927: NMM ethnologist Marius Barbeau had played a key role
in the *Exhibition of Canadian West Coast Art, Native and Modern* of that
year, and the museum had also advised and lent to the Indians of Canada
Pavilion during mid-1960s. Taylor was receptive, and he and his staff agreed
to work with Evrard and Rothschild to identify suitable objects for the exhibition. At the time of Evrard's visit, however, the NMM was in the process of
moving out of the Victoria Memorial Building, the original home of both the
National Museum and the National Gallery, so that its exhibition galleries
could be renovated, and it thus could not serve as the Canadian venue for the
show. The National Gallery, however, had moved permanently into the Lorne
Building in downtown Ottawa several years earlier and was in a position to
accommodate the exhibition. The clear implication of the extant documents
is, then, that if not for this problem of timing, *Masterpieces*, although an
exhibition whose purpose was to feature historic Indigenous objects as art,
would have been shown at a museum of anthropology not only in Paris but
also in Ottawa.[11]

The context for Taylor's willingness to embrace an aestheticized display of
"ethnographic" objects is illuminated by the planning that was in progress
for the reinstallation of the NMM's exhibitions after the renovation. Meeting minutes show that the staff ethnologists had been giving serious consideration to the inclusion of a permanent "Primitive Art Exhibit" of objects
from around the world to complement the Canadian ethnology exhibits. The
agenda of a 1964 curatorial meeting called for a discussion of whether this
component (the only one with a non-Canadian scope) should be conceived
as "a straight Art exhibit pure and simple; or as an ethnological exhibit."[12] A
draft proposal written by scientist-in-charge Eugene Arima in 1967 recommended "an exhibition of primitive art which would not only be ethnologic-
ally sound and informative, but which would have great aesthetic appeal as
well."[13] Arima also suggested the kinds of items that would be included from
the National Museum's collections: the "magnificent collection of Northwest
Coast art would certainly serve as the foundation for such an exhibition. In
addition, we have a fine collection of Eskimo carvings and prints, Iroquois
false face masks, beadwork – a wide assortment of art objects from all the
cultural areas of Canada." He also listed archaeological specimens in the museum's collection and suggested using "for comparative or contrastive purposes" the "art work from New Guinea" then on loan to the museum and
"a representative collection of primitive art from all over the world."[14] This
display of "primitive art" did not, in the end, materialize, although a few non-
Canadian pieces, such as the NMM's Benin brass bell, were integrated into

a general introduction to cultural history. The genres of Canadian Native art that Arima listed are, however, very similar to those chosen by Evrard, Rothschild, and the NMM staff for *Masterpieces*. The 186 objects borrowed from eleven Canadian museums were divided into almost identical regional groupings: "the Eskimos," "the Indians of the Northwest Coast," "the Indians of the Plains," and "the Indians of the Eastern Region."

The ready acceptance with which Canadian collaborators greeted the use of a distinctively European and modernist Primitive Art paradigm in the *Masterpieces* exhibition suggests that older ways of thinking about Indigenous arts had been eroding for some time. The NMM curators were undoubtedly aware not only of contemporary academic debates over the virtues of the art and artifact display paradigms but also of mid-twentieth-century developments in the major art centres of the West.[15] In the 1950s, French lovers of Primitive Art had successfully lobbied to have the Musée de la France d'Outre-mer, located in the elaborate art deco building constructed for the 1931 French Colonial Exhibition, recast as the Musée national des arts d'Afrique et d'Océanie (MAAO) in order to provide Paris with a venue where ethnographic objects could be displayed as art.[16] During the late 1930s and 1940s, the Museum of Modern Art in New York had organized a series of large, temporary exhibitions of African, Native American, and Oceanic arts.[17] In 1957 René d'Harnoncourt, who had been a key organizer of these shows, joined forces with Nelson Rockefeller to found a new Museum of Primitive Art, which displayed Rockefeller's private collection. In 1969, the same year that *Masterpieces* was shown at the National Gallery, these collections were in turn offered to the Metropolitan Museum of Art, where they formed the core of a new wing opened in 1982. As Aldona Jonaitis has shown, during the mid-twentieth century New York's American Museum of Natural History had also been combining aestheticized "art" installations with its ethnographic displays, sometimes within the same hall.[18] By the 1960s, then, museum goers in Paris and New York could see the same kinds of objects exhibited as both art and artifact in a range of prestigious venues.

Masterpieces of Indian and Eskimo Art from Canada was one of the two major exhibitions presented by the National Gallery during 1969 and 1970.[19] Although it had become an NGC project by default rather than by intention, its transfer moved it into the domain of the NGC's designers. The high modernist "white cube" installation created by Jack Macgillivray was typical of art galleries during this decade, and it introduced an even more radical mode of decontextualization than had been employed in earlier exhibitions of Primitive Art (figs. 14.2 and 14.3). The Museum of Modern Art's *Indian Art of the United States (1941)*, for example, had shown Native North American art forms against abstract panels of colour, and maps and contextual labels were integrated into a number of sections. Macgillivray's approach, which he seems to have developed with no input or interference from the National Museum's ethnologists, rigorously isolated the objects against luxurious expanses of stark white wall in order to promote the unimpeded viewing and intense visual experiences typical of the high modernist formalism of the

14.2 (*above*)   Installation of Plains clothing and war shirts at the National Gallery of Canada's *Masterpieces of Indian and Eskimo Art from Canada* exhibition in 1969. Photo © National Gallery of Canada, Ottawa

14.3 (*below*)   Installation of Northwest Coast carvings at the National Gallery of Canada's *Masterpieces of Indian and Eskimo Art from Canada* exhibition in 1969. Photo © National Gallery of Canada, Ottawa

decade. Label text was kept to a minimum, moving the representative of one lending museum to write a letter complaining that the public could not find out who owned the individual pieces.[20] The NMM ethnologists' responses to this display are hinted at by an unsigned note penciled on the bottom of a memo distributed to National Gallery staff to inform them of a television feature on the exhibition that had been aired on the local CBC evening show. "This was interesting," the note reads. "Charlotte Gobeil interviewed Bill Taylor. (first question – what did he think of the 'awful' installation, WT saying that it wasn't *that* exactly but it was 'clinical'; Did mention that we present objects as art."[21]

When this installation is considered alongside the picture captions and essays written for the catalogue by the NMM's ethnologists, the sharp difference between the ethnological and aesthetic approaches to Indigenous objects also becomes evident, despite the two national museums' apparent rapprochement. To give just one example, the catalogue entry for a pre-contact stone carving of a frog from British Columbia, reads: "Anthropomorphic carving on grandiorite. One end broadly convex, body edges convex, other end more convex and carved in the form of a face with a well defined nose and broad eyebrows. Two oval depressions, on either side of center of upper face appear eye-like." One wonders what Christian Zervos, the prominent French art critic who contributed the preface to the catalogue, made of such texts. His view of what was important about the objects on display was informed, in contrast, by romantic primitivism and modernist formalism. He wrote of the Northwest Coast totem poles, rattles, amulets, and canoes in the exhibition, for example, that "all are instruments for arousing mysterious forces and compelling them to appear. The call of the unknown and the supernatural vibrates in these objects."[22] He also argued that "scholarly elaboration … can only miss the essence of these objects" and that it is essential "to insist that the aesthetic value of the objects … is eminently worthy of consideration."[23] Aesthetic value, Zervos states in his final sentence, "whether it be 'primitive' or 'sophisticated,' can only result from a union of matter and creative ability; a union in which there is a ceaseless and reciprocal exchange expressed in universal language."[24]

Zervos's prose accords with the installation style created for the Paris venue. As Diana Nemiroff has noted, the Musée de l'Homme's display was "atmospheric and evocative," complete with Indian music and Eskimo drumming and dramatic areas of "spotlight and shadow" that "create[d] an impression of mystery and magic." "Distanced, therefore, in both time and place, the exhibition was hailed by the French press in terms that recalled the first European explorations, as a 'discovery' and a 'revelation' … It is revealing of the deep desire for experiences of the primitive that, when the exhibition came to the National Gallery of Canada, some reviewers complained that the objects, 'lit with the light of common day,' had lost their ambience, that is to say, some of their *otherness*."[25] Yet despite these differences of approach, both anthropological and art installations drew on understandings of the primitive that positioned Indigenous arts in what Johannes Fabian has termed the "ethnographic present," a fictive past time of authenticity forever cut off from contemporary life.

From a contemporary vantage point, the complete lack of Aboriginal voice in *Masterpieces* is striking. As we have seen, even as Evrard and Rothschild were journeying to Ottawa, Aboriginal artists were finding common cause with political activists and forcing the creation of a pavilion at Expo 67 that could serve as a site for the articulation of Native perspectives on history, culture, and art. In 1969 the focus of political activism shifted to Parliament Hill, where Aboriginal opponents of the Trudeau government's assimilationist White Paper on Indian policy successfully forced its withdrawal.[26] In contrast to these forms of activism, the disciplinary squabbles over art and artifact seem of minor moment. Yet at the same time the exhibition of Indigenous-made objects as high art at the National Gallery of Canada carried a significance that moved the politics of inclusion forward.[27] Although coming out of a primitivist tradition, the exhibition implicitly recognized Indigenous visual production as high art, and it set a precedent for the more permanent and differently conceptualized integration of Indigenous arts at the National Gallery and the Art Gallery of Ontario more than three decades later. As a precedent, however, *Masterpieces* raises a number of questions. How far do these new exhibitions move us away from the backward gaze of the primitive art lover? To what degree do Western formalist aesthetics continue to control the selection and the installation paradigm? And what impact has the presence of non-Western art works had on the curation of settler arts and on art-historical and museological narratives and conventions?

The National Gallery: Bridging the Third Solitude

The practice of the National Gallery of Canada is to refresh the Canadian galleries every two years by rotating the works on display. In the late 1990s the NGC began to plan for a historic expansion of the scope of these galleries by integrating Indigenous works of art into the rotation scheduled for 2003. The survey would now begin before European contact and continue, as before, through to 1985. (Works made after this period, both Indigenous and non-Indigenous, are displayed in the contemporary art galleries.) The break with past practice that this initiative represented was signalled by the similarly unprecedented naming of the new Canadian installations *Art of This Land / Art d'ici*. This title gestures in two directions at once. It reaffirms the territorial rootedness of the settler arts that continue to dominate the exhibition, while also referencing, if more subtly, the original ownership and continuing claims to land of Canada's Indigenous peoples. By using the term "art" in the singular, furthermore, the title also constructs an ideal unity that remains unrealized in Canadian geopolitics.

Denise Leclerc, curator of Modern Canadian Art, assumed responsibility for the Indigenous component of *Art of This Land*, and she has been assisted in its development by Greg Hill (Mohawk) and Linda Grussani (Algonquin).[28] Leclerc has traced the roots of the project back to discussions that began during the planning of the gallery's new building, which opened in 1988.[29] She notes that although the NGC had considered the inclusion of Indigenous arts at that time, the undertaking proved too complex in the midst of the gallery's comprehensive reinstallation. The momentum for change, however, continued to build. On one level, as Leclerc notes, since the early twentieth century modern artists – themselves inspired by non-Western arts – have been pushing against the confines of the traditional fine arts genres of painting, sculpture, and graphic media that art museums have traditionally featured. Active lobbying for the inclusion of contemporary Indigenous art in the NGC during the 1980s and early 1990s added to the momentum, as did three reports commissioned by key arts organizations which pointed out fundamental anomalies in institutional policies related to the collecting and exhibiting of Native arts.[30] "As the result of a process of internal logic," Leclerc writes, "since contemporary Aboriginal art was slowly but surely gaining ground within the institution (notably through acquisitions), it was becoming increasingly urgent that our historical Canadian exhibition galleries also reflect the contributions of historical Aboriginal art."[31]

The official mandates given to the national museums by the federal government had assigned responsibility for collecting and exhibiting Indigenous arts to the National Museum of Man and for Western and Asian arts to the National Gallery. Revisiting the NGC's mission to "make known … a collection of works of art, both historic and contemporary, with special, but not exclusive, reference to Canada," its curators discovered there a more elastic and inclusive possibility. During the late 1990s Leclerc began to approach possible lenders and to identify individual works for the first installation of *Art of This Land*, and she also brought Indigenous and non-Indigenous specialists to Ottawa to discuss with NGC staff the issues of representation and display that are specific to Indigenous arts.[32] The schedule of biennial rotations means that the selection of works in *Art of This Land* has changed three times since 2003 – in 2005, 2007, and 2009 – placing heavy demands on NGC staff. Continuous borrowing is expensive in curatorial travel, loan fees, insurance, and other costs, and the fragility and light-sensitivity of many of the items can make museums reluctant to lend them for the full two years. But beyond such practical concerns, the project's reliance on loans also means that the curatorial narratives of the Euro-Canadian and Indigenous art components cannot be controlled in the same ways. While only some of the Euro-Canadian oil paintings, sculptures, and silver in the NGC's own collection are rotated out of the installations every two years, *all* of the Indigenous items must be changed. The virtue of this necessity is that Leclerc and her colleagues have been able to expose viewers to a wide range of new works, many of which have rarely been exhibited, even by their home institutions. The difficulty, however, is that the relationships she can construct between Indigenous and settler art works must inevitably depend to a degree on opportunity and serendipity. The regular turnovers also mean that a rigorous discussion of *Art of This Land* would require a careful consideration of each installation separately, a task that is beyond the scope of this chapter. I will, rather, sample the successive iterations in order to explore the advantages and disadvantages of the chronological-survey structure as a mode of inclusion.

The suite of thirty-three rooms in the NGC's Canadian section is structured as a series of large galleries opening out sequentially from one another, with smaller, more intimate side galleries leading off to one side. This classic linear visitor path has been common to public art museums since the early nineteenth century. As Carol Duncan has written, it causes visitors to "follow a route through a programmed narrative" that is political and ideological.[33] Movement forward through the rooms, in other words, is a progress through time and space not only in a literal but also in a metaphorical sense. Prior to 2003, this journey began with the arrival of French settlers, in a room devoted to the ecclesiastical arts of Quebec whose focal point was a large and elaborately gilded eighteenth-century tabernacle. To create a new space for the "Art of the Ancient Ones," this gallery was divided in half by a new wall built across the middle. In and of itself, this yielding up of space in a federal institution that has always had to strive for a judicious balance in the representation of French and British histories in Canada is earnest of the seriousness of the NGC's new commitment.

The artifacts now showcased in the first of the Canadian galleries presented the NGC's designers with an unprecedented challenge. In contrast to the church furniture, oil paintings, and marble sculptures they were accustomed to displaying, the archaeological record of the millennia that preceded the arrival of Europeans is contained in small artworks made of durable, monochromatic materials. In the inaugural 2003 installation the stone, bone, antler, and ceramic sculptures looked dull, lifeless, and lost, but by 2009 many of the initial problems had been resolved. The gallery was painted a buttery yellow that fills it with a sunny day–lit warmth. In the centre of the wall facing the entrance the designers placed a Kwakwaka'wakw stone piledriver carved in the shape of a dogfish whose strong contours draw the eye and lead it up to lines of text that now stand out against the yellow wall. These link the artifacts of the past to stories and songs still alive in Aboriginal traditions: "Our elders say that the old people are speaking to us through the stories and songs they left behind long ago. It is time to listen and hear their story."

In the centre of the floor, four symmetrically placed cases suggest the cardinal directions that define Indigenous cosmology, ritual, and spiritual orientation. The exquisitely carved fishing lures, pipes, pendants, and other items on display come from the four quarters: the ancient Thule and Dorset peoples of the Arctic, the Newfoundland Beothuk, who were hastened into extinction by the genocidal policies of settlers, the Onkwehonwe from the eastern Great Lakes region, and the peoples of the western Plains. The aesthetic experience made available to the visitor by this design strategy evokes neither the impression of distance and mystery created by the chiaroscuro Paris installation of *Masterpieces* nor the austere formalism of its Ottawa installation but, rather, an impression of order, rationality, and connection.

As the visitor moves beyond this first gallery into the subsequent centuries of contact, the representational challenges change. Like other art museums, the National Gallery positions works of art both as objects of aesthetic contemplation and enjoyment and as products of historically contingent developments that are internal and, at the same time, external to particular artistic traditions. It creates its narratives, as Michael Baxandall and Mieke Bal have shown us, through the triangulated relationship of viewer, object, and curatorial text and through the sequencing and juxtapositions of these units of display.[34] The incorporation of Indigenous art into a settler museum brings with it, however, the further need to engage with the processes of cross-cultural interaction that have been produced over time as a result of the shifting power relations of colonialism.

In the four rotations that have thus far been mounted of *Art of This Land*, four different kinds of relationships have been structured, I would argue, by the selection and placement of works and texts. One kind of grouping has directly evoked specific episodes of intercultural and artistic exchange. A second has been more documentary, displaying Indigenous arts side by side with settler images in which similar garments, weapons, and other items are depicted, juxtapositions that can evoke ritual, aesthetic, or economic contexts to which they belong. A third kind suggests formal affinities among Indigenous and Euro-Canadian works, while a fourth simply brings into conjunction works of art that come from the same time and place but have no apparent interrelationship.

Two memorable examples of historical interconnection were included in the inaugural 2003 installation. A small side gallery that leads off the eighteenth-century Quebec installations displayed two self-portraits in oils by the nineteenth-century self-taught Huron-Wendat painter Zacharie Vincent together with oil portraits of Vincent painted by Quebec artists Eugene Hamel and Antoine Plamondon. Intermingled with these paintings, Leclerc placed cases containing a wampum belt, a feathered headdress, embroidered moccasins, trade-silver ornaments, and a type of sash known as a ceinture fléchée. These accoutrements of Huron-Wendat diplomacy and ceremonial dress appear in the portraits; their representation was a central concern of Vincent's artistic project, which was motivated by his desire to preserve traditions that were in decline. A further resonance was evoked by Hamel's portrait of Vincent. The Québécois painter came from a neighbouring village, and his example and tutelage stimulated Vincent to become a painter. Similarly, settler and Indigenous interrelationship and colonial exchange as registered in art were suggested by the placement of the well-known wooden sculpture of an angel attributed to Tsimshian artist Frederick Alexcie inside the Rideau Chapel, a salvaged Franco-Ontarian architectural interior installed in the National Gallery's Canadian section (fig. 14.4). While the sculpture's imagery fitted the ecclesiastical setting, its distinctive Northwest Coast formline

style contrasted with the chapel's ornate nineteenth-century decoration, setting it off in a way that effectively conveyed the distinctive qualities and separations that have characterized Indigenous and settler Christian communities and practices.

The strategy that I have termed documentary has been deployed particularly in gallery A104, which shows "Art in the Maritimes and Ontario, 1800–1860," and in gallery A105, devoted to Paul Kane and the Plains artists. The placement of a Mi'kmaq quilled basket adjacent to a well-known painting of a Mi'kmaq fishing encampment presents the visitor with a real example of an Indigenous art form that is depicted in the work of the anonymous settler artist. In a similar way, examples of Plains and Métis beaded and painted clothing have been grouped together with Paul Kane's paintings of mid-nineteenth-century Native life in western Canada. In such groupings the documentary intent of the Euro-Canadian paintings, which were often made to preserve a record of "vanishing" Indigenous peoples, are reinforced by the addition of the historical Indigenous arts, many of which were collected with the same purpose. Together they stand as evidence of the more distanced ethnographic project of the nineteenth century, rather than of histories of intercultural entanglement.

14.4 (*also colour plate 15*) The Rideau Chapel with sculpture of an angel attributed to Tsimshian carver Frederick Alexcie (on loan from the University of British Columbia Museum of Anthropology) in *Art of This Land*. Photo © National Gallery of Canada, Ottawa

14.5   A Kwakwaka'wakw crooked beak of heaven mask by Willie Seaweed (1945), on loan from the Glenbow Museum, juxtaposed with Alfred Pellan's *Blossoming* (1950), from the National Gallery, in the 2003–5 installation of *Art of This Land*. Mask reproduced with the permission of the Glenbow Museum. Photo © National Gallery of Canada, Ottawa

A reliance on formalist resonance has characterized some of the installations in gallery A107, which is devoted to "Early 20th Century Modernisms and Pacific-Northwest Coast Aboriginal Peoples." Leclerc has borrowed a series of outstanding examples of Northwest Coast masks, headdresses, button blankets, painted drums, and other objects for this room, and in the course of the four rotations, a number of the juxtapositions with settler paintings have suggested visual affinities of line, form, and colour harmony between European and Indigenous works. As reported in an article on the 2005 installation in the NGC members' magazine, the goal was to reveal "aesthetic associations linking Aboriginal and Euro-Canadian works," illustrated, for example, by the way in which "the circular motifs in Willie Seaweed's spectacular *Mask* (c. 1945) resonate with a nearby painting by Alfred Pellan, *Blossoming* (c. 1950) and with Robert Roussil's poplar sculpture *Gesticulation* (1954)"[35] (fig. 14.5). Such resonances do not evidence historical interactions, but are, Leclerc has stated, fundamental to the National Gallery's approach as an art museum. "The Gallery's interest in these objects … is primarily aesthetic," she has said. "We see them as works of art, rather than as artifacts, and attempt to work through visual associations that are both rational and interpretative."[36]

In accordance with this approach, the introductory text panels placed near the entrances of the main galleries provide only brief and generalized information about history and artistic development. The text panel in Gallery A107 is representative. The first paragraph characterizes Native life and art in the region and the changes that were taking place in the period being represented:

> Beginning more than three thousand years ago, many different Aboriginal peoples of Canada's Pacific Northwest coast and interior developed rich artistic traditions that employed the region's natural resources, in particular, red and yellow cedar. Using the wood, bark, and roots of these trees, along with other materials from the land and the sea, they carved canoes, poles, and house posts, and made containers, ceremonial objects, and clothing. Although the styles of embellishment varied these peoples generally followed aesthetic traditions that reflected heraldic kinships and spiritual beliefs. In spite of Government repression and the 1884 to 1951 outlawing of the potlatch – a gift-giving ceremony that was central to West Coast Aboriginal people and that encouraged production of highly developed art – they continued to create works of exceptional merit.

This text is followed by a second paragraph that provides similar information for settler art and history. It is, of course, impossible to convey the complexity of historical processes in short exhibition texts, but the level of generalization here seems particularly reductive. It flattens and effectively silences not only the histories of cultural loss and deprivation visited upon First Nations community members by settlement, losses of land and resources, religious conversion, and residential schooling, but also the local and specific nature of resistance to assimilationist pressures. To characterize the potlatch as a "gift-giving ceremony" without noting its centrality as a social and political institution, for example, falls dangerously close to the kind of stereotyped representation that lay behind its prohibition in the 1884 Indian Act.

The fourth kind of juxtaposition that occurs in *Art of This Land* has been particularly evident in gallery A106, which showcases Inuit and Dene arts. Here the media and practices of the Indigenous and Western artists in the room are so different as to suggest neither specific historical interrelationships nor general formal affinities. Rather, the viewer experiences them as belonging to separate but parallel worlds (fig 14.6). Such a "disconnect effect" can perhaps be considered an accurate reflection of the actual human and social separations enforced by the reserve system and differential rates of modernization. Where such juxtapositions occur, however, the result is to

14.6   A Cree beaded hood shown with contemporaneous paintings by members of the Group of Seven in *Art of This Land*. Photo © National Gallery of Canada, Ottawa

introduce a kind of third solitude to the two of French and English histories in Canada that the gallery has traditional sought to align and interrelate.

Following these galleries, the visitor path leads, finally, to seven galleries devoted to the paintings of the Group of Seven. It is not, perhaps, accidental that these are the only rooms in which Indigenous arts are absent. In standard histories of Canadian art, this foundational moment of Canadian modernism has been positioned as a culmination of the settler nation's search for identity. In *Art of This Land* it remains undisturbed as the triumphal moment in the development of the nation's art.[37] Yet the years during which the Group of Seven rose to prominence as a national school coincide with the period during which Aboriginal communities were experiencing assimilationist pressures at their most intense, together with the worst horrors of residential schooling. As the exhibition continues to develop, it will be important to consider the mounting body of revisionist critiques of this standard narrative of Canadian history in light of their particular implications for an exhibit that now embraces the works of Indigenous artists.[38]

Art of This Land is a new and brave initiative, and it will undoubtedly grow and develop over time. The gesture of inclusion it makes constitutes, in and of itself, a long overdue recognition of the presence of Indigenous people and art making over thousands of years in "the vast territories now known as Canada," as the introductory panel puts it. In this context, the comprehensiveness of the NGC's approach and its integration of Aboriginal artists into almost all the Canadian galleries insists on Indigenous and setter arts as continuous and contingent presences and acknowledges that both bodies of art change and evolve over time. And despite the problems of interpretation, the presentation of Indigenous works as art in the same relatively decontextualized mode as settler art does important work because it places both traditions on parallel planes of aesthetic achievement. Although each of these points seems almost embarrassingly simple and obvious, all have been implicitly denied by the prior absence of Indigenous arts from the national narrative of Canadian art. The contrast with the *Masterpieces* exhibition of 1969, which froze the authenticity of Indigenous arts in the ethnographic present and rendered them as remote and mysterious objects of Western desire and nostalgia, makes clear the great distance the NGC has travelled.

Yet other problems remain to be worked out. Deprived of information, the viewer falls back on admiration. This is, of course, not a bad thing in itself, but it inevitably consigns the lesser known traditions to a status that Brian O'Doherty's has termed "provincial." As he wrote in his classic analysis of the modernist white cube space of the art gallery (the paradigm to which the NGC adheres even if it now paints the walls in all the colours of Farrow and Ball), "The mark of provincial art is that it has to include too much – the context can't replace what is left out, there is no system of mutually understood assumptions."[39] True inclusivity, I would argue, cannot avoid the responsibility to overcome this knowledge gap, and this challenge, as I also argue, will require the NGC to revisit not only issues of historical contextualization but also its definition of art itself.

Aboriginal people – both contemporary artists and those knowledgeable about historical cultural traditions – have eloquently affirmed the holistic nature of Indigenous expressive culture. Northwest Coast masks convey their meanings and their full aesthetic impact in dance and when accompanied by the songs and stories inherited through the lineages of great families. The artistry of a quilled basket or beaded dress may also be fully revealed only through the aroma of the sweetgrass woven into it or the rain-like tinkling of its metal cone fringe and in terms of the knowledge imparted in the process of its making.[40] Not only aesthetic experience but also judgments of quality are bound up with such relationships. At the NGC, as in most Western art galleries, however, both definitions of art and criteria of quality remain uninterrogated. This issue was raised in the winter of 2010 when NGC director Marc Mayer was questioned by a CBC reporter about the gallery's lack of inclusion of artists from diasporic communities. His answer – "We just look for excellence. We don't care who makes it." – begged the question of the ways in which secular and ocular-centric traditions of Western modernity may occlude whole realms of aesthetic expression and meaning, counter to the ideal of inclusivity that Canada's official multiculturalism establishes.[41]

Another contrast between *Art of This Land* and *Masterpieces* is the presence in the new exhibition of numerous examples of the textile arts that feature prominently in Aboriginal art traditions, especially in the Woodlands and Subarctic, regions that were barely represented in the earlier exhibition because it privileged the Western fine art genres of sculpture and painting. Yet as Anne Whitelaw argues in her critique of *Art of This Land,* the Aboriginal works on display "remain overdetermined by the discourse of the art museum which privileges modes of seeing,"[42] and "the basis for the selection of Aboriginal works thus appears to be closely linked to how well they would fit in with the already existing narrative of Canadian art."[43] She urges that the opportunity offered by inclusion is to "rethink the *narrative* of Canadian art history ... and to reflect on the conceptions of aesthetic value – as they pertain to both Aboriginal and Euro-Canadian objects – that underpin the objects."[44] It is good, in other words, that an elaborately beaded nineteenth-century Cree headdress can be seen in the National Gallery, but the logical implication of this inclusion, in Whitelaw's view, is "the potential for rupture" of Euro-Canadian museological conventions. A logical extension of the display of Indigenous textile arts would thus be to introduce the needlework arts of settler women as well.

Potential for rupture is also implied by the multi-sensory and synesthetic nature of Indigenous arts. What implications might there be for the displays of seventeenth-century Quebec religious art if a future installation of Northwest Coast masks or rattles could be made to convey the dance movements, songs, and oral narratives to which, in Northwest Coast societies, the carved object is merely an adjunct? *Art of This Land* suggests such questions, but they have not yet been answered.

Memory, Myth, and Power at the Art Gallery of Ontario

When the redesigned and expanded Art Gallery of Ontario opened in November 2008, the public was presented with installations that were as dramatically changed as the new and greatly expanded Frank Gehry–designed building. Almost half the works now on display are new to the AGO, and this enlargement is primarily the result of the historic donation of Kenneth Thomson's collections of Euro-Canadian, Indigenous, and European art. In conformity with the donor's wishes, the Thomson collections will be exhibited in separate galleries for a set number of years and organized within them by artist. Cases containing his Aboriginal art, primarily Northwest Coast and Inuit, are placed in the middle of a number of the Thomson galleries. As at the National Gallery, these carvings, selected with the eye of the Western art connoisseur, are displayed to maximize their aesthetic impact and have only minimal "tombstone" labels.

AGO director Matthew Teitelbaum has explained that the classical art gallery approach required for the Thomson collections enabled the AGO's curators to "think of the other Canadian installations in a different way" and to ask themselves "what stories we want to tell."[45] Their response to this challenge was to draw on the three decades of critical reflexivity and revisionism within the discipline that began with the "new art history" of the 1970s and 1980s and to bring to bear on the installations its critical insights into the way that art history and its institutions have been complicit in inscribing hegemonic constructs of class, race, and gender. In the ground-floor installations of European art this post-structuralist and postcolonial orientation has resulted in a strategic intermingling of selected Canadian, American, European, and Indigenous arts in a series of thematic rooms that bear titles such as "Encounters with Diversity," "History and Her Story," "Arcadian Land Seized and Lost," and "Memory of War." "Encounters with Diversity" exemplifies the ways in which the selected works of art and their text panels and captions directly interpellate visitors. The introductory text underlines the past and present operation of "oppositions based on gender, class, and ethnicity" that "often leads to the exclusion, marginalization, and stereotyping of the social 'other.'" In winter 2009 Pieter Breughel the Younger's *The Peasants' Wedding,* a nineteenth-century genre scene of Quebec Indians by Cornelius Krieghoff, and other works were juxtaposed with an Inuit print by Napachie Pootoogook and video pieces by contemporary African-American installation artist Kara Walker. Similarly, in "Arcadian Land Seized or Lost," paintings by Claude Lorraine and Group of Seven artists A.Y. Jackson and Lawren Harris were hung together with a contemporary photographic representation of an open-pit coal mine by Edward Burtynsky and Cree artist Kent Monkman's repainting of a nineteenth-century pioneer landscape scene, *The Rape of Daniel Boone Junior* (2002). As these examples suggest, the combination of the chronological and "canonical" Thomson galleries (to use Teitelbaum's term) with the thematic approach used elsewhere has produced a kind of "both/and" solution to installation in which Indigenous and contemporary art are intermingled thematically in the galleries showing the AGO's permanent collection and in more orthodox installations in the galleries dedicated to the Thomson collections.

The thematic approach highlights the centrality of social, political, and discursive critique to the work of many contemporary artists. It also acknowledges the "conversational community" in which they participate together with critics, curators, and art historians.[46] As at the National Gallery, the inclusion of works by Indigenous artists has had a number of precedents at the AGO. These include *Gauguin to Moore: Primitivism in Modern Sculpture*, a comparative exhibition of modern and Primitive Art similar in content to the earlier Evrard exhibition at the Musée de l'Homme, which was organized in 1981 by AGO curator Alan Wilkinson.[47] A second precedent was the landmark 1984 exhibition *From the Four Quarters*, organized by Dennis Reid and

Joan Vastokas to mark the official bicentennial of Ontario.[48] This show juxta-posed what were effectively two historical surveys, one of Indigenous and the other of settler arts. In retrospect, and even though it did not carry these sequences forward into the contemporary period, the exhibition was a highly innovative project that anticipated the approach taken more recently by the NGC. During the 1980s and 1990s, the AGO also experimented with a num-ber of interventions by contemporary Indigenous artists. Prominent among these are Anishinaabe artist Robert Houle's *Anishinaabe Walker Court* (1993), which was created in response to Lothar Baumgarten's 1985 site-specific work commissioned by the AGO for its historic central space, the Walker Court, and entitled *Monument for the Native Peoples of Ontario*.[49] Even more dir-ectly relevant to the current innovations in the Canadian galleries were the interventionist installations that Reid and his colleagues Anna Hudson and Richard Hill commissioned of Onondaga photographic artist Jeffrey Thomas and Anishinaabe installation artist Rebecca Belmore during the 1990s.[50] An-other important precedent for the reframing of the AGO's canonical collec-tion of paintings by the Group of Seven was the provocative and controversial "OH! Canada" program of interactive activities and counter-installations by community arts groups, including the First Nations group Ge ni yo gwê dage (Four People Together), that the AGO organized to accompany its showing of the NGC's travelling exhibition *The Group of Seven: Art for a Nation* in 1996.[51]

Memory, Myth, and Power in Canadian Art

The AGO's transcultural and postcolonial approach is borne out even more rigorously in the Canadian installations on the second floor, reconceptual-ized by the curator of Canadian Art, Gerald McMaster (Plains Cree), and Dennis Reid, who was director of Collections and Research at the time.[52] Here the works are organized according to three sweeping themes of mem-ory, myth, and power. Entering from a central space that also leads into the Thomson Galleries, visitors begin with a meditation on memory that tele-scopes the history of Indigenous arts within the confines of a narrow cor-ridor gallery. Two panels of projectile points are elegantly mounted along a timeline that stretches back through "11,000 years of visual expression, trad-ition, and memory." As at the NGC, the power of oral tradition to create con-tinuity is invoked: "The memories of previous generations were often kept alive through stories, language, and art. They reveal a past which continues to shape the future." On a video screen across from this installation curators, artists, and Indigenous scholars speak to us about oral traditions, museums, and memory. The cases and contemporary paintings that follow take us through successive historic phases of Indigenous presence, enforced absence (represented by an empty case), and contemporary resurgence.

In the "Myth" and "Power" thematic sections, historical Indigenous art works are strategically positioned to force the viewer to look at familiar settler arts in new ways, creating the kind of rupture that Anne Whitelaw advocates.

Two pairings in "Myth" suggest the degree to which the curators have been willing to take risks. In one, two eighteenth-century Anishinaabe bags displaying quill-embroidered images of the Thunderbird and the Misshipeshu (or Underwater Panther), the most powerful beings of the upper and under zones of the Anishinaabe cosmos, are displayed next to Tom Thomson's *The West Wind*, one of the most iconic of all Group of Seven paintings (fig. 14.7). To implicate both Anishinaabe and settler icons in the realm of the mythic brings all three works fully into the secular space of the modern art gallery; as a levelling and demystifying gesture, it has the potential to offend true believers in both communities. A second juxtaposition positions a nineteenth-century Plains painted buffalo hide near a painting by Jack Chambers and links both to the possession of land. This installation suggests a different kind of difficulty that tends to haunt thematic approaches. In selecting one among several meanings contained in a work of art, thematic groupings can seem arbitrary and even capricious. The type of buffalo hide on display, for example, is usually understood as a record of the deeds and achievements of its owner, and it could therefore fit just as well if not better into the "Memory" section.

14.7   Anishinaabe bags, datable to c. 1800, displaying images of the most powerful *manitos* (spirit powers) of the upper and under worlds, juxtaposed with Tom Thomson's *The West Wind* (1916–17), in the "Myth" section, Canadian galleries, Art Gallery of Ontario. Photo © Art Gallery of Ontario, Toronto

14.8 (*also colour plate 16*)
Kent Monkman's *The
Academy* (2008) anchors
one of the galleries of the
"Power" section of the
Canadian galleries. Photo
© Art Gallery of Ontario,
Toronto

The curatorial structuring of the "Power" section is particularly tight and compelling. The introductory text panel
reads: "Relationships of power are complex and dynamic.
They are at play in our institutions and governments, as well
as in our social and cultural groups. These dynamics are often
documented through art, while art has frequently been used
to promote the values of those in power. As you examine the
works in these galleries, contemplate the forces that might be
at play. Consider how they may have shaped both Canadian
art and identity. How do the power dynamics around you
play themselves out in your life?"

One of the two main galleries in this section is dominated by a large especially commissioned painting by Kent
Monkman. *The Academy* (2008) fills one end wall and works
to deconstruct the way in which settler art history and institutions have imposed Eurocentric norms on Indigenous
lands (fig. 14.8). Monkman sets the scene in a nineteenth-
century art school in which artists were traditionally trained
in the Western classical tradition by copying from canonical
Greek and Roman sculptures. He has, however, transposed
his "academy" from the expected Western architectural in-

terior to a Mandan earth lodge copied from a well-known painting of the 1830s by American artist George Catlin.[53] The painting is a tour de force of art-historical quotation, and the puzzle of locating the sources of each of the figures within the AGO's installations proves irresistible to many visitors.[54] A quick look around the room, for example, reveals that portraits of William Henry Boulton and his wife, Harriet, hanging nearby are the sources for the seated man in the left foreground and the bride standing next to him. Harriet Boulton, later Smith, was the prominent Torontonian who bequeathed The Grange, the house left her by Boulton, to the Art Gallery of Toronto as its first home. She holds a wreath in her outstretched arm, a motif borrowed from Nicholas Andre Monsiau's *Zeuxis Choosing His Models*, displayed on the floor below, but Monkman has represented it as a circle of sweetgrass, used by Aboriginal people in rituals of purification. Her gesture directs the eye to the centre of the canvas, which is occupied by models posed as the Laocoön, the Hellenistic sculptural group that is one of the most admired and imitated works in the history of Western art. The art "students" appear to be painting from these models, yet on closer examination the images on one easel are revealed as drawings of Indigenous rock art. Other pieces of Indigenous art – a Pueblo pot, a model totem pole, and a Northwest Coast mask – are seen spilling from a large green sack that evokes acts of looting. (The birchbark handbag in front of the Pueblo pot is a slyer allusion to a parodic installation of Monkman's own which included birchbark handbags stamped with Louis Vuitton logos.)[55]

The Laocoön stands here not only as an icon of academic classicism and the Western art tradition against which Canadian settler artists have historically measured themselves, but also as a quintessential image of heroic human struggle, pain, and death. By introducing it into a space of Indigenous dwelling and ritual, Monkman establishes a context in which its reference can be broadened. The artist has painted himself into the picture on the far right, where he is seen in three-quarter view, top-hatted in the manner of his nineteenth-century forebears and wearing a painted hide coat similar to a splendid example displayed in a glass case across from the painting. His arms are extended, enclosing the young settler artist standing next to him in a near embrace. With one he gestures toward the Laocoön group, while with the other he points to the artist seated at his easel. This figure is the only artist in the picture who is actually painting, and the face reflected in the mirror attached to his easel identifies him clearly as the pioneering Anishinaabe painter Norval Morrisseau (1932–2007). The painting on Morrisseau's easel, furthermore, is his *Self Portrait Devoured by Demons* (1964), now in the AGO's collection. The uncanny similarity between this portrait and one of Laocoön's sons, standing on the right of the group, provides *The Academy*'s punctum. Monkman, who is an assiduous miner and parodist of the Western artistic canon, clearly intends us to draw a parallel between the tragic fate of the Trojan priest Laocoön, victimized and tortured by invading Greeks, and that of Morrisseau, who, raised in poverty, caught between two religions and two cultures, and afflicted by addictions to alcohol and drugs, has come to be emblematic of the struggles of many Indigenous people of his generation.[56] Through this realignment, Monkman assigns the role of the representing subject to the Indigenous artist and relegates the settler figures to spectatorial roles, inverting the normal ordering of the North American settler narrative of art history.

Monkman's device snaps into place a link between two histories that have always already been intertwined.[57] Yet his intention in pointing to the coincident images of human torment created by the Greek and the Anishinaabe artists is not, I would argue, to establish an identity between them. Rather, he insists on the need to privilege – or at the minimum to include – art histories that are native to the geopolitical space in which the art museum is situated. By assigning Morrisseau a central place in the academy and himself the role of authoritative guide, Monkman directs our gaze not only within the painting but also outside it. *The Academy* dominates the room in which it hangs. It estranges not only the settler portraits and religious paintings arranged around the other three walls but also the Indigenous clothing and carvings in their glass cases, reminding us of the centrality of art, material culture, and museums to Western representations of Indigenous cultures, while also causing us to read them in terms of Monkman's messages of decontextualization, theft, and loss.

As the art critic for the Toronto *Globe and Mail* wrote in a review of the AGO's new Canadian galleries, the installations express "a powerful sense of mission: the drive to create an account of history that is not a master narrative but which, rather, allows for a kind of productive doubt, and multiple points of entry. The viewer must navigate between opposing views, and make meaning … One suddenly sees the exotic white man from the indigenous perspective."[58] Such an approach does important cultural work in early twenty-first-century Canada, and it is categorically opposed to the teleological and progressivist narratives that have perpetuated the modernist, nationalist, and primitivist distancing of Indigenous peoples. Yet it too silences other important ways of understanding. It suppresses any sense of the historical meanings or development of artistic expression over time in either Euro-Canadian or Indigenous tradition. The viewer standing in front of a case holding the carved model totem pole or the magnificently painted and quill-embroidered Cree man's outfit is given even less entree into their cultural and historical worlds than is provided by the brief contextual panels at the NGC (fig. 14.5). The exclusive focus on a single theme also elides the episodes of artistic exchange that are integral to the story of colonialism. These losses are most evident where the curatorial control has been most successful. In the "Power" section, for example, it is impossible to see the historical paintings and Aboriginal works of art in any terms other than those decreed by the curators, and the implied disrespect for the creative achievements of the artists is problematic. Repeat visitors, having figured out the puzzles and understood the critical points, will, finally, want to go on to something new. At the AGO, as at the National Gallery, it will be necessary for the installations to continue to evolve in tandem with the external political and social worlds they have chosen to reference.

The National Gallery of Canada and the Art Gallery of Ontario are following different routes as they explore the new terrain of inclusivity. At the NGC, as we have seen, we travel along a path from past to future. Although we are presented with new things to look at, they are framed in ways that allow us to see only the kinds of aesthetic qualities that Western art connoisseurs have prized. The route that visitors travel at the AGO is non-linear, and it produces disturbing images of a Canadian past in which all has *not* been harmonious and progressive – a past that is truer to the best representations that contemporary historians and art historians have been producing. Yet here, too, definitions of art remain determined by the Western aesthetic systems and genres in which the contemporary Indigenous artists whose works are responsible for the critique have been trained. Ivan Gaskell's discussion of strategies of inclusivity is helpful in thinking through the cognitive and ethical implications of these different strategies. In discussing his juxtaposition of a seventeenth-century Algonkian bow with European works of art in a temporary exhibition of art from Harvard University's Fogg Art Museum, he identifies three different possible approaches:

> When a thing moves from one society to another, one or more of three attitudes is in play: (1) the new users employ and interpret it solely on their own terms without regard to the uses and interpretations of its earlier users, either oblivious to those earlier uses, or purposefully to expunge them; (2) the new users discern familiar characteristics that they value, and that they assume earlier users also discerned and valued; (3) the new users attempt to learn the terms of use, interpretation and value of the earlier users, acknowledging that these may differ from their own wholly or in part, but in the belief that their acquisition will bring them advantages. I term these three attitudes respectively *supersession*, *assumption*, and *translation*.[59]

In Gaskell's terms, the NGC's *Art of this Land* makes use of all three approaches, while the AGO relies primarily on translation. Yet, as Gaskell also notes, each approach carries risks that include "depriving or withholding from subordinated social groups artifacts that are properly their own, mistreating or unwarrantably exposing artifacts that have sacred significance, and using artifacts to promote or uncritically perpetuate asymmetrical power relationships." Even translation, which might appear the least appropriative, is, as Gaskell writes, "a species of new use."[60] We will need such tools of analysis as the NGC and the AGO continue to develop their exhibitions and as other institutions venture into the territory of inclusivity.

The historian Daniel Richter has also drawn a distinction that is helpful in thinking about projects of inclusivity. "Thanks to a growing body of investigators," he writes, "many readers' understanding of colonial North America may have been *revised* in a multicultural direction, but for the most part they have not yet been *re-visioned*."[61] In the four decades since *Masterpieces of Canadian Indian and Eskimo Art* was mounted, not only the National Gallery and the Art Gallery of Ontario but other Canadian art museums as well have taken great strides forward in the work of revision. If we pursue the logical implications of these important initiatives, we will achieve the work of *re-vision*.

15

The Digital (R)Evolution of Museum-Based Research

Museums as Research Sites

The exhibition is the public face of the museum, and it is thus not surprising that museum exhibitions have served as primary sites for protest, revisionist experimentation, and critical analysis.[3] Like the skin of a living organism, however, the exhibition is also a surface upon which changes in the museum's state of being are visibly registered, and its qualities can therefore be read as symptoms of the health of the institution's internal generative processes. Research remains the most important of these processes, despite a loss of prestige in recent years resulting from shifting priorities and the need to broaden audiences and increase revenue. Without good research, good exhibitions, publications, websites, educational programs, and even good gift shops cannot come into being. "Good" research in this sense involves both the generation of accurate information and the ability to make a museum's collections comprehensible in terms of the historical consciousness of its visitors. In a pluralist and decolonizing society such as Canada, historical consciousness is also, of course, plural, and research models and processes must accommodate this reality. In the early twenty-first century we are, furthermore, experiencing the profound impacts of two large-scale changes, one technological and one demographic. We are in the midst of a digital revolution that is affecting all cultural, educational, and research sectors, and we are adjusting to a demographic change that is shifting Canada's political, cultural, and social points of reference from a corner of northern Europe to a fully global compass. I will argue in this

In many communities, few cultural materials remain; the very word "museum" is often a reminder of what has been lost to Aboriginal people, not what has been preserved for their use ... This makes it all the more important that Aboriginal people have access to mainstream museums and the items they hold. Aboriginal people must be involved in cataloguing museum holdings and consulted on appropriate modes of display and interpretation.
– Royal Commission on Aboriginal Peoples (1996)[1]

People and their theories and methodologies come and go, but the objects in the Museum provide a lasting resource for finding out about the world, if only we give them the attention they deserve.
– Chris Gosden and Frances Larson (2007)[2]

chapter that as these epochal processes unfold, museum collections can have a constructive and unique agency. I will also urge that a key strategy lies in harnessing the power of digital technologies to new collaborative models of museum-based research.

Digital-imaging, database, and search technologies developed with dramatic rapidity during the 1990s, just as Canadian museums were looking for ways to implement the new models of partnership mandated by the report of the Task Force on Museums and First Peoples. The improvement of this technology has been particularly momentous for collections research because of its reliance on visual access to unique artifacts and documents scattered among many different and distant institutions. The negative effects for Indigenous communities of the comprehensive removal of their heritage items was stressed by the Royal Commission on Aboriginal Peoples. "The very word 'museum,'" its report stated, "is often a reminder of what has been lost to Aboriginal people, not what has been preserved for their use." Electronic technologies offer unprecedented tools with which to reassemble and create new forms of access to dispersed cultural materials. Furthermore, in the context of collaborative museology, remote access can begin to level the playing field by displacing the museum as the unique site for the study of these materials and mediating entrenched hierarchies of privileged access and complicated protocols of permission, vetting, and security.

In this chapter I will describe two digital projects that seek to take advantage of these potentials, the Reciprocal Research Network (RRN) and the GRASAC Knowledge Sharing database (GKS). I have been involved in the development of both projects – with the RRN from 1999 to 2002, at its initial stage of conceptualization and funding, and with the GKS from 2003 to the present, from conceptualization to implementation. Although the full potential of both projects is still unfolding, they are already beginning to change the terms on which museum-based research is conducted and to suggest the new understandings of Indigenous intellectual traditions and expressive culture that can result.

The Research Legacy of Modernist Museum Anthropology

The problems that these two new tools address are legacies of past museum practice, and it will be useful to begin by briefly reviewing the characteristic assumptions and approaches that have historically informed modernist museum-based research. Research was entrenched as a core mandate of major North American anthropology museums from the time of their foundation in the late nineteenth and early twentieth centuries. Following American models, Canadian institutions such as the Royal Ontario Museum and the National Museum of Canada created curatorial hierarchies that mimicked those of universities.[4] The professional advancement of their curators was, like that of academics, dependent on research and publication, although they were also expected to communicate their research to the general public through exhibitions.

In his 1911 essay "An Anthropological Survey of Canada," Edward Sapir, the founder of the National Museum of Canada's ethnology division, announced a research agenda representative of the museum culture of the period. He outlined his plans for a systematic and multidisciplinary program of collecting and documentation whose end product would be a "reconstructed culture-history" of Canada's Indigenous peoples.[5] He tallied the research that had already been accomplished, culture area by culture area, and listed that which remained to be done, ending with a ringing appeal that expressed his sense of urgency: "Now or never is the time in which to collect from the natives what is still available for study … With the increasing material prosperity of Canada the demoralization or civilization of the Indians will be going on at an ever increasing rate. No shortsighted policy of economy should be allowed to interfere with the thorough and rapid prosecution of the anthropological problems of the dominion. What is lost now will never be recovered again."[6] Sapir's paper epitomizes the positivist scientific paradigm and the ethos of salvage anthropology that framed anthropological research in the early twentieth century. In keeping with this agenda, the NMC, like other research-oriented anthropology museums in the United States and Canada, sent out staff and contract ethnographers to Indigenous communities to assemble large and comprehensive collections that documented the "remnants" of historic Indigenous cultures through interviews, artifacts, photographs, and recordings of language and song.

Despite Sapir's hopes, a government "policy of economy" did limit the scope of field research, and the situation was soon further aggravated by the outbreak of World War I. Anthropologists who had chosen to base themselves in museums were frustrated in their efforts to work in accordance with evolving anthropological approaches for other reasons as well. Like his teacher and mentor Franz Boas, Sapir had found it impossible to represent the comprehensive and multidisciplinary model that informed his division's research program within the confines of museum exhibitions.[7] After a decade of employment as a curator at the American Museum of Natural History, Boas had come to the conclusion that museum research was too closely tied to the study and presentation of material culture, and that this genre, on its own, could not convey broader cultural systems and histories to the public. Exhibitions, he concluded, inevitably simplified complex social processes in order to meet the needs of visitors who come to the museum in search of "entertainment." "Intelligibility is too often obtained by slurring over unknown and obscure points," Boas wrote in 1908, three years after resigning his position at the AMNH to teach full time at Columbia University.[8] In 1925 Sapir followed suit, leaving the National Museum of Canada for the University of Chicago.

The devaluation and marginalization of the collections research mandate at the NMC and other similar institutions during the middle decades of the twentieth century was also the product of far-reaching changes in the discipline of anthropology that led to the de-emphasis of material culture study. As a result, museums came to be regarded as a backwater of anthropological practice, a view that has by no means disappeared within the discipline. Inevitably, the work of many curators in anthropology museums followed the trends of the mother discipline and became increasingly detached from research on their museums' collections. As the twentieth century wore on, the exhibitions on view in many of these museums, still shaped by controlling paradigms of scientific positivism and salvage anthropology, looked increasingly outdated.[9] They continued to structure displays as continental surveys organized according to a standard system of culture areas and subgroups and to represent Indigenous peoples in an imaginary pre-modern epoch that Johannes Fabian terms the "ethnographic present."[10] Generalized, impersonal, and clinical, these "permanent" displays presented the appearance of closed systems which, once installed, could be left in place for decades.

Where museums did attempt to communicate more broadly based cultural processes and to represent material objects as a part of multi-sensory and performative systems, the results could be mixed. Diane Losche, for example, has argued that in the 1960s, when Margaret Mead and her associates reinstalled the Pacific Hall at the American Museum of Natural History, their efforts to represent this wider range of sensory experience was, ultimately, a failure.[11] In this case, as in the earlier experiences of Boas and Sapir, the difficulty of exhibiting holistic cultural formations reflected, in part, the limitations of the available technology to convey language, oral narratives, performance, and other multi-sensory expressive modes. On a more fundamental level, however, the Western museum's traditional privileging of visual experiences – its self-definition as a "way of seeing," as Svetlana Alpers has phrased it – continued to constrain such efforts.[12]

As art museums began to take up the display of "primitive art" in both permanent and temporary exhibits during these same decades, curators in anthropology museums introduced a more explicit focus on aesthetic quality, and their research, somewhat paradoxically, also began to address some of the connoisseurial problems of attribution and dating that anthropology museums had been largely ignoring. As we have seen in earlier chapters of this book, however, during the 1980s both aestheticizing art gallery exhibits and contextualizing anthropology displays presented ripe targets for postcolonial and post-structuralist critiques. Indigenous critics have viewed the privileging of material objects in both kinds of institutions through a Marxist lens of fetishization and sought alternatives to the object-centred exhibitions of the past in major reinstallations such as those at the National Museum of the American Indian (2004) and the Canadian Museum of Civilization (2003) (see chapter 12). The place of object display in contemporary museums remains a subject of debate. In his discussion of the NMAI's opening exhibits, for example, Steven Conn argued that to abandon object display was to evacuate the museum of its fundamental representational strategy. "Museums have always tried to tell stories with objects," he noted, for "the notion that original objects can convey an immediacy and a 'realness' to a narrative is at the very heart of what a museum is."[13] We have, it seems, been going through a deconstructive phase during which the actions of past museums stimulated equal and opposite reactions.

Other recent reinstallations suggest, however, that we are emerging from this deconstructive period. For example, the University of British Columbia's Museum of Anthropology's reinstalled Multiversity Galleries, a hybrid of storage and exhibition that replaces the earlier open storage facilities, and the National Museum of the American Indian's long-term exhibition *An Infinity of Nations* (opened in January and October 2010 respectively) are both object-dense installations that focus on material expressions of culture and that required considerable collections research. The difference, of course, is that the two installations were organized by fully collaborative curatorial teams composed of Indigenous and non-Indigenous curators and fully engaged Indigenous perspectives in processes of selection, arrangement, and interpretation.[14]

Even as debates around the role of objects in exhibitions continue, the tremendous value of the artifacts, photographs, field notes, wax cylinder recordings, and other forms of documentation preserved in museum storages and archives continues to be reaffirmed in other contexts. On the one hand, Indigenous researchers are reactivating collections-based research as a resource for urgent contemporary projects ranging from land-claims negotiations to Indigenous language renewal and the recovery of lapsed artistic traditions and technologies. On the other hand, a new era of collections research is being stimulated by a trans- and interdisciplinary renewal of academic interest in materiality and visual culture. Chris Gosden and Frances Larson have drawn on actor-network theory and work on art and agency to reposition museums and their collections in networks of collectors, museum workers, visitors, and professional technologies that exert agency on each other and on still wider social worlds. They also affirm the value of collaborative models in enhancing and extending the interconnections they trace historically, and they locate the museum's unique potentials for trans-temporal agency in its collections: "Many avenues for exploration remain – including making new objects for use, or allowing the originals to be handled in controlled circumstances – and these activities can be especially productive when pursued in partnership with originating communities. People and their theories and methodologies come and go, but the objects in the Museum provide a lasting resource for finding out about the world, if only we give them the attention they deserve."[15]

Museum-based research, then, is being revitalized both by such new approaches and by Indigenous cultural politics. Yet both groups of researchers still find themselves having to confront obstacles that arise from early twentieth-century collecting and archiving practices and mid-twentieth-century neglect. The dispersal of collections amongst different institutions is, as noted, one of the greatest problems, and it is a direct by-product of the typological approach associated with late nineteenth- and early twentieth-century cultural evolutionism. Museums sought to present their visitors with universal sequences that demonstrated the hierarchical development of human societies, and they thus needed to acquire an array of object types representative of the major culture areas of the world. Accordingly, field anthropologists typically divided up their collections, selling or trading "duplicates" amongst an informal network of anthropology museums that stretched from Philadelphia, Boston, Ottawa, Washington, DC, and Chicago to Europe and Australia.[16]

The further disarticulation that occurred once a collection entered the museum was the result of Western technologies of preservation and archiving that assign separate storages and cataloguing systems according to materials and genres, placing, for example, photographs, wax cylinder recordings, and material artifacts in different sections of a museum. Within artifact storage, furthermore, light-sensitive fabrics, furs, and metals may be stored separately so that environmental conditions can be optimized, and paper records are usually subdivided into separately indexed files of fieldwork notes, letters, and accession and donor information. Such procedures are effective technologies for preservation and organization, but they also disrupt the original integrity of collections, and they can cause us to lose sight of the multidisciplinary approaches of earlier generations of fieldworkers. The highly catholic range of their research interests comprehended food preparation, plant cultivation, ethnobotany, language, archaeology, kinship structures, ceremonies, art, and craft technologies, a list that resonates strongly with the holistic understandings of traditional knowledge which are being urged by many contemporary Indigenous scholars[17] (fig. 15.1).

In addition to the challenge of recovering the original integrity of historical collections, contemporary researchers must address the imprecise or inaccurate attributions that were originally recorded for many items in ethnographic collections. Early contact-period items were often collected as curiosities and entered collections with only the vaguest attributions to place of origin. The later typological system assigned objects to generic and often arbitrary slots in a highly artificial table of culture areas and subgroups. As successive generations of cataloguers recopied the original information and transferred it to electronic catalogues, furthermore, data could be omitted and new errors could creep in. Few museums have been able to employ curators with specialist knowledge of the different regions represented in their museums, and collections research became a luxury rather than a central part of most curators' job descriptions.[18] As a result, these attributions were, by and large, left in place until the late twentieth century. Taken together, then, the challenges posed by distance and dispersal, inadequate documentation, and the *sui generis* nature of each institution's organizational systems make it clear that a new era of museum research will require fresh and more powerful research tools.

In 1972 the Canadian government initiated a National Inventory Program for museums (NIP), which soon led to the creation of an integrated computerized database that brought together the collections of the country's major

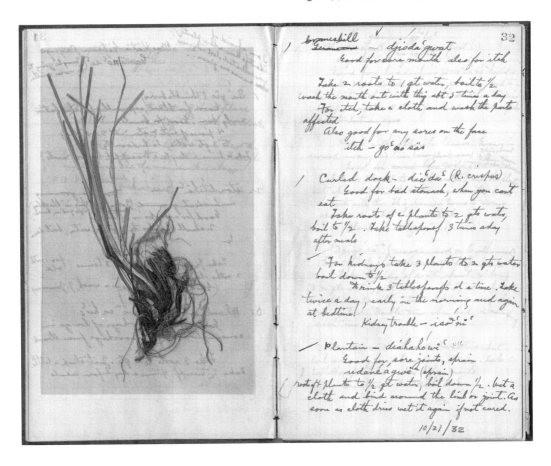

museums. The Canadian Heritage Information Network, or CHIN database, as it is commonly known, was an innovative tool that allowed museum-based researchers to search across the collections of its contributing museums.[19] Yet computerization could not provide a magic bullet in and of itself. Museums entered their existing information complete with its inadequacies and early twentieth-century typological systems of classification. Furthermore, because the technology of the period did not permit the attachment of images to CHIN records – and in any case only a very small percentage of ethnographic collections had been photographed – users of the database could not refine and correct records. The federal government terminated further development of the database in the early 1990s and gave participating museums funds to purchase their own database software. The museums proceeded – to borrow a phrase from Stephen Leacock – to "ride madly off in all directions." Most purchased proprietary and expensive software systems that were incompatible, complicated, and accessible only to their own staff members.

15.1   Pages 31 and 32 of a field notebook belonging to F.W. Waugh with a plant specimen and notes on Indigenous knowledge recorded during his 1912 field trip to the Six Nations of the Grand River for the National Museum of Canada. Archives, Canadian Museum of Civilization, Ethno, III-I-89M, box 200 f.20. Photo © Canadian Museum of Civilization, IMG-2011-0016-0001Dm

As we have seen, the report of the Task Force on Museums and First Peoples, with its call for increased access to museum collections and its guidelines for repatriation, was issued in 1992, just as the CHIN database was being shut down. From a research perspective, the government's decision was regressive, re-erecting barriers to efficient museum research by removing the ability to conduct integrated searches or modify records just at the moment when these capacities were most urgently needed.[20] The report of the Royal Commission on Aboriginal Peoples four years later underlined the urgency of museum access and research in the context of Indigenous peoples' need to recover from the long period of colonial oppression, but it also stressed the ongoing custodial responsibility of museums: "Aboriginal people have so many urgent day-to-day needs that establishing a community-controlled museum, although important and desirable, is often not the top priority." The report continued:

> This makes it all the more important that Aboriginal people have access to mainstream museums and the items they hold. Aboriginal people must be involved in cataloguing museum holdings and consulted on appropriate modes of display and interpretation. This provides an opportunity for non-Aboriginal professionals to gain more insight into Aboriginal culture. Further, these collections must be accessible to Aboriginal people. Here we do not simply mean an open-door policy on the part of museums, inviting Aboriginal people to visit the displays. Rather, any facility that benefits from the display of Aboriginal culture should put something back into the Aboriginal community.[21]

By the turn of the new century, then, the difficulty of reassembling the heritage items originating in a particular community or region had often increased rather than decreased, and the challenge of creating access had become a major preoccupation for many museum professionals. How, they asked, could the problems of distance, the lack of visual documentation and images, and the idiosyncrasies of archival and collecting practices be overcome?

The Reciprocal Research Network

When I became director of the University of British Columbia's Museum of Anthropology (MoA) in 1997, I had the honour to follow in the footsteps of distinguished curators and directors who had established a tradition of collaboration with Indigenous communities. Founders Harry and Audrey Hawthorn and my predecessor, Michael Ames, had built a small university collection into a museum with an international reputation for its innovative practices and magnificent installations of Northwest Coast art. Almost from the moment of their arrival in the late 1940s, the Hawthorns had sought to establish relationships with living Northwest Coast Indigenous artists and to use the museum's collections to support the continuation of traditional arts.[22] The museum had thus been working collaboratively with contemporary Indigenous researchers, artists, and curators well before the task force report was issued. After 1992 it began to explore even more radical ways of sharing power and developing multivocal understandings of collections.

In 1976, when MoA moved into its famous Arthur Erickson–designed building, it introduced a Research Collections area with publicly accessible "open storage" in which visitors could view the museum's collections in glass-fronted cases and Plexiglas-topped drawers. As the years passed, however, it became evident that what had seemed a radical democratization of access was still only partial because the only information that could be provided in the public viewing area consisted of binders containing the minimal records printed out from the old CHIN database. There was no mechanism for enriching or correcting these records by adding the new information that was being generated through each successive collaboration with an artist or a community group. When an exhibition ended, only a small part of the research it had generated was systematically captured and recorded in a form that could be made available to future researchers. As one MoA curator commented, for all its popularity and apparent openness, visible storage functioned much like a cabinet of curiosities, putting intriguing objects on view without offering meaningful interpretation. The lack of comprehensive photographic documentation of the museum's collection – also typical of the situation in other museums – meant that researchers had to make the trip to Vancouver in person to find and study collections of interest to them.

The year 1997 also brought the announcement of an ambitious new federal program initiated by the government of Prime Minister Jean Chrétien. The Canada Foundation for Innovation (CFI) was established with a $2.5-billion-dollar fund to support the creation of innovative research infrastructure in Canadian non-profit institutions. This initiative led me and museum staff to revisit the traditional research mandate of the museum – and especially the university museum – in light of recent developments in Canadian museology. In particular, we asked what were the implications for the research infrastructure of an anthropology museum of collaborative research models, ethical and policy requirements for Indigenous access, and the renewed academic interest in material culture and museums.

We accepted the challenge of submitting an application to the CFI that would reimagine the twenty-first-century needs of a Canadian anthropology museum holding important collections of First Nations and world heritage. The application was grounded in an affirmation of the research potential of museum collections and the staying power of collaborative research as the dominant model for museums in the future. "Museum collections have assumed dramatically renewed significance in the contemporary world," we wrote. "The power of cultural materials to trigger memory is proving to be an invaluable key to the recovery of orally transmitted information retained in originating communities. Bringing together globally dispersed collections,

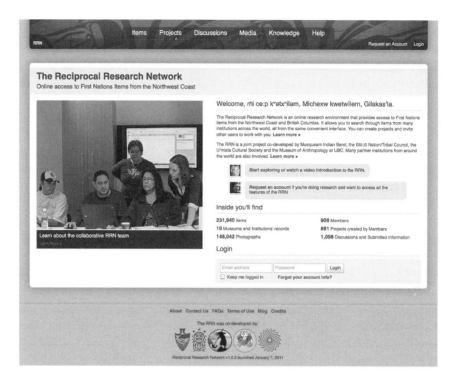

15.2   Welcome page, Reciprocal Research Network website

originating communities, and advanced analytical models thus creates synergies needed for the production of new knowledge."[23] We also argued that because the design of existing museum research spaces had been intended to support individual researchers and hierarchical authority structures, it "resists community participation and impede[s] the kind of critical research on cultural heritage that First Nations and other communities need and want."[24]

We proposed the creation of two new capacities, one physical and the other virtual. The physical spaces of the museum would be expanded and reconfigured to accommodate multidisciplinary forms of investigation and research teams as well as individuals. A new virtual-space research tool, the Reciprocal Research Network (RRN), would extend the reach of the museum's collections and resources beyond its physical building in two different ways. First, it would deliver digital images and information about the ethnographic and archaeological collections held at MoA to other research sites, including both Indigenous communities and other museums[25] (fig. 15.2). Second, it would link MoA's electronic catalogue with those of other institutions holding Northwest Coast and British Columbia material in North America and Europe and make it possible for researchers to search them simultaneously. Through the creation of interactive software capacities, the RRN would support collaborative research among distant partners. This new resource would also provide interfaces appropriate to different kinds of users, find electronic solutions to accommodate culturally sensitive information and materials, and develop protocols for shared management of the network. The application of electronic technology to First Nations research contexts would be, in itself, a research focus:

> New technologies offer exciting research opportunities, but also pose ethical and philosophical questions for collaborative research that are especially challenging in relation to indigenous peoples ... A Reciprocal Research Network has the potential to de-centre the traditional structures and hierarchies of knowledge that have defined relations between museums and First Nations communities for over a century. Yet it can only realize this potential, first, if it provides adaptable, culturally appropriate mechanisms for protecting and sharing indigenous knowledge, and, second, if it makes the network accessible and acceptable for community research by adapting taxonomies of knowledge embedded in its structure to community knowledge systems.[26]

We submitted our application, entitled "A Partnership of Peoples," to the CFI in 2000, together with three First Nations partners or "co-developers" – the Musqueam Indian Band, the Sto:lo Tribal Council and Sto:lo Nation, and the U'mista Cultural Society – who undertook to work with MoA to create infrastructure that would serve the full range of British Columbia's peoples. At a memorable meeting prior to the submission of the application, MoA Curator of Education Jill Baird and I presented the concept of the RRN to the Musqueam Band Council and asked formally for their participation. We illustrated the proposed network's potential for reuniting and making available images of historical Musqueam heritage by showing three digital slides of important stone carvings that had come from the rich Marpole archaeological site in Musqueam territory. One is now in the Vancouver Museum, another in the Royal British Columbia Museum, and a third at the Seattle Art Museum, but none remains at Musqueam itself. One of the council members commented approvingly that the RRN component of the infrastructure would be a form of "virtual repatriation," a phrase I would not, until that moment, have ventured to use myself. The band council endorsed our request and voted to partner on the project.

I have subsequently come to use the term "digital repatriation" for electronic projects like the RRN, since it seems to me to make a clearer distinction between the kinds of access that can be provided by electronic tools and those that cannot. A digital heritage repository cannot replicate the unique nature of the relationships and spiritual connections that come into being when people and heritage items are brought into each other's physical presence. Nor does it allow the full range of studies and analyses that a researcher might want to undertake. Digital repatriation is not intended to be a substitute for the actual transfer of ownership of cultural property through repatriation negotiations. However, digital access can accomplish a first level of image and text repatriation, returning to originating communities infor-

15.3 (*see also colour plate 17*) The Multiversity Galleries at the Museum of Anthropology, University of British Columbia, opened January 2010. Photo by Bill McLennan

mation about their history and cultural achievements. As an ethical gesture, it responds to people's right to own their pasts. Equally, as a research tool, it is a way of supporting the development of new knowledge and understandings of those pasts that are informed by Indigenous perspectives, memory, and knowledge.

I left MoA shortly after the award of the CFI grant, which contributed forty per cent of the $41.5 million budgeted for the project, the largest grant the foundation had given to a social sciences and humanities research-infrastructure project.[27] The detailed implementation of the general concepts we had developed for the RRN was innovatively and creatively undertaken during the next five years by a steering group made up of Susan Rowley, curator, Arctic and Public Archaeology at MoA; Leona Sparrow, representing the Musqueam Indian Band; Dave Schaepe, representing the Sto:lo Tribal Council and Sto:lo Nation; and Andrea Sanborn, from the U'mista Cultural Society. They in turn worked with a team of computer specialists, Nicholas Jakobsen and Ryan Wallace. One of the project's first accomplishments was a charter that articulates a commitment to create an environment of mutual respect and to choose technology that enables the widest possible access and affirms the open-ended and ongoing nature of the RRN. In a 2008 article the key contributors outlined the RRN's purpose and process of development in detail, emphasizing its decentred structure of authority and reiterating its model of co-development and co-management.[28] They also affirmed a relationship between new museum technologies and community-building that resonates strongly with Gosden and Larson's historical analysis of the Pitt Rivers Museum as a networked agent of social formations, to which I have already referred. The RRN, its developers stress, is not merely an electronic structure but will work to create social structures that "facilitate relationship building across user groups through the provision of a collaborative research environment."[29] Launched in 2010, the RRN can be consulted by visitors to the museum in the new Multiversity Galleries that have replaced the former open-storage facility (fig. 15.3). It can also be accessed outside the museum by password over the Internet by researchers and Indigenous community members.

The GRASAC Knowledge Sharing Database

My own research focuses on the Great Lakes region of North America, and my return to Carleton University in 2003 gave me the opportunity to begin a parallel project that would support research in this area. Historian Heidi Bohaker and Indigenous law scholar Darlene Johnston had been thinking along the same lines, and we decided to collaborate to create a shared database that would build further on the disciplinary complementaries of our own research. Again with support from the CFI and matching funds from the Ontario Innovation Trust (although of a smaller order of magnitude than in the RRN project), we invited about thirty researchers in the field to come together in 2005 to form the Great Lakes Research Alliance for the Study of Aboriginal Arts and Cultures, or GRASAC. Two key founding partners have been the Woodland Cultural Centre (WCC) and the Ojibwe Cultural Foundation (OCF). These are the two largest and oldest Indigenous cultural centres in Ontario and serve primarily Onkwehonwe and Anishinaabe communities respectively. The steering committee that saw the project through its initial stages included, in addition, Alan Corbiere, whose research focuses on Anishinaabe history and oral tradition and who is also executive director of the OCF; Janis Monture, a Mohawk museologist who is the executive director of the WCC; and Anishinaabe legal scholar John Borrows, a specialist in Indigenous law. In its developmental stages the project also benefited from the expertise of anthropologist and material culture specialist Cory Willmott, in addition to other GRASAC members.

Over the next three years we commissioned Idéeclic, specialists in cybermuseology, to create software comprised of open-source components for the GRASAC Knowledge Sharing database, or GKS (fig. 15.4). We also initiated a series of research visits to North American and European museums by interdisciplinary GRASAC teams. They took a fresh look at collections, created thorough photographic documentation, updated information, and assembled the layers of catalogue information that are associated with many items. Because so much historic Great Lakes material culture is undocumented or inaccurately identified, creators of GKS records are asked to fill in drop-down

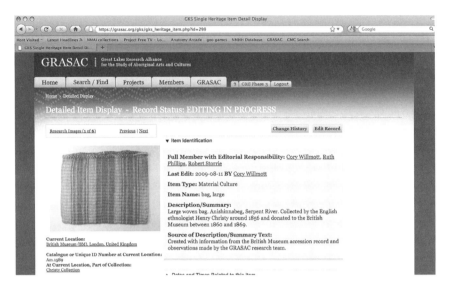

15.4   A record page from the GRASAC Knowledge Sharing database

fields where they provide the reasons for their attributions to peoples, places, and time periods. The GKS seeks also to counter the anonymity of earlier ethnographic classification by ensuring that each record, comment, or attribution is signed by the contributor. On-site research can, of course, involve only small groups or individuals, but each record has a comment field where other GRASAC members can enter corrections, additional information, or comments. The interactivity of this field is intended to be dynamic, resulting in changes to fields in the database where appropriate.

GRASAC researchers come from three different sectors – universities, Indigenous communities, and museums and archives. The GKS serves as a platform for individual and collaborative research projects, with shared online space dedicated to specific projects where record sets can be saved, new research discussed, and ideas exchanged. We conceive of GRASAC as a network of researchers that can grow indefinitely – there are almost two hundred at this writing. The fundamental qualification for membership is the ability and interest in contributing, whether that consists of sharing images and data, creating records, or adding comments – all members are contributors and all contributors are members – and all researchers with legitimate interests are welcome. We anticipate that knowledge sharing will benefit members in different ways. For example, museums and archives that lack specialist curators gain access to Indigenous perspectives and more accurate information about the Great Lakes items in their collections. In turn, Indigenous community members gain digital access to their ancestral heritage and to updated information about these items.

The GKS, as will be evident, is a child of the RRN, but as in all parent-child relationships, it exhibits unique features as well as general family resemblances. As noted, rather than the model adopted by the RRN of harvesting records from existing databases and then, over time, adding to them interactively, GRASAC's members review, add to, and correct existing information through first-hand study of collections at the time that records are created. Perhaps the most notable difference, however, is the inclusion of different kinds of heritage items in the same database. Bohaker and Johnston conceptualized its design around one long and comprehensive table which is used to describe all "heritage items," whether they take the form of material items, text, or visual images. In its first phase of development, the GKS brought together material culture, historical documents, photographs, and prints and paintings. Beginning in 2011 a new language module is being added which will integrate indigenous terminology and historical linguistic research, a key source for the recovery of Indigenous concepts and knowledge. At a deep level of structure the GKS thus acknowledges an inherent relationship amongst all forms of data, but users can also reconfigure records in conventional ways according to media and genres. The fields currently used in the database reflect Western ways of classifying knowledge, but we hope that, as the project develops, these will be modified in accordance with the comments contributed to the records and insights into Indigenous traditions of classification that emerge from the integration of Indigenous language research.

The GKS design is thus a mechanism for promoting the reassociation of heritage items that are historically, geographically, and culturally related. A search on "Cayuga" and "basket," for example, might pull up images of baskets, historical photographs of people making them, and terms and phrases used in Cayuga to name and talk about baskets. Similarly, a search on "Robinson-Huron treaty" might bring up an image of the original treaty document, a medal presented to one of the Anishinaabe signatories, and a photograph of one of his descendants wearing the medal as ongoing affirmation of the diplomatic agreement that was reached. Ideally, as the database grows, searches on "wampum belts" will bring digital images of belts together with the council minutes of speeches made during the negotiation and the treaty agreements signified by the belts' original presentation. Records might also include video links that allow users to hear contemporary elders, artists, or other Aboriginal community members discussing the meanings and qualities of historical items in the GKS. This relational capacity invokes academic interdisciplinarity to approximate the holism of Indigenous thought and systems of expressive culture.

At the time of this writing in 2011, the GKS has been available for little more than two years, the more than three thousand records are still being edited, and the commenting process is only just getting started. Yet even at this early stage, its potential for enriching, deepening, and changing current understandings of Great Lakes heritage items is emerging. Asked to speak about GRASAC at an academic conference, Heidi Bohaker and I singled out three moments of connection that occurred during a visit to Britain in 2007 which suggest the project's future potential.[30]

First Anecdote: Local Knowledge in a Universal-Survey Museum

In December 2007, ten GRASAC members spent eight days studying the important Great Lakes collections at the British Museum. Among the items in a collection that had come from Stoneyhurst College was a group of quill-embroidered birchbark mats, bowls, and other items acquired in 1879 by an English Jesuit, Father Edward Purbrick, during an inspection tour of Jesuit missions in the Canadian Great Lakes region. From Purbrick's report we know that he visited northern Ontario Anishinaabe communities at Garden River, Sault Ste Marie, and Fort William (Thunder Bay). He does not, however, record where he acquired the quilled bark items, nor have the specialist anthropologists and art historians who have studied the collection in past years been able to establish a specific provenance.[31] During our visit all the pieces were brought out, photographed, and described for the GKS. Turning over one bowl, Alan Corbiere read out the penciled name on its base – Mani-ian Pakwatchikwe Shawana – and said, "That's a name from Wikwemikong, Manitoulin." Turning over another, he commented, "Sophie Agowisse [Oh-gowisse] – that's a family at M'chigeeng."[32] The reliability of Corbiere's attribution was undoubted: his rigorous archival and linguistic research over many years has resulted in an unparalleled knowledge of the history of the Manitoulin Anishinaabe.

The moment was electrifying for those of us who had long known the Stoneyhurst collection, both because so few examples of historic Great Lakes arts are documented to particular places and because we have even fewer for which the artists' names are known. To the art historians and material culture specialists in the group, who brought a comparative framework of other Great Lakes visual arts and who were experienced in the work of stylistic analysis, it was immediately evident that, on the basis of these identifications, the whole collection could be attributed to Manitoulin Island and probably to two or three individual hands. In theory, an outside scholar with extensive field experience at Wikwemikong and M'chigeeng could have identified the makers with a particular locale, but it is far more likely that such knowledge will come from community-based researchers deeply invested in the histories of their communities. Such local knowledge is, then, the necessary complement of the panoptical survey and the comparative approach embedded in Western disciplinary traditions. In the work of attribution, reclamation, and reconnection both are needed, and neither is adequate in itself. What is perhaps most important is the subsequent archival research that Corbiere has done in nineteenth-century documents written in English, French, and Ansihinabemowin to reveal the relationship between the presentation made to Father Purbrick and the long tradition of diplomatic gift exchange in the Great Lakes. Placed in this context, these quilled bark baskets and mats – which I have written about in the context of market-oriented souvenir exchange – assume an entirely new set of meanings which I, from my outsider perspective, had missed.[33]

Second Anecdote: Meeting the Beings

After their return, the participants in the British Museum trip found in their email inboxes a paper written by Lindsay Borrows, then a second-year university student who had joined our team as a volunteer assistant. She had written her essay, entitled "Nanabush in London: Context, Life, Words, and Cultures in the British Museum," for one of her courses, and she sent it to us as the trip report we had requested from all the participants. Instead of adopting a conventional Western narrative form, Borrows wrote in the third person as a female Nanabush, the trickster figure of Anishinaabe oral tradition. She assigned us all Anishinaabe names and described her experiences at the British Museum as a profoundly moving visit to family and friends, the "beings" who "have been left sleeping in confining boxes on distant shelves for too long." As Nanabush, Borrows experienced research in a museum vault as a family reunion between human and other-than-human kin. Here is her description of our work on the Stoneyhurst collection: "As Bine [Alan Corbiere] advanced, he read a name on the bottom. It was from his home. This drum was his brother" (fig. 15.5).

In her writing Borrows reveals a fundamental tension at play in GRASAC between Indigenous and non-Indigenous perspectives. When we enter a museum or archival storage area, with what, or with whom, are we working? During our first workshop in 2005, Anishinaabe legal historian and GRASAC co-founder Darlene Johnston had raised the problem of the English term "objects" in light of Anishinaabe discursive traditions in which modes of material and expressive culture can assume animacy. The notion that Indigenous peoples employ a broader category of personhood than do other cultural traditions is hardly new. Anthropologist Irving Hallowell, for example, explored this concept in depth during his research in northern Ontario in the 1930s.[34] As an intercultural collaboration, however, GRASAC must make operative the notion of other-than-human persons, and we have struggled together to find terms through which we can acknowledge the existence of a drum as both a musical instrument and a brother or a relative – a "being," to use Lindsay Borrows's word. At times our struggles to escape our language-determined ways of thinking have devolved into the semi-comical, and we now, for lack of a better term in any language, often refer collectively to objects/artifacts/potential other-than-human beings as "heritage items." The very awkwardness of the term serves as a reminder of the problems of cultural translation.

Such fundamental differences in cultural categories have also proven challenging throughout the design of our database and web interface. Finding ways of naming, presenting, and structuring Aboriginal heritage that privilege neither Aboriginal nor Western traditions at the expense of the other is one of the major underlying challenges of projects such as the GKS and the RRN. It invites us to engage fully in pluralism, with all the perils and possibilities that are posed by such an approach, such as the inclusion in individ-

15.5   British Museum and GRASAC researchers studying Great Lakes items in the British Museum's collection. Left to right: British Museum conservation scientist Dr Caroline Cartwright, Woodlands Cultural Centre executive director Janis Monture, legal historian Darlene Johnston, and student Lindsay Borrows. Photo by Ruth Phillips

ual records of contradictory statements. We look forward to the addition of the Indigenous languages module to the GKS because it will provide a capacity to address these issues more directly in terms of Indigenous discourse.

Third Anecdote: Closing the Distance

On a late grey afternoon in Oxford, a group of GRASAC researchers and Pitt Rivers Museum staff experienced what has thus far been the most dramatic demonstration yet of the ability of new technology to close the distances that have impeded the understanding of historic Aboriginal collections. Through a video-conferencing hookup established between the museum's new state-of-the-art research facility and the Ojibwe Cultural Foundation on Manitou-lin Island, the researchers in England were able to consult Elder Eddie King in Canada (fig. 15.6). King had agreed to discuss a group of items whose uses and meanings had puzzled us during the preceding days of work. Seated at a table at the OCF, he used his remote control to move the camera in Oxford so that he could examine details of a rare and remarkable eighteenth-century bag attributed to the Illini. Finger-woven of buffalo hair, it has interwoven white glass trade beads that form a line of anthropomorphic figures. The bag

is unusually large and wide, and King suggested that it could have been used to hold extra pipe stems employed in funerals and other important Anishinaabe rituals. The layered histories of use associated with these pipes are carefully remembered across generations, and King's commentary thus introduced potential meanings and historical resonances that had not previously been suggested by the many researchers who have examined, exhibited, and published the bag over the years. As the headline of an article that appeared a little while later in the *Manitoulin Expositor* put it, through technology we collectively experienced "Reconnecting Roots."[35]

Conclusion

On a fundamental level, GRASAC is a project of reclamation and recovery, reconnection and reintegration. It mitigates the separation of people from heritage and the enforced losses of traditional knowledge that continue to have serious consequences for Aboriginal identity and spiritual and mental health and to hinder non-Aboriginal understandings of Indigenous knowledge systems that are needed now more than

15.6   Alan Corbiere, executive director of the Ojibwe Cultural Foundation, at the Pitt Rivers Museum, Oxford University, and Elder Eddie King at the Ojibwe Cultural Foundation, M'chigeeng, Ontario, discussing items from the museum's collection via a video-conferencing link in December 2007. Photo by Malcolm Osman, courtesy of the Pitt Rivers Museum

ever. The three anecdotes that are recounted here suggest the radical poten-tial of the dialogue and multivocality that both GRASAC and the RRN seek to promote. Each describes a moment when the multiple and repeated sep-arations produced by the action of Western scientific and objectifying para-digms seemed suddenly to have been bridged.

As postcolonial theorists such as James Clifford, Mary Louise Pratt, and Thomas Richards have made clear, gestures of separation have served as strategies of colonial empowerment. As I have argued in this chapter, in cer-tain contexts such strategies can be a productive – and necessary – condi-tion of academic research.[36] To perform her analysis, the humanist or social scientist must separate herself from the subject of her study; art, materiality, economy, polity, or language must be considered as discrete systems in order to be analyzed; data must be removed from their places of origin to distant sites of analysis – offices, studies, laboratories, archives, museums – and the physical preservation of documents, photographs, and material artifacts de-pends on their separate storage in dedicated environments. GRASAC does not deny the analytical power and value achieved by such technologies of knowledge production. Rather, we seek to complement them by the equally compelling and necessary gestures of reintegration and holistic framing that digital technologies can help us to realize.

16

"Learning to Feed off Controversies"

Meeting the Challenges of Translation and Recovery in Canadian Museums

The epochal changes that are transforming relationships between museums and communities in many settler nations in the early twenty-first century are the products of a series of controversies that shook up the museum world during the last decades of the twentieth.[2] Boycotts, demonstrations, media storms, protest art, questions asked in Parliament, and budget cuts in Congress stimulated the reflexivity, critical analysis, and activism necessary for change. Yet in the aftermath of these tumults, museums have become wary of controversy, and many now tend to regard exhibitions that could provoke debate as risks not worth taking. A situation in which museums try to avoid new controversies, even as they (and their government sponsors) celebrate the changes produced by old ones is more than a paradox. When museums decide to play it safe, they risk losing their efficacy as actors in the social worlds within which they function.

I have borrowed the phrase "learning to feed off controversies" from the introductory chapter of Bruno Latour's 2005 book, *Reassembling the Social: An Introduction to Actor-Network Theory*. In this concluding chapter I will explore the argument Latour makes there for the value of controversy in social process and its relevance to the dialectical process of debate and reform that museums in Canada and other settler societies have experienced since the 1980s. I will also argue for the usefulness to the analysis of museums as social institutions of the concepts of "translation," "hybridity," and "imbroglio" that Latour and others have advanced through actor-network theory.[3] This discussion is informed by an ass-

When we usually think of politics, we think only of a very small series of attitudes that suppose a gathering of people around the question of the representation of people. These perspectives have little to do with things, nor are they related to other ways of gathering. The only thing we want from the [exhibition] visitors is for them to recognize that there are many other ways of assembling, and that most of this assembling – this politics – is about things.
– *Bruno Latour on the exhibition* Making Things Public *(2005)*[1]

umption that anthropology and art museums can and should contribute to contemporary projects of decolonization, Indigenous recovery, and broader inclusivity. "Recovery," here, has a double sense, referring both to acts of *reclaiming* that which has been lost or forgotten through invasion, colonization, and violence and to *healing* the damage to psychic and physical health inflicted by those losses. In the latter part of this chapter I will discuss a number of exhibitions that seem to me to illustrate the positive social value that exhibitions can have when they embrace, rather than occlude, the effective networks of social, material, and technological interconnectedness that actually exist. In so doing, as actor-network theory urges, such exhibitions encourage rather than suppress the revelatory potential of controversies.

Museums, Networks, and Translation

Actor-network theory, or ANT, is a de-essentializing and de-objectifying approach to the sociology of organizations, power structures, and processes of social reproduction. Museums, needless to say, can and should be considered under all three of these headings. ANT describes a world in constant flux and movement, a world in which activity occurs through the networking of heterogeneous entities that we normally think of as separate and distinct – humans, natural phenomena, machines, material objects. As sociologist John Law puts it, "To the extent that 'society' reproduces itself it does so because it is materially heterogeneous. And sociologies that do not take machines and architectures as seriously as they do people will never solve the problem of reproduction."[4] The hyphen between "actor" and "network" expresses the instability of these heterogeneous entities, both human and non-human, and insists on the necessity of considering them in association with each other. Law writes, for example, that "thinking, acting, writing, loving, earning – all the attributes that we normally ascribe to human beings, are generated in networks that pass through and ramify both within and beyond the body. Hence the term, actor-network – an actor is also, always, a network."[5] Another key ANT term, "translation," refers to the process by which heterogeneous actors form into networks. As Law explains, "'translation' is a verb which implies transformation and the possibility of equivalence, the possibility that one thing (for example an actor) may stand for another (for instance a network)."[6]

Well-functioning networks and successful processes of translation mask their own inherent instability and appear as single entities, or actors, through a process known as punctualization. As Latour argued in his 1991 book, *We Have Never Been Modern*, we have been habituated to think about the world in terms of punctualized or discrete entities (such as objects), pure categories (such as art or science), and autonomous systems (such as the art world, the government, or museums). We usually do not see the networks of interconnection that run through and constitute these actors and networks as functioning systems until they meet some form of resistance. When we think of a museum – as we usually do – as a solid and unified entity that serves as a container for "collections" of other solid and autonomous entities, we are experiencing punctualization. ANT's focus on the effective relationships among actors, rather than on punctualization effects, leads us to reimagine the museum as a networked system of people, things, and technologies that is connected to a host of other similarly heterogeneous networks.

Latour's understanding of the modernist paradigm as one which promotes pure categories that mystify the actuality of heterogeneity also usefully glosses twentieth-century tensions between Western disciplines (notably art history and anthropology) and holistic Indigenous knowledges, and it provides an explanation for the museum dilemmas to which these tensions have led. "The proliferation of hybrids," he stresses, "has saturated the constitutional framework of the moderns."[7] When blurrings, convergences, or clashes arise, they are indications that our categories – art/artifact, modern/primitive, object/person, Western/non-Western – can no longer contain the accumulated contradictions bred by their own fictive nature. Latour notes that "when the word 'modern,' 'modernization,' or 'modernity' appears, we are defining, by contrast, an archaic and stable past. Furthermore, the word is always being thrown into the middle of a fight, in a quarrel where there are winners and losers."[8]

Latour argues that in order to reconnect that which has been severed by the modern "work of purification," we must substitute a "work of translation" in which we engage actively in identifying those networks that have, all along, connected the multifarious phenomena of the world. As he writes, "The word 'modern' designates two sets of entirely different practices which must remain distinct if they are to remain effective, but have recently begun to be confused. The first set of practices, by 'translation,' creates mixtures between entirely new types of beings, hybrids of nature and culture. The second, by 'purification,' creates two entirely distinct ontological zones: that of human beings on the one hand; that of nonhumans on the other … The first set corresponds to what I have called networks; the second to what I shall call the modern critical stance."[9] As this passage makes clear, the kind of translation Latour advocates is radically different from that of modernist art historians or cultural anthropologists who have rigorously contained their studies within the parameters of iconological traditions or localized cultural systems.

Interdisciplinarity, Hybridity, and the Museum of Art-thropology

Latour's notion of the counter-modern, with its foregrounding of mixtures and hybridity, accounts, furthermore, for the marked trend toward the melding of art and artifact paradigms in museum display that began during the last years of the twentieth century and has been gaining momentum at the beginning of the twenty-first. Art museums increasingly provide extended labels, maps, and contextual photos that instruct viewers about the meaning of iconographic motifs and ritual contexts, while anthropology museums regularly exhibit contemporary art as a strategy for incorporating Indigen-

16.1   Detroit Institute of Arts installation of Great Lakes clothing incorporating didactic text panels, extended labels, and contextualizing photographs and images (2007). Photo courtesy of the Detroit Institute of Arts

ous perspectives on history and culture and as evidence both of the survival of traditional world views and of active engagement with global art markets. The new exhibits of African and Native-American art opened by the Detroit Institute of Arts in 2007 are a prime example, featuring many of the contextual elements once found only in anthropology museums (fig. 16.1).

The current hybridity that characterizes art history and anthropology and the museums they sponsor is not really new, for their categorical opposition has always been something of a false dichotomy. In their origins, both disciplines drew on a common repertoire of aesthetic and scientific constructs in order to contribute to evolutionist and progressivist metanarratives of human history, and both adopted a comparative methodology based on visual description and analysis that was derived from natural science and for which collections of material objects and visual images were essential.[10] Both judged value in terms of similar standards of aesthetic quality grounded in Kantian aesthetics, and both imposed a characteristically Western hierarchy of fine and applied arts on objects produced in other times and by other cultures. In the early twentieth century, through the parallel projects of Franz Boas and Alois Riegl, both disciplines also began to move toward more relativist modes of analysis and understanding.

The attempt to maintain categorical purity was most rigidly imposed during the high-modernist middle decades of the twentieth century, during which time academic anthropologists moved away from the study of material culture and the anthropology of art and art historians adhered to their traditional focus on the European tradition and "great civilizations." The representation of Indigenous arts was left, by default, largely to modernist artists and critics, whose deep appreciation of Primitive Art was narrowly defined by their formalist aesthetic concerns and their disenchantment with industrial modernity. When art history and anthropology began to re-engage with Indigenous art and material culture in the 1970s and 1980s, both responded to a set of interlocking political, economic, and social movements of the postwar period – the dismantling of colonial empires, the civil and human rights movements, the growing pluralism of Western nations, identity politics, and economic and cultural globalization.

As one of modernity's key tools of separation and purification, the museum became a target of contestation, and the big museum controversies that took place during the 1980s are quintessential demonstrations of Latour's argument that hybridity and controversy occur when pure categories are revealed as having always been fictive. The Ur-museum debates that erupted around the Museum of Modern Art's *"Primitivism" in 20th Century Art: Affinity of the Tribal and the Modern* (New York, 1984) and the Glenbow's *The Spirit Sings* (Calgary, 1988) did so when the narrower concerns traditionally addressed by modernist art and anthropology museums overflowed their carefully maintained boundaries into realms of politics, ethics, and practice to which they had initially seemed unrelated (see chapter 2). These controversies were renewed by the opening of the Louvre's Pavillon des Sessions in 2000 and the Musée du quai Branly in 2006. To many critics, the long-term exhibitions at both sites seemed throwbacks to outdated traditions of modernist primitivism that are even more anomalous in the early twenty-first century.[11]

Actor-network theory offers not only diagnostic and analytical tools but also prescriptive strategies. By focusing, as Latour recommends, on the activities of translation that take place in museums, we are better positioned to affect the complex and apparently heterogeneous social, political, economic, and natural chains of activity in which they participate. For proponents of ANT, it is *necessary* to identify the real and existing linkages among human and non-human actors in order to achieve effective understandings of the social. It is here that controversies – "imbroglios" – are useful. Latour writes:

> When you wish to discover the new unexpected actors that have more recently popped up and which are not yet bona fide members of "society," you have to travel somewhere else and with very different kinds of gear … Instead of taking a reasonable position and imposing some order beforehand, ANT claims to be able to find order much better after having let the actors deploy the full range of controversies in which they are immersed. It is as if we were saying to the actors: "We won't try to discipline you, to make you fit into our categories; we will let you

deploy your own worlds, and only later will we ask you to explain how you came about settling them."[12]

As they unfolded, the above-mentioned exhibition protests seemed to many museum professionals to raise issues tangential to the content of the exhibitions, but in each case the controversy revealed integral connections between the historical representations inside the museum's walls and the contemporary racial tensions, radical social inequalities, economic deprivations, identity politics, and political struggles that troubled the world outside. The finding of the new order of the postcolonial museum as a social agent was the work of the task forces, academic conferences, consultation meetings, and negotiations that followed moments of disturbance in pre-existing systems. In Latour's sense, their reports and conclusions made it possible to map the contours of underlying topographies travelled by his "new and unexpected actors."

In ANT terms, a museum controversy is a sign of resistance in the network that links the museum to the communities it serves and of the need for a new process of translation. The guidelines of the Canadian Task Force on Museums and First Peoples (1992) and the regulations of the US Native American Graves Protection and Repatriation Act (1990), I would argue, constitute such translations (see chapter 7). Even when the initial reaction to a controversy is conservative, it can produce change indirectly.[13] The controversial 1991 exhibition *The West as America: Reinterpreting Images of the Frontier, 1820–1920*, organized by the Smithsonian Institution's National Museum of American Art, is a good example. Its postcolonial reinterpretations of nineteenth-century American art elicited sufficient negative reaction to force the museum to change some of its original captions, but the museum's 2003 exhibition *George Catlin and His Indian Gallery*, which offered similar rereadings, went unchallenged.[14] Furthermore, in 2004 the National Museum of the American Indian inaugurated, without controversy, an installation of Catlin's portraits in which Plains Cree actor-playwright Floyd Favel delivers a nuanced but even more comprehensive and sharply postcolonial critique of the stereotypical and romanticized images they convey than that offered in *The West as America*.

The Mask in the Museum and the Unmasking of the Museum

Over the past three decades, items in museum collections to which originating communities attribute power and personhood have also served as sites of resistance and controversy. In some cases, for example, artists have worked with conservators in new ways to restore masks from which important attachments had been removed. Intended to function as multi-sensory social interventions in their original contexts of use, masquerades are typically made of fabric, fibre, animal parts, and other signifying and kinetically active elements, but they have been stripped down to their carved headpieces in order to create displays that focus on their "pure" sculpted forms. In many Indigenous traditions, furthermore, masquerades embody spiritual power and are considered to have forms of agency that can be destructive when misdirected. In chapter 14 I recounted the difficulties that members of the Great Lakes Research Alliance for the Study of Aboriginal Arts and Cultures have had in finding English words with which to replace the terms "object" and "artifact." This discussion reopened an issue that had first arisen for me when I encountered a parallel problem of translation during my doctoral fieldwork in West Africa in the 1970s.

While working in Mende villages in Sierra Leone, I requested permission to photograph masks used by members of the women's Sande Society in order to document their histories and patterns of stylistic and iconographic development. My focus on the carved headpiece, however, proved to be very un-Mende, for like most African peoples, they do not have a separate word for "mask." To speak of the headpiece separately from the rest of the masquerade costume, or to articulate the masked being's identity as an *ngafa*, or spirit, separable from the material and mechanical components of its dramatic realization by a human impersonator, implies a distinction which the Mende do not verbalize in public discourse.[15] I learned that the phrase that most closely translates the English "*sowei* mask" is *sowo wui*, which means, literally, "the head of the *sowei*." In more "modern" villages the Sande women did not object to my seeing, measuring, and studying these heads – although sometimes in an enclosed area that men could not enter. In villages where traditional protocols were more strictly observed, however, Sande officials "pulled" the fully masked and costumed figures, each accompanied by her attendants and heralded by the musical, high-pitched chanting of her name. Early on in my fieldwork, I tried to explain to a chief who had arranged my meeting with Sande women in one such village that for my needs it wasn't necessary to go to all this trouble. He gently responded that *ndoli jowei* (literally, "dancing *sowei*") could only be seen when fully and correctly garbed, and to drive home the point he asked me, "Could you go out without your head?"[16]

This exchange impressed on me the need to attend to the moments when translation proves difficult, and it also changed the way I came to see these masks in museums. I have never since been able to look at a museum installation in which a *sowei* mask has been stripped bare of her raffia, white head tie, protective amulets, jewellery, and black body costume without feeling that a violation has taken place amounting to a kind of voyeuristic stripping bare or amputation. For anyone with a training in art history, such an apprehension is inevitably also informed by Marcel Duchamp's fundamental insight that the Western system of art and museums operates as a machine for the production of economies of desire and commodification, while at the same time preventing the fulfillment of those desires. Like the Bride in *The Bride Stripped Bare by Her Bachelors, Even*, the African mask, displayed as a bare headpiece, cannot satisfy the viewer's hunger to possess the Other. Decapitated and stripped, the mask fatally frustrates access to the knowledge of the Other which is at the heart of the satisfaction of desire. The universalizing process of formalist appreciation that is imposed under the rubric of modernist primitivism occludes localized identities, denatures the exotic, and reduces it to sameness. Equally importantly, such modernist installation strategies prevent viewers from recognizing the historical and contemporary networks of interconnection amongst world cultures – whether they be networks of artistic exchange or the underlying political and economic processes that have delivered up exotic artifacts to the Western gaze.

My small epiphany in West Africa is paralleled by the experiences of many other historians of non-Western art who have gone "into the field" both in distant countries and in their own backyards. The hybridity of recent museum displays to which I referred earlier often involves the reversal of past processes of stripping away and the revision of modernist notions of authenticity. It can also involve the retranslation of Western practices of conservation. The example of masks is again emblematic. At the Fenimore Art Museum in Cooperstown, New York, Yu'pik artist and performer Chuna McIntyre has replaced the feathers and other elements that were lost decades earlier from Yu'pik masks.[17] The Metropolitan Museum of Art commissioned a new raffia and fabric body costume for a mask displayed in its Rockefeller wing.[18] The University of British Columbia Museum of Anthropology and the Royal British Columbia Museum regularly lend old masks in their collections for use in potlatches and other events, allowing artists to refurbish them so that they can be returned to a state appropriate for performance. Such restorations of individual masks align themselves with exhibition projects that seek to restore the mask to its synesthetic context of masquerade and the masquerade to its holistic expressive function within networks of social agency and intervention. Let us turn to two exhibitions, one in Canada and one in Australia, which move toward such goals.

Mask versus Masquerade: *The Village Is Tilting* and *Dhari a Krar*

In February 2007 the University of British Columbia Museum of Anthropology opened a small exhibition about the Chewa masquerade cycle known as the Gule Wamkulu, or Great Dance. This exhibit, entitled *The Village Is Tilting: Dancing AIDS in Malawi,* focused on the way the Chewa have adapted these masquerades to address the AIDS pandemic and its devastating impact on their lives. Photographer Douglas Curran worked with Carol Mayer to curate the exhibition, which featured both mask headpieces and costumes and large-scale colour photographs of masquerades drawn from the comprehensive photographic documentation that Curran has made during more than a decade of travel in Malawi.[19] The central theme was introduced at the exhibit entrance through interviews with Chewa people projected on a video monitor and statements printed on a semi-transparent fabric wall that lined the ramp leading into the exhibition. "When the men were going to work in the mines, this is when this disease started to come to us," states

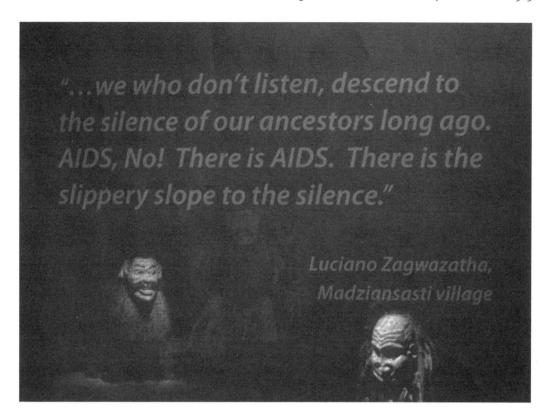

Mai Karonga. "We who don't listen, descend to the silence of our ancestors long ago. AIDS, NO! There is AIDS. There is the slippery slope to the silence," says a man from another village, Luciano Zagwazatha. "Men, women and boys and girls are not following the rules of life set out by our ancestors … today no young girl runs away from a man," comments Mai Alphonsina Kumilambe" (fig. 16.2).

Text panels in the main space of the exhibition explained that the masked spirits, or *nyau*, provide access to ancestral spirits who have power over fertility and life. Although colonial administrators banned the Wamkulu as an obscene "national evil," Chewa have successfully preserved their masquerade traditions and adapted them to reinforce positive social values and trans-generational continuities. "As the AIDS virus has permeated their society," a text panel told visitors, "the forms of the Chewa spirits have been regenerated again, providing new contemporary frameworks through which to understand the broader social implications and responses to the pandemic." Masks that represent characters such as "Chadzunda, The old deaf man/The chief," who embodies ideals of dignity and modesty, and "Akupha Aonongo, The

16.2   Introductory texts for *The Village Is Tilting: Dancing AIDS in Malawi* (2007), Museum of Anthropology, University of British Columbia, Vancouver. Photo by Ruth B. Phillips

16.3 (*see also colour plate 18*) Installation of mask and photographs by Douglas Curran in *The Village Is Tilting: Dancing AIDS in Malawi* (2007), Museum of Anthropology, University of British Columbia, Vancouver. Photo by Ruth B. Phillips

killers are destroyers," were displayed and their attributes and relevance to the AIDS crisis explained. Akupha, for example, "exemplifies the Chewa "anti-aesthetic": his "appearance indicates he is a carrier. His face is not smooth and well-oiled as is the Chewa ideal: instead, his dusty, ashen skin is delineated with many wrinkles, and atop his head is a tumor." The designer of the exhibition, Skooker Broome, painted the walls a deep rusty blood red that suggested the danger and power invoked both by AIDS and the Wamkulu. This saturated colour and the spotlighting of the individual masks intensified the sense of enclosure and drama, while the juxtaposition of the masks with Curran's photographic panels evoked a sense of immediacy that was further enhanced by a video of masquerade performances (fig. 16.3).

Masks are also the subject of a long-term exhibition opened in 2005 at the National Museum of Australia in Canberra. *Dhari a Krar: Headdresses and Masks from the Torres Strait* was conceptualized by staff curator Anna Edmonson in collaboration with two Torres Strait Islanders, curator-designer Brian Robinson and program coordinator Carly Jia.[20] Strikingly, the exhibit adopts some of the same strategies as *The Village Is Tilting* to contextualize the mask headpieces on display and to evoke the dynamic role played by masquerades as social mediators both historically and in the present.

Nineteenth-century Torres Strait masks are canonical objects of Primitive Art. Collectors removed the famous tortoise shell and wooden masks from the islands in the late nineteenth and early twentieth centuries following the arrival of missionaries in 1871 (an event known to Torres Strait Islanders as the "Coming of the Light"), and none remains in Torres Strait communities. Yet masquerade traditions continued to evolve and adapt in these communities in response to new spiritual and political needs. By foregrounding this process of change and innovation, *Dhari a Krar* demystifies what Joseph Alsop has termed the "rare art tradition" at the heart of Western connoisseurship and collecting practices.[21] The exhibition also offers an example of the way in which the Western connoisseur's habit of stripping away appendages to reveal the underlying carved forms can denature, for its original users, a mask's very identity and aesthetic impact. As a text panel on trading patterns tells us, wooden masks known as *mawa* or *buk* were traded from Papua New Guinea in an undecorated state. It was only when Torres Strait people added ochre designs, human hair, feathers, fibres, and seeds that they acquired specific identities and could be used in performance.

The exhibition emphasizes the cosmopolitan history of Torres Strait Islanders and the role of innovative masquerades in secular strategies of social integration, rather than focusing on the ritual/spiritual contexts, such as initiation, that are usually favoured by Western writers. It privileges, in other words, creative hybridity and adaptation, rather than the purity of lost authenticity. One text panel within the exhibit reads: "Unlike ceremonial dances, Torres Strait secular dances have always been innovative in their choreography and costume. From the mid 1800s the establishment of missions and the pearling industry brought people from around the globe including Japanese, Malays, Filipinos, Micronesians, Polynesians and Europeans. Torres Strait Islanders took advantage of this mix of cultures to create new repertoires of songs and dances. Today Torres Strait Islander dancers continue to draw on a diverse range of influences."

Other texts emphasize the role played by traditional "old-fashioned" dance in the re-enactment and preservation of historical memory and the equal importance of "dances incorporating newer elements (such as Polynesian dance styles introduced by missionaries in the late-19th century) … known as *ailan dans* (island dance)."

The walls of the *Dhari a Krar* gallery are painted black, and as in *The Village Is Tilting*, this colour choice and other design features are important in realizing the exhibition's messages. Blackness suggests the traditional forest ambience of Torres Strait Island initiation rituals and the dramatic, sudden appearances of masked beings amongst the trees that impress initiates with their mystery and power. In sections of the exhibition that display individ-

16.4   Large video screen with Torres Strait dance performance, in *Dhari a Krar: Headdresses and Masks from the Torres Strait*. Photo © National Museum of Australia, Canberra

ual mask headpieces, this colour choice also supports the "art hang" that Edmonson requested from the designers for a set of late nineteenth-century mask headpieces and allows their formal qualities to be highlighted.[22] As well, the dark gallery interior sets off the virtual performance space at the centre of the exhibition, which consists of a large screen on which masquerade performers are projected at near life size (fig. 16.4). The large panel of electronic light draws visitors in to sit and watch the dancers. As spectators at a virtual performance, they experience the event in real time, absorbing the message that Torres Strait masquerades are not only historical but also contemporary. The music that emanates from this performance space fills the gallery, animating the masks on display in the wall cases.

The Village Is Tilting and *Dhari a Krar* are relatively small exhibitions that were created with modest budgets. Yet both effectively insist on the dynamic nature of masquerade traditions as expressive forms that enable their creators to adapt to the changing conditions of life in the contemporary world.

They evoke the synesthetic nature, theatricality, and per-
formativity of masquerades and avoid fetishizing the mask
headpieces as objects of desire while still making them available for aesthetic appreciation as products of an individual
carver's skill and imagination (fig. 16.5). Neither exhibition,
finally, segregates "art" or traditional material culture from
the historical and contemporary human actors, biological
microbes, or global demographic movements with which
they are inextricably bound up.

The Spirit Sings: Twenty Years After

A set of contemporary exhibits on view at Calgary's Glenbow
Museum in 2008 also provided me with an opportunity to
assess the changes that have taken place in that institution
during the twenty years since it hosted *The Spirit Sings*.[23]
Four exhibitions about Indigenous history, art, and culture
were on display, two long-term and two temporary. The largest of these is *Niitsitapiisinni: Our Way of Life*, which opened
in 2002 after four years of development. *Niitsitapiisinni* is a
large, collaborative, community-curated exhibition that is representative of similar processes employed in recent years at
many other Canadian museums.[24] Charles Taylor's notion of

16.5   Display of nine-
teenth-century tortoise-
shell masks in *Dhari a
Krar: Headdresses and
Masks from the Torres
Strait*, National Museum of
Australia, Canberra. Photo
by Ruth B. Phillips

the politics of recognition is immediately evident in Glenbow curator Gerald Conaty's account of the way the project was initiated: "In 1998 we invited 17 Blackfoot people to work with us in developing an exhibit that would reflect their culture and history as they know it." The elders and traditional-knowledge specialists made it clear that their primary purpose was to provide an educational site for the young of their own community, and Glenbow's agreement that a joint project should contribute benefits defined by the community partner, as prescribed in participatory action research, suggests that its staff shared this orientation.[25]

Numerous meetings followed, both at the museum and in Blackfoot communities, whose goal, Conaty explains, was "to discover the essential elements of Blackfoot culture, elements that are intuitive to the Blackfoot but may not be at all obvious to a non-Blackfoot person."[26] A key principle of the project was that "it was not an exhibition about Glenbow's collection of Blackfoot artefacts" but "an exhibit about Blackfoot culture." Out of this process of patient listening, the Glenbow staff developed a storyline and approaches to design and took them back to their Blackfoot partners for critique and revision. Patience, as Conaty stresses, was required on all sides, for Blackfoot contributors were as unfamiliar with museum culture and protocols as Glenbow staff were with Blackfoot ways of working. Once the exhibition was completed, however, Conaty reports that the Blackfoot "were well satisfied at how their ideas had been given form. It was a process that was new to all of us and, in the end, the Blackfoot were able to say that the museum had 'got it right.'"[27]

The product of this extensive collaborative process is a complex exhibition that conveys traditional cosmology, seasonal rhythms, and beliefs in the interdependency of humans, plants, and animals. The main areas of the exhibition feature recreated pre-contact land and skyscapes in which teepee-shaped glass cases containing historical artifacts are embedded as supports for storytelling and teaching (figs. 11.2 and 11.3). The success with which the traditional life on the land is evoked is such that, upon leaving these open spaces and entering the rectangular rooms of the reserve house and the residential schools that came with colonization, the visitor experiences a visceral sense of confinement. In the last section of the exhibition, visitors again enter a circular space where, in Conaty's words, "Young and old explain their current challenges and reveal the pride they feel for their [Blackfoot] culture and traditions."[28] Like the Canadian Museum of Civilization's First Peoples Hall, *Niitsitapiisinni* established a fresh model of collaboration for the museum, and both the museum and the community have been able to develop new projects more quickly and easily because of the mutual knowledge and trust that were gained through the process of exhibition development.

Adjacent to *Niitsitapiisinni* is the Glenbow's overview of Canadian Aboriginal peoples, entitled *Native Cultures of the Four Directions*. According to curator Beth Carter, the exhibit was initiated at the request of the museum's Native Advisory Council to provide a context for the Blackfoot exhibit. Less

than a third the size of *Niitsitapiisinni*,[29] the *Native Cultures* gallery reflects the museum's decision to put its major focus on the Indigenous people of the immediate region, rather than on the universal or even continental surveys typical of twentieth-century ethnographic museums – and to feature peoples its collections would support. As in *Niitsitapiisinni*, the four quadrants into which the gallery is divided reflect Indigenous cosmology. Yet its broader scope also entails a trade-off, for in contrast to the immediacy and intimacy conveyed by first-person voices in collaborative exhibitions such as *Niitsitapiisinni*, the more conventional typologies of the *Native Cultures* gallery create a mood of more distanced objectification.

The *Native Cultures* gallery is animated by the small temporary exhibit area at its centre. It is designed as a circular space in the middle of which is a display case with vitrines facing in four directions. In 2008 an exhibition entitled *Situation Rez: Kainai Students Take Action with Art* was installed in this space (fig. 16.6). It displayed two art projects created by students in art classes at the Kainai High School in Standoff, Alberta, working in collaboration with the Red Cross and the Glenbow Museum. One class made paintings in the traditional Blackfoot pictographic style used on hide and in ledger books, while the other made papier mâché bowls

16.6   *Situation Res,* Glenbow Museum, Calgary, 2008. Photo by Ruth B. Phillips

painted with traditional motifs. In both projects the students address the
HIV/AIDS epidemic affecting Blackfoot and other Aboriginal communities.
Through the use of traditional imagery, the students linked the HIV/AIDS
crisis to the epidemics of infectious diseases their ancestors had endured and
to traditional teachings that promote health and well-being. Labels movingly
express the interconnections the students discovered. Joseph Iron Shirt's
wellness bowl, for example, read: "Wellness is a part of life. We all represent
wellness in our lifetime. There are times when we will do good stuff for other
people. But we all have to be aware of HIV/AIDS because by 2008, 30% of our
people will have this. So we have to be more careful of what we do now, and
treat other people with wellness."

The final Glenbow exhibition related to Indigenous cultures that was on
view in 2008 was a temporary show, *Tracing History: Presenting the Un-presentable,* which was organized with specific reference to the twentieth an-niversary of *The Spirit Sings*. It consisted of works by four contemporary Ab-original artists – Faye HeavyShield, Adrian Stimpson, Terrance Houle, and
Tanya Harnett – who were invited by curator Quyen Hoang to explore and
respond to works in the Glenbow's collection. In its own way, each of the four
new art works destabilized fixed meanings that museums have attached to
artifacts and enriched them with other understandings.

Terrance Houle's video work *Aakaisttsiiksiinaakii: Many Snake Woman: "The Daughters after Me"* meditates on a portrait of his grandmother, Mary
Snake Woman, painted during the 1930s by German artist Winold Reiss (fig.
16.7). In the video, his sister, mother, grandmother, and small daughter come
in, sit down, rearrange their blankets, shift in their chairs, sneeze, and look
out at the camera, achieving and then losing the formal pose of their ances-tor in the Reiss portrait. We are led to think about the process by which a
living subject becomes a painted object through the artist's brush or camera
and the arresting of flux, mobility and time that occurs. "I often find," Houle
writes in his artist's statement, "that these portraits don't tell much about the
people in it … I wanted to make a video that showed the same woman and
her lineage, three generations of daughters … The lineage brings life to my
grandmother's portrait and is not just a simple portrait in a two dimensional
sense like Reiss's. It tells a story of a Blackfoot woman and the ideas of sur-vival, identity, and time. I wanted to make a work that spoke to the objects
in a museum and how those objects still live and breathe and have life and
stories to them."[30]

Tanya Harnett chose to comment on a nineteenth-century ledger-book
painting made in the 1880s by Hongeyeesa, an Assiniboine artist from her
own Carry the Kettle reserve in Saskatchewan. The drawing depicts a steam-boat with a horned animal at the prow and strange black figures on its decks.
For her 1993 catalogue of Hongeyeesa's paintings, Valerie Robertson con-sulted with contemporary members of the Carry the Kettle First Nation to in-terpret this drawing, and she identified the boat as probably having been one
of the new steamboats that had recently appeared on the nearby Milk River.[31]

16.7 (*see also colour plate 19*) Terrance Houle, *Aakaist-tsiiksiinaakii: Many Snake Woman: "The Daughters after Me"* (2008), video; shown in *Tracing History: Presenting the Unpresentable*, 2008. Reproduced with permission of the artist; photo © Glenbow Museum, Calgary

Harnett's work proposes another possible explanation. Her piece, *Skull Mountainettes*, consists of two photographs of the hilly area on the reserve bearing the same name, a locale that is identified in oral tradition as the burial place of the victims of the two devastating smallpox epidemics that decimated the Assiniboine in 1781 and 1838, reducing the population by as much as eighty per cent (fig. 16.8). In between the photographs she positioned a pedestal case whose glass top was filled with mist produced by the same kind of machine she had used to create the fog or miasma that hangs in front of the Skull Mountainettes in her photographs. Harnett writes in the exhibition brochure: "The slough Hongeeyesa lived near was about 100 yards away from the Skull Mountainettes and he would have lived with the story about the smallpox … There were many steamboats that travelled up the Missouri during this period and there is no direct evidence to tie the ledger drawing to the smallpox epidemic and there is no one to inform us what Hongeeyesa was trying to depict. The story is lost. Still, I think there are stories that want to be told." Through Harnett's intervention, new resonances emerge that join the Hongeeyesa painting to collective memory, enveloping and filling gaps in the museum's own documentation so as to enlarge the potential meanings of his drawing without fixing or closing off other interpretations.

16.8 (*see also colour plate 20*) Tanya Harnett, *Skull Mountainettes* (2008), digital photographic prints mounted on Plexiglas, shown in *Tracing History: Presenting the Unpresentable*, 2008. Reproduced with permission of the artist; photo © Glenbow Museum, Calgary

Museum Experiments: Networking the Object in the Twenty-First-Century Exhibition

The exhibitions I have discussed resulted from processes of negotiation and experimentation that participate in what I have called, following Latour, instances of "retranslation." As they have decided which new projects to initiate over the past three decades, many museums have come to accept a criterion of social contingency, according to which the timeliness of a topic is determined not just in relation to the research interests of curators or the strengths of a collection but in terms of priorities defined by community partners. In the course of such engagements, many new actors have been identified and new kinds of accommodations have been proposed for their specific needs. The relationships that are formed through the new partnerships are flatter and more reciprocal than older top-down models of consultation, as is implied by the term "network." Where good collaborations have occurred, the creation of an exhibition or other project does not end the relationships that have been established. Museums come to be involved in the long-term work of communities, and communities come to factor museums into their projects of postcolonial recovery. Some of these actors are human ("non-traditional" museum researchers and visitors), and some are non-human (collections, new technologies). Actor-network theory, for which "actors" can be both human and non-human, has no difficulty with such practices.

Although I have sought to emphasize the different ways in which certain recent exhibitions can open up standard subjects of museum representation to new meanings, it is likely that the average museum visitor continues to experience these exhibits as having *resolved* the controversies that lie in their background – that is, as stable, "punctualized" entities. In two recent curatorial projects Latour, in collaboration with Peter Weibel, has sought to demonstrate the way in which museum exhibitions can maintain or promote an awareness of what he calls the politics or social relations that are implied in and created through assemblies of things. In *Iconoclash* (2002) and *Making Things Public* (2005), Latour and Weibel treated the museum space as a laboratory that could be used to demonstrate the interconnection between images, things, and arenas of disciplinary specializations such as science and art.[32] In standard museum practice, they have written, "exhibitions ... act merely as a site for manifesting the autonomy of preformed curatorial tastes," while in their own exhibition experiment, "everyone submits to the risks and interests of heterotonomy."[33] *Making Things Public* they assert, constituted a microcosm of the social within the gallery space:

> It showed that implicitly any exhibition was an assembly – an assembly with a political character. It also showed dramatically and transparently what essentially constitutes every public assembly that is "thing"-based: a complex set of technologies, interfaces, platforms, networks, media, and "things," which gave rise to a public sphere. Precisely in this way, the exhibition itself becomes the model of an "object-oriented democracy": a "gathering," a "thing" in itself. The visitor's behaviour triggers influences, responses, and changes at every moment, repeatedly creating new public spheres.[34]

Many of the themes of this chapter come together in Weibel and Latour's account of their two exhibitions. Because *Making Things Public* was conceived as an experiment, the organizers had to be prepared for the possibility that they might fail, a condition that is closely related to the notion of controversy as a potentially productive process. They also urge the value of understanding the postmodern exhibition as a *performative* event in which "the work disappears and is replaced by instructions for enactment, for the communicative action, and for options for action. Open fields of enactment mean new alliances arise between author, work, and observer, in which new actants such as machines, programs, multiple users, and visitors operate on the same level."[35]

The openness described in this passage suggests in turn the new relationship between research and exhibitions that is emerging in postcolonial museums. As users bring ever more diverse cultural and professional formations to their engagements with museums, these institutions must increasingly function in ways that parallel Weibel and Latour's experimental exhibitions by fostering and recognizing the ongoing need to re-form (and reform) the networks that link humans, things, and knowledges in response to a world that is ever in flux. In accordance with such a position, we must reimagine the museum as an ever-shifting array of actors who participate in networks that extend beyond its physical boundaries. Each network, as already noted, is the result of a process of translation that connects human and non-human actors – new electronic technologies, older museum cataloguing technologies, artifacts, and the overlapping categories of culturally diverse community partners and museum professionals – in a new way. Perhaps most difficult to accept is the notion that when exhibitions (or research projects) fail, we should regard these failures as positive contributions to our museological future because they have the power to expose in fruitful ways the contradictions that riddle real life.

As Latour and Weibel also remind us, museum exhibitions can support a democratic and levelling politics by working with the growing hybridity of the contemporary world – democratic, technological, aesthetic. We are all, in Latour's view, either modern or not modern to equivalent degrees, and our shared condition of hybridity is the inevitable result of lives lived in multiple cultural worlds. If we are aware of this process more keenly today, it is not so much because it is new as because of the speed with which people, capital, technologies, and modes of expressive culture can now move across vast geographical distances. But what is new is also old, and one potential bonus of a growing consciousness of interconnection in our common late- or post- or non-modernity is that we that we may be more able to engage in translational processes, in both the literal and the ANT senses, with the holistic thought-worlds of Aboriginal peoples. Blackfoot elder and teacher Leroy Little Bear has written, "Aboriginal paradigms include ideas of constant flux, all existence consisting of energy waves/spirit, all things being animate, all existence being interrelated, creation/existence having to be renewed, space/place as an important referent, and language, songs, stories, and ceremonies as repositories for the knowledge that arise out of these paradigms."[36] If Little Bear's article were not headed "Aboriginal Paradigms: Implications for Relationships to Land and Treaty Making," we could easily attribute this paragraph to Bruno Latour – and perhaps vice versa.

NOTES

Preface

1 Harold Cardinal, *The Rebirth of Canada's Indians* (Edmonton: Hurtig, 1977), 8.

2 Indian Association of Alberta, *Citizens Plus* (Edmonton: Indian Association of Alberta, 1970). On the White Paper and the Red Paper, see Dale Turner, *This Is Not a Peace Pipe: Towards a Critical Indigenous Philosophy* (Toronto: University of Toronto Press, 2006), 13–37; and Michael D. Behiels, "Aboriginal Nationalism in the Ascendancy: The Assembly of First Nations' First Campaign for the Inherent Right to Self-government, 1968–1987," in Norman Hillmer and Adam Chapnick, eds, *Canadas of the Mind: The Making and Unmaking of Canadian Nationalisms in the Twentieth Century* (Montreal: McGill-Queen's University Press, 2007), 160–85.

3 Library and Archives Canada, Royal Commission on Bilingualism and Biculturalism fonds, "Biography / Administrative history," http://www.collectionscanada.gc.ca/pam_archives/public_mikan/index.php?fuseaction=genitem.displayItem&lang=eng&rec_nbr=251&rec_nbr_list=251; accessed 4 April 2011.

4 The speech was entitled "Canada: A Multicultural Nation" and was the maiden speech in the Senate of Canada by Senator Paul Yuzyk on 3 March 1964. Senator Yuzyk's promotion of a multicultural model is discussed in the obituary written by Michael B. Bociurkiw: "Senator was architect of multiculturalism," *Ukranian Weekly*, 13 July 1986, http://www.yuzyk.com/weekly-death-e2.shtml; accessed 15 June 2010. Ukranian Canadians had, however, been using the term "multiculturalism" since the 1950s. See Peter Henshaw, "John Buchan and the British Imperial Origins of Canadian Multiculturalism," in Hillmer and Chapnick eds, *Canadas of the Mind*, 204. See also Laura Weir, "The Making of a Multicultural Imaginery: The Ukrainian Canadian Community's Role in Redefining the Nation during the Royal Commission on Bilingualism and Biculturalism" (MA research essay, Department of History, Carleton University, 2009). Weir argues that the confidence inspired by the 1966 celebration of the immigration of Ukranians to Canada was an important factor in their recommendations to the B and B Commission.

5 Canada, Royal Commission on Bilingualism and Biculturalism, *Report* (Ottawa: Queen's Printer, 1967–70), vol. 4.

6 Pierre Elliott Trudeau, Robert L. Stanfield, David Lewis, and Réal Caouette, in House of Commons, *Debates*, 8 October 1971, 8545–8; reproduced at http://www.abheritage.ca/albertans/speeches/trudeau.html; accessed 15 June 2010.

7 For critiques of Canada's official state multiculturalism, see Richard J.F. Day, *Multiculturalism and the History of Canadian Diversity* (Toronto: University of Toronto Press, 2000); and Gerald Kernerman, *Multicultural Nationalism: Civilizing Difference, Constituting Community* (Vancouver: University of British Columbia Press, 2005).

8 Adrienne Clarkson was appointed governor general in 1999 and Michaëlle Jean in 2005.

9 John Porter, *The Vertical Mosaic: An Analysis of Social Class and Power in Canada* (Toronto: University of Toronto Press, 1965). In the 1930s John Murray Gibbon had termed this social configuration a mosaic and compared it favourably to the more homogeneous ideal of the melting pot fostered in the United States in his book *Canadian Mosaic: The Making of a Northern Nation*. (Toronto: McClelland & Stewart, 1938).

10 Charles Taylor, "The Politics of Recognition," in Amy Gutman, ed., *Multiculturalism: Examining the Politics of Recognition* (Princeton: Princeton University Press, 1994), 25–73.

11 John Ralston Saul, *A Fair Country: Telling Truths about Canada* (Toronto: Viking Canada, 2008).

12 An adequate analysis of the distinctive ways in which different settler societies have addressed multiculturalism and the claims of Indigenous peoples requires a much longer discussion than is possible here. It invites, in particular, rigorous comparative study with other former British colonies such as New Zealand, Australia, and South Africa. Some useful points of departure for such a study are Kylie Message, *New Museums and the Making of Culture* (New York: Routledge, 2006); Bain Atwood, "Contesting Frontiers: History, Memory and Narrative in a National Museum," in *reCollections: Journal of the National Museum of Australia* 1, no. 2 (2006): 103–14; Paul Williams, "Te Papa: New Zealand's Identity Complex," *Journal of New Zealand Art History* 24 (2003): 11–24; Elizabeth Rankin and Leoni Schmidt, "The Apartheid Museum: Performing a Spatial Dialectics," *Journal of Visual Culture* 8, no. 1 (2009): 76–102; Elizabeth Rankin and Carolyn Hamilton, "Revision; Reaction; Re-vision: The Role of Museums in (a) Transforming South Africa," *Museum Anthropology* 22, no. 3 (1999): 3–13; and Annie Coombes, *History after Apartheid: Visual Culture and Public Memory in a Democratic South Africa* (Durham, NC: Duke University Press, 2003).

13 See catalogue of same title (Kleinburg, Ont.: McMichael Canadian Collection, 1984).

14 In its parallel presentation of the two artistic traditions, the exhibition, which was entitled *From the Four Quarters: Native and European Art in Ontario, 5000 BC to 1867 AD*, was ahead of its time and bears comparison with the new and inclusive installations of Canadian art at the National Gallery of Ontario and the Art Gallery of Ontario that are discussed in chapter 15 of this book. It was curated by Dennis Reid and Joan Vastokas, who also co-authored a small publication of the same title.

15 The Department of Communications (now Canadian Heritage) had responsibility for museums.

16 Task Force on Museums and First Peoples, *Turning the Page: Forging New Partnerships between Museums and First Peoples* (Ottawa, 1992).

17 Personal communication, Robin Wright, August 1989. See her edited catalogue for the exhibition: *A Time of Gathering: Native Heritage in Washington State* (Seattle: Burke Museum and University of Washington Press, 1991).

18 Jane Peirson Jones, "The Colonial Legacy and the Community: The Gallery 33 Project," in Karp, Christine Mullen Kreamer, and Steven D. Lavine, eds, *Museums and Communities: The Politics of Public Culture* (Washington, DC: Smithsonian Institution Press, 1994), 221–41.

19 Alison Mayes, "Exhibit Shines Light on Manitoba's Filipinos," *Winnipeg Free Press*, 17 June 2010.

20 Ibid.

21 Ivan Karp and Steven D. Lavine, eds, *Exhibiting Cultures: The Poetics and Politics of Museum Display* (Washington, DC: Smithsonian Institution Press, 1991).

22 Susan Vogel, ed., *Art/artifact: African Art in Anthropology Collections* (New York: The Center for African Art, 1988), and Sally Price, *Primitive Art in Civilized Places* (Chicago: University of Chicago Press, 1989).

23 Arjun Appadurai, ed., *The Social Life of Things: Commodities in Cultural Perspective* (New York: Cambridge University Press, 1986).

24 James Clifford and George E. Marcus, eds, *Writing Culture: The Poetics and Politics of Ethnography* (Berkeley: University of California Press, 1986); and James Clifford, *The Predicament of Culture: Twentieth Century Ethnography, Literature and Art* (Cambridge, Mass.: Harvard University Press, 1988) and *Routes: Travel and Translation in the Late Twentieth-Century* (Cambridge, Mass.: Harvard University Press, 1997)

25 Annie Coombes, *Reinventing Africa: Museums, Material Culture, and Popular Imagination in Late Victorian and Edwardian England* (New Haven, Conn.: Yale University Press, 1994); and Nicholas Thomas, *Entangled Objects: Exchange, Material Culture, and Colonialism in the Pacific* (Cambridge, Mass.: Harvard University Press, 1991) and *Colonialism's Culture: Anthropology, Travel and Government* (Princeton: Princeton University Press, 1994).

26 Oliver Impey and Arthur MacGregor, eds, *The Origin of Museums: The Cabinet of Curiosities in Sixteenth- and Seventeenth-Century Europe* (Oxford: Clarendon, 1985); Krzysztof Pomian, *Collectors and Curiosities: Paris and Venice, 1500–1800*, trans. Elizabeth Wiles-Portier (Cambridge, Mass.: Polity Press 1990); Horst

Bredekamp, *The Lure of Antiquity and the Cult of the Machine: The Kunstkammer and the Evolution of Nature, Art and Technology,* trans. Allison Brown (Princeton: Markus Wiener, 1995).

27 George W. Stocking Jr, ed., *Objects and Others: Essays on Museums and Material Culture* (Madison: University of Wisconsin Press, 1988); and Curtis M. Hinsley, *Savages and Scientists: The Smithsonian Institution and the Development of American Anthropology, 1846–1910* (Washingon, DC: Smithsonian Institution Press, 1981).

28 Eilean Hooper-Greenhill, *Museums and the Shaping of Knowledge* (London and New York: Routledge, 1992); Tony Bennett, *The Birth of the Museum: History, Theory, Politics* (London and New York: Routledge, 1995); and Carol Duncan, *Civilizing Rituals: Inside Public Art Museums* (London and New York: Routledge, 1995).

29 Aldona Jonaitis, *Chiefly Feasts: The Enduring Kwakiutl Potlatch* (Seattle and New York: University of Washington Press and American Museum of Natural History, 1991).

30 Michael M. Ames, *Museums, the Public and Anthropology: A Study in the Anthropology of Anthropology* (Vancouver: University of British Columbia Press, 1986) and *Cannibal Tours and Glass Boxes: The Anthropology of Museums* (Vancouver: University of British Columbia Press, 1992).

31 Ames, *Cannibal Tours,* 4.

32 The Exhibition Histories series published by Afterall Press in London incorporates elements of the case-study model I advocate. Each volume in the series focuses on a historic exhibition of contemporary art that has "changed the way art is seen and made." Each includes not only essays but also interviews with curators and others involved, "key texts from the time (such as reviews) and comprehensive visual documentation." http://www.afterall.org/books/; accessed 4 April 2011.

Introduction to Part One

1 The first two chapters in Part One expand on my essay "Show Times: De-celebrating the Canadian Nation, Decolonising the Canadian Museum, 1967–92," in Annie E. Coombes, ed., *Rethinking Settler Colonialism: History and Memory in Australia, Canada, New Zealand*

and South Africa (Manchester: Manchester University Press, 2006), 121–39.

2 Karen Coody Cooper, *Spirited Encounters: American Indians Protest Museum Policies and Practices* (New York: Altamira Press, 2008), 3.

3 An example of this caution is the Canadian Museum of Civilization's decision to postpone the opening of its exhibition of Arab-Canadian immigrant art, *The Lands within Me,* shortly after the 2001 attacks on the World Trade Center and the Pentagon. In this case the federal government, anxious to distinguish between terrorists and the general Muslim-Canadian population, ordered the museum to open as originally planned. See Elayne Oliphant, "'Il n'y a pas de "potentially hot issues"': Paradoxes of Displaying Arab-Canadian Lands within the Canadian Museum of Civilization Following 9.11" (MA thesis, Department of Political Economy, Carleton University, 2005).

Chapter One

1 The term "Indians" in this chapter reflects usage common among both Indigenous and non-Indigenous people during the 1960s. It also conveys a necessary distinction between the Inuit, who were not included in the pavilion, and the other Indigenous peoples of Canada. Displays about the Inuit were included in the Canada Pavilion, and a large exhibition of contemporary Inuit art was installed in its restaurant.

2 One of the first points noted in the minutes of the first meeting of the Indian Advisory Council that oversaw the pavilion's development was that "though the Indian is not celebrating a One Hundredth Birthday, as are White Canadians, it may be a useful approach to show the way of life and progress of Indians during the past hundred years." Kanien'kehaka Raotitiohkwa Cultural Centre (KRCC), Quebec, library files, "Minutes of the First Meeting of the Indian Advisory Council," Ottawa, 14–17 March 1966.

3 Tony Bennett, "1988: History and the Bicentenary," *Australian-Canadian Studies* 7, nos. 1–2 (1989): 156.

4 Sherry Brydon, "The Indians of Canada Pavilion at Expo 67," *American Indian Art Magazine* 22, no. 3 (1997): 54–7.

5 Expo 67 opened on 27 April 1967 and closed on 29 October of that year. The Indians of Canada Pavilion had originally been designed so that it could be dismantled and reassembled on another site for use as a friendship or arts and craft centre. A number of viable proposals were put forward by reserves and other organizations, but in the end the Department of Indian Affairs and Northern Develpment (DIAND) was unwilling to spend the $300,000 required to relocate it. Ownership was transferred to the City of Montreal on condition that Indian displays be maintained in the building for at least five years. The building was torn down in the late 1970s, although the totem pole remained in place. Art commissioned for the exterior of the pavilion has been in inaccessible storage in federal buildings since the late 1960s.

6 Sherry Brydon, "The Indians of Canada Pavilion at Expo 67: The First National and International Forum for Native Nations" (Honours essay, Department of Art History, Carleton University, 1991). Brydon's paper is grounded in exhaustive research in the major archival sources held in Library and Archives Canada (LAC), Indian and Northern Affairs Canada (INAC), and the library of the KRCC. It contains a more comprehensive citation of texts and photographs. We are grateful to Tom Hill, Joseph Francis, Alex Janvier, and Russell Moses, who generously agreed to be interviewed by Brydon; to Andrew Delisle, who gave an interview to Phillips; and to Bill Kretzel, Kerry Abel, and H. Blair Neatby for their help in elucidating the broader historical context.

7 The history of the administration of the other Canadian pavilions demonstrates a tendency toward devolution that parallels the history of the Indians of Canada Pavilion described here. The Centennial Commission, composed of federal civil servants, was initially set up under the federal Secretary of State to oversee all the Canadian pavilions except the Canada Pavilion itself. As planning proceeded, the provinces and regions took over development of their own pavilions directly, and ultimately the commission oversaw only the Indians of Canada Pavilion. The federal administrative structure for Indians also changed during the years that Expo 67 was being developed. In 1965 the Indian Affairs Branch was transferred from the Department of Citizenship and Immigration to the Department of Northern Affairs and National Resources. One year later the Department of Indian and Northern Affairs, later the Department of Indian Affairs and Northern Development (DIAND), was created. See James S. Frideres, *Native People in Canada* (Scarborough: Prentice-Hall Canada, 1983), 18. The department is now called Indian and Northern Affairs Canada (INAC).

8 INAC Archives, 1/43-3 V. 1, Letter of June 1963 from H.M. Jones, Acting Deputy Minister, DIAND, to J.A. Roberts, Deputy Minister, Department of Trade and Commerce.

9 This kind of origin story has been typical of other settler societies. Official Australian celebrations of the country's bicentennial in 1988, for example, also considered aborigines as an earlier wave of "immigrants," and Aboriginal opposition to this narrative in Australia paralleled that which developed around the original Expo 67 storyline. As Bennett recounts, "this inclusive invitation was tellingly resisted, and its double-dealing rhetoric just as tellingly exposed, by the slogan governing the Aboriginal protest against the First Fleet re-enactment: 40,000 years don't make a Bicentennial." Bennett, "1988: History and the Bicentenary," 160.

10 INAC Archives, 1/43-3 V.1, "Storyline, Government of Canada Pavilion, Montreal 1967," December 1963.

11 Ontario, Quebec, the Maritimes, the Yukon, the western provinces, and the Northwest Territories all had separate pavilions.

12 Characteristically, earlier official displays celebrated the "progress" of Aboriginal people toward "civilization" as programmed by directed assimilation policies. In earlier fairs, Aboriginal people usually participated in the areas set aside for popular amusements, where troupes of professional entertainers from different parts of North America set up Indian villages and performed dances, most often using stereotypical Plains Indian props and costumes. See, for example, Aaron Glass, "Conspicuous Consumption: An Intercultural History of the Kwakwaka'wakw Hamat'sa" (PhD dissertation, Department of Anthropology, New York University, 2006).

13 LAC, RG 71, v. 447, J.W. Francis, Chief Architect and Project Co-ordinator, "Indians of Canada Pavilion – Expo 67, Press Conference – Ottawa,

July 1966; Presentation of Theme and Design Concept."

14 For status Indians, the successors of the National Indian Council were the National Indian Brotherhood, formed in 1968, and the Assembly of First Nations, formed in 1982. Other organizations have also come into existence to represent the special interests of Métis, non-status Indians, and Native women. See Frideres, *Native People in Canada*, 139; and Sally Weaver, *Making Canadian Indian Policy: The Hidden Agenda, 1968–70* (Toronto: University of Toronto Press, 1981), 42.

15 INAC Archives, 1/43-3 V. 1, 19, Letter of June 1964 from R.F. Battle, Director of the Indian Affairs Branch, to R. Letendre, Administrator of Exhibits, Canadian Corporation for the 1967 World Exhibition, 3.

16 LAC, RG 10/8575 1/1-2-2-18, pt. 2, "Participation in Canada's Centennial by People of Indian Ancestry – Some Policy Considerations" (unsigned), 24 September 1964, 2.

17 Ibid, 7.

18 Personal communication to Ruth Phillips, Kahnawake, Quebec, 6 May 1992.

19 LAC, RG 69, v. 607, "Minutes of the Indian Advisory Council, 4/5 March 1967, 10.

20 According to the minutes of its first meeting, the establishment of the Indian Advisory Council had been recommended by the National Indian Advisory Board at its meetings of 10–12 January 1966. The primary mandate of this board was to make recommendations concerning changes to the Indian Act, while the task of the IAC was to advise DIAND on plans for Expo 67 and to ensure that the plans for the Indian pavilion would be informed by Aboriginal input and participation. The members of the IAC were Wallace Labillois, Howard Beebe, Chief Wilfred Bellegarde, Cornelius Bignell, Chief Baptiste Cazon, James Debassige, Chief Magella Gros-Louis, and George Manuel (regarding the chairmanship of Dr Gilbert Montour, see note 23).

21 Harold Cardinal, *The Unjust Society: The Tragedy of Canada's Indians* (Edmonton: Mel Hurtig, 1969), 104.

22 George Manuel and Michael Posluns, *The Fourth World: An Indian Reality* (New York: The Free Press, 1974), 165.

23 Ibid., 172. Gilbert Montour was the original chairman-designate. According to the minutes

of the first meeting of the IAC, the council confirmed Dr Montour's appointment after "some members strongly expressed a concern over the means being permitted Council to select its own Chairman, though members made it clear that this concern in no way involved questioning the merits of the nomination by the Branch of Dr. Montour." The minutes of IAC meetings, however, report only that Dr Montour subsequently resigned to accept an appointment at the United Nations. His successor as chairman was Wallace Labillois. See LAC, RG 69, v. 607, "Minutes of the Indian Advisory Council, 4/5 March 1967," 10.

24 INAC Archives, 1/43-3-4, Memo of 4 March 1966 from Robert Marjoribanks to Director of Development re "Title for Head of Indians of Canada Pavilion." Marjoribanks wrote, "There is some feeling among Indians that [the title of commissioner] does not accurately reflect the independent status of the Indian Pavilion or Chief Delisle's position." Andrew Delisle recalled that the recommendation was at first resisted by the minister of Indian Affairs and finally approved only as the result of direct application to the prime minister, supported by Montreal's mayor, Jean Drapeau. Personal communication to Ruth Phillips, Kahnawake, Quebec, 8 May 1992.

25 KRCC library files, "Minutes of the First Meeting of the Indian Advisory Council for The Indians of Canada Pavilion – Expo 67," 14–17 March 1966, 8–9.

26 Francis noted that visitors "will have been subjected to an overwhelming array of multi-screen projections, electronic gadgets, and other paraphernalia of the technological age ... It is our purpose, therefore, to offer the visitor a change of pace and a rather different experience." LAC, RG 71, v. 447, J.W. Francis, "Indians of Canada Pavilion – Expo 67, Press Conference – Ottawa, July 1966: Presentation of Theme and Design Concept," 3.

27 Ibid.

28 Ibid.

29 Ibid.

30 Neil Harris, "Great American Fairs and American Cities: The Role of Chicago's Columbian Exposition," in Harris, *Cultural Excursions: Marketing Appetites and Cultural Tastes in Modern America* (Chicago: University of Chicago Press, 1990), 126.

31 Susan Stewart, *On Longing: Narratives of the Miniature, the Gigantic, the Souvenir, the Collection* (Baltimore: Johns Hopkins University Press, 1984), 71.

32 Ibid., 86.

33 Robert Venturi, Denise Scott Brown, and Steven Izenour, *Learning from Las Vegas: The Forgotten Symbolism of Architectural Form* (Cambridge, Mass.: MIT Press, 1972).

34 Francis referred to the role of signs in his statements during this period: "There will be little need, we hope, for our Pavilion to bear a label or sign to identify itself, for its total impression, including the landscape on which it rests, will be unmistakably Indian, but in a curiously contemporary way." LAC, RG 71, v. 447, 3, "Indians of Canada Pavilion – Expo 67; Introduction to Theme and Design Concept," 3–4.

35 See Brydon, "The Indians of Canada Pavilion at Expo 67," (Honours essay).

36 Janvier later retitled this work *Beaver Crossing Indian Colours*. He recounted that after he had completed his painting and returned home, he had a phone call from Joe Garland, a pavilion administrator, complimenting him but asking him to give it another title. He said that the nine-mile walk to the telephone at the general store at Beaver Crossing inspired the new title, which he thought DIAND would appreciate. Personal communication to Sherry Brydon, 21 February 1991.

37 LAC, RG 71, v. 447, "Murals for the Indians of Canada Pavilion" (n.d.), notes by Carol Wabegijig.

38 See, for example, W. Jackson Rushing III, *Native American Art and the New York Avant-Garde: A History of Cultural Primitivism* (Austin: University of Texas Press, 1995); and Ann Temkin, ed., *Barnett Newman* (New Haven, Conn.: Yale University Press, 2002).

39 During the Expo 67 project Morrisseau had recurrent problems with alcoholism, and much of his design was executed by Carl Ray. See Lister Sinclair and Jack Pollock, *The Art of Norval Morrisseau* (Toronto: Methuen, 1979), 32.

40 See Ruth B. Phillips, "Norval Morrisseau's Entrance," in Greg Hill, ed., *Norval Morrisseau: Shaman Artist: Negotiating Primitivism, Modernism, and Anishinaabe Tradition* (Ottawa: National Gallery of Canada, 2006), 42–77; and Valda Blundell and Ruth B. Phillips,

"If It Isn't Shamanic Is It Sham?" *Anthropologica* 25, no. 1 (1986): 117–32.

41 See Lee-Ann Martin, *The Art of Alex Janvier: His First Thirty Years, 1960–1990* (Thunder Bay, Ont.: Thunder Bay Art Gallery, 1994).

42 Some of these artists made works that were displayed in the interior. It has not been possible to assemble a complete list of what these were from the archival evidence uncovered so far.

43 The late Jackson Beardy, a Cree artist from Manitoba, was consulted on the pavilion. He spoke to Ruth Phillips on a number of occasions during the 1980s of the great importance his participation had had for him, even though he was not commissioned to make any of the art. Kenneth Hughes has written that in Montreal Beardy "mixed with Indian jewellers, wood carvers, sculptors, and painters from different parts of the country. Any doubts he may have had about the validity of pursuing art disappeared as he saw the variety and richness of the collective heritage of many Indian tribes in the process of being reborn and transformed." Hughes attributes Beardy's failure to be awarded a commission to make art for the pavilion to the drinking in which he – and other artists – engaged while in Montreal. Kenneth Hughes, *The Life and Art of Jackson Beardy* (Winnipeg: Canadian Dimension Publishers, 1979), 13.

44 Quoted in "Manitoulin '78, the Art Conference," *The Native Perspective* 3, no. 2 (1978): 48.

45 Personal communication to Sherry Brydon, Ottawa, 18 March 1991.

46 Quoted in Sinclair and Pollock, *The Art of Norval Morrisseau*, 30.

47 David Staples, "Artist Alex Janvier," *Edmonton Journal*, 31 January 1988.

48 "A Retrospect of Indian Art," *The Native Perspective* 3, no. 2 (1978): 36.

49 Chief George explained, "There is a longing among the young of my nation to secure for themselves and their people the skills that will provide them with a sense of purpose and worth. They will be our new warriors." See George, "Our Sad Winter Has Passed," reprinted in Kent Gooderam, ed., *I am an Indian* (Toronto: J.M. Dent and Sons, 1969), 19.

50 INAC Archives, 1/43-3, v.3, Letter from A.G. Leslie, Director of Development, to Assistant Deputy Minister of Indian Affairs, 9 August 1967, 2.

51 Personal communication to Ruth Phillips, Kahnawake, Quebec, 8 May 1992.

52 Canada, Controller of Stationery, *Indians of Canada Pavilion – Expo 67* (1967). The brochure was ten pages in length and contained an expanded version of the text panels mounted in the installations.

53 See, for example, Curtis M. Hinsley, "The World as a Marketplace: Commodification of the Exotic at the World's Columbian Exposition," in Ivan Karp and Steven D. Lavine, eds, *Exhibiting Cultures: The Poetics and Politics of Museum Display* (Washington, DC: Smithsonian Institution Press, 1991), 344–65.

54 This was the first point noted during the discussion of the pavilion's content that followed the presentation of the architectural plans to the IAC. Its importance is reinforced by the sentence that follows: "The Past may appear more evident than the others in the present stage of design only because this is the section initiated in the design work … the theme of the Present actually has been assigned a greater physical area than the Past." KRCC library files, "Minutes of the Second Meeting of the Indian Advisory Council," held at Montreal, 20–22 April 1966, 6.

55 Personal communication to Sherry Brydon, Ottawa, 18 March 1991. No photograph of this section has been located.

56 LAC, RG 71, v. 447, J.W. Francis, Chief Architect and Project Co-ordinator, "Indians of Canada Pavilion – Expo 67, Press Conference – Ottawa, July 1966; Presentation of Theme and Design Concept – Indians of Canada Pavilion – Expo 67."

57 Canada, Controller of Stationery, *Indians of Canada Pavilion*, 5.

58 *Indian News* 10, no. 1 (April 1967): 5.

59 LAC, RG 71, v. 447, J.W. Francis, Chief Architect and Project Co-ordinator, "Indians of Canada Pavilion – Expo 67, Press Conference – Ottawa, July 1966; Presentation of Theme and Design Concept," 5.

60 The brochure's section on the arrival of the white man continued in this deconstructive vein: "These were the so-called 'savages' whom the Europeans met when they 'discovered' North America." Canada, Controller of Stationery, *Indians of Canada Pavilion*, 6.

61 LAC, RG 71, v. 447, J.W. Francis, Chief Architect and Project Co-ordinator, "Indians of Canada Pavilion – Expo 67, Press Conference – Ottawa, July 1966; Presentation of Theme and Design Concept," 6.

62 In connection with this aspect of the installation, Andrew Delisle noted that in the 1960s the major political concern of Aboriginal peoples was with the protection of treaty rights, rather than the recognition of Aboriginal rights or sovereignty that later became a central goal (personal communication to Ruth Phillips, Kahnawake, Quebec, 8 May 1992). Aboriginal people had reason to be concerned, for the federal government's White Paper, issued only two years later, advocated the abolition of reserves and other special provisions for Aboriginal peoples. See Alan C. Cairns, *Citizens Plus: Aboriginal Peoples and the Canadian State* (Vancouver: University of British Columbia Press, 2000).

63 Quoted in "Canadian Indians at EXPO '67," *Sanity* (Montreal), July–August 1967.

64 Canada, Controller of Stationery, *Indians of Canada Pavilion*, 9.

65 Ibid.

66 The exhibition brochure was even more explicit: "School curricula and text books are usually designed for children of a European background and have very little relationship to the Indian child's home experience" (ibid.).

67 LAC, RG 71, v. 447, Rosemary Speirs, "Indian pavilion shocks complacent non-Indians," unlabelled newspaper clipping [probably from the *Montreal Star*].

68 Personal communication from Tom Hill to Ruth Phillips, Ottawa, 18 March 1991.

69 "Pavilion Tells Indians' Story," *Indian News* 10, no. 1 (April 1967): 5.

70 INAC Archives, Working Files, Indian Art Centre, Indians of Canada Pavilion, Expo 67, Exhibition Design Copy (n.d.).

71 The minutes report this visit, which occurred on the second day of the three-day meeting, without further comment. KRCC library files, "Minutes of the First Meeting of the Indian Advisory Council," Ottawa, 14–17 March 1966, 7.

72 Homi Bhabha, "Of Mimicry and Man: The Ambivalence of Colonial Discourse," in Bhabha, *The Location of Culture* (New York: Routledge, 1994), 85–92.

73 INAC Archives, 1/43-3, v. 1, Andre Nault, Executive Assistant, 18 April 1967.

74 Personal communication to Ruth Phillips, Kahnawake, Quebec, 8 May 1992.

75 INAC Archives, 1/43-3, v. 3, Letter to Mr. R.A.J. Phillips, Director, Special Planning Secretariat, Office of the Privy Council, Ottawa, 12 December 1967.

76 Michael McGarry, "Indians Speak with Straight Tongue," in *The Winnipeg Tribune's Weekend Showcase*, 24 June 1967.

77 Harris, *Cultural Excursions*, 129.

Chapter Two

1 Glenbow Archives (GA), *The Spirit Sings (TSS)*, box F, folder 4, p. 3, Bernard Ominayak, quoted in "Selected Chronology of Events Relating to Lubicon Land Claim" (typescript), 3.

2 GA, *TSS*, box F, folder 5, Letter of 25 August 1986, sent by Duncan Cameron to directors of museums from which loans to *The Spirit Sings* exhibition had been requested.

3 Stuart Hall, "Whose Heritage? Un-settling the 'Heritage,' Re-imagining the Post-nation," in Jo Littler and Roshi Naidoo, eds, *The Politics of Heritage: The Legacies of "Race"* (New York: Routledge, 2005), 28.

4 The first part of this chapter is an expanded version of "Three Propositions about *The Spirit Sings*: Power, Representation, History," delivered at "Legacies and Futures: Beyond *The Spirit Sings*," organized to mark the exhibition's twentieth anniversary by the Alberta College of Art and Design and the Glenbow Museum, 13–14 March 2008. The section entitled "Third Proposition: The Public Relations Wrap" is a revision of "The Public Relations W(rap): Learning from the Experience of 'The Spirit Sings,'" *Inuit Art Quarterly* 5, no. 2 (1990): 13–21.

5 Karen Coody Cooper, *Spirited Encounters: American Indians Protest Museum Policies and Practices* (New York: Altamira Press, 2008), ix, 27. Cooper's book title also considers the referentiality of the term "spirit," which, as she states, combines "key words taken from two exhibitions highly protested by American Indians" (ix).

6 For example, the Kwakwaka'wakw treasures confiscated in 1922 after Chief Dan Cranmer's potlatch had been returned only in 1979 by the Canadian Museum of Civilization, in 1987 by the Royal Ontario Museum, and in 1993 and

2002 by the National Museum of the American Indian. The history of protests against the display of medicine, or "False Face," masks is summarized in chapter 6.

7 See Julia Harrison's, Michael Ames's, and Bruce Trigger's statements in "Museums and Politics: *The Spirit Sings* and the Lubicon Boycott," *MUSE*, Special issue on Museums and the First Nations, 6, no 3 (Fall 1988): 12–25. See also Julia Harrison, "Completing a Circle: The Spirit Sings," in Noel Dyck and James B. Waldram, eds, *Anthropology, Public Policy, and Native Peoples in Canada* (Montreal: McGill-Queen's University Press, 1993), 334–57.

8 GA, *TSS*, box F, folder 5, ICME Newsletter, no. 7, 3. Reproduced as part of a package of supporting documents circulated by the organizers of the Lubicon boycott.

9 Erasmus had been national chief of the Assembly of First Nations when it decided to support the boycott. The conference was held from 3 to 5 November at Carleton University in Ottawa with the support of the Canadian Museums Association, the Canadian Museum of Civilization, and the Assembly of First Nations and was funded by the then Department of Communications (now the Department of Canadian Heritage). Erasmus's statement was used as the opening epigraph for Task Force on Museums and First Peoples, *Turning the Page: Forging New Partnerships between Museums and First Peoples* (Ottawa, 1992).

10 For an analysis, see Valda Blundell and Laurence Grant, "Preserving Our Heritage: Getting beyond Boycotts and Demonstrations," *Inuit Art Quarterly,* Winter 1989, 12–16.

11 Task Force on Museums and First Peoples, *Turning the Page*. See also Trudy Nicks, "Partnership in Developing Cultural Resources: Lessons from the Task Force on Museums and First Peoples," *Culture* 12, no. 1 (1992): 87–94; and Thomas Wilson and David Penney, "Museums and First Peoples in Canada," *Museum Anthropology* 16, no. 2 (1992): 6–11.

12 A few years later, the Australian museum community would take the Canadian guidelines as a model for a parallel process of its own (personal communication from Francesca Cubillo, then senior curator, Aboriginal Art and Material Culture, Museum and Art Gallery

of the Northern Territory, Darwin, Australia, January 2008, Melbourne). See, for example, http://www.visualarts.net.au/files/VARCes.pdf; accessed February 2009.

13 Veena Das, *Critical Events: An Anthropological Perspective on Contemporary India* (Oxford: Oxford University Press, 1995), 5.

14 Robyn Gillam, *Hall of Mirrors: Museums and the Canadian Public* (Banff, Alta: Banff Centre Press, 2001), 131.

15 For a critique of the culture-area approach, see Alfred Young Man's book review "*The Spirit Sings: Artistic Traditions of Canada's First Peoples,*" *American Indian Quarterly* 14, no. 1 (Winter 1990): 71–3.

16 GA, *TSS*, box F, folder 3, Mark Lowey, "Crooked-nosed Mohawk mask has long history," *Calgary Herald*, 28 January 1988, quoting from court documents.

17 The same mask, given to the Royal Ontario Museum by Evelyn Johnson, an Onondaga from the Six Nations of the Grand River and sister of Pauline Johnson, had been included in *Masterpieces of Canadian Indian and Inuit Art,* shown in Paris and Ottawa in 1968–69 (see chapter 14) and had also been displayed by the Royal Ontario Museum.

18 See Gloria Cranmer Webster, "The Potlatch Collection Repatriation," *University of British Columbia Law Review*, no. 14 (1995): 137–41, and "From Colonization to Repatriation," in Gerald McMaster and Lee-Ann Martin, eds, *Indigena: Contemporary Native Perspectives* (Vancouver: Douglas and McIntyre, 1992), 25–39; and Tina Loo, "Dan Cranmer's Potlatch: Law, Coercion, Symbol, and Rhetoric in British Columbia, 1884–1951," *Canadian Historical Review* 123, no. 2 (1992): 125–65.

19 *Potlatch: A Strict Law Bids Us Dance* (1975), directed and produced by Dennis Wheeler.

20 Donna McAlear, "Repatriation and Cultural Politics: Australian and Canadian Museum Responses to First Peoples' Challenges for Cultural Property Ownership" (PhD dissertation, Griffith University, Australia, 1999), 107–15.

21 The Lubicon Cree boycott of the exhibition was called two years before the opening of the games and the exhibition, after it had become apparent that a general boycott of the games was not viable and after the exhibition's corporate sponsor had been announced to be a company, Shell Oil, that was drilling on traditional Lubicon lands.

22 See Robert Redfield's classic essay "Art and Icon," in Robert Goldwater, ed., *Aspects of Primitive Art* (New York: Museum of Primitive Art, 1959); for a key set of reflexive discussions on these two paradigms and their histories, see Susan Vogel, ed., *Art/artifact: African Art in Anthropology Collections* (New York: Center for African Art and Prestel Verlag, 1988).

23 Aldona Jonaitis, *From the Land of the Totem Poles: The Northwest Coast Indian Art Collection at the American Museum of Natural History* (Seattle: University of Washington Press, 1988), 22–61.

24 On these debates, see, for example, James Clifford, "Histories of the Tribal and the Modern," in Clifford, *The Predicament of Culture: Twentieth-Century Ethnography, Literature, and Art* (Cambridge, Mass.: Harvard University Press, 1988); Hal Foster, "The 'Primitive' Unconscious of Modern Art, or White Skin Black Masks," in Foster, *Recodings: Art, Spectacle, Cultural Politics* (Seattle, Wash.: Bay Press, 1985), 180–208; and Thomas McEvilley, "Doctor, Lawyer, Indian Chief," in McEvilley, *Art and Otherness: Crisis in Cultural Identity* (Kingston, NY: McPherson and Company, 1992), 27–56.

25 Vogel, *Art/artifact.*

26 See Audrey Hawthorn, *Labour of Love: The Making of the Museum of Anthropology, UBC, The First Three Decades, 1947–1976* (Vancouver: UBC Museum of Anthropology, 1993).

27 Wilson Duff, *Arts of the Raven: Masterworks by the Northwest Coast Indian: An Exhibition in Honour of the One Hundredth Anniversary of Canadian Confederation* (Vancouver: Vancouver Art Gallery, 1967). Montreal's Mayor Drapeau invited curator Audrey Hawthorn to mount this exhibition as a follow-up to Expo 67's successful art exhibitions, and it, in turn, helped to build support for the creation of a dedicated building for the UBC Museum of Anthropology. See Hawthorn, *Labour of Love,* 67–74.

28 M.D. McLeod, "Treasures of Ancient Nigeria, London, Royal Academy," *Burlington Magazine* 125, no. 960 (March 1983): 185. The exhibition was organized by the Nigerian National Museum and the Detroit Institute of Arts.

29 In "Four Northwest Coast Museums: Travel Reflections," Clifford writes: "Treatment of artifacts as fine art is currently one of the most effective ways to communicate cross-culturally a sense of quality, meaning, and importance." James Clifford, *Routes: Travel and Translation* (Cambridge, Mass.: Harvard University Press, 1997), 121.

30 Aboriginal art was prominent in Dorothy K. Burnham's exhibition and catalogue *The Comfortable Arts: Traditional Spinning and Weaving in Canada* (Ottawa: National Gallery of Canada, 1981). Other exceptions were two exhibitions mounted for the Ontario bicentennial in 1984: the Art Gallery of Ontario's *From the Four Quarters* and the McMichael Canadian Collection's *Patterns of Power: The Jasper Grant Collection and Great Lakes Indian Art of the early 19th Century.*

31 GA, TSS, box B2.2, Planning Proposals, folder 3, "Olympic Exhibition Working Group Recommendations to Management."

32 GA, TSS, box B1, folder 1, "The Spirit Sings, Design Proposals for the Exhibition and Related Events and Programs," prepared by Rick Budd, Head, Exhibit and Graphic Design, and dated 21 August 1986, 5.

33 GA, TSS, box B1, Design, folder 11, Letter from Beth Carter, Glenbow Assistant Curator, to Librarian, Radio-Canada Service du Québec nordique, 20 May 1987.

34 Personal communication, Winter 1986.

35 On "Into the Heart of Africa," see Shelley Ruth Butler, *Contested Representations: Revisiting "Into the Heart of Africa"* (Peterborough, Ont.: Broadview Press, 2007); Jeanne Canizzo, "Exhibiting Cultures: 'Into the Heart of Africa,'" *Visual Anthropology Review* 7, no. 10 (1991): 150–60; Linda Hutcheon, "The Post Always Rings Twice: The Postmodern and the Postcolonial," *Textual Practice* 8, no. 2 (Summer 1994): 205–38; Henrietta Riegel, "Into the Heart of Irony: Ethnographic Exhibitions and the Politics of Difference," in Sharon Macdonald and Gordon Fyfe, eds, *Theorizing Museums* (Oxford: Blackwell, 1996), 83–103; and Enid Schildkraut, "Ambiguous Messages and Ironic Twists: 'Into the Heart of Africa' and 'The Other Museum,'" *Museum Anthropology* 15, no. 2 (1991): 16–23.

36 Linda Hutcheon, *Irony's Edge: The Theory and Politics of Irony* (New York: Routledge, 1994), 202.

37 GA, TSS, box C. All comments are quoted in full from cards stamped 1 May 1988.

38 The concept of "wrapping" in this sense is developed by Aldona Jonaitis, working from theory developed by Frederick Jameson, in her essay "Franz Boas, John Swanton, and the New Haida Sculpture at the American Museum of Natural History," in Janet Catherine Berlo, ed., *The Early Years of Native American Art History: Essays on the Politics of Scholarship and Collecting* (Seattle: University of Washington Press, 1992), 22–61.

39 The latter title appears in a comprehensive binder entitled "Glenbow Project, OCO '88, Progress Spring 1984," in GA, TSS, box B2.

40 Ibid., "National Treasures Exhibition, Organizational Meeting October 17–18, 1983." Cameron began his career at the Royal Ontario Museum and served as director of the Brooklyn Museum, both "universal history" museums with collections of world art. Alone among Canadian museum directors, he had, a few years earlier, secured for the Glenbow *Treasures of Ancient Nigeria*, a landmark international touring exhibition of Ife and Benin art from the national museum of Nigeria and the British Museum.

41 GA, TSS, box F, folder 5, Memorandum to R.W. Force and Curatorial Council of 16 June 1986.

42 Reid was initially invited to curate the Northwest Coast section, but his illness made it difficult for him to travel or attend meetings, and he continued to participate through his wife.

43 GA, TSS, box B1, folder 8.

44 The drum and the rest of the Beltrami collection remained unpublished until 1987, when the Museo Civico E. Caffi issued a handsome catalogue: Leonardo Vigorelli, *Gli oggetti indiani raccolta da G. Costantino Beltrami: Un catalogo* (Bergamo: Museo Civico E. Caffi, 1987).

45 See, for example, Raymond William Stedman, *Shadows of the Indian: Stereotypes in American Culture* (Norman: University of Oklahoma Press, 1982).

46 Clifford, in *The Predicament of Culture,* 191.

47 Ibid., 193. Clifford comments on modernism's "taste for redeeming otherness, for constituting non-Western arts in its own image."

48 Lis Smidt Stainforth, "Did the Spirit Sing? An Historical Perspective on Canadian Exhibitions of the Other" (MA thesis, Department of Art History, Carleton University, 1992).

49 John Borrows, *Recovering Canada: The Resurgence of Indigenous Law* (Toronto: University of Toronto Press, 2002).

50 Rita Joe, *Song of Eskasoni: More Poems of Rita Joe* (Charlottetown, PEI: Ragweed Press, 1988).

Chapter Three

1 Arjun Appadurai, *Modernity at Large: Cultural Dimensions of Globalization* (Minneapolis: University of Minnesota Press, 1996), 43.

2 For example, in *Civilizing Rituals: Inside Public Art Museums* (New York: Routledge, 1995) Carol Duncan has traced the origin of standard museological narratives of national schools of art (and culture) to Napoleon's transformation of the Louvre into a public museum and the repository of his imperial conquests. Tony Bennett, in *The Birth of the Museum: History, Theory, Politics* (New York: Routledge, 1995), explores the use of museums to discipline citizens to the state's structures of power and class.

3 See James Clifford, "Museums as Contact Zones," in Clifford, *Routes: Travel and Translation in the Late Twentieth Century* (Cambridge, Mass.: Harvard University Press, 1997), 188–219.

4 Sharon Macdonald, "Theorizing Museums: An Introduction," in Sharon Macdonald and Gordon Fyfe, eds, *Theorizing Museums: Representing Identity and Diversity in a Changing World* (Oxford: Blackwell, 1996), 2.

5 The Museum of Anthropology is the largest university museum in Canada and also serves as the anthropology museum for the city of Vancouver. During the 1990s it received up to 180,000 visitors every year and offered programs to about 15,000 schoolchildren.

6 See W. Wesley Pue, ed., *Pepper in Our Eyes: The APEC Affair* (Vancouver: University of British Columbia Press, 2000).

7 See Susan Roy, "History Visible: Culture and Politics in the Presentation of Musqueam

History" (MA thesis, Department of History, Simon Fraser University, 1999); and "Performing Musqueam Culture at British Columbia's 1966 Centennial Celebrations," *BC Studies* (Autumn 2002): 55–90.

8 See chapter 2 for an analysis of *The Spirit Sings* and chapter 2, note 35, for references to analyses of *Into the Heart of Africa*.

9 Task Force on Museums and First Peoples, *Turning the Page: Forging New Partnerships between Museums and First Peoples* (Ottawa, 1992). See also Trudy Nicks, "Partnerships in Developing Cultural Resources: Lessons from the Task Force on Museums and First Nations," *Culture* 12, no. 1 (1992): 87–94.

10 *From under the Delta* was on view from April 1997 until April 1999. *Written in the Earth* was at the Museum of Anthropology during 1996 and 1997, after which it toured smaller museums in British Columbia. The two exhibitions received awards from, respectively, the Canadian Museums Association and the British Columbia Museums Association. On *From under the Delta*, see Margaret Holm and David Pokotylo, "From Policy to Practice: A Case Study in Collaborative Exhibits with First Nations," *Canadian Journal of Archaeology* 21 (1997): 1–12. On *Written in the Earth*, see Michael Ames, "How to Decorate a House: The Re-negotiation of Cultural Representations at the University of British Columbia Museum of Anthropology," *Museum Anthropology* 22, no. 3 (1999): 41–51.

11 See Elizabeth Lominska Johnson and Kathryn Bernick, *Hands of Our Ancestors*, Museum Note no. 16 (Vancouver: UBC Museum of Anthropology, 1986); and Lizanne Fisher and Elizabeth L. Johnson, "Bridging the Gaps: A Museum Based Heritage Awareness Program," *Museum Anthropology* 12, no. 4 (1988): 1–8.

12 The text of this protocol is not made public by request of the Musqueam First Nation.

13 Quoted from an exhibition text panel for *Written in the Earth*.

14 See Audrey Hawthorn, *A Labour of Love: The Making of the Museum of Anthropology, UBC, The First Three Decades, 1947–1976* (Vancouver: UBC Museum of Anthropology, 1993).

15 At the time of the APEC meeting the museum had also begun planning for a more permanent acknowledgment of its special relationship to

the Musqueam First Nation through a reinstallation of Musqueam and other Coast Salish
monumental sculptures. Although these had
always been placed at the beginning of the visitor path through the permanent exhibitions,
the relationship between the Musqueam community and the museum/university site was not
explicitly stated. The new installation, opened
in June 1999, presents a housepost transferred
to the university by Vincent Stogan's father with
a new weaving commissioned from Musqueam
weavers Deborah and Robyn Sparrow. The
interpretive signage provides statements by
Vincent Stogan (Tsimele'nuxw) and other
Musqueam community members.

16 See Ruth B. Phillips and Christopher B. Steiner,
"Art, Authenticity and the Baggage of Cultural
Encounter," in Ruth B. Phillips and Christopher
B. Steiner, eds, *Unpacking Culture: Art and
Commodity in Colonial and Postcolonial Worlds*
(Berkeley: University of California Press, 1999).

17 Appadurai, *Modernity at Large*, 178.

18 "Memorandum for the Prime Minister:
Letter to Musqueam Indian Band on APEC
Involvement," from Ronald Bilodeau, marked
"Confidential" and dated 3 September 1997. I
was given a copy of this document by one of the
complainants in the APEC inquiry described
below. The reference to the Talking Stick appears to be a confusion of customs observed
by more northerly First Nations, such as the
Kwakwaka'wakw, with those of the Musqueam
and other Coast Salish. For an excellent discussion of Musqueam leaders' use of art in the
public presentation of community interests
during the twentieth century, see Roy, "History
Visible."

19 Quoted from the text of Chief Sparrow's speech,
released by the Musqueam Indian Band to
the Canadian Broadcasting Corporation on 4
December 1997, a copy of which I received.

20 "Officials cancel chief's message to APEC leaders," *Vancouver Sun*, 26 November 1997, A15.

21 For example, the deployment of landscape
representations has been much analyzed in relationship to the early twentieth-century painting
of Canada's Group of Seven; see, for instance,
Robert Linsley, "Landscapes in Motion: Lawren
Harris, Emily Carr and the Heterogeneous
Modern Nation," *Oxford Art Journal* 19 (1996):
80–95. On the use of the image of the totem

pole, see Ronald Hawker, *Tales of Ghosts: First
Nations Art in British Columbia, 1922–1961*
(Vancouver: University of British Columbia
Press, 2003); and Aldona Jonaitis and Aaron
Glass, *The Totem Pole: An Intercultural
History* (Seattle: University of Washington
Press, 2010). See also Daniel Francis, *National
Dreams: Myth, Memory, and Canadian History*
(Vancouver: Arsenal Pulp Press, 1997); and
Eva Mackey, *The House of Difference: Cultural
Politics and National Identity in Canada*
(Toronto: University of Toronto Press, 2002),
34–6.

22 This is a paraphrase of the beginning of the
speech, which was audible to myself and the
nine other museum staff members allowed to be
present in the Great Hall during the morning
press conference in order to ensure the security
of the collections.

23 Two prominent examples were the major
museum exhibitions *Indigena* and *Land, Spirit,
Power*, shown respectively at the Canadian
Museum of Civilization and the National
Gallery of Canada in 1992 (see chapter 8).

24 See Richard Ericson and Aaron Doyle,
"Globalization and the Policing of Protest: The
Case of APEC 1997," *British Journal of Sociology*
50 (1999): 587–606.

25 Richard Ericson, "The Policing of Signs," paper
presented to the "Protest, the Public Sphere, and
Public Order" conference, Geneva, Switzerland,
1998.

26 A notable precedent for the willing commodification of visual signifiers of national identity
was the RCMP's sale to the Disney Corporation
in the 1980s of the rights to the use of its image
outside Canada.

27 Appadurai, *Modernity at Large*, 39.

28 MoA Archives, Letter of 29 January 1998
from Alicia Westergard-Thorpe, Media
group, "Democracy Street," to Jennifer Webb,
Programme Coordinator and Assistant to
Director, Museum of Anthropology.

29 Scott Lash and John Urry, *Economies of Signs
and Space* (London: Sage, 1994), 3.

Introduction to Part Two

1 *Chocolate, the Exhibition,* developed by the
Field Museum of Chicago, opened in 2002 and
toured widely. *Pearls*, also a touring exhibition,

was organized by the American Museum of Natural History with the Field Museum and opened in New York in 2001. One of the most recent such exhibitions is *Water,* developed by the American Museum of Natural History and shown at the Royal Ontario Museum in 2011 with added Canadian content.

2 Shelly Errington, *The Death of Authentic Primitive Art and Other Tales of Progress* (Berkeley: University of California Press, 1998).

3 Joseph Alsop, *The Rare Art Traditions: The History of Art Collecting and Its Linked Phenomena Wherever These Have Appeared* (New York: Harper and Row, 1982).

4 Ruth B. Phillips, *Trading Identities: The Souvenir in Native North American Art from the Northeast, 1700–1900* (Montreal and Seattle: McGill-Queen's University Press and University of Washington Press, 1998).

5 Johannes Fabian, *Time and the Other: How Anthropology Makes Its Object* (New York: Columbia University Press, 1983).

6 On the Western construction of the relationship between "selves" and "objects," see Susan Stewart, *On Longing: Narratives of the Miniature, the Gigantic, the Souvenir, the Collection* (Baltimore: Johns Hopkins University Press, 1984); and James Clifford, "Objects and Selves – An Afterword," in George Stocking Jr, ed., *Objects and Others: Essays on Museums and Material Culture* (Madison: University of Wisconsin Press, 1985), 236–46.

Chapter Four

1 This chapter was first written for the meeting of the International Committee on Museum Ethnography at Quebec City in September 1992; it was then revised for publication in the *Cambridge Review* 114, no. 2320 (February 1993): 6–10.

2 Aldona Jonaitis, "Franz Boas, John Swanton, and the New Haida Sculpture at the American Museum of Natural History, in Janet Berlo, ed., *The Early Years of Native American Art History* (Seattle: University of Washington Press, 1992), 22–61.

3 See Spencer R. Crew and James E. Sims, "Locating Authenticity: Fragments of a Dialogue," in Ivan Karp and Stephen D. Lavine, eds, *Exhibiting Cultures: The Poetics and*

Politics of Museum Display (Washington, DC: Smithsonian Institution Press, 1991), 159–75.

4 The three institutions are the Canadian Museum of Civilization, the Royal Ontario Museum, and the McCord Museum of Canadian History. They have major holdings of historic material from the Woodlands, the area with which I am most familiar and therefore most able to assess in terms of the questions examined in this chapter. I am grateful to Brian Kwapil of the Public Museum of Grand Rapids and to Robert Klymasz, Stephen Inglis, Andrea Laforet, Moira McCaffrey, and Trudy Nicks for their help in my research.

5 Public Museum of Grand Rapids, accession numbers 117056–87. Quoted phrases are from the original accession list.

6 The careful preservation of three pairs of the Reverend Bingham's spectacles by his family is itself evidence of the intense Victorian appreciation of spectacles and other related technologies of seeing, brought for the first time within the reach of ordinary people; see Asa Briggs, *Victorian Things* (London: B.T. Batsford, 1988).

7 These new installations were created for the new Van Andel Museum Center, opened in 1994, which replaced the universal-survey ethnology display that had been installed the museum's former exhibition building. In contrast to the earlier comprehensive culture-area exhibits, the 1994 exhibition *Anishinabek: The People of This Place*, represents only tribes of western Michigan. It focuses on the strategies of resistance and survival that Michigan Anishinabek adopted after refusing to leave their homelands and move to the Indian territories established by the federal government in Kansas and Oklahoma, in accordance with the Indian Removal Act of 1830.

8 James Clifford, "On Collecting Art and Culture," in Clifford, *The Predicament of Culture: Twentieth-Century Ethnography, Literature, and Art* (Cambridge, Mass.: Harvard University Press, 1988), 215–51.

9 Barbara Kirschenblatt-Gimblett, "Objects of Ethnography," in Karp and Lavine eds, *Exhibiting Cultures*, 387.

10 Ames frequently used this phrase in our conversations about his decision to add the Koerner collection of European ceramics to the UBC Museum of Anthropology's permanent

exhibits. See also his essay "Are Museums of Anthropology Really Necessary Any More?" in Ames, *Cannibal Tours and Glass Boxes: The Anthropology of Museums* (Vancouver: UBC Press, 1992), 98–110.

11 Eilean Hooper-Greenhill, *Museums and the Shaping of Knowledge* (London: Routledge, 1992).

12 This lobbying effort resulted in a major exhibition in the National Gallery of Canada, *Land, Spirit, Power: First Nations at the National Gallery*, which opened in September 1992, as well as in the acquisition of contemporary Indian art for the permanent collection (see chapter 8).

Chapter Five

1 This chapter was first written for delivery at a meeting of the Association of Art Museum Directors in Raleigh, North Carolina, in June 1992; it was then revised for publication in *Museum Anthropology* 18, no. 1 (1994): 39–46. It is reprinted here with minor changes.

2 For a recent examination of this question in relation to museum displays, see Arthur Danto, "Artifact and Art," in Susan Vogel, ed., *Art/artifact: African Art in Anthropology Collections* (New York: The Centre for African Art, 1988), 18–32.

3 See chapter 2 for references on the MOMA "*Primitivism*" show and *Into the Heart of Africa* and for a discussion of *The Spirit Sings*. For *Circa 1492*, see Simon Schama, "They All Laughed at Christopher Columbus," *New Republic*, 6 October 1992; and Homi Bhabha, "Double Visions," *Artforum* 30, no. 5 (January 1992): 85–9.

4 I have discussed the relationship between the "new" art history and the study of Native North American art in more detail in "What Is 'Huron Art'? Native American Art and the New Art History," *Canadian Journal of Native Studies* 9, no. 2 (1989): 161–86.

5 John Tagg, *Grounds of Dispute: Art History, Cultural Politics and the Discursive Field* (Minneapolis: University of Minnesota Press, 1992), 8.

6 Virginia Dominguez, "Invoking Culture: The Messy Side of 'Cultural Politics,'" *South Atlantic Quarterly* 9, no. 11 (1992): 19–20.

7 Ibid., 24–5.

8 My supervisors, Guy Atkins and John Golding, were also present. More than my arguments, it was their breadth of vision and support that guided the project through the academic shoals.

9 A small number of African artists were also beginning to engage with Western modernism at this time, largely in formal art school programs set up by former colonial regimes, but the movement was not widespread and was virtually non-existent in Sierra Leone.

10 Recognition from the world of high art only began to come on a large scale around 1990, with such shows as the Centre Pompidou's *Magiciens de la Terre* in 1989 and the Center for African Art's *Africa Explores* in 1991.

11 Michael Baxandall, *Painting and Experience in Fifteenth-Century Italy* (Oxford: Oxford University Press, 1972); and Svetlana Alpers, *The Art of Describing: Dutch Art in the Seventeenth Century* (Chicago: University of Chicago Press, 1983).

12 Baxandall, *Painting and Experience*.

13 Alpers, *The Art of Describing*, xv.

14 Donald Preziosi, *Rethinking Art History: Meditations on a Coy Science* (New Haven, Conn.: Yale University Press, 1989), 36.

15 Historical writing, also responding to a loss of faith in the scientific paradigm of knowledge, has been influenced by Geertzian anthropology, as manifested in a parallel trend toward micro-history and the "revival of narrative." See Lawrence Stone, "The Revival of Narrative: Reflections on a New Old History," *Past and Present* 85 no. 1 (1979): 3–24.

16 George E. Marcus and Michael M.J. Fischer, *Anthropology as Cultural Critique: An Experimental Moment in the Human Sciences* (Chicago: University of Chicago Press, 1986), 24.

17 See Svetlana Alpers, "The Museum as a Way of Seeing," in Ivan Karp and Steven D. Lavine, eds, *Exhibiting Cultures: The Poetics and Politics of Museum Display* (Washington, DC: Smithsonian University Press, 1991), 25–32. Material culture studies initially occupied a central place within anthropology. This area began to become marginalized in the 1920s, when field anthropologists shifted their primary concern to kinship studies and other aspects of social organization, although material culture studies have remained an important area within

anthropological archaeology. Recently, with the work of scholars such as Appadurai, Thomas, and Stocking, a renewed interest in objects has grown. See Curtis M. Hinsley Jr, *Savages and Scientists: The Smithsonian Institution and the Development of American Anthropology, 1846–1910* (Washington, DC: Smithsonian Institution Press, 1981); Arjun Appaduarai, ed., *The Social Life of Things: Commodities in Cultural Perspective* (Cambridge: Cambridge University Press, 1988); Nicholas Thomas, *Entangled Objects: Exchange, Material Culture, and Colonialism in the Pacific* (Cambridge, Mass.: Harvard University Press, 1991); and George W. Stocking Jr, *Objects and Others: Essays on Museums and Material Culture* (Madison: University of Wisconsin Press, 1985). In art history, in contrast, the object continued to be central, and only recently has a strong theoretical interest manifested itself within the discipline.

18 See Richard Wollheim, "Giovanni Morelli and the Origins of Scientific Connoisseurship," in Wollheim, *On Art and Mind* (London: Lane, 1973), and "Carlo Ginzburg, Morelli, Freud, and Sherlock Holmes: Clues and the Scientific Method," *History Workshop* 9 (1980): 5–36.

19 I have discussed this issue further in my essay "'Catching Symbolism': Studying Style and Meaning in Native American Art in the 1990s," *Arctic Anthropology* 28, no. 1 (1991): 92–100.

20 As Preziosi writes, "Objects of surveillance are understandable through removal from their social and historical contexts. Such a fragmentation and bracketing necessarily gives priority to the formal, morphological, and surface characteristics of the observed objects." See his *Rethinking Art History*, 36.

21 For a discussion of Boas's concept of culture, see George W. Stocking Jr, *Race, Culture, and Evolution: Essays in the History of Anthropology* (Chicago: University of Chicago Press, 1982), 195–233. For discussions of Riegl, see Robert Goldwater, *Primitivism in Modern Art*, rev. ed. (New York: Vintage, 1967), 26–7; and Michael Ann Holly, *Panofsky and the Foundations of Art History* (Ithaca, NY: Cornell University Press, 1984), 74.

22 One outstanding example of the introduction of multivocality and interdisciplinarity to a major museum of natural history is the exhibition of Franz Boas's Kwakiutl collec-

tions, *Chiefly Feasts: The Enduring Kwakiutl Potlatch*, organized in 1991 by Aldona Jonaitis and co-curated by Gloria Cranmer Webster (a Kwakwaka'wakw museum professional) for the American Museum of Natural History. For further discussion of the problematics of such exhibitions, see Janet Catherine Berlo and Ruth B. Phillips, "'Vitalizing the Things of the Past': Museum Representations of Native North American Art in the 1990s," *Museum Anthropology* 16, no. 1 (1992): 29–43; and Aldona Jonaitis, "Chiefly Feasts: The Creation of an Exhibition," in Jonaitis, ed., *Chiefly Feasts: The Enduring Kwakiutl Potlatch* (Seattle: University of Washington Press, 1991), 21–71.

23 I use the term "tribal" here and below with the reservations articulated by James Clifford in *The Predicament of Culture: Twentieth Century Ethnography, Literature and Art* (Cambridge, Mass.: Harvard University Press, 1988), 191n1: "A catchall, the concept of tribe has its source in Western projection and administrative necessity rather than in any essential quality or group of traits. The category thus denoted is the product of historically limited Western taxonomies." My use of the term in this chapter, like Clifford's, "reflects common usage while suggesting ways in which the concept is systematically distorting." For more general discussions of primitivism and "primitive" art, see Richard L. Anderson, *Art in Primitive Societies* (Englewood Cliffs, NJ: Prentice Hall, 1979); Rashid Araeen, "From Primitivism to Ethnic Arts," in Susan Hiller, ed., *The Myth of Primitivism: Perspectives on Art* (New York: Routledge, 1991), and the other essays in that volume; Sally Price, *Primitive Art in Civilized Places* (Chicago: University of Chicago Press, 1989); and Mariana Torgovnik, *Gone Primitive: Savage Intellects, Modern Lives* (Chicago: University of Chicago Press, 1990).

24 See Johannes Fabian, *Time and the Other: How Anthropology Makes Its Object* (New York: Columbia University Press, 1983).

25 In this sense, the celebration of the essential purity of unique and fixed tribal styles is directly analogous to the celebration of great artist-innovators in the scheme of Western art. "For both the Palladian villa and the Benin bronze," writes Preziosi, "the same lines of disciplinary power and knowledge converge in the quest for

authorship and homogeneous Selfhood." See his *Rethinking Art History*, 33.

26 Robert Redfield, "Art and Icon," in Robert Goldwater, ed., *Aspects of Primitive Art* (New York: Museum of Primitive Art, 1959), 18.

27 Robert Goldwater was one of the most notable of this small band of art historians. His books on the arts of the Western Sudan illustrate the total reliance on anthropological documentation in art-historical writing on African art during that period. The books also display the inadequacy and lifelessness of textual representations produced by art historians working exclusively from secondary sources and without direct experience in the field. See Goldwater, *Sculptures from Three African Tribes: Senufo, Baga and Dogon* (New York: Museum of Primitive Art, 1959), and *Bambara Sculpture from the Western Sudan* (New York: Museum of Primitive Art, 1960).

28 Barbara Braun, "Surrealists and the 'Primitive' Art Market in 1940s New York," paper presented to the College Art Association, Houston, Texas, 1988.

29 Robert Goldwater, "Judgments of Primitive Art, 1905–1965," in Daniel Biebuyck, ed., *Tradition and Creativity in Tribal Art* (Berkeley: University of California Press, 1969), 24–41; and William Rubin, ed., *Primitivism in 20th-Century Art: Affinities of the Tribal and the Modern* (New York: Museum of Modern Art, 1984). See also my essays "Moccasins into Slippers: Traditions and Transformations in Nineteenth-Century Woodlands Indian Textiles," *Northeast Indian Quarterly* 7, no. 4 (1989): 26–36, and "Glimpses of Eden: Iconographic Themes in Huron Pictorial Tourist Art," *European Review of Native American Studies* 5, no. 2 (1991): 19–28.

30 I include in the category of anthropology the work of art historians who began to do fieldwork in Africa and other parts of the world in the 1960s. The history of the relationship among their studies, curatorial projects, and the development of contemporary American art has yet to be written. It would be interesting, for example, to trace the influence of such events as *African Art in Motion*, the exhibition organized in 1974 by art historian Robert Farris Thompson at the National Gallery of Art, on anthropological representations.

31 Hans Belting, *The End of the History of Art?* trans. Christopher S. Wood (Chicago: University of Chicago Press, 1987), 3–5.

32 See my essay "Why Not Tourist Art? Significant Silences in Native American Museum Representation," in Gyan Prakash, ed., *After Colonialism: Imperialism and the Colonial Aftermath* (Princeton: Princeton University Press, 1994), 98–125.

33 James Clifford, "Traveling Cultures," in Lawrence Grossberg, Cary Nelson, and Paula Treichler, eds, *Cultural Studies* (New York: Routledge, 1992), 96–116.

34 This research was conducted in January 1992 by Trudy Nicks of the Royal Ontario Museum and myself in connection with the interdisciplinary project in which we were engaged: to document and analyze the production of art by Indigenous people in northeastern North America for sale to non-Natives. The project was funded by a Senior Research Fellowship from the J. Paul Getty Trust and by a Research Grant from the Social Sciences and Humanities Research Council of Canada.

35 Franz Boas, *Primitive Art* (reprint of 1st ed., New York: Dover Publications, 1955), 9.

36 Evan Maurer, "Determining Quality in Native American Art," in Edwin L. Wade, ed., *The Arts of the North American Indian: Native Traditions in Evolution* (New York: Hudson Hills Press, 1986), 142–55.

Chapter Six

1 William N. Fenton, "Museum and Field Studies of Iroquois Masks and Ritualism," *Explorations and Fieldwork of the Smithsonian Institution in 1940* (Washington, DC, 1941), 100.

2 Quoted in "Slow but Steady Progress Reported in Return of Artifacts to Indians," *Indian Trader*, November 1995. George was referring to an Onkwehonwe request to the New York State Museum for the return of masks. The quotation begins: "A concern the Museum has is that since these items are so great historically, what assurances can we offer that they'd be preserved? And our response is that …"

3 See T.J. Ferguson and B. Martza, "The Repatriation of Zuni *Ahayu:da*," *Museum Anthropology* 14, no. 2 (1990): 7–15; W.L. Merrill, E.J. Ladd, and T.J. Ferguson, "The Return of

the *Ahayu:da*: Lessons for Repatriation from Zuni Pueblo and the Smithsonian Institution," *Current Anthropology* 34, no. 5 (1993): 523–67; George H.J. Abrams, "The Case for Wampum: Repatriation from the Museum of the American Indian to the Six Nations Confederacy, Brantford, Ontario, Canada," in Flora E.S. Kaplan, ed., *Museums and the Making of "Ourselves": The Role of Objects in National Identity* (London: Leicester University Press, 1994); Zena Pearlstone, *Katsina: Commodified and Appropriated Images of Hopi Supernaturals* (Los Angeles: Fowler Museum of Cultural History, 2002); and Catherine Bell et al., "First Nations Cultural Heritage: A Selected Survey of Issues and Initiatives," in Catherine Bell and Val Napoleon, eds, *First Nations, Cultural Heritage and Law: Cases Studies, Voices, Perspectives* (Vancouver: UBC Press, 2008), 367–415.

4   The names for these masked beings differ in the languages of the six modern Onkwehonwe nations. I use the Seneca name as given by Fenton.

5   For recent discussions of the methods and goals of visual studies and visual anthropology, see W.J.T. Mitchell, "Showing Seeing: A Critique of Visual Culture," *Journal of Visual Culture* 1, no. 2 (2002): 166–7; Nicholas Mirzoeff, " Introduction," in *An Introduction to Visual Culture* (New York: Routledge, 1998); and Marcus Banks and Howard Morphy, "Introduction: Rethinking Visual Anthropology," in Banks and Morphy, eds, *Rethinking Visual Anthropology* (New Haven, Conn.: Yale University Press, 1997). For model studies of museum and popular "seeing," see Annie Coombes, *Reinventing Africa: Museums, Material Culture and Popular Imagination*, (New Haven, Conn.: Yale University Press, 1994); and Mirzoeff, *An Introduction to Visual Culture*, chapter 4.

6   See, among others, Tim Barringer and Tom Flynn, eds, *Colonialism and the Object: Empire, Material Culture and the Museum* (New York: Routledge, 1998); Coombes, *Reinventing Africa*; Thomas Richards, *The Imperial Archive: Knowledge and the Fantasy of Empire* (London: Verso, 1993); James Clifford, *The Predicament of Culture: Twentieth-Century Ethnography, Literature and Art* (Cambridge, Mass.: Harvard University Press, 1988), and *Routes: Travel and Translation*, (Cambridge, Mass.: Harvard

University Press, 1997); and Nicholas Thomas, *Entangled Objects: Exchange, Material Culture, and Colonialism in the Pacific* (Cambridge, Mass.: Harvard University Press, 1991), and *Possessions: Indigenous Art/Colonial Culture* (London: Thames and Hudson, 1999).

7   See Brian W. Dippie, *The Vanishing American: White Attitudes and U.S. Indian Policy* (Middletown, Conn.: Wesleyan University Press, 1982).

8   See George W. Stocking Jr, ed., *Objects and Others: Essays on Museums and Material Culture* (Madison: University of Wisconsin Press, 1985); James Clifford, "On Collecting Art and Culture," in Clifford, *The Predicament of Culture*; Sally Price, *Primitive Art in Civilized Places* (Chicago: University of Chicago Press, 1989); Shelly Errington, *The Death of Authentic Primitive Art and Other Tales of Progress* (Berkeley: University of California Press, 1998); Susan Hiller, ed., *The Myth of Primitivism: Perspectives on Art* (New York: Routledge, 1991); and Shepard Krech III and Barbara A. Hail, eds, *Collecting Native America, 1870–1960* (Washington, DC: Smithsonian Institution Press, 1999).

9   See my "Why Not Tourist Art: Significant Silences in Native American Museum Representations," in Gyan Prakash, ed., *After Colonialism: Imperial Histories and Postcolonial Displacements* (Princeton: Princeton University Press, 1995), 98–127; Johannes Fabian, *Time and the Other: How Anthropology Makes Its Object* (New York: Columbia University Press, 1983); and Errington, *The Death of Authentic Primitive Art*. See also Robert Young, *Colonial Desire: Hybridity in Theory, Culture, and Race* (London: Routledge, 1995).

10 For an overview of these developments, see Laura Peers and Alison K. Brown, eds, *Museums and Source Communities: A Routledge Reader* (New York: Routledge, 2003).

11 The Smithsonian's plans to change this exhibit were halted by budget cuts during the early 1990s. The museum closed the 1950s North America hall in 2004, although modifications to it had been made previously in response to requests from Native Americans.

12 Christian F. Feest, "From North America," in William Rubin, ed., *"Primitivism" in 20th Century Art: Affinity of the Tribal and the*

Modern (New York: Museum of Modern Art, 1985); and W. Jackson Rushing III, *Native American Art and the New York Avant-Garde: A History of Cultural Primitivism* (Austin: University of Texas Press, 1995).

13 William Fenton tabulated the major museum holdings of carved and husk face masks he examined as numbering 1,509. See his *The False Faces of the Iroquois* (Norman: University of Oklahoma Press, 1987), 20–1.

14 I derive the number of masks from Fenton's comprehensive table "Museums Visited and Mask Collections Seen and Studied" (ibid.). The immense projects of ethnological collecting that began in the mid-nineteenth century tailed off rather abruptly around 1930, and Fenton's "sample" was exhaustive. On the museum collecting of the period, see William Sturtevant, "Does Anthropology Need Museums?" *Proceedings of the Biological Society of Washington* 82 (1969): 619–50. Sally Weaver estimates that between the 1860s and the 1960s Longhouse membership in the largest community, the Six Nations Reserve in Ontario, was roughly 23 per cent of a population that fluctuated between 3,000 and 4,500 in the period 1860 to 1930. See her "Six Nations of the Grand River," in *Handbook of the North American Indian*, vol. 15, *The Northeast*, ed. Bruce Trigger (Washington, DC: Smithsonian Institution Press, 1978), 527, 530. I add to this figure the same percentage of the roughly 10,000 Onkwehonwe living on other reserves (ibid., St Lawrence Lowlands Region, 466–546).

15 See Douglas Cole, *Captured Heritage: The Scramble for Northwest Coast Artifacts* (Seattle: University of Washington Press, 1985); Janet Catherine Berlo, ed., *The Early Years of Native American Art History* (Seattle: University of Washington Press, 1991); Diana Fane, Ira Jacknis, and Lisa M. Breen, *Objects of Myth and Memory: American Indian Art at the Brooklyn Museum* (Seattle: University of Washington Press, 1991); and Krech and Hail, *Collecting Native America, 1870–1960*.

16 "Report on the Fabrics, Inventions, Implements and Utensils of the Iroquois, Made to the Regents of the University, January 22, 1851," Assembly Document no. 122, *New York State Cabinet of Antiquities Annual Report* 5 (1852): 66–117.

17 *Ga:goh:sah* translates as "face," as it does in all the other Onkwehonwe languages except for Onondaga, which uses a form of the name Hadui. The scholarly studies are tabulated and enumerated by Fenton in *The False Faces of the Iroquois*, 87–9.

18 Frederick W. Hodge, ed., *Handbook of American Indians North of Mexico* (Washington, DC: Government Printing office, 1907), 2: 490. The entry is signed with the initials of the director of the Bureau of American Ethnology, W.H. Holmes.

19 The *ga:goh:sah* appear on three different kinds of occasions: the semi-annual Traveling Rites, the Midwinter Festival, and private ceremonies (Fenton, *The False Faces of the Iroquois*, 267).

20 The strategy used by Onkwehonwe carvers recalls Robert Thompson's discussion of the Yoruba anti-aesthetic as an inversion of ideal standards of beauty, or a "sanctioned expression of artistic ugliness," adopted for highly specific expressive purposes. See Thompson, "Aesthetics in Tropical Africa," in Carol F. Jopling, ed., *Art and Aesthetics in Primitive Societies: A Critical Anthology* (New York: Dutton, 1971). As Fenton further explains, however, the relationship between the forms of a mask and the being it represents through time is not fixed. Older Common Faces can eventually come to represent Hadui, a phenomenon that almost exactly parallels the changing identities of masks among the Liberian Dan documented by Eberhardt Fisher in "Dan Forest Spirits: Masks in Dan Villages," *African Arts* 10, no. 2 (1978): 22–7.

21 For a compilation of these early descriptions, see Fenton, *The False Faces of the Iroquois*, 72–82.

22 For an important historical perspective on the application of the term "grotesque" to non-Western art, see Frances S. Connelly, *The Sleep of Reason: Primitivism in Modern European Art and Aesthetics, 1725–1907* (University Park: Pennsylvania State University Press, 1999).

23 Within cultural evolutionist discourse a distinction was made between carving and the higher form of sculpture. The less tool-like the carved object, the more sculptural it became. The 1907 *Handbook of the American Indians*, for example, noted a "strong sculptural tendency" in "the stone pipes, ornaments, and images of

the mound-builders of the Mississippi valley, the carvings of the pile-dwellers of Florida, the masks, utensils, and totem poles of the N. W. coast tribes, and the spirited ivory carvings of the Eskimo. Sculpture, the fine art, is but a higher phase of these elementary manifestations of the esthetic." See W.H. Holmes, "Art," in *Handbook of American Indians*, 1: 95.

24 Fenton has written that his first articles on the masks in the late 1930s and early 1940s "reached a wide audience outside of ethnology and promptly went out of print … Masks evidently hold an especial fascination for a wide range of people in the creative arts, whereas shamanism has implications for medicine and professions concerned with the human psyche" (*The False Faces of the Iroquois*, 13–14).

25 The False Faces, furthermore, are represented by multiple examples in contrast to other types of objects which appear as unique pieces. The books surveyed included Oliver LaFarge et al., *Introduction to American Indian Art* (Glorieta, NM: Rio Grande Press 1985; reprint [1931]); Frederic H. Douglas and Rene D'Harnoncourt, *Indian Art of the United States* (New York: Museum of Modern Art, 1941); Frederick J. Dockstadter, *Indian Art in America: The Arts and Crafts of the North American Indian* (New York: Promontory Press, n.d.); Wolfgang Haberland, *The Art of North America* (New York: Greystone Press, 1968); Ralph T. Coe, *Sacred Circles: Two Thousand Years of North American Indian Art* (London: Arts Council of Great Britain, 1976); Evan Maurer, *The Native American Heritage: A Survey of North American Indian Art* (Chicago: Art Institute of Chicago, 1976); Walker Art Gallery, *American Indian Art: Form and Tradition* (New York: E.P. Dutton, 1972); Richard Conn, *Native American Art in the Denver Art Museum* (Denver: Denver Art Museum, 1979); Norman Feder, *American Indian Art* (New York: Harrison House/Harry N. Abrams, 1982); Christian F. Feest, *Native Arts of North America* (New York: Oxford University Press, 1980); and Glenbow Museum, *The Spirit Sings: Artistic Traditions of Canada's First Peoples: A Catalogue of the Exhibition* (Toronto: McClelland and Stewart, 1987).

26 On the MoMA exhibit see W. Jackson Rushing III, "Marketing the Affinity of the Tribal and the Modern," in Berlo, *The Early Years of Native American Art History*; and on the Exposition of Indian Tribal Arts see Molly H. Mullins, "The Patronage of Difference: Making Indian Art 'Art, Not Ethnology,'" in George Marcus and Fred Myers, eds, *The Traffic in Culture: Refiguring Art and Anthropology* (Berkeley: University of California Press, 1995), 166–98.

27 LaFarge et al., *Introduction to American Indian Art*, 160–1. The MoMA catalogue is more restrained, noting that the False Faces were "exceptions" to the general simplicity of Onkwehonwe crafts, and it mentions in passing only their "twisted and exaggerated features and … profusion of wrinkles" (Douglas and D'Harnoncourt, *Indian Art of the United States*, 154, 157).

28 Dockstadter, *Indian Art in America*, caption accompanying plate 223. The book illustrates the collections of New York's old Museum of the American Indian, now the Smithsonian Institution's National Museum of the American Indian.

29 Coe, *Sacred Circles*, 85. When ethnologists contributed to art catalogues, as has often occurred, they sometimes contested a narrowly aesthetic presentation of the masks. In an important 1972 exhibition catalogue Robert Ritizenthaler was asked to contribute one essay on False Face masking alone and another of the same length to cover all the rest of "Woodland Indian Art." He ended the essay on the masks with the statement "When worn by actors performing their rites before an appreciative audience of members of their own society the masks then constitute an entity that vanishes when they are kept in a museum or simply regarded as art objects" (Walker Art Center, *American Indian Art*, 47).

30 Of another mask Conn wrote that its "lively sense of rhythm and design maximizes the emotional impact of this striking mask" (*Native American Art*, 48).

31 In the catalogue caption to the mask (which, as discussed below, was later removed from the show at the request of Mohawk representatives) I wrote that the False Faces "are portrayed in a plastic and expressionistic style quite unlike the restrained naturalism that marks effigy clubs and utensils. Sharp contrasts are set up between concave and convex forms, smooth surface and deeply grooved."

32 See Svetlana Alpers, "The Museum as a Way of Seeing," in Ivan Karp and Stephen D. Lavine, eds, *Exhibiting Cultures: The Poetics and Politics of Museum Display* (Washington, DC: Smithsonian Institution Press, 1991), 26.

33 James Clifford, "On Collecting Art and Culture," in Clifford, *The Predicament of Culture*. See also Berlo, *The Early Years of Native American Art History*; Janet Catherine Berlo and Ruth B. Phillips, "Our (Museum) World Turned Upside-Down: Re-presenting Native American Arts," *Art Bulletin* 77, no. 1 (1995): 6–10; Joan Vastokas, "Native Art as Art History: Meaning and Time from Unwritten Sources," *Journal of Canadian Studies* 21, no. 4 (1986): 7–36; Ruth B. Phillips, "Art History and the Native-Made Object: New Discourses, Old Differences?" in Rushing, *Native American Art in the Twentieth Century*, 97–112.

34 M. Nourbese Philip, "Social Barbarism and the Spoils of Modernism," in Philip, *Frontiers: Selected Essays and Writings on Racism and Culture, 1984–1992* (Stratford, Ont.: Mercury Press, 1992), 96.

35 Fenton, *The False Faces of the Iroquois*, 454. Photographs in the collection of the Woodland Cultural Centre at Brantford, Ontario, show False Face masks displayed for sale at the craft shop run by the Jamieson sisters on the Six Nations Reserve.

36 Both photos are reproduced in Ruth B. Phillips, "Performing the Native Woman: Primitivism and Mimicry in Early Twentieth-Century Visual Culture," in Lynda Jessup, ed., *Policing the Boundaries of Modernity* (Toronto: University of Toronto Press, 2001), 26–49.

37 The letter, written by Kanatiio (Allen Gabriel), appeared in the *Ottawa Citizen*, 20 April 1996, H6.

38 *Globe and Mail*, 17 April 1996, A8.

39 See Tony Bennett, *The Birth of the Museum: History, Theory, Politics* (New York: Routledge, 1995); Carol Duncan, *Civilizing Rituals: Inside Public Art Museums* (New York: Routledge, 1995); Eilean Hooper-Greenhill, *Museums and the Shaping of Knowledge* (New York: Routledge, 1992); and Aldona Jonaitis, *From the Land of the Totem Poles* (Seattle: University of Washington Press, 1988).

40 I am greatly indebted to Dr Trudy Nicks of the Royal Ontario Museum, who has generously shared her long-term research into popular visual culture representations of Indians and who has brought many of the examples cited in this essay to my attention.

41 The hotel was located at Times Square between 44th and 45th streets. Designed by Clinton and Russell, it opened in 1904.

42 *Hotel Astor Indian Hall* (souvenir booklet designed and executed by A. Malcolm, 164 Fifth Avenue, New York; unsigned, undated, and unpaginated), [3].

43 Ibid., [15].

44 The credits name Charles Turbyfill, Dr Blossom, and Professor Coffin specifically.

45 Lillian Davids Fazzini, *Indians of America* (Racine, Wisc.: Whitman Publishing, 1935), 2.

46 Ibid., 7.

47 *Native Asset – Native Design* (Montreal: Canadian Pulp and Paper Association, 1956).

48 Barbeau and other ethnologists working for the National Museum of Canada engaged in similar projects aimed at promoting industrial applications of Canadian Native art and encouraging prominent Canadian artists to adopt Native themes in their work. See Harlan I. Smith, *An Album of Prehistoric Canadian Art* (Ottawa: F.A. Acland, 1923); and Sandra Dyck, "'These Things Are Our Totems': Marius Barbeau and the Indigenization of Canadian Art and Culture in the 1920s" (MA thesis, School for Studies in Art and Culture: Art History, Carleton University, 1995).

49 See Idées Paris, *Art Deco Jewelry Designs in Full Color* (New York: Dover, 1993), plate 24.

50 Private collection, Toronto.

51 Jean Baudrillard, "The System of Collecting," trans. Roger Cardinal, in John Elsner and Roger Cardinal, eds, *The Cultures of Collecting* (Cambridge, Mass.: Harvard University Press, 1994).

52 *National Geographic* 101, no. 3 (1952).

53 Catherine A. Lutz and Jane L. Collins, *Reading "National Geographic"* (Chicago: University of Chicago Press, 1993).

54 See Anthony F.C. Wallace, *The Death and Rebirth of the Seneca* (New York: Random House, 1969).

55 Fenton, *The False Faces of the Iroquois*, 186.

56 Canadian Museum of Civilization, Canadian Ethnology Service, file E7-6R, Memo from Michael K. Foster to Dr Barrie Reynolds, Chief

Ethnologist, Canadian Ethnology Service, 10 March 1975. I am grateful to Judy Hall for her help in reconstructing this history.

57 Ibid., Memo from Sandra Gibb, Senior Exhibits Coordinator, 9 April 1980. The masks were removed on 14 April. The exhibition was taken down ten years later when the museum moved to its new building.

58 These are Onondaga, Tuscarora, Tonawanda (Seneca), and Akwesasne (Mohawk). According to Fenton, a letter articulating this policy was first sent to museums known to have False Face masks by the Grand Council in March 1981. I cite a statement sent to me by Peter Jemison in 1996.

59 This text is now online at http://www.peace4turtleisland.org/pages/maskpolicy.htm; accessed 9 April 2011.

60 The specific arrangements made by different museums vary, depending on their discussions with different Onkwehonwe consultants. At the McCord Museum of Canadian History in Montreal, Onkwehonwe representatives recommended that the masks be stored facing the wall. At the George Gustav Heye Centre of the National Museum of the American Indian in New York a special room with restricted access has been set aside for them.

61 Akwesasne Mohawk elder Ernest Benedict responded to a question on this subject by noting that the Grand Council had discussed the matter and was divided (personal communication, October 1994).

62 UBC Museum of Anthropology, Museum files, Letter of 8 February 1995 from Tom Hill to Michael Ames, Director.

63 "Spirits Speaking Through: Canadian Woodland Artists," *Spectrum Series*, Canadian Broadcasting Corporation.

64 Bruce G. Trigger, review of *The False Faces of the Iroquois*, by William N. Fenton, *Canadian Historical Review* 69 (June 1988): 256–7.

65 Joel Montour, review of *The False Faces of the Iroquois,* by William N. Fenton, *Northeast Indian Quarterly* 6, no. 4 (Winter 1989): 60–1.

66 Ibid.

67 "Questions of Tradition: An Interdisciplinary Symposium," organized by Mark Phillips and Gordon Schochet, took place from 13 to 16 November 1997 in New Brunswick, New Jersey, and was sponsored by the *Journal of the History*

of Ideas and the International Society for Intellectual History.

68 Surveys of the history of art, furthermore, are the products of such processes of surveillance.

69 Clifford, "On Collecting Art and Culture," 215–51.

70 Personal communication, Carleton University, c. 1995.

71 For Mirzoeff, for example, "a history of visual culture would highlight those moments where the visual is contested, debated and transformed as a constantly challenging place of social interaction and definition in terms of class, gender, sexual and racialized identities" (*An Introduction to Visual Culture*, 4).

72 See Mieke Bal, "A Postcard from the Edge," in Bal, *Double Exposures: The Subject of Cultural Analysis* (New York, Routledge, 1997), 195–224.

73 Rita Reif, "A Law, a Legacy, and Indian Art," *New York Times*, 6 November 1995, 39.

74 I am grateful to Diana Loren of the Peabody Museum of Anthropology and Ethnology for providing me with the information presented here (personal communication, Cambridge, Mass., 26 April 2010).

Chapter Seven

1 *Report of the Royal Commission on Aboriginal Peoples* (Ottawa, 1996), vol. 3, *Gathering Strength*, chapter 6, "Arts and Heritage." Available at http://www.collectionscanada.gc.ca/webarchives/20071211060616/http://www.ainc-inac.gc.ca/ch/rcap/sg/si56_e.html#1.2%20Sacred%20and%20Secular%20Artifacts; accessed 27 January 2010.

2 "Introduction," in Elazar Barkan and Ronald Bush, eds, *Claiming the Stones, Naming the Bones: Cultural Property and the Negotiation of National and Ethnic Identity* (Los Angeles: Getty Research Institute, 2002), 15.

3 "Preface," in S. Douglass S. Huyghue, *The Nomades of the West; or, Ellen Clayton* (London: Richard Bentley, 1850), 1: v–vi.

4 Today's Museum Victoria unites within one institution a number of museums devoted to natural history, industry, science, and technology. In Australia, as elsewhere, ethnographic materials were usually preserved as adjuncts of natural history, geological, or industrial collections until the late nineteenth century, when

anthropology was established as a separate academic discipline. The Huyghue collection was first accessioned into the Art Collection Register on 22 December 1879 (email from Dr Lindy Allen, Museum Victoria, 2 March 2010). For a recent history of the museum, see Carolyn Rasmussen, ed., *A Museum for the People: A History of Museum Victoria and Its Predecessor Institutions, 1854–2000* (Melbourne: Scribe Publications and Museum Victoria, 2001).

5   In its 1996 recommendations on repatriation, for example, the *Report of the Royal Commission on Aboriginal Peoples* in Canada states, "Legislation also played a role: laws were enacted to suppress religious practices, such as the potlatch ceremony of west coast nations, and items with spiritual import were often confiscated" (vol. 3, *Gathering Strength*, chapter 6: "Arts and Heritage," http://www.collectionscanada.gc.ca/webarchives/20071211060616/ http://www.ainc-inac.gc.ca/ch/rcap/sg/ si56_e.html#1.2%20Sacred%20and%20Secular %20Artifacts; accessed 27 January 2010).

6   An early example is Jeanette Greenfield's *The Return of Cultural Treasures* (Cambridge: Cambridge University Press, 1996); and the concept has been further elaborated in recent works such as Ana Filipa Vrdoljak, *International Law, Museums and the Return of Cultural Objects* (Cambridge: Cambridge University Press, 2008), which has particular reference to Australia; and, in relation to Canada, Catherine Bell and Robert K. Patterson, eds, *Protection of First Nations Cultural Heritage: Laws, Policy, and Reform* (Seattle: University of Washington Press, 2008).

7   The "Relational Museum Project" was directed by Chris Gosden and Mike O'Hanlon and is discussed in Chris Gosden and Frances Larson, *Knowing Things: Exploring the Collections at the Pitt Rivers Museum, 1884–1945* (Oxford: Oxford University Press, 2008).

8   The revised Australian document, issued by the successor organization, Museums Australia, is entitled "Continuous Cultures, Ongoing Responsibilities." For a critique of the Australian policy and its development, see Vrdoljak, *International Law*, 282–6. On NAGPRA see, for example, Peter Welsh, "Repatriation and Cultural Preservation: Potent

Objects, Potent Pasts," *University of Michigan Journal of Law and Reform* 25 (1992): 837–65; and C. Timothy McKeown, "Implementing a 'True Compromise': The Native American Graves Protection and Repatriation Act after Ten Years," in Cressida Fforde, Jane Hubert, and Paul Turnbull, eds, *The Dead and Their Possessions: Repatriation in Principle, Policy and Practice* (New York: Routledge, 2002), 108–32.

9   Excerpts from Task Force on Museums and First Peoples, *Turning the Page: Forging New Partnerships between Museums and First Peoples* (Ottawa, 1992) are annexed to the *Report of the Royal Commission on Aboriginal Peoples* at http://caid.ca/RRCAP3.6.A.pdf; accessed 27 January 2010. For *Previous Possessions, New Obligations* (Museums Australia, 2000), see http://www.history.sa.gov.au/history/about_us/ collections_policy/Appendix1cJuly05.pdf; accessed 27 January 2010. The Native American Graves Protection and Repatriation Act, Public Law 101-601, is reprinted in Tamara L. Bray, ed., *The Future of the Past: Archaeologists, Native Americans, and Repatriation* (New York: Garland, 2001), 233–44.

10 Bray, *The Future of the Past;* Laforet, "Narratives of the Treaty Table: Cultural Property and the Negotiation of Tradition," in Mark Salber Phillips and Gordon Schochet, eds, *Questions of Tradition* (Toronto: University of Toronto Press, 2004), 33–55.

11 For examples of local lobbying campaigns, see, for example, Gloria Cranmer Webster, "The U'mista Cultural Centre," *Massachusetts Review* 31, no. 1/2 (Spring/Summer 1990): 132–43; Richard W. Hill Sr, "Regenerating Identity: Repatriation and the Indian Frame of Mind," in Bray, *The Future of the Past*, 127–38; See also *Protecting Knowledge: Traditional Resource Rights in the New Millennium* (Union of British Columbia Indian Chiefs, desktop publication produced for the conference of the same title held at the University of British Columbia, 23–26 February 2000).

12 For arguments that advance repatriation based on comprehensive human rights arguments, see Vrdoljak, *International Law*; Catherine Bell and Robert Paterson, "Aboriginal Rights to Cultural Property in Canada," *International Journal of Cultural Property* 8, no. 1 (1999): 167–211; and Catherine Bell and Robert Paterson, "Aboriginal

Rights to Repatriation of Cultural Property," in Ardith Walkem and Halle Bruce, eds, *Box of Treasures or Empty Box*: *Twenty Years of Section 35* (Penticton, BC: Theytus Books, 2003), 104–54.

13 Michael Fisher and Margaret Bruchac write of NAGPRA, "It encourages museums to part with Native collections but also gives them great latitude to assign tribal affiliations to these materials. It sometimes fosters conflict among Native peoples by forcing recognized and un-recognized tribes to advance competing claims to ancestral remains. It puts in public view sensitive information about religious practices that many Native Americans feel should not circulate beyond the boundaries of their com-munities. It encourages the misplaced belief that all elements of culture, including intan-gible ones, can be returned to their original source." From Fisher and Bruchac, "NAGPRA from the Middle Distance: Legal Puzzles and Unintended Consequences," in John Henry Merryman, ed., *Imperialism, Restitution and the Law* (Cambridge: Cambridge University Press, 2006), 193–217.

14 Ann M. Tweedie, *Drawing Back Culture: The Makah Struggle for Repatriation* (Seattle: University of Washington Press, 2002), 119.

15 Ibid., 99–100.

16 Thomas's example is the 1999 discovery of a frozen and preserved human body in northern British Columbia, Kwäday Dän Ts'ínchi, or "long-ago person found." See "Finders Keepers and Deep American History: Some Lessons in Dispute Resolution," in Merryman, ed., *Imperialism, Restitution and the Law*, 218–53.

17 See Judy Thompson and Ingrid Kritsch, *Yeenoo Dài' K'ètr'ijilkai' Ganagwaandaii: Long Ago Sewing We Will Remember – The Story of the Gwich'in Traditional Caribou Skin Clothing Project*, Mercury Series Ethnology Paper 143 (Gatineau, Que.: Canadian Museum of Civilization, 2005); and Ingrid Kritsch and Karen Wright-Fraser, "The Gwich'in Traditional Caribou Skin Clothing Project: Repatriating Traditional Knowledge and Skills," *Arctic* 55, no. 2 (2002): 205–11.

18 See also Ruth B. Phillips and Elizabeth Lominska Johnson, "Exorcising the 'Ghosts of History': Canadian Museums, First Nations and the Negotiation of Repatriation," in John Torpey, ed., *Politics and the Past: On Repairing*

Historical Injustices (Boulder, Colo.: Rowan and Littlefield, 2003), 149–68.

19 Karen Wright Fraser, "My People Did This: The Re-Making of a Gwich'in Garment," in Judy Thompson, Judy Hall, and Leslie Tepper, in collaboration with Dorothy K. Burnham, *Fascinating Challenges: Studying Material Culture with Dorothy Burnham* (Hull, Que.: Canadian Museum of Civilization, 2001), 99–106.

20 On the Gwich'in project see Thompson and Kritsch, *Yeenoo Dài' K'ètr'ijilkai'*. On Dorothy Burnham's work at the CMC on Aboriginal textile and clothing traditions, see Thompson et al., *Fascinating Challenges*.

21 The canoe is unusually large and came into the collection of the James Mitchell Museum at the National University of Ireland in 1852, donated by the family of its collector, a military officer named Captain Stepney St. George. Although the precise conditions of acquisi-tion are not known, painted decorations on the canoe suggest it may have been made for a former British lieutenant governor of New Brunswick. Some contemporary Maliseet greeted it as a returning ancestor, in accord-ance with traditional beliefs that canoes, like other items, can be "other-than-human" per-sons and embody spirits. See "Maliseet Canoe Back in Canada," *Windspeaker*, 1 August 2007; http://www.accessmylibrary.com/coms2/summary_0286-34378889_ITM, accessed 27 January 2010; and Shawn Berry, "Canoe to Stay in Canada: University in Ireland to Return Birchbark Canoe," *Daily Gleaner* (Fredericton, NB), 3 June 2009.

22 The case involved a collection of items from Pauingassi, Manitoba, many of which were sacred items related to Fair Wind, which were deposited in the museum in 1970 to preserve them from harm. See Office of the Auditor General of Manitoba, "Investigation of Missing Artifacts at the Anthropology Museum of the University of Winnipeg," June 2002, http://www.oag.mb.ca/reports/UofMANTH_JUN02.pdf; accessed 27 January 2010; and Jennifer H.S. Brown's discussion of the history of the collection and the intentions of Fair Wind's descendant, Charlie George Owen, that they remain in the museum in "retirement": "Doing Aboriginal History: A View from

Winnipeg." *Canadian Historical Review* 84, no. 4 (December 2003): 613–35. See also the comprehensive analysis of this case in Maureen Anne Matthews, "Repatriating Agency: Animacy, Personhood and Agency in the Repatriation of Ojibwe Artifacts" (PhD thesis, Institute of Social and Cultural Anthropology, University of Oxford, 2009).

23 The following account of Huyghue's life is based on Gwendolyn Davies's biography in the *Dictionary of Canadian Biography,* vol. 12 (http://www.biographi.ca/009004-119.01-e.php?&id_nbr=6178&interval=25&&PHPSESSID=6cnbvlhuncf6mehrsat4ve9807; accessed 27 January 2010), and her introduction to the reprint of Huyghue's first novel, *Argimou: A Legend of the Micmac*, by "Eugene" (Sackville, NB: R.P. Bell Library, Mount Allison University, 1977), i–x.

24 *Argimou* was published in instalments in a short-lived Saint John, New Brunswick, monthly literary periodical entitled *Amaranth* between January 1841 and December 1843 under the pseudonym "Eugene." It was republished as a novel in 1847 by the *Halifax Morning Courier.* The passages in this chapter are quoted from the 1977 reprint of *Argimou,* ed. Gwendolyn Davies. *The Nomades of the West; or, Ellen Clayton*, 3 vols. (London: Richard Bentley, 1850) was published under the name of S. Douglass S. Huyghue. A historical novel set in the late seventeenth century, it narrates the travels of two young white orphans and their Abenaki, Mohawk, and French-Canadian companions, whose adventures take them across the North American continent to a lost utopian community of refugees from the Aztec empire found deep in the Rocky Mountains.

25 Huyghue, *Argimou*, 2–3.

26 Ibid., 4.

27 Ibid., 2.

28 Information cited from Nova Scotia Museum, Mi'kmaq Portraits Collection, http://museum.gov.ns.ca/mikmaq, records MP0148 and MP0149. These are some of the earliest identified portraits of individual Mi'kmaq people.

29 L.F.S. Upton, *Micmacs and Colonists: Indian-White Relations in the Maritimes, 1713–1867* (Vancouver: University of British Columbia Press, 1979), 137.

30 Between the 1820s and 1850s, Aboriginal peoples of the Maritimes regularly presented chiefs' outfits to those white men made honorary chiefs. Lieutenant Governor Sir Howard Douglas, for example, was given an outfit in Fredericton in the 1820s whose whereabouts are not now known. Other coats, leggings, hats, and moccasins exist, but are not currently associated as outfits (personal communication from Stephen Augustine, Ottawa, October 2007).

31 On the Mi'kmaq and Maliseet iconographic and design traditions, see Ruth Holmes Whitehead, "I Have Lived Here Since the World Began: Atlantic Coast Artistic Traditions," in *The Spirit Sings: Artistic Traditions of Canada's First Peoples* (Toronto: McClelland and Stewart, 1987), 17–31. We lack precise information about the symbolism of these designs for Maritime peoples, but scholars have persuasively argued that for the neighbouring Innu, double curves have symbolic meanings related to the animals and plants on which hunting peoples depend. See Ted J. Brasser, *Bo'Jou Neejee! Profiles of Canadian Indian Art* (Ottawa: National Museum of Canada, 1976); Dorothy K. Burnham, *To Please the Caribou: Painted Caribou-Skin Coats Worn by the Naskapi, Montagnais, and Cree Hunters of the Quebec-Labrador Peninsula* (Toronto: Royal Ontario Museum, 1992); and Alika Podolinski Webber, "Ceremonial Robes of the Montagnais-Naskapi," *American Indian Art Magazine* 9, no. 1 (1993): 60–9.

32 Frank Speck, *Double-Curve Motive in Northeastern Algonkian Art*, Memoir 42, Anthropological Series (Ottawa: Geological Survey of Canada, 1914).

33 Frank Speck, *Penobscot Man: The Life History of a Forest Tribe in Maine* (Philadelphia: University of Pennsylvania Press, 1940).

34 Ruth Holmes Whitehead has extensively documented and analyzed museum collections of Mi'kmaq and Maliseet textiles. See, for example, "I Have Lived Here Since the World Began" and "The Maritimes," in exhibition catalogue volume *The Spirit Sings: Artistic Traditions of Canada's First Peoples, A Catalogue of the Exhibition* (Toronto: McClelland and Stewart, 1987).

35 Christina Morris was at one stage of her life married to another Mi'kmaq chief, Louis L.B.

Paul, who had an association with Perley; Stephen Augustine suggests a possible attribution of the Huyghue coat to her.

36 W.A. Spray, "Moses Henry Perley," *Dictionary of Canadian Biography*, vol. 11 (http://www.biographi.ca/009004-119.01-e.php &id_nbr=4652&&PHPSESSID=jq18ol3tho821 dcvmgv706ug43; accessed 27 January 2010).

37 Gwendolyn Davies, "Introduction," in Huyghue, *Argimou*, iii.

38 A Captain Rolland was also present at the 1841 ceremony in Miramichi, but it is not known whether he also received an outfit (Personal communication from Stephen Augustine, Ottawa, October 2007).

39 Huyghue, *Argimou*, 10.

40 Huyghue described this trip in "A Winter's Journey" in *Bentley's Miscellany* (1849): 630–8; and in "My First Winter in the Woods of Canada," *Bentley's Miscellany* 27 (1850): 152–60.

41 Museum Victoria Archives, Melbourne Museum, R.E. Johns papers XM 1495, S.D.S. Huyghue papers, "Some Account of Wampum." One copy is signed "Ballarat 1860" and the other "Hawthorne [now a suburb of Melbourne], in 1879," the year of Huyghue's retirement.

42 Ibid., [2].

43 See Mallery's "Picture Writing of the American Indians," in *Tenth Annual Report of the Bureau of Ethnology to the Secretary of the Smithsonian Institution, 1888–'89, by J. W. Powell, Director*, 2 vols. (Washington, DC: Government Printing Office, 1893; Dover Reprint, 1972), 1: 223–30.

44 Museum Victoria Archives, Johns papers, Huyghue, "Some Account of Wampum," [3].

45 Ibid.

46 See Moira G. Simpson, *Making Representations: Museums in the Postcolonial Era* (New York: Routledge, 1996), 216–18; George H.J. Abrams, "The Case for Wampum: Repatriation from the Museum of the American Indian to the Six Nations Confederacy, Brantford, Ontario, Canada," in Flora E.S. Kaplan, ed., *Museums and the Making of "Ourselves": The Role of Objects in National Identity* (Leicester: Leicester University Press, 2000); and Tom Hill with Paul Williams, *Council Fire: A Resource Guide* (Brantford, Ont.: Woodland Cultural Centre, 1989).

47 For a discussion of Huyghue's documentation of the Huron-Wendat wampums, see Jonathan C.

Lainey, *La "monnaie des Sauvages": les colliers de wampum d'hier à aujourd'hui* (Sillery, Que.: Septentrion, 2004), 108–12.

48 See Ruth B. Phillips, *Trading Identities: The Souvenir in Native North American Art of the Northeast, 1700–1900* (Seattle: University of Washington Press, 1998).

49 Huyghue, *Nomades of the West*, 1: 133.

50 Schoolcraft's *Historical and Statistical Information Respecting … the Indian Tribes of the United States* was published in six volumes between 1851 and 1857.

51 See Philip J. Deloria's discussion of Morgan in "Literary Indians and Ethnographic Objects," in Deloria, *Playing Indian* (New Haven, Conn.: Yale University Press, 1998), 71–94.

52 For example, the University of Pennsylvania Museum collection includes two birchbark baskets ornamented with porcupine quills that Schoolcraft presented to the family with whom his daughter boarded while attending school in Philadelphia, and Morgan collected a group of similar baskets while on a boat tour of the central Great Lakes circa 1860. See my article "Quilled Bark from the Central Great Lakes: A Transcultural Art History," in Christian F. Feest, ed., *Studies in American Indian Art: A Memorial Tribute to Norman Feder* (Altenstadt, Germany: European Review of Native American Studies, 2001), 118–31.

53 See Adam Kuper, *The Invention of the Primitive: Transformations of an Illusion* (New York: Routledge, 1988).

54 Ibid.

55 Tony Bennett, *The Birth of the Museum: History, Theory, Politics* (New York: Routledge, 1995), 59.

56 Museum Victoria Archives, Melbourne Museum, R.E. Johns papers XM 1498, S.D.S. Huyghue papers.

57 The coat was exhibited in 2006 in *Threading the Commonwealth: Textile Tradition, Culture, Trade and Politics* and published in the catalogue of the same title, edited by Suzanne Davies et al. (Melbourne: RMIT Gallery, 2006), 21.

58 Kwame Anthony Appiah, *Cosmopolitanism: Ethics in a World of Strangers* (New York: W.W. Norton, 2006), xii.

59 Ibid., 129.

60 World History Association, Mission Statement, http://www.thewha.org/history_mission.php; accessed 27 January 2010.

61 James Elkins, "Introduction," in *Is Art History Global?* (New York: Routledge, 2007), 22.

62 Charles Taylor, "The Politics of Recognition," in Amy Gutman, ed., *Multiculturalism and the Politics of Recognition* (Princeton: Princeton University Press, 1994), 25–74.

63 Chika Okeke-Agulu, "Art History and Globalization," in Elkins, *Is Art History Global?* 202–7.

64 The chief's coat from the Huyghue collection was reproduced in colour in the main exhibition publication (see Whitehead, "I Have Lived Here Since the World Began," 44) as well as in the catalogue volume. For the latter, see *The Spirit Sings: Artistic Traditions of Canada's First Peoples: A Catalogue of the Exhibition*, 21, E42 and E43.

65 Other Mi'kmaq people have also viewed the outfit while in Australia, including Viviane Gray, who is a member of the Restigouche Mi'kmaq, one of the communities that conferred chief's status on Moses Perley in the 1840s.

66 Glooscap Heritage Centre, Mission Statement, http://www.glooscapheritagecentre.com/index.php; accessed 27 January 2010.

67 Ibid.

68 The statement regarding the repatriation of non-Australian materials in this label is somewhat misleading, as Museum Victoria considers requests from overseas and Australian claimants on the same basis (email from Dr Lindy Allen, 2 March 2010).

69 Colonial Office archives 217/179, ff. 406–8, Louis-Benjamin Peminuit Paul to Queen Victoria, received by the Colonial Office, London, 25 January 1841; reprinted in Ruth Holmes Whitehead, *The Old Man Told Us: Excerpts from Micmac History, 1500–1950* (Halifax, NS: Nimbus Publishing, 1991), 218–19. See Upton, *Micmacs and Colonists*, 188–92, for photographs.

70 For the text of Canada's Statement of Apology to Former Students of Indian Residential Schools, as well as related statements, see http://www.ainc-inac.gc.ca/ai/rqpi/apo/index-eng.asp; accessed 27 January 2010.

71 For example, in *Report of the Royal Commission on Aboriginal Peoples*, vol. 3, *Gathering Strength*, chapter 3, "Health and Healing," a number of those who presented briefs to the commission made the connection explicit: "These speakers and many others articulated a vision of health care in which each person is considered as a whole, with health and social problems that cannot be cured in isolation from one another, and with resources for achieving health that come not just from expert services but also from the understanding and strength of family, community, culture and spiritual beliefs." Available at http://www.collectionscanada.gc.ca/webarchives/20071207000748/http://www.ainc-inac.gc.ca/ch/rcap/sg/si21_e.html#2.1%20Aboriginal%20Perspectives%20on%20Health%20and%20Healing; accessed January 2010.

72 John Henry Merryman, "Introduction," in Merryman, ed., *Imperialism, Art and Restitution* (Cambridge: Cambridge University Press, 2006), 3.

73 For example, see two of the essays in Merryman's *Imperialism, Art and Restitution*: in "View from the Universal Museum," James Cuno defends the idea of the universal museum by invoking "our common artistic patrimony" (19) with no reflexivity about who "we" are in modern postcolonial, multicultural, and globalizing societies; in "The Beautiful One Has Come – To Stay" Stephen K. Urice contends that Berlin's Egyptian Museum has the legal right to retain the famous bust of Nefertiti because it was legally exported in the early twentieth century under "Egyptian law," without acknowledging that Egyptian law was, at the time, controlled by a British colonial regime (143).

Introduction to Part Three

1 Louis Althusser, "Ideology and Ideological State Apparatuses (Notes towards an Investigation)," in Althusser, *Lenin and Philosophy, and Other Essays* (New York: Monthly Review Press, 1971), 166.

2 See, for example, Eva Mackey, *The House of Difference: Cultural Politics and National Identity in Canada* (London: Routledge 1999); and Daina Augaitis et al., *Questions of Community: Artists, Audiences, Coalitions* (Banff, Alta: Banff Centre Press, 1995).

3 Robyn Gillam, "The Spirit Sings: A Sour Note in the Museum's Halls," in Gillam, *Hall of Mirrors:*

Museums and the Canadian Public (Banff, Alta: Banff Centre Press, 2001), 132. This essay, it should be noted, contains many factual errors regarding not only the genesis of the task force report but also *The Spirit Sings* exhibition that gave rise to it.

4 Althusser, "Ideology and Ideological State Apparatuses," 147.

5 Eilean Hooper-Greenhill, *Museums and the Interpretation of Visual Culture* (New York: Routledge, 2000), 162.

6 I discuss the notion of rehearsal in more detail in "Re-placing Objects: Historical Practices for the Second Museum Age," *Canadian Historical Review* 86, no. 1 (March 2005): 84–110.

7 Carol Mayer, "University Museums: Distinct Sites of Intersection for Diverse Communities," *Museologia* (Museu de Ciência da Universidade de Lisboa), no. 3 (2003): 106.

8 On *The Spirit of Islam* see Mayer, "University Museums," 101–6; and Jill Baird, "Local Options – Towards a Postcolonial Museum," in Rita L. Irwin, Kit Grauer, and Michael J. Emme, eds, *Revisions: Readings in Canadian Art Teacher Education*, 3rd ed. (Boucherville, Que.: Canadian Society for Education through Art, 2007), 121–37.

9 Personal communication from John Halani, community co-chair of the advisory committee, Vancouver, 2007. See also *The Spirit of Islam* website: http://www.moa.ubc.ca/spiritofislam/.

10 Mayer, "University Museums," 103.

11 The curatorial team was not only intercultural but also interdisciplinary. Co-ordinating curators Moira McCaffrey and Sandra Olsen were trained in archaeology and art history respectively. Kanatakta (Kahnawake Mohawk) is a historian, Kate Koperski a folklore specialist, Trudy Nicks an anthropologist, Ruth Phillips an art historian, and Jolene Rickard (Tuscarora) an artist and art historian.

12 The organizing institution was Montreal's McCord Museum of Canadian History working with the Castellani Museum of Niagara University in Buffalo, New York. The McCord partnered with the Kanien'kehaka Raotitiohkwa Cultural Centre at Kahnawake, and the Castellani worked closely with members of the Tuscarora Community. The exhibition was shown between 1999 and 2003 at the McCord (18 June 1999 to 9 January 2000), the Castellani (2 July to 19 November 2000), the Canadian Museum of Civilization (8 June to 4 November 2001), the National Museum of the American Indian (9 December 2001 to 19 May 2002), the Royal Ontario Museum (21 June to 14 October 2002), and the Mashuntucket Pequot Museum (16 November 2002 to 16 February 2003). See Morgan Perkins, "Continuity and Creativity in Iroquois Beadwork," *American Anthropologist* 106, no. 3 (Sept. 2004): 595–9.

13 Duncan F. Cameron, "The Museum, a *Temple* or the *Forum*," *Curator* 14, no. 1 (1971): 11–24.

14 Paul Basu and Sharon Macdonald, "Introduction," in *Exhibition Experiments* (Oxford: Blackwell, 2007), 11.

15 Ibid., 17.

Chapter Eight

1 *Indigena: Contemporary Native Perspectives on Five Hundred Years* was shown at the Canadian Museum of Civilization in Gatineau, Quebec, from 16 April to 12 October 1992; it then travelled to the Winnipeg Art Gallery; the Dalhousie Art Gallery, Halifax; the Windsor Art Gallery; the Heard Museum, Phoenix; and the Glenbow Museum, Calgary. See Gerald McMaster and Lee-Ann Martin, eds, *Indigena: Contemporary Native Perspectives* (Vancouver: Douglas and McIntyre, 1992).

2 *Land, Spirit, Power: First Nations at the National Gallery of Canada* was shown from 22 September to 22 November 1992 at the National Gallery of Canada in Ottawa. It was displayed at the MacKenzie Art Gallery in Regina from 27 August to 8 November 1993; the Contemporary Arts Museum in Houston, Texas, from 4 June to 7 August 1994; and the Nickle Arts Museum, Calgary, from 24 September to 27 November 1994. See Diana Nemiroff, Charlotte Townsend-Gault, and Robert Houle, *Land, Spirit, Power: First Nations at the National Gallery of Canada* (Ottawa: National Gallery of Canada, 1992).

Chapter Nine

1 See Lena Williams, "Black Memorabilia: The Pride and the Pain," *New York Times*, 8 December 1988, C1.

2 On *Into the Heart of Africa* see Shelley Ruth
   Butler, *Contested Representations: Revisiting
   "Into the Heart of Africa"* (Peterborough, Ont.:
   Broadview Press, 2007); Jeanne Canizzo, "Ex-
   hibiting Cultures: 'Into the Heart of Africa,'"
   Visual Anthropology Review 7, no. 10 (1991):
   150–60; Linda Hutcheon, "The Post Always
   Rings Twice: The Postmodern and the Postcol-
   onial," *Textual Practice* 8, no. 2 (Summer 1994):
   205–38; Henrietta Riegel, "Into the Heart of
   Irony: Ethnographic Exhibitions and the Pol-
   itics of Difference," in Sharon Macdonald and
   Gordon Fyfe, eds, *Theorizing Museums* (Oxford:
   Blackwell, 1996), 83–104; Enid Schildkraut,
   "Ambiguous Messages and Ironic Twists: 'Into
   the Heart of Africa' and 'The Other Museum,'"
   Museum Anthropology 15, no. 2 (1991): 16–23;
   and M. Nourbese Philip, "Social Barbarism and
   the Spoils of Modernism," "Museum Could
   Have Avoided Culture Clash," and "Letter:
   January, 1990/NOW," in Philip, *Frontiers: Essays
   and Writings on Racism and Culture, 1984–1992*
   (Stratford, Ont.: Mercury Press 1992), 93–109.

3 See Schildkraut, "Ambiguous Messages
   and Ironic Twists"; and Linda Hutcheon,
   Irony's Edge: The Theory and Politics of Irony
   (Routledge: New York, 1994), 198–9.

4 Norman Bryson, *Vision and Painting: The Logic
   of the Gaze* (New Haven, Conn.: Yale University
   Press, 1983), 141.

5 Ibid., 142.

6 The related exhibition publications are Jeanne
   Canizzo, *Into the Heart of Africa* (Toronto:
   Royal Ontario Museum, 1989); Lisa G. Corrin,
   *Mining the Museum: An Installation by
   Fred Wilson* (Baltimore: The Contemporary
   Museum; and New York: New Press, 1994);
   and *Art/artifact: African Art in Anthropology
   Collections* (New York: Center for African Art,
   1988).

7 *Fluffs and Feathers* was originally mounted
   in 1988 by Tom Hill and Deborah Doxtator at
   the Woodland Cultural Centre Museum. It
   was then remounted in partnership with the
   Royal Ontario Museum, shown at the ROM
   in 1992, and between 1993 and 1995 toured to
   the McCord Museum of Canadian History,
   the Canadian Museum of Civilization, the
   Manitoba Museum of Man and Nature, Quebec
   City's Musée de la Civilisation, the New York
   State Museum, and the Glenbow Museum. The
   accompanying book, originally published by the
   Woodland Cultural Centre in 1988, was reissued
   in conjunction with the touring exhibition.
   See Deborah Doxtator, *Fluffs and Feathers: An
   Exhibit on the Symbols of Indianness, A Resource
   Guide* [rev. ed.] (Brantford, Ont.: Woodland
   Cultural Centre; and Toronto: Royal Ontario
   Museum, 1992). See also Riegl, "Into the Heart
   of Irony," 94–9; and Deborah Doxtator, "The
   Rebirth of a Native Exhibit inside a White
   Institution: *Fluffs and Feathers* Goes to the
   ROM" (paper presented at the Canadian
   Anthropological Society annual conference,
   Toronto, May 1993).

8 *Savage Graces* was first shown at the UBC
   Museum of Anthropology in 1992. It toured
   to the Ottawa Art Gallery, the Winnipeg
   Art Gallery, the Edmonton Art Gallery,
   the Memorial University Art Gallery,
   Saskachewan's Wanuskewin Heritage Park, the
   Southern Alberta Art Gallery, and the Windsor
   Art Gallery. See the special issue of *Harbour:
   Magazine of Art and Everyday Life* devoted
   to *Savage Graces*: 3, no. 1 (Winter 1994); and
   Crystal Parsons, "Museum, Gallery and Other
   Institutions in Contemporary Canadian First
   Nations Art" (MA thesis, Carleton University,
   School for Studies in Art and Culture, 2006).

9 Mieke Bal, "The Politics of Citation," *diacritics*
   21, no. 1 (Spring 1991): 21.

10 Personal communication, Ottawa, 1994.

11 Bryson, *Vision and Painting*, 107.

12 Svetlana Alpers, "The Museum as a Way of
   Seeing," in Ivan Karp and Steven D. Lavine,
   eds, *Exhibiting Cultures: The Poetics and
   Politics of Museum Display* (Washington, DC:
   Smithsonian Institution Press, 1991), 25–32.

13 Bal, "The Politics of Citation," 26.

14 Ibid.

15 See Lawrence Weschler, *Mr. Wilson's Cabinet of
   Wonder* (New York: Pantheon, 1995).

Chapter Ten

1 Personal communication from Leslie Tepper,
   the exhibit curator, 1995.

Chapter Eleven

1 Paolo Freire, *Pedagogy of Freedom: Ethics,
   Democracy, and Civic Courage*, trans. Patrick
   Clarke (New York: Rowman and Littlefield,
   1998), 42.

2 Eilean Hooper-Greenhill, *Museums and the Interpretation of Visual Culture* (New York: Routledge, 2002), 162.

3 This chapter was originally published as the introduction to Section 3 of a collection edited by Laura Peers and Alison K. Brown: *Museums and Source Communities: A Routledge Reader* (New York: Routledge, 2003), 155–71. The case studies by Michael Ames ("How to Decorate a House: The Renegotiation of Cultural Representations at the University of British Columbia Museum of Anthropology"), Anthony Shelton ("Curating *African Worlds*"), Anita Herle ("Objects, Agency and Museums: Continuing Dialogues between the Torres Strait and Cambridge"), Stephanie Moser et al. ("Transforming Archaeology through Practice: Strategies for Collaborative Archaeology and the Community Archaeology Project"), and Gerald Conaty ("Glenbow's Blackfoot Gallery: Working towards Co-existence") are to be found in that volume, and page references given here are taken from that publication. I am grateful to Michael Ames, Sarah Casteel, Mark Phillips, and Judy Thompson for their helpful readings of preliminary drafts of this chapter.

4 Key studies of museum exhibits and their socio-political functions include Carol Duncan, "Art Museums and the Ritual of Citizenship," in Ivan Karp and Steven D. Lavine, eds, *Exhibiting Cultures: The Politics and Poetics of Museum Display* (Washington, DC: Smithsonian Institution Press, 1991), 88–103; Tony Bennett, *The Birth of the Museum: History, Theory, Politics* (London: Routledge, 1995); Donna J. Harroway, "Teddy Bear Patriarchy: Taxidermy in the Garden of Eden, New York City, 1908–36," in Amy Kaplan and Donald Pease, eds, *Cultures of United States Imperialism* (Durham, NC: Duke University Press, 1994), 237–91; and Shelly Ruth Butler, *Contested Representations: Revisiting "Into the Heart of Africa"* (London: Gordon and Breach, 1999). For studies of museum practices as also inscribing Western values and on the development of new paradigms, see Miriam Clavir, *Preserving What Is Valued: Museums, First Nations, and Conservation* (Vancouver: University of British Columbia Press, 2001); and Nancy Rosoff, "Integrating Native Views into Museum Procedures: Hope and Practice at the National Museum of the American Indian," in Peers and

Brown, *Museums and Source Communities*, 72–80.

5 See Herbert Gans, *Popular Culture and High Culture: An Analysis and Evaluation of Taste* (New York: Basic Books, 1974); and Howard Becker, *Art Worlds* (Berkeley: University of California Press, 1982).

6 Pierre Bourdieu, "The Field of Cultural Production," trans. Richard Nice, in Bourdieu, *The Field of Cultural Production: Essays on Literature and Art* (New York: Columbia University Press, 1993), 37.

7 *Kaxlaya Gvilas: The Ones Who Uphold the Laws of Our Ancestors* displayed the most important extant Heiltsuk collection made in the colonial period, assembled by medical missionary R.W. Large in the early twentieth century. The collection is now in the Royal Ontario Museum, which organized the exhibit. See Martha Black, *Bella Bella: A Season of Heiltsuk Art* (Toronto: Royal Ontario Museum, 1997). The exhibit's Vancouver showing was made possible by support from the Audain Foundation and the Department of Canadian Heritage.

8 About 50 per cent of Indigenous people in Canada now live in cities, and the Heiltsuk follow this pattern.

9 Carol Duncan's analysis of the art museum as a ritual space, in "Art Museums and the Ritual of Citizenship," applies equally to museums of anthropology and history.

10 This was the second time such efforts had been expended, since a large group of Heiltsuk had also made the even longer journey to Toronto for the opening of the exhibit at the Royal Ontario Museum two years earlier.

11 Victor Turner, "Introduction," in Turner, ed., *Celebration: Studies in Festivity and Ritual* (Washington, DC: Smithsonian Institution Press, 1982), 14.

12 This statement describes a general pattern. There have been early experiments in community collaboration outside North America. For example, see *The Living Arctic* at the Museum of Mankind in 1989, curated by J.C.H. King with Canadian First Nations partners; *Paradise: Portraying the New Guinea Highlands* in 1993, also at the Museum of Mankind, curated by Michael O'Hanlon with partners from New Guinea; and the reinstallation of North American exhibits curated by Peter Bolz at the Ethnographische Museum, Berlin. See also Jane

Pierson Jones, "The Colonial Legacy and the Community: The Gallery 33 Project," in Ivan Karp, Christine Mullen Kreamer, and Steven D. Lavine, eds, *Museums and Communities: The Politics of Public Culture* (Washington, DC: Smithsonian Institution Press, 1992), 221–41, for a description of a 1990 project at the Birmingham Museum and Art Gallery.

13 See note 3 to this chapter for details about these articles. I was fortunate to have been able to see all of these exhibitions and to have spoken with some of the collaborators. My remarks are therefore based not only on their essays but also on several discussions and interviews and on my own observations. I did not, however, know I would be writing about all of the exhibits when I saw them, and I therefore apologize to the authors for any unevenness in my text.

14 See chapter 2 for a discussion of the task force. On its recommendations see Trudy Nicks, "Partnerships in Developing Cultural Resources: Lessons From the Task Force on Museums and First Peoples," *Culture* 12, no. 1 (1992): 87–94.

15 Ames, "How to Decorate a House," 175.

16 Catherine E. Bell and Robert E. Patterson, "Aboriginal Rights to Cultural Property in Canada," *International Journal of Cultural Property* 8, no. 1 (1999): 167–211.

17 Shelton, "Curating *African Worlds*," 184.

18 Ibid., 192.

19 Moser et al., "Transforming Archaeology," 208.

20 Ames, "How to Decorate a House," 175.

21 Conaty, "Glenbow's Blackfoot Gallery," 231.

22 Michael Robinson, "Shampoo Archaeology: Towards a Participatory Action Research Approach in Civil Society," *Canadian Journal of Native Studies* 16, no. 1 (1996): 125–38, note 1.

23 Joan Ryan and Michael Robinson, "Community Participatory Research: Two Views from Arctic Institute Practitioners," *Practicing Anthropology* 18, no. 4 (1996): 7–11; quotation from 8.

24 Ames, "How to Decorate a House," 177.

25 Shelton, "Curating *African Worlds*," 188.

26 See Ruth B. Phillips, "The Public Relations W(rap): What We Can Learn from *The Spirit Sings*," *Inuit Art Quarterly* 5, no. 2 (1990): 13–21, and chapter 2 in this volume.

27 Hooper-Greenhill, *Museums and the Interpretation of Visual Culture*, 152–3.

28 Aldona Jonaitis, *Chiefly Feasts: The Enduring Kwakiutl Potlatch* (Seattle: University of Washington Press, 1992), 251.

29 James Clifford, *Routes: Travel and Translation in the Late Twentieth Century* (Cambridge, Mass.: Harvard University Press, 1997), 194.

30 Moser et al., "Transforming Archaeology," 225.

31 Ruth B. Phillips, "Where Is 'Africa'?: Re-Viewing Art and Artifact in the Age of Globalization and Diaspora," *American Anthropologist* 104, no. 3 (2002): 11–16.

32 Freire, *Pedagogy of Freedom*, 76–7.

33 See Robert Redfield, "Art and Icon," *Aspects of Primitive Art* (New York: Museum of Primitive Art, 1959); Phillips, "Where Is 'Africa'?"; and chapter 5 in this volume.

34 For example, Richard West Jr, the Native American director of the Smithsonian's National Museum of the American Indian (an institution administered by Indigenous people), said repeatedly in public speeches that, unlike the mid-twentieth-century installations of the same collection at the old Museum of the American Indian, those in the new museum built on the Mall in Washington, DC, would not be object-centred. (One such occasion was a lecture delivered at the symposium "Native Women and Art: Survival and Sovereignty," at the Cantor Arts Centre, Stanford University, 9 May 2002.)

35 Shelton, "Curating *African Worlds*," 187.

36 This response was recorded in comment cards filled out in the exhibition (personal communication from Kenneth Lister, assistant curator, Department of Anthropology, Royal Ontario Museum, 25 April 2002).

37 An exhibit is always a process of negotiation and "translation." Even without community involvement, exhibits are always negotiations among collaborators with different and at times conflicting practices. Disparate logics must be reconciled (for example, the desire to preserve an object intact versus the acceptance of the risk of alteration through display and handling), and information must be converted from textual and academic format into a narrativized and spatialized language of objects, colours, forms, light, movement, and sound. The late Audrey Hawthorn, founding curator of the UBC Museum of Anthropology, for example,

was fond of saying that an exhibition was 60 per cent curatorial content and 60 per cent design.

38 Conaty and other Glenbow staff are credited on another, smaller and less-prominent text panel. The Blackfoot members of the team, however, wanted the key Glenbow staff members' photos to be included in the large wall on the same basis as themselves and to be acknowledged as full members of the team (personal communication from Gerry Conaty, 11 May 2002).

39 Stephen Greenblatt, "Resonance and Wonder," in Ivan Karp and Steven D. Lavine, eds, *Exhibiting Cultures: The Poetics and Politics of Museum Representation* (Washington, DC: Smithsonian Institution Press, 1991), 42–56.

40 Robert Young, *Colonial Desire: Hybridity in Theory, Culture and Race* (London: Routledge, 1995), 23–4.

41 Simon During, "Postmodernism or Postcolonialism Today," in Bill Ashcroft, Gareth Griffiths, and Helen Tiffin, eds, *The Postcolonial Studies Reader* (New York: Routledge, 1995), 127. During uses the notion of the museum metaphorically to convey a concept of frozen reification in developing this argument: "From the side of the post-colonizer, a return to difference is projected, but, from the side of post-modernity, English (multinational capitalism's tongue) will museumify those pre-colonial languages which have attached themselves to print and the image so belatedly" (128).

42 Shelton, "Curating *African Worlds*," 188.

43 Hooper-Greenhill, *Museums and the Interpretation of Visual Culture,* 162.

44 Shelton, "Curating *African Worlds*," 192.

Chapter Twelve

1 This chapter is reprinted with minor changes from Amy Lonetree and Amanda J. Cobb, eds, *The National Museum of the American Indian: Critical Conversations* (Lincoln: University of Nebraska Press, 2008), 405–30. Reprinted by permission of the University of Nebraska Press. Copyright 2008 by the Board of Regents of the University of Nebraska. The chapter incorporates and expands upon two shorter discussions: "Disrupting Past Paradigms: The National Museum of the American Indian and the First Peoples Hall at the Canadian Museum of Civilization," in "Review Roundtable: The National Museum of the American Indian," *Public Historian* 28, no. 2 (2006): 75–80; and "Double Take: Contesting Time, Place, and Nation in the First Peoples Hall of the Canadian Museum of Civilization," co-authored with Mark Salber Phillips, *American Anthropologist* 107, no. 4 (December 2005): 694–704. A version of this chapter was also delivered as a lecture at the University of Illinois at Urbana-Champaign in October 2005.

2 On Cardinal's architecture, see Trevor Boddy, *The Architecture of Douglas Cardinal* (Edmonton: NeWest Press, 1989).

3 Douglas E. Evelyn. "The Smithsonian's National Museum of the American Indian: An International Institution of Living Cultures," *Public Historian* 28, no. 2 (2006): 53.

4 Signalled by the Smithsonian Institution Press's *Exhibiting Cultures: The Poetics and Politics of Museum Display,* edited by Ivan Karp and Steven D. Lavine (Washington, DC: Smithsonian Institution Press, 1991); and *Museums and Communities* (which features Cardinal's CMC building on its cover), edited by Ivan Karp, Christine Mullen Kreamer, and Steven D. Lavine (Washington, DC: Smithsonian Institution Press, 1992). See also Donald Preziosi and Claire Farrago, eds, *Grasping the World: The Idea of the Museum* (Aldershot, UK: Ashgate Press, 2004).

5 Johannes Fabian has termed this concept the "ethnographic present" in *Time and the Other: How Anthropology Makes Its Object* (New York: Columbia University Press, 1983). For an example of cultural evolutionist narrative in the Onkwehonwe displays of the Museum of the American Indian during the 1980s, see Ruth B. Phillips, *Trading Identities: The Souvenir in Native North American Art from the Northeast, 1700–1900* (Seattle: University of Washington Press, 1998), 50–2.

6 Tony Bennett, *Pasts beyond Memory: Evolution, Museums, Colonialism* (New York: Routledge, 2004).

7 On the controversy raised by *The Spirit Sings,* see chapter 2 in this volume and Julia Harrison, "Completing a Circle: *The Spirit Sings,*" in Noel Dyck and James B. Waldram, eds, *Anthropology, Public Policy, and Native*

Peoples in Canada (Montreal and Kingston: McGill-Queen's University Press, 1993). On the task force, see chapter 2 and Trudy Nicks, "Partnerships in Developing Cultural Resources: Lessons from the Task Force on Museums and First Peoples," *Culture* 12, no. 1 (1992): 87–94. For a comparison of initial impacts of NAGPRA and the task force report, see Michael M. Ames, "Are Changing Representations of First Peoples in Canadian Museums and Galleries Challenging the Curatorial Prerogative?" in *The Changing Presentation of the American Indian: Museums and Native Cultures* (Seattle: University of Washington Press, 2000), 73–88.

8　Aboriginal bands that never concluded treaties for the alienation of their land can negotiate for the return of cultural property held by federal and provincial institutions as part of the larger land-claims process.

9　The term "commemoration" is used advisedly; Indigenous protest against the original intention to celebrate the occasion changed the tone of anniversary-year events in many locations. See Pauline Turner Strong, "Exclusive Labels: Indexing the National 'We' in Commemorative and Oppositional Exhibitions," *Museum Anthropology* 21, no. 1 (1997): 42–56.

10　For a discussion of *Indigena* and *Land, Spirit, Power* see chapter 8.

11　See Jolene Rickard, "Cew Ete Haw I Tih: The Bird that Carried Language Back to Another," in Lucy R. Lippard, ed., *Partial Recall: Photographs of Native North Americans* (New York: The New Press, 1992), 105–11. Truman Lowe, one of the artists featured in *Land, Spirit, Power,* is another linking figure between these 1992 exhibits and the NMAI. As curator of Contemporary Art at the NMAI, he organized its opening temporary art exhibition, *Native Modernism: The Art of George Morrison and Alan Houser.*

12　The Human History Division of the National Museum of Canada was split off from the natural history divisions and renamed the National Museum of Man in 1968. It was again renamed in 1986, becoming the Canadian Museum of Civilization.

13　On the differences in power relations, see Michael M. Ames, "How to Decorate a House: The Renegotiation of Cultural Representations at the University of British Columbia Museum

of Anthropology," *Museum Anthropology* 22, no. 3 (1999): 41–51, discussed in chapter 11.

14　See Judith Ostrowitz, "Concourse and Periphery: Planning the National Museum of the American Indian," *Museum Anthropology* 25, no. 2 (2002): 21–37. The author participated in several of these vetting sessions.

15　The National Museum of African Art employs an art paradigm, in contrast to the artifact paradigm that was used in the National Museum of Natural History (NMNH)'s African exhibits at the time of its creation. Similarly, when the NMAI was created, the NMNH's North American collections resembled the modernist Museum of the American Indian and National Museum of Canada exhibits described earlier in this essay. Plans to redo the North American exhibits at the NMNH exhibits were in progress, but they were never funded and had to be cancelled. As a result, the NMAI is currently the only Smithsonian museum that has long-term displays of Native American materials. The African exhibits at the NMNH were reconceptualized using collaborative curatorial approaches that led to the *African Voices* exhibit, which opened in September 1999. See Mary Jo Arnoldi, Christine Mullen Kreamer, and Michael Atwood Mason, "Reflections on 'African Voices' at the Smithsonian's National Museum of Natural History," *African Arts* 34, no. 2 (2001): 16–35, 94; and Ruth B. Phillips, "Where Is 'Africa'? Re-Viewing Art and Artifact in the Age of Globalization," *American Anthropologist* 104, no. 3 (2002): 11–19.

16　Timothy Luke, *Museum Politics: Power Plays at the Exhibition* (Minneapolis: University of Minnesota Press, 2002).

17　Ibid., 226–7.

18　Alan Cairns, *Citizens Plus: Aboriginal Peoples and the Canadian State* (Vancouver and Toronto: UBC Press, 2000), 51–3; Sally Weaver *Making Canadian Indian Policy: The Hidden Agenda, 1968–1970* (Toronto: University of Toronto Press, 1980).

19　This process is administered by the Branch of Acknowledgment and Research in the Department of the Interior and the Bureau of Indian Affairs. It requires applicants or communities to prove continuous identification as American Indians from historical times, evidence of a governing system, political influence, and a list of tribal members whose status has never been formally terminated and who are not members of any other tribe. See http://www.bia.gov/idc/groups/public/documents/text/idc-001219.pdf. Accessed 4 July 2011.

20 For a summary of the Indian Arts and Crafts Act, see http://www.doi.gov/iacb/act.htm.

21 Between 2003 and about 2010 this mural was printed in monochromatic grey tones washed in pink and overprinted with the welcome message. The original version has since been replaced with a full colour rendering with the welcome message moved to the side, giving greater prominence to the image but less to the Kitigan Zibi elders' words.

22 I elaborate on the nature of multivocal versus community-curated collaborative exhibitions in chapter 11.

23 Paul Richard, "Shards of Many Untold Stories," *Washington Post*, 21 September 2004, C1.

24 Ibid., C2.

25 Edward Rothstein, "Museum with an American Indian Voice," *New York Times*, 21 September 2004, http://www.nytimes.com/2004/09/21/arts/design/21muse.html.

26 See note 32 to chapter 11. Richard West Jr, the Native American director of the Smithsonian's NMAI (an institution administered by Indigenous people), has said that, unlike the mid-twentieth-century installations of the same collection at the old Museum of the American Indian, those in the new museum would not be object-centred. One such occasion was a lecture delivered at the symposium "Native Women and Art: Survival and Sovereignty," Cantor Arts Centre, Stanford University, 9 May 2002.

27 "CMC Principles for Development of the First Peoples Hall," created in 1998, edited in 2002, copy provided to the author by Dr Andrea Laforet.

28 Steven Conn, "Heritage vs History at the National Museum of the American Indian," *Public Historian* 28, no. 2 (Spring 2006): 71.

29 Louis Althusser, "Ideology and Ideological State Apparatuses (Notes towards an Investigation)," in Althusser, *Lenin and Philosophy, and Other Essays* (New York: Monthly Review Press, 1971), 147.

30 Charles Taylor, *Multiculturalism and "the Politics of Recognition": An Essay*, ed. Amy Gutmann (Princeton: Princeton University Press, 1992).

31 Andrew Barry, quoted in Bennett, *Pasts beyond Memory*, 108.

Introduction to Part Four

1 William Sturtevant, "Does Anthropology Need Museums?" *Proceedings of the Biological Society of Washington* 82 (1969): 619–50. I have developed the notion that we are in a second, renewed age of museum development in my essay "Re-placing Objects: Historical Practices for the Second Museum Age," *Canadian Historical Review* 86, no. 1 (2005): 83–110.

2 James Clifford, "On Collecting Art and Culture," in Clifford, *The Predicament of Culture: Twentieth-Century Ethnography, Literature, and Art* (Cambridge, Mass.: Harvard University Press, 1988), 215–51.

3 Jeanne Inch, "Forward," in *Preserving Aboriginal Heritage: Technical and Traditional Approaches: Proceedings of Symposium 2007* (Ottawa: Canadian Conservation Institute, 2008), vii.

4 Gilbert W. Whiteduck, "Message from the Advisory Commitee," ibid., xv.

Chapter Thirteen

1 Versions of this chapter were delivered at the Universities Art Association of Canada conference in 2005 and at the National Portrait Gallery of London in 2007. I am grateful to Lilly Koltun and Johanna Mizgala for their helpful readings of the text.

2 At http://www.portraits.gc.ca/; accessed October 2005. Koltun's statement has since been removed from the website.

3 At http://www.tbs-sct.gc.ca/rma/dpr/03-04/pch/PCHd3401_e.asp; accessed 11 November 2009.

4 These arguments are advanced in new theorizations of cosmopolitanism. See, for example, Ulrich Beck, *The Cosmopolitan Vision* (Cambridge: Polity Press, 2006).

5 For different analyses of multiculturalism, see Richard J.F. Day, *Multiculturalism and the History of Canadian Diversity* (Toronto: University of Toronto Press, 2000), and Will Kymlicka, *Multicultural Citizenship* (Oxford: Clarendon Press, 1995).

6 Nathan Glazer, *Affirmative Discrimination: Ethnic Inequality and Public Policy* (New York: Basic Books, 1974).

7 Minister's Forum on Diversity and Culture, 22–23 April 2003. The performance was held on 13 April in the auditorium of the Canadian Museum of Civilization.

8 *Oxford English Dictionary* (online edition); accessed November 2009.

9 Ibid.

10 The more recent actions were, in part, responses to another landmark event of the 1990s, the issuing in 1996 of the report of the Royal Commission on Aboriginal Peoples.

11 Charles Taylor, "The Politics of Recognition," in Amy Gutman, ed., *Multiculturalism: Examining the Politics of Recognition* (Princeton: Princeton University Press, 1994), 25–74.

12 Ibid., 42. For responses to Taylor, see the other essays in Gutman, ed., *Multiculturalism*, and Day, *Multiculturalism and the History of Canadian Diversity*.

13 See Gilles Havard, *The Great Peace of Montreal of 1701: French-Native Diplomacy in the Seventeenth Century* (Montreal: McGill-Queen's University Press, 2001).

14 See Heidi Bohaker, *"Nindoodemag*: The Significance of Algonquian Kinship Networks in the Eastern Great Lakes Region, 1600–1701," *William and Mary Quarterly*, 3rd series, 63, no. 1 (January 2006): 23–52.

15 Tomson Highway, *Comparing Mythologies* (Ottawa: University of Ottawa Press, 2003), 44.

16 For an introduction to the portraits of the Four Indian Kings, see John G. Garratt with Bruce Robertson, *The Four Indian Kings* (Ottawa: Public Archives Canada, 1985); and Johanna Mizgala, "First Impressions, Lasting Consequences," http://www.portraits.gc.ca/009001-2101-e.html; accessed 11 November 2009.

17 Shearer West, *Portraiture* (New York: Oxford University Press, 2004), 11.

18 Svetlana Alpers, "The Museum as a Way of Seeing," in Ivan Karp and Steven D. Lavine, eds, *Exhibiting Cultures: The Poetics and Politics of Museum Display* (Washington, DC: Smithsonian Institution Press, 1991), 25–32.

19 Personal communication from Elizabeth Mackenzie, Rae, NWT, July 2005.

20 See Kristina Huneault, "Always There: First Peoples and the Consolation of Miniature Portraits in British North America," in Tim Barringer, Geoff Quilley, and Doug Fordham, eds, *Art and the British Empire* (Manchester: Manchester University Press, 2007).

21 In addition, a gallery entitled "Through Karsh's Lens," displaying a range of twentieth-century portraits, and additional focus galleries were planned as part of the long-term installations.

Chapter Fourteen

1 I capitalize Primitive Art in this chapter to refer to a specific discursive construct within modernism, rather than to characterize the objects to which it refers as "primitive." See Shelly Errington, *The Death of Authentic Primitive Art and Other Tales of Progress* (Berkeley: University of California Press, 1998), xxv–xxvii.

2 See Diana Nemiroff, "Modernism, Nationalism, and Beyond: A Critical Reading of Exhibitions of First Nations Art," in Diana Nemiroff, Charlotte Townsend Gault, and Robert Houle, eds, *Land, Spirit, Power: First Nations at the National Gallery of Canada* (Ottawa: National Gallery of Canada, 1992), 16–41; and Leslie Dawn, *National Visions, National Blindness: Canadian Art and Identities in the 1920s* (Vancouver: University of British Columbia Press, 2006).

3 National Gallery of Canada, *Exhibition of Canadian West Coast Art: Native and Modern*, (Ottawa: National Gallery of Canada, 1927), 2.

4 For a comprehensive listing of exhibitions at the NGC that included Aboriginal art, see Jessica Hines, "Art of This Land and the Exhibition of Aboriginal Art at the National Gallery" (MA thesis, School for Studies in Art and Culture: Art History, Carleton University, 2006).

5 The Department of Northern Affairs wanted to enhance the marketability of Inuit art as a source of economic development, while the Department of External Affairs organized international travelling exhibitions of Inuit art as a useful strategy of Cold War diplomacy. See Norman Vorano, "Creators: Negotiating the Art World for over 50 Years," *Inuit Art Quarterly* (2004): 9–17, and "Inuit Art in the Qallnaat World: Modernism, Museums and the Popular Imaginary, 1949–1962" (PhD dissertation, Visual and Cultural Studies, University of Rochester, 2007).

6 Judy Hall, "Charles Gimpel: Early Promotion of Inuit Art in Europe," *Inuit Art Quarterly* 24, no. 1 (Spring 2009): 34–42.

7 I am grateful to the National Gallery of Canada for the award of a research fellowship in historic

Canadian art in 1996–97, which allowed me to conduct archival research on the *Masterpieces* exhibit. I have also profited from the subsequent research of Linda Grussani on this exhibition. See her "Constructing the Image of Canada as a Nation: The International Presentation of Aboriginal Art Exhibitions (1969–1990)" (MA thesis, School for Studies in Art and Culture: Art History, Carleton University, 2003).

8   See Herbert J. Gans, *Popular Culture and High Culture: An Analysis and Evaluation of Taste* (New York: Basic Books, 1974).

9   See Kent Minturn, "Dubuffet, Lévi-Strauss, and the Idea of Art Brut," *RES: Anthropology and Aesthetics*, no. 46 (Autumn 2004): 247–58, and Minturn's translation of Dubuffet's 1951 talk at the Evrard Gallery, "In Honor of Savage Values," ibid., 259–68.

10 See William Taylor and George Swinton, "The Silent Echoes: Pre-historic Canadian Eskimo Art," *The Beaver* 298 (Autumn 1967): 32–47.

11 The summary presented here is based on files in the National Gallery of Canada (NGC) Archives and an examination of the personal papers of Dr Taylor.

12 NGC Archives, 12-4-418, "Human History Branch, National Museum of Canada: Minutes of a meeting of the Director, Assistant Director and Division Chiefs, held 12 May 64, to discuss the Overall Gallery Plan."

13 Ibid., "Suggested Programme for Ethnological Exhibits – 1967, "An Exhibition of Primitive Art."

14 Ibid.

15 Robert Redfield's essay "Art and Icon," in Robert Goldwater, ed., *Aspects of Primitive Art*, (New York: Museum of Primitive Art, 1959), 11–40, remains one of the best statements of this debate.

16 In 2003 the museum's collection was merged into the Musée du quai Branly. See Bernard Plossu et al., *MAAO mémoires* (Paris: Marval, 2002).

17 On MoMA's Indian Arts of the Americas, see W. Jackson Rushing Jr, "Marketing the Affinity of the Primitive and the Modern: René d'Harnoncourt and 'Indian Art of the United States,'" in Janet Catherine Berlo, ed., *The Early Years of Native American Art History* (Seattle: University of Washington Press, 1992), 191–236.

18 Aldona Jonaitis, *From the Land of the Totem Pole: The Northwest Coast Indian Art Collection at the American Museum of Natural History* (Vancouver: Douglas and McIntyre, 1988).

19 *Masterpieces* was shown in Paris from March to September 1968 and in Ottawa from 21 November 1969 to 11 January 1970.

20 NGC Archives, 12-4-418, Letter from Hugh Dempsey to William Taylor, 27 November 1969.

21 Ibid., "'Something Else Tonight' Mon 1 Dec [1969] at 7:05 pm."

22 Christian Zervos, "Preface," in *Masterpieces of Indian and Eskimo Art from Canada* (Ottawa: National Gallery of Canada, 1969), unpaginated.

23 Ibid.

24 Ibid.

25 Nemiroff, "Modernism, Nationalism, and Beyond," 33–4; italics in the original. This reconstruction of the Paris installation (which I saw and which I remember in just this way) is strongly evocative of the deep shadows and isolated spot-lighting of objects at the Musée du quai Branly.

26 See Harold Cardinal, *The Unjust Society* (Vancouver: Douglas and McIntyre, 1969); and Alan Cairns, *Citizens Plus: Aboriginal People and the Canadian State* (Vancouver: UBC Press, 2000), 51–69.

27 See, for example, James Clifford, "Quai Branly in Process," *October* 120 (Spring 2007): 3–23; Sally Price, *Paris Primitive: Jacques Chirac's Museum on the Quai Branly* (Chicago: University of Chicago Press, 2007); Benoît de l'Estoile, *Le goût des autres, de l'Exposition coloniale aux Arts premiers* (Paris: Flamarion, 2007); and Anthony Alan Shelton, "The Public Sphere as Wilderness: Le Musée du quai Branly," *Museum Anthropology* 32, no. 1 (2009): 1–16.

28 Hill became the first Audain Curator of Indigenous Arts in 2007.

29 Denise Leclerc, "Art of This Land at the National Gallery of Canada," trans. Judith Terry, *National Gallery of Canada Review* 7, forthcoming.

30 These reports were the *Report on Indian and Inuit Art at the National Gallery of Canada*, commissioned by the NGC in 1983; *Politique d'inclusion et d'exclusion: l'art contemporain autochtone dans les musées d'art du Canada*, written by Lee-Ann Martin for the Canada Council; and the report of the Task Force on Museums and First Peoples in 1992 (see chapter 2 in this volume).

31 Leclerc, "Art of This Land."

32 The consultants were Indigenous museum professionals Stephen Augustine, Tom Hill, Gerald McMaster, and François Vincent and non-Indigenous art historians and museum professionals François-Marc Gagnon, Marie Routledge, Judy Thompson, and myself. We met twice: in 2001 and 2002.

33 See Carol Duncan, "Art Museums and the Ritual of Citizenship," in Ivan Karp and Steven D. Lavine, eds, *Exhibiting Cultures: The Politics and Poetics of Museum Display* (Washington, DC: Smithsonian Institution Press, 1991), 88–103.

34 See Michael Baxandall, "Exhibiting Intention: Some Preconditions of the Visual Display of Culturally Purposeful Objects," in Karp and Lavine, *Exhibiting Cultures*, 33–41; and Mieke Bal, "Postcards from the Edge," in Bal, *Double Exposures: The Subject of Cultural Analysis* (New York: Routledge, 1996).

35 Dilys Leman, "Making Connections: Phase Two of *Art of This Land*," *Vernissage* (Winter 2006): 19.

36 Ibid.

37 See Anne Whitelaw, "Whiffs of Balsam, Pine, and Spruce: Art Museums and the Production of a Canadian Aesthetic," reprinted in John O'Brian and Peter White, eds, *Beyond Wilderness: The Group of Seven, Canadian Identity, and Contemporary Art* (Montreal: McGill-Queen's University Press, 2007), 175–80.

38 See O'Brian and White, *Beyond Wilderness*.

39 Brian O'Doherty, *Inside the White Cube: The Ideology of the Gallery Space* (Santa Monica, Calif.: Lapis Press, 1986), 79.

40 See Deborah Doxtator, "Basket, Bead and Quill and the Making of 'Traditional' Art," in Janet Clark, ed., *Basket, Bead and Quill* (Thunder Bay, Ont.: Thunder Bay Art Gallery, 1992), 11–21. Cory Willmott provided aural evidence for the rain-like sound of older metal cones in "Shape, Rattle and Roll: Forms and Functions of Metal in Anishinaabe Aesthetic Traditions" (paper delivered to the Native American Art Studies Association, Norman, Oklahoma, October 2009).

41 Jelena Adzic, "Diaspora Art," aired on CBC's *The National*, 2 February 2010. Mayer's remarks stimulated an organized protest from the Aboriginal Curatorial Collective and other Canadian artists and critics.

42 Anne Whitelaw, "Placing Aboriginal Art at the National Gallery of Canada," *Canadian Journal of Communication* 31 (2006): 198.

43 Ibid., 201.

44 Ibid., 205.

45 Matthew Teitelbaum, "Thinking about Canada, While Imagining a New Art Gallery of Ontario with Frank Gehry," Canada Program Seminar, Weatherhead Center for International Affairs, Harvard University, 21 September 2009.

46 The recognition of such conversational communities – a phrase borrowed by Griselda Pollock from Thomas Kuhn – has been a key feature of "new" art-historical work since its inception. See, for example, Pollock's dialogue with artist Mary Kelly in her feminist classic *Vision and Difference: Femininity, Feminism, and Histories of Art* (New York: Routledge, 1988) and Hans Belting's use of a Hervé Fischer performance piece to launch *The End of the History of Art?* (trans. Christopher S. Wood, Chicago: University of Chicago Press, 1987), his influential postmodern critique of art-historical meta-narratives.

47 See John Tancock's review "Toronto, Primitivism in Modern Sculptures: Gauguin to Moore," *Burlington Magazine* 24, no. 948 (March 1982): 195; and Alan G. Wilkinson, *Gauguin to Moore: Primitivism in Modern Sculpture* (Toronto: Art Gallery of Ontario, 1981).

48 Dennis R. Reid and Joan M. Vastokas, *From the Four Quarters: Native and European Art in Ontario, 5000 BC to 1867 AD* (Toronto: Art Gallery of Ontario, 1984).

49 On Houle's piece, see my essay "Settler Monuments, Indigenous Memory: Dismembering and Re-membering Canadian Art History," in Robert Nelson and Margaret Olin, eds, *Monuments and Memory: Made and Unmade* (Chicago: University of Chicago Press, 2003), 281–304.

50 See Jeff Thomas and Anna Hudson, "Edmund Morris: Speaking of First Nations," and Robin K. Wright, "The Cunningham Collection of Haida Argillite at the Art Gallery of Ontario," in Linda Jessup and Shannon Bagg, eds, *On Aboriginal Art in the Art Gallery* (Hull, Que.: Canadian Museum of Civilization, 2002), 127–48 and 163–79 repectively.

51 On "OH! Canada" see Peter White, "Out of the Woods," in O'Brian and White, eds, *Beyond*

Wilderness, 11; and John Grande, "Canada. Eh?" *Art Papers* 21, no. 92 (May–June 1997).

52 Indigenous artists have lobbied since the 1980s for the appointment of Aboriginal curators in museums. Where this has happened, these curators have most often been appointed to positions dealing with Indigenous art or culture. McMaster, who is also an artist, had previously served as curator of Contemporary Canadian Indian Art at the Canadian Museum of Civilization and then as deputy assistant director for Cultural Resources at the Smithsonian's National Museum of the American Indian. As his predecessor in the post of curator of Canadian Art, Reid, who is the author of a major survey of Canadian art history as well as numerous studies of historical and twentieth-century Euro-Canadian art, had co-curated with Joan Vastokas the AGO's pioneering 1984 exhibition *From the Four Quarters*, noted above.

53 *Interior View of the Medicine Lodge, Mandan O-kee-pa Ceremony* (1832), Museum of American Art, Smithsonian Institution, 1985.66.504. Monkman may also be referencing a similar scene painted by Karl Bodmer.

54 I am grateful to Anne De Stecher, Heather Igloliorte, and Mark Phillips for lending their eagle eyes to help decode some of the references in *The Academy*.

55 It can be viewed at http://web.mac.com/ eoin.murphy/iWeb/site/monkman.html.

56 This point was made by Selwyn Dewdney, one of Morrisseau's mentors, in a biographical sketch published around the time that this self-portrait was made: "Norval Morriseau [*sic*] is neither a 'bush bum' nor a 'picturesque aborigine,' but a sensitive, intelligent human being, faced with the agonizing problem of integrating within his own person the conflicting elements of two deeply dissimilar cultures. Sometimes he can cope with the moods of black despair that this dichotomy brings on by taking long walks in the bush. Sometimes it drives him to drink, to achieve the temporary but real relief that is, perhaps, our most significant gift to his people." See "The World of Norval Morrisseau," in *Legends of My People, the Great Ojibway*, ed. Selwyn Dewdney (Toronto: McGraw-Hill Ryerson, 1965), viii–xxii.

57 It is a view shared by other Indigenous artists, including curator Gerald McMaster. In several essays he has urged the need to ac-

knowledge shared but difficult histories. See his "Our (Inter) Related History," in Lynda Jessup with Shannon Bagg, eds, *On Aboriginal Representation in the Gallery* (Hull, Que.: Canadian Museum of Civilization, 2002), 3–8.

58 Sarah Milroy, "Unmasking Art's Dazzling Pleasures – and Its Complexities," *Globe and Mail*, 15 November 2008, R7.

59 Ivan Gaskell, "Museum Display, an Algonquian Bow, and the Ship of Theseus" (unpublished paper presented to the colloquium "Materiality and Cultural Translation," Weatherhead Center for International Affairs, Harvard University, May 2010). Gaskell has also presented his formulation in "Encountering Pacific Art," *Journal of Museum Ethnography*, no. 21 (March 2009): 202–10.

60 Gaskell, "Museum Display."

61 Daniel K. Richter, *The Ordeal of the Longhouse: The Peoples of the Iroquois League in the Era of European Colonization* (Chapel Hill: University of North Carolina Press, 1992), 2.

Chapter Fifteen

1 Canada, *Report of the Royal Commission on Aboriginal Peoples*, vol. 3, *Gathering Strength*, 6, "Arts and Heritage," 1.2, "Sacred and Secular Artifacts," http://www.collectionscanada.gc.ca/ webarchives/20071211060616/http://www.ainc-inac.gc.ca/ch/rcap/sg/si56_e.html; accessed 9 April 2010.

2 Chris Gosden and Frances Larson with Alison Petch, *Knowing Things: Exploring the Collections at the Pitt Rivers Museum, 1884–1945* (Oxford: Oxford University Press, 2007), 240.

3 Part of this chapter was delivered in a co-presentation with Alan Corbiere at the December 2009 annual meeting of the American Anthropological Association in Philadelphia.

4 See Cory Willmott, "The Historical Praxis of Museum Anthropology: A Canada/ US Comparison," in Julia Harrison and Regna Darnell, eds, *Historicizing Canadian Anthropology* (Vancouver: UBC Press, 2006), 212–25.

5 Edward Sapir, "An Anthropological Survey of Canada," *Science*, new series, 34 (1911): 790.

6 Ibid., 793.

7 See Franz Boas, "Some Principles of Museum Administration," *Science*, new series, 25, no. 650 (14 June 1907): 921–33.

8 Ibid., 922.

9 See George W. Stocking Jr, ed., *Objects and Others: Essays on Museums and Material Culture* (Madison: University of Wisconsin Press, 1988).

10 Johannes Fabian, *Time and the Other: How Anthropology Makes Its Object* (New York: Columbia University Press, 1983).

11 Diane Losche, "The Fate of the Senses in Ethnographic Modernity: The Margaret Mead Hall of Pacific Peoples at the American Museum of Natural History," in Elizabeth Edwards, Chris Gosden, and Ruth B. Phillips, eds, *Sensible Objects: Colonialism, Museums and Material Culture* (London: Berg, 2006), 223–44.

12 Svetlana Alpers, "The Museum as a Way of Seeing," in Ivan Karp and Steven D. Lavine, eds, *Exhibiting Cultures: The Poetics and Politics of Museum Display* (Washington, DC: Smithsonian Institution Press, 1991), 25–32.

13 Steven Conn, "Heritage vs History at the National Museum of the American Indian," *Public Historian* 18, no. 2 (Spring 2006): 71.

14 In an advance announcement of *An Infinity of Nations: Art and History in the Collections of the National Museum of the American Indian*, which opened in 2010 at the NMAI's New York venue, the museum's website described it as "a spectacular permanent exhibition of 700 works of art from throughout Native North, Central and South America" that "will demonstrate the great depth of the museum's collections and explore the historic importance of many of these magnificent objects." See http://blog.nmai.si.edu/main/an-infinity-of-nations/; accessed 9 April 2010.

15 Gosden and Larson, *Knowing Things*, 240.

16 The following are a few examples of the scope of this network: Robyn Sloggett has documented Leonhard Adam's active trading of Australian Aboriginal items with fellow ethnology curators in the United States and Europe in "Dr. Leonhard Adam and his Ethnographic Collection at the University of Melbourne" (PhD dissertation, School of Culture and Communications, University of Melbourne, 2009); in the early twentieth century, field-collected Onkwehonwe clothing was traded to the Peter the Great Museum of Ethnology in St Petersburg; and Harry Hawthorn arranged for trades of Northwest Coast items from the University of British Columbia's Museum of Anthropology with the museum at the University of Otago in New Zealand.

17 On holistic approaches in Indigenous scholarship, see, for example, John Borrows, *Recovering Canada: The Resurgence of Indigenous Law* (Toronto: University of Toronto Press, 2002); Deborah Doxtator, "Basket, Bead and Quill, and the Making of 'Traditional' Art," in Janet Clark, ed., *Basket, Bead and Quill* (Thunder Bay, Ont.: Thunder Bay Art Gallery, 1995), 11–21; and Linda Tuhuwai Smith, *Decolonizing Methodologies: Research and Indigenous Peoples* (New York: Zed Books, 1999).

18 There are, of course notable exceptions to this pattern, such as the meticulous cataloguing project undertaken at the National Museum of Canada by Judy Hall and Judy Thompson during the 1970s and 1980s.

19 The creation of the National Inventory Program (NIP) was part of a new National Museums Policy, which was in turn a response to the UNESCO Convention on Means of Prohibiting and Preventing the Illicit Import, Export and Transfer of Ownership of Cultural Property of 1970. It became the Canadian Heritage Information Network in 1982. "The mandate of NIP was to create a computerized national inventory of Canadian cultural and scientific collections, to facilitate the sharing of collections information, to conduct applied research and development on information management standards and technology, and to advise museums and the heritage community in these areas ... At first, museums sent their paper collections catalogues to CHIN for automation but, as technology advanced, the National Inventories were maintained by the participating museums through dial-up access to CHIN's mainframe computer, with support from CHIN. The National Inventories became not only an important resource for research, comparative cataloguing, and exhibition planning, but also a tool for collections management within individual institutions. CHIN also provided museums with the capability to share information through electronic mail long before the Internet made this a common practice." See http://www.rcip-chin.gc.ca/apropos-about/histoire-history/complete-narrative-eng.jsp; accessed 9 April 2010.

20 Task Force on Museums and First Peoples, *Turning the Page: Forging New Partnerships*

between *Museums and First Peoples* (Ottawa, 1992). The federal government's decision to shut down CHIN froze the existing database and turned it into an archival resource.

21 Canada, *Report of the Royal Commission on Aboriginal Peoples*, vol. 3, *Gathering Strength*, 6, "Arts and Heritage," 1.2, "Sacred and Secular Artifacts."

22 Audrey Hawthorn, *A Labour of Love: The Making of the Museum of Anthropology, UBC: The First Three Decades, 1947–1976* (Vancouver: UBC Museum of Anthropology, 1993).

23 "A Partnership of Peoples: A New Infrastructure for Collaborative Research at the University of British Columbia's Museum of Anthropology" (application submitted to the Canada Foundation for Innovation, 2000), 3A–3B.

24 Ibid., 3A.

25 The Museum of Anthropology also houses the collections of a separate institution, UBC's Laboratory of Archaeology.

26 "A Partnership of Peoples," 4F.

27 The CFI grant of $17.5 million, awarded in 2001, was matched by an equivalent grant from the British Columbia Knowledge Development Fund and funds from the University of British Columbia.

28 Lee Iverson (UBC), Susan Rowley (UBC), Leona Sparrow (Musqueam Indian Band), Dave Schaepe (Sto:lo Research and Resource Management Centre), Andrea Sanborn (U'mista Cultural Society), Ryan Wallace (UBC), Nicholas Jakobsen (UBC), and Ulrike Radermacher (UBC), "The Reciprocal Research Network," in J. Trant and D. Bearman, eds, *Museums and the Web 2008: Proceedings* (Toronto: Archives & Museum Informatics, 2008), http://www.archimuse.com/mw2008/papers/iverson/iverson.html; accessed 9 April 2010.

29 Ibid.

30 The remainder of this chapter is based on Heidi Bohaker and Ruth B. Phillips, "Bringing Heritage Home: Aboriginal Perspectives in Western Repositories," presented at the annual conference of the Canadian Anthropology Association, Carleton University, Ottawa, May 2008.

31 I discussed Purbrick and his collection in more detail and wrongly suggested that the quilled bark wares may have come from Garden River in *Trading Identities: The Souvenir in Native*

North American Art from the Northeast, 1700–1900 (Seattle: University of Washington Press, 1998), 150, 182.

32 The name translates as Mary Ann Bgoji-kwe Shawana; Bgoji-kwe means wild or natural woman (personal communication from Alan Corbiere).

33 Alan Corbiere and I presented this research in our paper "Complement and Compliment: Assembling Western and Indigenous Knowledges in Digital Space," at the American Anthropological Association annual meeting, Philadelphia, 4 December 2009.

34 See A. Irvin Hallowell, "Ojibwa Ontology, Behavior, and World View," in Raymond D. Fogelson et al., eds, *Contributions to Anthropology: Selected Papers of A. Irving Hallowell* (Chicago: University of Chicago Press, 1976), 357–90; Julie Cruikshank, *Life Lived Like a Story: Life Stories of Three Yukon Native Elders* (Vancouver: University of British Columbia Press, 1991); and Maureen Anne Matthews, "Repatriating Agency: Animacy, Personhood and Agency in the Repatriation of Ojibwe Artifacts" (PhD dissertation, Institute of Social and Cultural Anthropology, University of Oxford, 2010). See also Fiona Cameron's related argument for the digital object as an independant creative work rather than a mere "replicant": "Beyond the Cult of the Replicant: Museums and Historical Digital Objects – Traditional Concerns, New Discourses," in Fiona Cameron and Sarah Kenderdine, eds, *Theorizing Digital Cultural Heritage: A Critical Discourse* (Cambridge, Mass.: MIT Press, 2007), 49–76.

35 Lindsay Kelly, "Reconnecting Roots," *Manitoulin Expositor*, 16 January 2008, 5.

36 See James Clifford, "Introduction: Partial Truths," and Mary Louise Pratt, "Fieldwork in Common Places," in James Clifford and George E. Marcus, eds, *Writing Culture: The Poetics and Politics of Ethnography* (Berkeley: University of California Press, 1986), 1–26 and 27–50 respectively; and Thomas Richards, *The Imperial Archive: Knowledge and the Fantasy of Empire* (New York: Verso, 1991).

Chapter Sixteen

1 María J. Prieto and Elise S. Youn, "Interview with Bruno Latour: Decoding the Collective Experiment," in Nader Vossoughian, ed.,

Agglutinations.com: Interviews and Reviews about Urbanism, Politics, and Society (5 July 2004), http://agglutinations.com/archives/000040.html; accessed 6 May 2010.

2 This chapter incorporates material from two previously published essays of mine: "The Mask Stripped Bare by Its Curators: The Work of Hybridity in the Twenty-First Century," in Thierry Dufrene and Anne-Christine Taylor, eds, *Cannibalismes disciplinaires: Quand l'histoire de l'art et l'anthropologie se rencontrent* (Paris: Musée du quai Branly and INHA, 2009), 379–96 (available online at http://actesbranly.revues.org/336); and "The Museum of Art-thropology: Twenty-First Century Imbroglios," *RES: Anthropology and Aesthetics* 52 (Autumn 2007): 8–19.

3 Bruno Latour, *Reassembling the Social: An Introduction to Actor-Network Theory* (New York: Oxford University Press, 2005).

4 John Law, "Notes on the Theory of the Actor Network: Ordering, Strategy and Heterogeneity" (Centre for Science Studies, Lancaster University, 1992), 7, http://www.lancs.ac.uk/fass/sociology/papers/law-notes-on-ant.pdf; accessed 6 May 2010; also published in *Systems Practice* 5 (1992): 379–93.

5 Ibid., 4.

6 Ibid., 5–6.

7 Bruno Latour, *We Have Never Been Modern*, trans. Catherine Porter (Cambridge, Mass.: Harvard University Press, 1993), 51; italics in original.

8 Ibid., 10.

9 Ibid., 10–11.

10 See Carlo Ginzburg, "Clues, Roots of an Evidential Paradigm," in Ginzburg, *Clues, Myths and the Historical Method* (Baltimore: Johns Hopkins University Press, 1989), 96–125.

11 See, for example, Sally Price, *Paris Primitive: Jacques Chirac's Museum on the Quai Branly,* (Chicago: University of Chicago Press, 2007); and James Clifford, "Quai Branly in Process," *October* 120 (Spring 2007): 3–23.

12 Latour, *Reassembling the Social*, 23.

13 Roy Miki has referred to the debates that can open up around pluralism and power as quagmires, but he has also pointed out that they can be useful because "all relationships are levelled in a quagmire; a kind of democratiza-tion occurs in a quagmire" (remarks made at the "Complicated Entanglements: Rethinking Pluralism in the 21st Century" conference, Carleton University, 5 April 2008, organized by the Carleton Centre for Transnational Cultural Analysis).

14 *George Catlin and His Indian Gallery* was shown at the Renwick Gallery in 2003 and then toured across the United States. The comments of George Horse Capture, Richard West Jr, Jaune Quick To See Smith, and Wilma Mankiller were not included in the exhibition publication but are integrated into the exhibition website: http://americanart.si.edu/exhibitions/online/catlinclassroom/cl.html.

15 See Ruth B. Phillips, "'Can You Go without Your Head?': Fieldwork as Transformative Experience," *Res* 39 (2001): 61–77.

16 Personal communication from Paramount chief Karkartuwa, village of Mende, Luawa chiefdom, Kailahun district, 3 November 1972.

17 Personal communication from Eva Fognell (curator of the Eugene and Clare V. Thaw Collection, Fenimore Art Museum) via email, 2007.

18 Personal communication from Alissa Lagamma, curator of African Art, Metropolitan Museum of Art, New York, 2002; personal communication from Frederick Lamp, New Haven, Conn., 2008.

19 *The Village Is Tilting* closed on 3 September 2007.

20 I am grateful to Anna Edmonson for her account of the development of the exhibition, on which the following discussion is based (personal communication, June 2007, Canberra, Australia).

21 Joseph Alsop, *The Rare Art Traditions: The History of Art Collecting and Its Linked Phenomena Wherever These Have Appeared* (New York: Harper and Row, 1982).

22 The low budget for the exhibition (of only $75,000) was, counter-intuitively, helpful to the curators in achieving their desired design. Without funding to install the more elaborate "house style" exhibition furniture used elsewhere in the museum, they could reuse older cases and paint them black.

23 My trip to Calgary was occasioned by an invitation to participate in "Legacies and Futures: Beyond *The Spirit Sings*," organized

by Benjamin Fullalove at the Alberta College of Art and Design in collaboration with the Glenbow Museum, 13–14 March 2008.

24 Gerald Conaty stresses that before the exhibition project was attempted, a positive relationship between the Blackfoot of southern Alberta and the Glenbow had been built up through successful school programs, repatriations of medicine bundles, and other joint efforts. See Conaty, "Glenbow's Blackfoot Gallery: Working towards Co-existence," in Laura Peers and Alison K. Brown, eds, *Museums and Source Communities: A Routledge Reader* (New York: Routledge, 2003), 227–41, also discussed in chapter 11 of this volume. For a comparative example involving other Alberta First Nations, see Catherine Bell, Graham Statt, and the Mookakin Cultural Society, "Repatriation and Heritage Protection: Reflections on the Kainai Experience," in Catherine Bell and Val Napoleon, eds, *First Nations Cultural Heritage and Law: Case Studies, Voices, and Perspectives* (Vancouver: University of British Columbia Press, 2008), 203–57.

25 Conaty, "Glenbow's Blackfoot Gallery," 230–1.

26 Ibid., 232.

27 Ibid., 234.

28 Ibid., 236.

29 *Niitsitapiisinni* occupies about 9,000 square feet, while *Native Cultures from the Four Directions* occupies roughly 2,500 square feet.

30 *Tracing History: Presenting the Unpresentable*, 16 February to 22 June 2008 (exhibition brochure, Glenbow Museum).

31 Valerie Robertson, *Reclaiming History: Ledger Book Drawings by the Assiniboine Artist Hongeeyeesa* (Calgary: Glenbow Museum, 1993).

32 *Iconoclash* and *Making Things Public* were exhibited at the Zentrum für Kunst und Medientechnologie in Karlsruhe, Germany, directed by Peter Weibel, in 2002 and 2005 respectively. In his catalogue essay for *Making Things Public*, Latour distinguishes between "things," understood in the Heideggerian sense as contingent entities whose meaning is dependent on other things with which they "assemble," and "objects," defined in the (illusory) modernist sense of autonomous and bounded entities that can be studied apart from other objects. He writes, for example: "the objects of science and technology, the aisles of supermar-kets, financial institutions, medical establishments, computer networks – even the cat walk for fashion shows! – offer paramount examples of hybrid forums and agoras, of the gatherings that have been eating away at the older realm of pure objects bathing in the clear light of the modernist gaze." See Latour, "Realpolitik to Dingpolitik, or How to Make Things Public," in Bruno Latour and Peter Weibel, eds, *Making Things Public: Atmospheres of Democracy* (Cambridge, Mass.: MIT Press, 2005), 14–43; also available at http://www.bruno-latour.fr/expositions/96-MTP-DING.pdf; accessed 12 May 2010.

33 Ibid., 95.

34 Peter Weibel and Bruno Latour, "Experimenting with Representation: *Iconoclash* and *Making Things Public*," in Sharon Macdonald and Paul Basu, eds, *Exhibition Experiments* (Oxford: Blackwell, 2007), 104.

35 Ibid., 107.

36 Leroy Little Bear, "Naturalizing Indigenous Knowledge: Synthesis Paper" (Aboriginal Knowledge Learning Centre, Canadian Council on Learning and University of Saskatchewan, 2009), 8, http://www.ccl-cca.ca/pdfs/ablkc/naturalizeIndigenous_en.pdf; accessed 30 April 2010.

INDEX

Page numbers in italics denote illustrations.
Colour plates and their numbers are also
italicized.

Pakwatchikwe Shawana, Maniian, 292, 355n32

Parker, Arthur, 128

Parker, Ely S., 145

Partial Recall, 209

"Participation in Canada's Centennial by People of Indian Ancestry" (Indian Affairs Branch), 31

participatory action research (PAR), 191

partnership between museums and originating communities. *See* collaborative models of museum practice

paternalism: and Indians of Canada Pavilion, 40, 43–5

Patterns of Power: The Jasper Grant Collection and Great Lakes Indian Art ... (McMichael Gallery), 11

Pauingassi, Man., 339n22

Paul, Louis-Benjamin Peminuit (Mi'kmaq chief), 151–2

Peabody Museum of Archaeology and Ethnology (Harvard): repatriating *ga:goh:sah,* 131

Pearson, Lester, 46

Peers, Laura, 160, 187

Pellan, Alfred: *Blossoming,* 264, *264*

Perley, Moses, 139–41, 151

Philip, M. Nourbese, 117–18

Phillips, Ruth B.: and *Across Borders,* 332n34, 343n11; and *Art of This Land,* 352n32; as director of MoA, 21, 75, 284–9; and GRASAC, 289–96; involvement with museum critique, 4–6, 8–9, 13–14, 21; Mende mask research, 104–5, 303–4; and Portrait Gallery of Canada, 233–4; and *The Spirit Sings,* 53; and Task Force on Museums and First Peoples, 13; writing on *ga:goh:sah,* 117, 130, 335n31

photographic documentation of collections: and accessibility, 283, 285; and preservation, 282; role in GKS of, 289

Pitt Rivers Museum, Oxford, 135; as agent of social formations, 289; and electronic research, 294–5; "Relational Museum Project," 338n7

Plains art and artists: in AGO installations, 271; in *Art of This Land,* 257, 261, 263; at Expo 67, 35; handling of medicine objects, 111; in *Masterpieces of Indian and Eskimo Art from Canada,* 256; and stereotypes, 34, 224; and *Spirit Sings* logo, 64, *plate 3*

Plamondon, Antoine: at NGC, 262

pluralism. *See* multiculturalism

Poitras, Edward: in *Indigena,* 165

Poitras, Jane Ash: in *Indigena,* 164–5

Pomian, Krzysztof, 19

Pootoogook, Napachie: at AGO, 269

popular culture: responding to, 124–5; and stereotypes, 173–5

Porter, John, 8

Portrait Gallery of Canada, 231–51; Arctic module, 241–3; Boethuk module, 246–8; collaborative process, 237; curatorial program for, 232–3, 248; Dene module, 244–6; "Facing the Other," 237–50, *238, plate 14;* Four Indian Kings ("Tangled Garden" section), 240–1, 248–50, *249, plate 14;* Great Lakes region module, 239–40; groupings dialogically structured, 238–9, 241–51; longevity grouping, 241; Northwest Coast region module, 243–4; origins of, 231–2; Phillips as guest curator, 15; proposed location for, 231, 232–3, *plate 13;* "Through Karsh's Lens," 350n21; understandings of portraiture, 237–8

Posluns, Michael: on Indians of Canada Pavilion, 32

powwow: in Indians of Canada Pavilion, 40

preservation and organization: and disarticulation of museum collections, 282

Preservation of a Species (Cardinal-Schubert), 165–7, *166, plate 5*

"Preserving Aboriginal Heritage: Technical and Traditional Approaches" (CCI conference), 229–30

"Preserving Our Heritage: A Working Conference for Museums and First Peoples," 51, 67, 324n9

Previous Possessions, New Obligations (Australia), 135

Preziosi, Donald, 105, 331n25

Price, Arthur: and *National Asset – Native Design,* 121

Price, Sally, 18

Primitive Art (Boas), 110

Primitive Art from Artists' Studios (Evrard), 254

Primitive Art/"primitive art": and art classification, 331n25, 332n29; and authenticity, 93; and "disappearing Indian," 113; exhibitions of modern and, 269–76; and Inuit carvings, 254; place of *ga:goh:sah* in, 114–17; reclassification process of, 11–12, 108, 254–9; use of term, 350n1. *See also* art

"Primitivism" in 20th Century Art (MoMA): in art and anthropology debate, 102; controversy over, 11–12, 48; as imbroglio, 301; and notion of affinity, 65–6; and *The Spirit Sings,* 56

progress. *See* civilization and progress

Proud to Be Musqueam (MoA), 73, *74*

public monuments: activism targeting, 25

public versus private: in architecture of Indians of Canada Pavilion, 34

punctualization, 298–9, 315

Purbrick, Edward, 292

Quseir al-Qadim, Egypt: collaborative museum project in, 188–204

rattles and masks: of the Coast Salish, 111
Ray, Carl, 35, 37, 322n39
Reciprocal Research Network (RRN): CFI funding for, 286–9, 355n27; charter of, 288–9; compared to GKS, 290–1; conceptualization of, 278; as digital repatriation, 287–9; website, 286
Redfield, Robert, 108
Reich and Petch Design International: and Portrait Gallery of Canada, 248
Reid, Bill, 37; and *The Spirit Sings*, 63, 326n42
Reid, Dennis: and AGO installations, 270; and Canadian art at AGO, 270, 353n52; curator of *From the Four Quarters* (AGO), 269–70
Reiss, Winold: portrait of Mary Snake Woman, 312
"Relational Museum Project" (Pitt Rivers Museum), 338n7
repatriation and recovery of cultural property: and Anishinaabe drum (*The Spirit Sings*), 65; Canada and US compared, 208; comprehensive-claim versus case-by-case approaches, 153–4; in context of globalization, 152–3, 342n73; definitions of cultural property, 135–6; and digital repatriation, 287, 296; and display of ceremonial items, 49; existing frameworks for, 135–41; in healing process, 152, 342n71; as issue of museum reform, 49; of Kwakwaka'wakw potlatch collection, 55, 324n6; and legislated acquisition practices, 338n5; Mi'kmaq coat as case study of, 132, 134–5, 138–54; museums' contribution to, 297–8; negotiated solutions, 137–8; and rise of Aboriginal activism, 53; and spectrum of ownership, 94; use versus preservation, 111, 332n2; and wampum, 142. *See also* appropriation; authenticity, sacrality, and possession; *ga:goh:sah* ("False Face" masks); Native American Graves Protection and Repatriation Act (NAGPRA, US)
research, museum-based: in application to CFI, 285–9; and collaborative practices, 193; on curators' job descriptions, 282, 354n18; digital influences on, 277–96; effect of CFI on, 285–9; exhibitions and role of, 277; interdisciplinary, 92; and participatory action research (PAR), 191; and public display of *ga:goh:sah*, 111–12; and *The Spirit Sings*, 52, 67–9
reserves: and Lubicon land claims, 49; represented in Indians of Canada Pavilion, 41–2, 323n62
Richard, Paul: review of NMAI, 224

Rickard, Jolene: and *Across Borders*, 343n11; curatorial work at National Museum of the American Indian, 209
Rideau Chapel (NGC), 262–3, *263, plate 15*
Riegl, Alois: concept of *Kunstwollen*, 106; and hybridity, 300
Ritzenthaler, Robert: on *ga:goh:sah*, 335n29
Robinson, Brian: curator of *Dhari a Krar*, 306
Robinson, Michael: on participatory action research, 191
Roth, Maria, 85
Rothschild, Alix de: and *Masterpieces of Indian and Eskimo Art from Canada*, 254–5
Rothstein, Edward: review of NMAI, 224
Roussil, Robert: *Gesticulation*, 264
Routledge, Marie: and *Art of This Land*, 352n32
Rowley, Susan: role in RRN, 288
Royal Canadian Mounted Police (RCMP): in Canadian identity, 80, 84
Royal Commission on Aboriginal Peoples: on Aboriginal access to museums, 277, 278; on accessibility and custodial responsibility of museums, 284; on healing through cultural property, 342n71; on legislated acquisition practices, 338n5; on museums, 132
Royal Commission on Bilingualism and Biculturalism, 6–7
Royal Ontario Museum (ROM): *Fluffs and Feathers*, 170; *Into the Heart of Africa*, 13; *Kaxlaya Gvilas*, 199; and multiculturalism, 148; return of wampum, 142
Ryan, Joan: on participatory action research, 191

sacrality: Nlaka'pamux "puberty veil," 183–4; in *The Spirit Sings* and Indians of Canada Pavilion, 54; and treatment of museum objects, 111; and Western categorization, 93–4. *See also ga:goh:sah* ("False Face" masks)
Sanborn, Andrea: role in RRN, 288
Sapir, Edward: "An Anthropological Survey of Canada," 279
Saul, John Ralston, 10
Savage Graces (McMaster), 168–78, *plates 7–8*; Cultural Amnesty box, 177; exhibition dates, 344n8; first room, *172*; as a *Gesamtkunstwerk*, 170; *HyperPhotogenics*, 173; "(Im)Polite Gazes" section, *173*, 173–4, *plate 8*; self-portrait, 176–8, *177*; structure of, 176; third section, *174*
SCANA. *See* Society of Canadian Artists of Native Ancestry (SCANA)
Schaepe, Dave: role in RRN, 288
Schoolcraft, Henry Rowe, 145, 341n52